WARDS OF COURT AND THE INHERENT JURISDICTION

This open access book explores the High Court's powers under its inherent jurisdiction and wardship in relation to children and incapacitous and vulnerable adults.

The book introduces the inherent jurisdiction and investigates its place in the modern law. Part 1 provides a comprehensive history of the inherent jurisdiction, before giving a detailed account of the core principles and procedure applicable today, and comparing the approaches taken in Scotland, Ireland, Canada, Australia and New Zealand. Part 2 considers the court's use of its inherent jurisdiction in specific categories of case, including child abduction, medical decision-making about children, child protection, incapacitous and vulnerable adults.

Despite its ancient roots, the inherent jurisdiction is relied on by High Court judges on a daily basis, in both everyday and cutting-edge cases. This book argues that the court's approach to some of these cases is justified, but that judges often make unnecessary and inappropriate use of the inherent jurisdiction.

Through its critical examination of the modern use of wardship and the inherent jurisdiction, the book is essential reading for practitioners and researchers working in this field.

Wards of Court and the Inherent Jurisdiction

Rob George

• HART •
OXFORD • LONDON • NEW YORK • NEW DELHI • SYDNEY

HART PUBLISHING

Bloomsbury Publishing Plc

Kemp House, Chawley Park, Cumnor Hill, Oxford, OX2 9PH, UK

1385 Broadway, New York, NY 10018, USA

29 Earlsfort Terrace, Dublin 2, Ireland

First published in Great Britain 2024

A catalogue record for this book is available from the British Library.

A catalogue record for this book is available from the Library of Congress.

Library of Congress Control Number: 2024944062

ISBN: HB: 978-1-50997-214-2
ePDF: 978-1-50997-216-6
ePub: 978-1-50997-215-9

Typeset by Compuscript Ltd, Shannon

FOREWORD

This is a remarkable book. It deserves to be read by all Judges in the High Court, Court of Appeal and (dare I say it) Supreme Court, who may be called upon to hear cases concerning children, or adults who lack the capacity to make a decision for themselves, or so-called vulnerable adults, and of course by the practitioners who conduct such cases and the academics who are interested in them. It does two things. First, it provides a comprehensive, scholarly and up-to-date account of the law and practice relating to wards of court and the inherent jurisdiction of the High Court in relation to these people. Second, it reveals how the jurisdiction is being used in ways in which it should not be used.

The author takes no issue with using the non-statutory powers of the High Court to fill unintended gaps in the statutory schemes relating to the care and upbringing of children and decision-making on behalf of people who are unable to make the decision for themselves, provided that these 'go with the grain' of the statutory scheme – for example, the tipstaff's powers to search for and secure the children in international child abduction cases. But he does take issue with using the inherent jurisdiction unnecessarily, when there are perfectly good statutory powers to achieve the same result – for example, to authorise medical treatment for a child to which the parents have refused their consent: Mrs Justice Booth pointed out as long ago as 1993 that a specific issue order under section 8 of the Children Act 1989 was designed for just that sort of case.

But much worse than that is using the inherent jurisdiction in ways which conflict with the principles of the relevant statutory scheme. A startling example is making children wards of court when they are being accommodated by a local authority under section 20 of the Children Act 1989. The 'cardinal feature' of such accommodation is that the parents can remove the child at any time. Yet if the child is a ward of court, they cannot do that without the leave of the court. An even more startling example is using the inherent jurisdiction to authorise the placement of children looked after by local authorities in settings which certainly restrict their liberty, and probably deprive them of it, when neither the criteria nor the procedural safeguards designed for such cases in section 25 of the Children Act 1989 are fulfilled. Not only that, the premises are not approved by the Secretary of State; they may even not be registered as a children's home and so the managers will be committing a criminal offence; and Parliament has recently forbidden local authorities to place children there. This flies in the face of the statutory scheme and may well violate article 5 of the European Convention on Human Rights because the power to do this is not sufficiently precise to be 'in accordance with the law'. Perhaps worse, it lets the government off the hook for their failure to provide adequate placements for some very troubled children.

But even that pales into insignificance alongside the bare-faced invention of a jurisdiction which does not exist. The Royal Warrant delegating to the High Court the Crown's jurisdiction in relation to both the property and the person of a mentally incapacitated adult was revoked in 1960. The House of Lords authoritatively decided in 1989 that the court had no jurisdiction to make decisions on behalf of such people apart from the statutory scheme in the Mental Health Act 1983. Parliament enacted a comprehensive scheme for decision-making on behalf of adults who lacked capacity in the Mental Capacity Act 2005. This laid down principles, criteria and safeguards. It did not abolish any inherent jurisdiction because none was thought to exist. Yet the High Court decided that it had the very jurisdiction that the House of Lords had decided that it did not have.

Worse still, the High Court then decided that it had a similar jurisdiction over adults who did not lack the capacity to make a decision for themselves but were in some way 'vulnerable'. Quite apart from the imprecision of its purpose, the definition of what is meant by vulnerable, and the powers it entails, which may be used against the wishes of the person concerned, this invention ignores the fact that Parliament deliberately decided not to enact a limited protective scheme, preserving the autonomy of the person concerned, which the Law Commission had proposed in 1995. Not only that, the jurisdiction has been used to remove such people from their homes against their will, despite the fact that Parliament had repealed the only statutory power to do so. This ignores the fundamental constitutional principle laid down in *Attorney-General v De Keyser's Royal Hotel* [1920] AC 508 – that where Parliament has occupied a space it is not for the courts to use the Royal Prerogative to circumvent the limits which Parliament has laid down – and it is worse still when there was no Royal Prerogative in the first place.

The author and I have no doubt that this is all being done for the very best of motives – to protect people whom the court is persuaded need its protection. But it is a cardinal principle of the Mental Capacity Act 2005 that a person is not to be treated as unable to make a decision simply because he makes an unwise one. Reading this book, I began to wonder whether I had wasted most of my time at the Law Commission – helping to devise carefully thought-out schemes for the care and upbringing of children and for decision-making on behalf of adults unable to make decisions for themselves. I well remember how controversial our recommendations for strictly limited emergency protection for adults who did not lack capacity were within the Commission. Of course, the great majority of cases are dealt with under those statutory schemes, which were certainly necessary. But what is the point of devising principles, criteria and limits if the High Court can simply ignore them? Is the undoubted wisdom and goodwill of the High Court Judges a good enough excuse?

Brenda Hale
Formerly President, Supreme Court of the United Kingdom

ACKNOWLEDGEMENTS

I am grateful to Lady Hale for writing the foreword to this book, and for her words of confidence while I was writing it.

Thanks to the British Academy for a Mid-Career Fellowship in 2018 that allowed me to work on this book, and to Melbourne Law School for hosting me as an Academic Visitor during some of that time.

I had two excellent Research Assistants at different stages of this project. Jack Palmer-Coole helped with archival research into the early history, and Katie Stephens collected and catalogued cases from Bailii from the last 20 years. Thank you both.

I have benefited enormously from many discussions with colleagues in academia and practice over the last few years, both directly and indirectly about the book. There will be people I have forgotten, but thank you to Edward Bennett, Gillian Black, Diana Bryant, Mehvish Chaudhry, Richard Cheesley, Edward Devereux, Alison Diduck, John Eekelaar, Belinda Fehlberg, Peter Harris, Mark Henaghan, the late Anne-Marie Hutchinson, Frances Judd, Alex Laing, Nathalie Lieven, Antony Mahon, Mavis Maclean, James Netto, Mary O'Dwyer, Emma Parsons, Nicola Taylor, Brian Tobin and Mark Twomey.

Victoria Butler-Cole, David Foster, Margaret George, Jo Miles and Emily Rayner are owed particular thanks for giving feedback on individual chapters (several, in some cases), as well as for other help.

Special thanks to Rob Marsh, for enormously helpful feedback on an entire draft of the book, for helping me to see both the wood and the trees, and for making this book (and more importantly, my life) better.

I have endeavoured to state the law as of July 2024.

CONTENTS

LIST OF ABBREVIATIONS

CA 1989	Children Act 1989
CoA	Court of Appeal
D	The respondent to an application in relation to P in adult welfare cases
DAA 2021	Domestic Abuse Act 2021
DAOP	Domestic Abuse Protection Order
DVPO	Domestic Violence Protection Order
ECHR	European Convention on the Protection of Human Rights and Fundamental Freedoms 1950
FLA 1986	Family Law Act 1986
FLA 1996	Family Law Act 1996
FPR 2010	Family Procedure Rules 2010
HC	High Court
HFEA 2008	Human Fertilisation and Embryology Act 2008
HL	House of Lords
LA	Local authority
LASPOA 2012	Legal Aid, Sentencing and Punishment of Offenders Act 2012
MCA 2005	Mental Capacity Act 2005
P	The person to be protected in adult welfare cases
PO	Parental order
PR	Parental responsibility
SSWB(W)A 2014	Social Services and Well-Being (Wales) Act 2014

Journal Abbreviations

CFLQ	Child and Family Law Quarterly
CLJ	Cambridge Law Journal
JSWFL	Journal of Social Welfare and Family Law
LQR	Law Quarterly Review
MLR	Modern Law Review
OJLS	Oxford Journal of Legal Studies

TABLE OF CASES

English cases

A

B

C

H

I

J

K

Q

R

Australian Cases

Canadian Cases

Irish Cases

New Zealand Cases

Scottish Cases

European Court of Human Rights Cases

TABLE OF STATUTES, STATUTORY INSTRUMENTS AND INTERNATIONAL MATERIAL

English statutes

English Statutory Instruments

Australian Statutes

Canadian Statutes

Irish Statutes

New Zealand Statutes

Scottish statutes

International Legal Instruments

PART I

General Principles

1

Introduction

1.1 The inherent jurisdiction is the term now used to describe the High Court's extensive non-statutory powers in relation to children and certain categories of adult. For children, one tool within this arsenal of powers is wardship, whereby a child comes under the protection of the court – but wardship is just 'machinery' to operate the wider powers of the inherent jurisdiction.[1] The inherent jurisdiction is part of the common law, 'the great safety net which lies behind all statute law and is capable of filling gaps left by that law, if and in so far as those gaps have to be filled in the interests of society as a whole'.[2] These powers have an ancient origin,[3] but have seen a new lease of life in the twenty-first century.

1.2 Wardship and the inherent jurisdiction are simultaneously widely used yet almost mythical – 'magic sparkle powers', as Andrew Pack describes them.[4] The *idea* of being a Ward of Court is surprisingly well known – though most probably think it an anachronistic part of legal history, from the era of Dickens (the wards in Bleak House's *Jarndyce v Jarndyce*, 1852) and Gilbert and Sullivan (Pirates of Penzance, 1879; Iolanthe, 1882). But wardship and the wider inherent jurisdiction continue to be an important part of English law.[5]

1.3 While there are many reported judgments invoking the inherent jurisdiction, it is hard to determine how wide-spread the court's use of these powers is. Until 1991, the court service collected administrative data about wardship, so it was possible to say how many children were warded in any given year. There are data showing a dramatic drop in the years following the implementation of the Children Act 1989 ('CA 1989'), from 2,815 inherent jurisdiction applications in 1985[6] to around 430 in each year from 1996 to 1999.[7] But no more recent data

[1] *Re L (An Infant)* [1968] P 119 (CoA), 156 (Lord Denning MR).
[2] *Re F (Mental Patient: Sterilisation)* [1990] 2 AC 1 (CoA), 13 (Lord Donaldson MR).
[3] See **ch 2**.
[4] See his Suesspicious Minds blog, suesspiciousminds.com (accessed 1 June 2024).
[5] I use England as a short-hand for the legal jurisdiction of England and Wales, except where otherwise indicated. For the approaches of other common law jurisdictions see **ch 5**.
[6] Law Commission, *Wards of Court*, WP No 101 (London: HMSO, 1987), para 3.3 ('Law Com WP 101'); see also N Lowe and R White, *Wards of Court*, 2nd edn (London: Barry Rose, 1986), 10 ('Lowe and White').
[7] J Mitchell, 'Whatever Happened to Wardship? Part I' [2001] *Fam Law* 130, 130.

exist about inherent jurisdiction applications.[8] It ought to be possible to know the number of wardship applications, at least, because the Family Procedure Rules require the court to record children who are warded in the *Register of Wards*[9] – but there is no evidence that this Register actually exists.[10] What is apparent, though, is that the court's use of the inherent jurisdiction has been 'rejuvenated' since 1999,[11] so the numbers from before then are surely a significant under-estimate now.[12]

Summary of the Argument

1.4 This book has two purposes. The first is to map the areas where the inherent jurisdiction is used in English law, and to determine the principles and limitations on its exercise. The second is to ask *why* this ancient jurisdiction remains part of the law, and whether its continued use is either necessary or appropriate.

1.5 I argue that there are occasions when the court has little alternative but to draw on its inherent jurisdiction – there are genuine lacunae in the law when the court is justified in drawing on its ancient powers to provide a remedy. These situations are either entirely novel, or the inherent jurisdiction is deployed in support of a statutory scheme, going 'with the grain' of legislation, to borrow a phrase from human rights law.[13]

1.6 However, I argue that, in two categories of case, the court makes far more use of its inherent jurisdiction than is justified. In the first, suitable statutory remedies exist, making recourse to the inherent jurisdiction unnecessary and inappropriate, both in principle[14] and at common law.[15] For some of these examples, the substantive outcome may be the same as would be available under statute, but the court disregards statutory powers and relies instead on its unenumerated, unrestricted inherent jurisdiction. There are also instances in this first category where the court reaches erroneous decisions based on its failure to consider its available statutory

[8] This is an example of a family law 'data black hole': see House of Lords Select Committee, *Children and Families Act 2014: A Failure of Implementation*, HL Paper 100 (London: TSO, 2022), para 126.

[9] FPR 2010, r 12.41.

[10] Following a freedom of information request, HMCTS initially stated that it had no 'business requirement' to know whether the Register exists or not, nor could it provide information about the number of wards. A later clarification stated that this information was held by the judiciary, not by HMCTS; however, no one that I contacted on behalf of the judiciary was able to provide any information. Informal enquiries suggest that the Register has ceased to exist.

[11] J Munby, 'Whither the Inherent Jurisdiction? Part I' [2021] *Fam Law* 215, 218; see **2.34** *et seq*.

[12] The only available number is that in the 12 months to June 2023, 1,389 inherent jurisdiction applications were made in relation to deprivation of liberty ('DOL') cases: see **10.3**. Of publicly reported cases in 2021–2023, DOL applications accounted for around a third of inherent jurisdiction cases, but the publicly available judgments represent only a small proportion of applications made.

[13] *Ghaidan v Godin-Mendoza* [2004] UKHL 30, [2004] 2 AC 557, [33], on legislative interpretation under HRA 1998, s 3.

[14] See **1.22–1.27**.

[15] *Attorney-General v De Keyser's Royal Hotel Ltd* [1920] AC 508 (HL); see **3.35** *et seq*.

remedies.[16] In the second category of case – in many ways more concerning – the court disregards constitutional limitations and acts as legislator,[17] making orders that either ride roughshod over statutory limitations set by Parliament or create remedies in situations where Parliament has decided not to do so.

1.7 As I discuss below,[18] the court justifies its continued use of the inherent jurisdiction based on the need to protect the vulnerable, with judges often tying themselves in knots to achieve their protective aim while purporting to apply fundamental principles that supposedly hold their powers in check. However, the constitutional implications of the court's decisions and its extensive use of its inherent jurisdiction is extraordinary. The court uses its inherent jurisdiction to affect the most fundamental aspects of people's lives, including when parental authority can be over-ridden by the court,[19] when a child can be deprived of their liberty,[20] who the parents of a child are,[21] and with whom a capacitous adult can associate and where they can live.[22] As Peter Harris has commented, if one were told that judges in another country had power to do these things, unlimited by statute and governed only by what the judges thought was best, it would cause outrage – but, because the inherent jurisdiction is operated by 'nice chaps in London', it is just accepted.[23] We need to stop accepting it quite so readily.

Terminology and Definitions

1.8 This book is about the High Court's non-statutory powers in relation to children (including wardship) and certain categories of adult (those who are *incapacitous* and, more questionably, those who are capacitous but *vulnerable*). These powers arose historically outside any statutory framework, and continue to be exercised without having been conferred by statute.[24]

1.9 The first challenge is that the label currently chosen for this legal phenomenon – 'the inherent jurisdiction' – is distinctly unhelpful. It is only since the 1990s that

[16] See, eg, **9.31–9.36**.
[17] On the constitutional role of the court, see **1.22–1.27**.
[18] See **1.19**.
[19] See **ch 9**.
[20] See **ch 10**.
[21] See **ch 11**.
[22] See **ch 14**.
[23] Personal correspondence, quoted with permission. Harris's phrase 'nice chaps' conveys the sense of being a trusted, establishment figure – 'one of us', as Sir Humphrey would say in *Yes, Minister*. It is not intended to carry a gendered connotation. Cf 'the good chap theory of government', that 'Ministers, Prime Ministers and others in positions of responsibility will share a certain understanding about appropriate standards of constitutional behaviour and will, for the most part, adhere to those standards': see M Elliott and R Thomas, *Public Law*, 5th edn (Oxford: OUP, 2024), 54.
[24] The continued *existence* of these non-statutory powers is seen in s 19(1)(b) of the Senior Courts Act 1981, confirming the ongoing availability of 'all such other jurisdiction … as was exercisable by [the High Court] immediately before the commencement of this Act …'.

this has been the term generally used to describe the legal issues in this book, and it can cause significant confusion. Most significantly, there are two quite different uses of the phrase 'the inherent jurisdiction' currently in use in relation to children and adults:[25]

i. The more common use – what I term the *general sense* – is an umbrella term for the substantive orders that the court can make, akin to the powers that exist under CA 1989, s 8 for example. By way of illustration, these are the powers used when the court authorises medical treatment or orders a child wrongfully brought to this country to be returned to their home state. Most of the book is about this general sense of the term.
ii. Less commonly, in the *specific sense*, 'the inherent jurisdiction' is used to mean a basis on which the court can claim *jurisdiction*, in the sense of the authority to make any decisions at all about a particular child or adult.[26] Used in this sense, the claim is based on the child or adult being a British national, and so to reduce confusion I term it *nationality-based jurisdiction*.[27] I address this in chapter six.

It is important not to confuse these two senses.

1.10 Four further issues arise about the label 'the inherent jurisdiction'. First, simply describing it by reference to its apparent source (ie, it is inherent in the court) says nothing about its purpose, scope or limitations. Previous labels, in particular the *parens patriae* label,[28] while unhelpful in using Latin, at least gave some sense of what the powers were about – the parental or paternal role of the state as protector of its citizens. Second, at least some aspects of what is called the inherent jurisdiction are not *inherent* at all, but are in fact *delegated* powers.[29] Third, and relatedly, by calling it *the* inherent jurisdiction, there is an impression that the issues covered are addressed under a single set of powers, but that is not the case. Finally, the term 'jurisdiction' is one of the most ambiguous in law. Lord Bridge once commented that few words 'have been used with so many different shades of meaning in different contexts or have so freely acquired new meanings with the development of the law as the word jurisdiction'.[30] As just noted, and as explored further in chapter six in particular, there are at least two different senses

[25] See *Re J (1996 Hague Convention) (Morocco)* [2015] EWCA Civ 329, [2015] 2 FLR 513, [75].

[26] This concept is usually just called 'jurisdiction', but elsewhere in this book I term it *authority-jurisdiction* to reduce confusion in a book about 'the inherent jurisdiction'.

[27] The phrase is used in *A v A (Children: Habitual Residence)* [2013] UKSC 60, [2014] AC 1, [70(v)] (Lord Hughes) and *Re B (Habitual Residence: Inherent Jurisdiction)* [2016] UKSC 4, [2016] AC 606, [61] (Lady Hale and Lord Toulson).

[28] This term is still used frequently, though sometimes (inaccurately) as if it has a more specific meaning akin to what I term nationality-based jurisdiction: see **ch 6**.

[29] On adults, see **2.42**. Since at least 1694, the court has sometimes claimed that its power over children is delegated from the Crown, but the historical accuracy of that claim is doubtful: see **2.11**.

[30] *Re McC (A Minor)* [1985] AC 528 (HL), 536.

of the word jurisdiction being used in the phrase 'the inherent jurisdiction', which creates confusion and error.

1.11 More specifically, it is necessary to distinguish the 'inherent jurisdiction' of the High Court in relation to children and some adults – the subject of this book – from wider powers which might be considered inherent in the court, and from 'inherent powers'.

Types of Inherent Jurisdiction Outside the Scope of this Book

1.12 There are numerous other 'inherent jurisdictions' which have nothing to do with the law relating to children and incapacitous or vulnerable adults (or, at least, which are not specific to them). To take a few illustrative examples, the court says that it has inherent jurisdiction: (i) to order the release on bail of a detained suspect, even if there is no statutory power to do so;[31] (ii) to stay proceedings;[32] (iii) for a final court of appeal to discharge or vary its own orders;[33] (iv) to make orders freezing the assets of a party to ensure that legal rights are protected and that judgments can be honoured;[34] and (v) to control vexatious litigation.[35] All of these issues can be called inherent jurisdiction, though some might more properly be termed inherent powers as discussed next; but either way, they are outside the scope of this book.

Inherent Jurisdiction and Inherent Powers

1.13 The terms inherent *jurisdiction* and inherent *powers* are sometimes used interchangeably,[36] and the strict delineation espoused in some contexts[37] is not necessarily applicable to the issues discussed in this book. But generally speaking, the idea of inherent powers can be seen to relate to 'all, but only, such powers as are necessary to enable a court to act effectively and uphold the administration of justice'.[38] As Lord Morris put it in *Connelly v Director of Public Prosecutions*,

[31] *R v Secretary of State for the Home Department, Ex p Turkoglu* [1988] 1 QB 398 (CoA); *Zaoui v Attorney-General* [2005] NZSC 38, [2005] 1 NZLR 577.

[32] Senior Courts Act 1981, s 49(3); see, eg, *Bain v R (New Zealand)* [2009] UKPC 4, [5] (Lord Hoffmann): 'The High Court has an inherent jurisdiction to stay criminal proceedings if it considers that their further prosecution would be an abuse of process.'

[33] *Bain*, ibid, [6]: 'The Privy Council, like other final courts of appeal, has an inherent jurisdiction to discharge or vary its own orders …'; *Taylor v Lawrence* [2003] QB 528 (CoA).

[34] *Mareva Compania Naviera SA v International Bulkcarriers SA* [1975] 2 Lloyd's Rep 509, [1980] 1 All ER 213 (CoA).

[35] *Grepe v Loam* (1887) 37 Ch D 168 (CoA); *Ebert v Venville* [2000] Ch 484 (CoA).

[36] See similar criticism by J Donnelly, 'Inherent Jurisdiction and Inherent Powers in the Irish Courts' (2009) 2 *Judicial Studies Institute Journal* 122, 125.

[37] See, eg, *Seimer v Solicitor-General* [2013] NZSC 68, [2013] 3 NZLR 441.

[38] ibid, [114] (citations omitted).

'a Court which is endowed with a particular jurisdiction has powers which are necessary to enable it to act effectively within such jurisdiction'.[39]

1.14 It is 'spectacularly unhelpful'[40] that one of the leading commentaries on inherent *powers*, an often-cited article by IH Jacob, is inappropriately titled: 'The Inherent Jurisdiction of the Courts'.[41] Joan Donnelly is right to comment that the article has 'spawned widespread confusion in common law jurisdictions on the concept of inherent jurisdiction, causing judges … to confuse it with a court's inherent powers'.[42]

Custodial and Protective Jurisdiction

1.15 Finally, in defining the scope of this book, it is necessary to consider the distinction between the court's 'custodial' and 'protective' powers,[43] more commonly discussed by judges in the mid-twentieth century. The label 'custodial' appears to be another way of describing the *parens patriae* powers over and the responsibility for children.[44] In *S v McC; W v W*, Lord MacDermott suggested that the welfare principle applies when determining 'custodial' issues, delineated by the scope of the statutory welfare principle – the child's custody, upbringing or property (as the language then put it).[45]

1.16 By contrast, Lowe and White describe 'little express attention' having been given to the protective jurisdiction of the court.[46] The authorities on this issue are far from clear, and even those cases that purport to engage with this question give unsatisfactory answers. For example, Lord MacDermott stated that the protective jurisdiction:

> recognises that the infant, as one not sui juris, may stand in need of aid. He must not be allowed to suffer because of his incapacity. But the aim is to ensure that he gets his rights rather than to place him above the law and make his rights superior to those of others. I shall refer to this duty and the powers of the court relative thereto as the 'protective jurisdiction'.[47]

The examples given include appointing or changing a guardian *ad litem* for the child, receiving payment into court of money received by a child from litigation,

[39] *Connelly v Director of Public Prosecutions* [1964] 1 AC 1254 (HL), 1301; see also *Scott v Scott* [1913] AC 917 (HL) and *Bremer Vulkan Schiffbau und Maschinenfabrik v South India Shipping Corpn Ltd* [1981] AC 909 (HL).

[40] P Joseph, *Constitutional and Administrative Law in New Zealand*, 3rd edn (Wellington: Brookers, 2007), 807.

[41] I Jacob, 'The Inherent Jurisdiction of the Courts' [1970] *Current Legal Problems* 23.

[42] Donnelly (n 36) 126.

[43] Lowe and White (n 6) ch 7.

[44] *S v McC; W v W* [1972] AC 24 (HL), 48.

[45] ibid, 48–9.

[46] Lowe and White (n 6) para 7.17.

[47] *S v McC; W v W* [1972] AC 24 (HL), 48.

and approving settlements agreed on a child's behalf.[48] This description appears to reflect largely procedural powers of the court, more akin to inherent powers than inherent jurisdiction.[49]

1.17 The main context in which the court continues to refer expressly to a protective approach is in cases where, exceptionally, the court has been persuaded to invoke its nationality-based jurisdiction to make orders concerning a child abroad.[50] But although the court sometimes says in this context that 'the focus nowadays must be on the *protective* rather than the *custodial* aspect of the inherent jurisdiction',[51] the use of those terms now seems to be quite different from that described by Lord MacDermott. The idea now seems to be that the court has taken an exceptional decision to make decisions about a child where the normal rules do not apply and, given that background, the focus is on protecting a child thought to be at substantial risk.[52] But there is no consistency. Wardship – whereby the *custody* of the child is vested in the court[53] – is expressly said to be available when exercising this *protective* jurisdiction.[54]

1.18 The terms are therefore used in inconsistent and often confusing ways, which have changed substantially over time. They do not serve any useful purpose, and it is unhelpful to continue using them.

Justification for the Continued Use of the Inherent Jurisdiction

1.19 The primary justification that is deployed for the continued existence and exercise of the inherent jurisdiction is *protection*.[55] As McFarlane P explained, 'a primary justification for the continued use of the inherent jurisdiction with respect to children in modern times is to provide *protection* for young people when their welfare demands'.[56] The same principle underlies the approach in relation to *incapacitous* adults, as Lord Brandon explained: 'the Crown as *parens patriae* had both the power and the duty to *protect* the persons and property of those unable to do so for themselves, a category which included both minors …

[48] ibid.
[49] See **1.13** *et seq.*
[50] See **ch 6**.
[51] *Re B (A Child) (Reunite International Child Abduction Centre and others intervening)* [2015] EWCA Civ 886, [2016] AC 606, [38] (rev'd on other grounds, [2016] UKSC 4, [2016] AC 608).
[52] This risk is what justifies the court's intervention at all, and therefore sets the limits of how the court should use its powers: see, eg, *GC v AS (No 2)* [2022] EWHC 310 (Fam), [2022] 2 FLR 756, [29] (Poole J).
[53] See **3.11**.
[54] *A v A* [2013] UKSC 60, [2014] AC 1, [28] (Lady Hale) and [70(iv)] (Lord Hughes).
[55] See also Law Commission (n 6) para 4.1.
[56] *Re T (Secure Accommodation)* [2018] EWCA Civ 2136, [2020] Fam 1, [6], quoted with approval [2021] UKSC 35, [2022] AC 723, [64] (Lady Black).

and persons of unsound mind'.[57] This *protective* approach underpins much of the court's thinking when it deploys its inherent jurisdiction. There are occasional notes of caution that the court should 'be careful to avoid the so-called *protective imperative*',[58] whereby the court is drawn towards an outcome that is *overly* protective of the adult or child concerned.[59]

1.20 At times, this protective rationale is further extended to capacitous but *vulnerable* adults: 'The court exercises a "protective jurisdiction" in relation to vulnerable adults',[60] whom it is said should be able to access the same 'protection' that the Mental Capacity Act 2005 ('MCA 2005') gives to adults who lack capacity.[61] However, a justification built around protection is more controversial when applied to capacitous adults. Reflecting the difficulty of justifying 'protecting' capacitous adults who have not asked for help, the court sometimes limits itself to a narrower aim – noting that capacitous adults are autonomous despite any (perceived) vulnerability, its purpose in some cases is said to be 'to protect and to facilitate their exercise of that autonomy'.[62]

1.21 While the court stresses that 'the distinctive inherent jurisdiction in relation to safeguarding children must nonetheless form a coherent part of the wider law',[63] the court seems willing to disregard fundamental legal principles when exercising this jurisdiction in some cases. As I will show through the book, in many cases the court's *protective imperative* towards children and adults comes through clearly, often at the expense of the coherent application of legal principles.

The Constitutional Role of Judges

1.22 I argue in this book that, through the inherent jurisdiction, the judiciary have tested – and at times exceeded – the limits of their constitutional role. It is therefore necessary to consider briefly the role of judges in the UK Constitution.

[57] *Re F (Mental Patient: Sterilisation)* [1990] 2 AC 1 (HL), 57; see also in the CoA, 26 (Lord Donaldson MR).

[58] *A Local Authority v BF* [2018] EWCA Civ 2962, [2019] COPLR 150, [22(10)] (Baker LJ) (emphasis added).

[59] See *PH v A Local Authority* [2011] EWHC 1704 (Fam), [2012] COPLR 128, [16(viii)] (Baker J), drawing from the 'child protection imperative' described in *Oldham MBC v GW and PW* [2007] EWHC 136 (Fam), [2007] 2 FLR 597, [97] (Ryder J).

[60] *Re SA (Vulnerable Adult with Capacity: Marriage)* [2005] EWHC 2942 (Fam), [2006] 1 FLR 867, [37] (Munby J).

[61] *Re L (Vulnerable Adults with Capacity: Court's Jurisdiction)* [2012] EWCA Civ 253, [2013] Fam 1, [65] (McFarlane LJ) and [79] (Kay LJ).

[62] *FS v RS and JS* [2020] EWFC 63, [2020] 4 WLR 139, [114] (Sir James Munby). See also **3.26**.

[63] *Re T (Secure Accommodation)* [2021] UKSC 35, [2022] AC 723, [188] (Lady Arden).

1.23 Most constitutional law thinkers consider that the UK's constitutional arrangements reflect the logic behind the principle of the separation of powers, namely that governmental power should not be over-concentrated in one body, and there should be checks and balances.[64] To that end, governmental power is exercised by three different institutions: Parliament (the legislature), government (executive) and the judiciary.

1.24 Broadly speaking, Parliament represents the views of the people and makes legislation; the government makes and implements public policy; and the judiciary interprets law and adjudicates legal disputes. However, there are overlaps – judges, for instance, exercise some legislative functions,[65] both when interpreting legislation and by developing the common law. Lord Reid wrote extra-judicially in 1972 that it is a 'fairy tale' to think that judges do not *make* law,[66] otherwise, as Lord Goff later put it, 'the common law would be the same now as it was in the reign of King Henry II'.[67]

1.25 It is not inherently problematic for the judiciary to exercise some legislative functions – what matters is if, in individual instances, power is ripe for abuse due to being over-concentrated in one body or there being insufficient accountability.[68] The risk of abuse of judicial power is reduced by certain generally applicable constitutional and legal principles:[69]

i. The common law only exists to the extent that the matter has not been dealt with by legislation, due to parliamentary sovereignty.[70]
ii. Judges are bound by the doctrine of precedent to follow earlier case law authority.
iii. Judges are bound by the rule of law which, even in its formal (as opposed to substantive) conception, entails that the law should not change too often and should be relatively certain.[71]
iv. The common law typically develops incrementally and by analogy with existing legal remedies.[72]

1.26 One interpretation of the limits on judges' lawmaking powers, proposed by Sir Robert Megarry V-C, is that the court is limited to 'extension of existing laws

[64] For the classic exposition of the separation of powers, see C Montesquieu, *The Spirit of the Laws* (Cambridge: CUP, 1989 [1748]), Book XI, ch 6. For alternative accounts of the UK's constitutional arrangements, *cf* W Bagehot, *The English Constitution* (Oxford: OUP, 2001 [1867]) and O Hood Phillips, 'A Constitutional Myth: Separation of Powers' (1977) 93 *LQR* 11.
[65] See Elliott and Thomas (n 23) 299–302.
[66] J Reid, 'The Judge as Law Maker' (1972–3) 12 *Soc of Public Teachers of Law* 22.
[67] *Kleinwort Benson LTC v Lincoln CC* [1999] 2 AC 349 (HL), 377.
[68] Elliott and Thomas (n 23) 113–115.
[69] ibid 301.
[70] *Attorney-General v De Keyser's Royal Hotel Ltd* [1920] AC 508 (HL); see **3.37** *et seq*.
[71] J Raz, *The Authority of Law* (Oxford: OUP, 1979), ch 11.
[72] *Caparo Industries v Dickman* [1990] 2 AC 605 (HL).

and principles'.[73] For him, while this allowed for the idea that 'there has to be a first time for everything', the judicial role is distinct from creating new law – 'it is no function of the courts to legislate in a new field'.[74] There are at least three reasons for this. First, judicial policy-making is undemocratic[75] – albeit it is always open to Parliament to legislate to reverse a judicial decision. Second, judges cannot be held accountable for their policy-making as easily as Parliament or the government. And third, the court is not institutionally suited to policy-making:[76] it does not generally have the relevant expertise;[77] judges cannot consult on possible changes to the law; and, when issuing judgments, judges are constrained by the facts of the case before them.[78]

1.27 For reasons of democracy, institutional competence, and good policy-making, therefore, the court generally recognises that, while it does perform a law-making function, it must exercise that power cautiously to prevent judicial over-reach. As Lord Phillips CJ put it in the first Annual Review of the Administration of Justice in 2008: 'We recognise the boundaries of our role and the need to accord proper respect to the respective roles of the other two branches of state … and we hope and expect that they will do the same'.[79] Similarly, in the context of the court's power to interpret legislation under s 3 of the Human Rights Act 1998 ('HRA 1998'), Lord Nicholls warned that judges should remain cognisant of their 'constitutional boundary' and should not 'make decisions for which they are not equipped'.[80] As I will explore throughout this book, however, the judiciary have not universally adhered to these limits when utilising the inherent jurisdiction, which makes more real the potential for the abuse of power.

Structure of the Book

1.28 The book is divided into two broad parts. The first (chapters one to five) covers general principles; the second (chapters six to fourteen) focuses on specific areas where the inherent jurisdiction is used. I draw together some of the threads in chapter fifteen.

1.29 Chapter two addresses the history of the inherent jurisdiction over children and adults, showing that the court's understanding of its inherent jurisdiction has changed over time. This is apparent in relation to children, but the history with

[73] *Malone v Metropolitan Police Comr* [1979] Ch 344, 372.
[74] ibid 372–3; see also *Midland Silicones Ldt v Scruttons Ltd* [1962] AC 446 (HL), 467.
[75] See, eg, P Devlin, 'Judges and Lawmakers' (1976) 39 *MLR* 1, 9.
[76] Elliott and Thomas (n 23) 302.
[77] Devlin (n 75) 11.
[78] See L Jaffe, *English and American Judges as Lawmakers* (Oxford: OUP, 1970), 35.
[79] N Phillips, *The Lord Chief Justice's Review of the Administration of Justice in the Courts*, HC 448 (London: TSO, 2008), para 1.4.
[80] *Ghaidan v Godin-Mendoza* [2004] UKHL 30, [2004] 2 AC 557, [33].

respect to adults is more remarkable, where the modern approach is properly seen as a new departure.

1.30 Chapter three analyses the core principles of the inherent jurisdiction. These are the fundamentals that apply – or, at least, ought to apply – whenever the inherent jurisdiction is invoked. I set out the scope of the jurisdiction, and the substantial constitutional limitations that exist to control its exercise. This links to chapter four, which sets out procedural issues that are informative about the nature and scope of the inherent jurisdiction.

1.31 Chapter five provides a comparison with other common law countries that have their own inherent jurisdictions (often with different names). This provides scope for considering different ways in which the jurisdiction may be used, and suggests that the English judges' commitment to and reliance on the inherent jurisdiction may not be as essential as they claim: other countries make far less use of it.

1.32 The second section of the book starts with a discussion of what I term 'nationality-based jurisdiction'. In this area, the court is using the inherent jurisdiction as a foundation for its claim to have authority to make decisions about a particular child in the first place. I address this issue in chapter six.

1.33 From there, I address substantive issues relating to children in chapters seven to twelve, covering child abduction, medical treatment, child protection, deprivation of liberty, adoption and surrogacy, and a range of miscellaneous topics including 'undesirable associations', private law parenting disputes, financial provision for children, restrictions on publicity, and the disposal of a deceased child's body. In all these areas, the inherent jurisdiction is used frequently – in most, I suggest far too often.

1.34 Chapters thirteen and fourteen are about adults. Chapter thirteen is about *incapacitous* adults. While the overall use that is made of the inherent jurisdiction in this context is limited because of the MCA 2005, the fact it is used at all is remarkable, since the court's authority to do so was withdrawn in 1960.

1.35 More remarkable still, the court claims that it has an 'inherent' jurisdiction over adults who are *capacitous* but *vulnerable*, which I address in chapter fourteen. This area of the inherent jurisdiction has no meaningful history, being created by the court around 2005 – its very existence is controversial, and the court has failed to articulate any clear principles that set out when the power is exercisable or on what basis decisions are made.

1.36 I pull these threads together in chapter fifteen, concluding that while some invocations of the inherent jurisdiction are justifiable, the majority of the issues explored in this book show its use to be excessive and inappropriate. I hope that this book draws attention to what the court has been doing, and leads to hard questions about how much of what is happening is actually acceptable.

2

The History of the Court's Inherent Jurisdiction

2.1 The origins of the court's inherent jurisdiction have long been debated. Simpson's *Law and Practice Relating to Infants* in 1875 describes 'much learned discussion' of it,[1] while a century later Sir George Baker P said extra-judicially that the history was 'shrouded in the mists of the Middle Ages and in the feudal system'.[2] With those murky origins in mind, this chapter sets out a broad history.

2.2 I note from the outset that, until the twenty-first century, the term 'inherent jurisdiction' was not generally used. Judges and commenters used phrases such as 'parental jurisdiction',[3] '*parens patriae* jurisdiction', or 'prerogative jurisdiction'.[4]

2.3 I start this chapter with the history of the jurisdiction in relation to children. I then consider the history of the court's powers over adults without capacity to make a particular decision, before addressing adults who have capacity but who are 'vulnerable'.

The Inherent Jurisdiction in Relation to Children

Early History

2.4 Excellent accounts of the origins of wardship and the court's *parens patriae* powers in relation to children are found in Nigel Lowe and Richard White's *Wards of Court* ('Lowe and White');[5] in John Seymour's article *Parens Patriae and Wardship Powers: Their Nature and Origin* ('Seymour');[6] and for the more recent history, in

[1] A Simpson, *A Treatise on the Law and Practice Relating to Infants* (London: Stevens and Haynes, 1875), 136.

[2] Foreword to N Lowe and R White, *Wards of Court*, 1st edn (London: Barry Rose, 1979).

[3] *R v Gyngall* [1893] 2 QB 232 (CoA), 239 (Lord Esher MR); B Bicknell, *The Law and Practice in Relation to Infants* (London: Solicitors' Law Stationery Society, 1928), 85.

[4] Law Commission, *Wards of Court*, WP No 101 (London: HMSO, 1987), para 2.3.

[5] 2nd edn (London: Barry Rose, 1986).

[6] (1994) 14 *OJLS* 159.

Stephen Cretney's *Family Law in the Twentieth Century: A History* ('Cretney').[7] While there are differences of emphasis, these accounts are broadly similar – my work draws on these fuller analyses.

2.5 Wardship originated in feudal times. There were two forms of land tenure in medieval England: *military tenures* and *socage tenures*. Under *military tenures*, when a tenant died leaving an infant heir, the landowning lord gained rights over the heir's person and property, and responsibilities to provide for the infant's maintenance and upbringing during their minority. These rights were saleable and assignable, and could yield large payments for the lord. By contrast, when a *socage tenant* died leaving an infant heir, the heir and the land was placed under the wardship of the nearest relative who was not in line to inherit the property. By at least the thirteenth century, the guardian could not profit from the land and had to account for it to the heir.

2.6 The Crown's involvement in taking a share of the profits in these early wardship cases started with Magna Carta (1215)[8] and the Statute of Marlborough (1267),[9] extended by Edward II in 1322.[10] Seymour explains that, because of the high costs of maintaining infant heirs, lords sought to limit their liability to the Crown, arranging for land to be held under a 'use' – or *trust* as it might now be called. Consequently, the Crown passed the Statute of Uses 1535, the Statute of Wills 1540 and the Act for the Explanation of the Statute of Wills 1542, and set up the Court of Wards to administer and enforce the Crown's rights in relation to land.[11] The Court of Wards (later termed the Court of Wards and Liveries) thus had rather unedifying origins as an administrative machine to increase Crown revenue.[12]

2.7 The Court of Wards did benefit wards by claiming primary jurisdiction over them and thereby protecting them from legal actions in other courts. Nevertheless, the court's interest in wards' wider welfare was limited – 'the protective [function] took second place to the profit-making' that was the court's main purpose.[13] The Court of Wards had jurisdiction only in relation to infants who were knights with land tenure over whom the Crown exercised prerogative wardship. Disputes concerning other infants remained in the Court of Chancery.[14]

[7] (Oxford: OUP, 2003).

[8] Clauses 4–5 (provisions against king and other guardians committing waste in their wards' lands).

[9] Clauses 6 (prohibition of the creation of 'collusive' feoffments to uses to evade wardship) and 17 (compelling a guardian to account when the heir came of age).

[10] Edw II, c 9, *Prerogativa Regis* (1322). See J Baker, *Introduction to English Legal History*, 5th ed (Oxford: OUP, 2019), 261. In relation to adults, see **2.42**.

[11] Henry VIII, c 46, An Act for the Establishment of the Court of the King's Wards (1540).

[12] H Bell, *An Introduction to the History and Records of the Court of Wards and Liveries* (Cambridge: CUP, 2011 [1953]), ch 1.

[13] ibid 114.

[14] W Holdsworth, *History of English Law*, Vol V (London: Methuen and Co, 1924), 309–10, 315.

2.8 The Court of Wards was formally abolished by the Tenures Abolition Act 1660, having ceased to function from 1645–46 when the Commonwealth Parliament passed an Ordinance for its abolition.[15] The 1660 Act allowed 'the law to build on a notion of wardship which involved a fiduciary duty'[16] – in other words, a duty to act in the heir's interests.

2.9 Seymour suggests that it may have been in the eighteenth century that the procedure of making a child a ward *of the court* arose.[17] The principal characteristics of being a ward of court in the modern era – the vesting of custody in the court and the 'no important steps' rule[18] – originated in the earliest feudal wardship cases, where the guardian gained powers and duties in relation to the infant's upbringing including issues such as marriage. It is likely, therefore, that the court gained significant powers over the person of the ward as well as their property by this period.

2.10 It is a matter of debate when the connection between wardship and the court's broader *parens patriae* jurisdiction was first made.[19] The two jurisdictions only began to merge after the Court of Wards was abolished, when the 'parental' approach – originally only within the *parens patriae* jurisdiction – began to feature in wardship cases as well.[20] Even in the 1820s wardship remained premised on the ward having property, although the court had begun to suggest that this was more about practicality – providing resources from which to enforce orders – than principle.[21]

2.11 Seymour explores differing explanations for the origins and scope of the Court of Chancery's broader *parental* or *parens patriae* role.[22] Although some judges equated the position of children with that of incapacitous adults, the history is different. As addressed below,[23] control over the estates of the mentally incompetent was expressly delegated to the Lord Chancellor by each monarch by Royal Warrant, whereas no such history exists in relation to the court's powers over children. Moreover, when Lord Somers LC first made the claim that the two were connected in *Falkland v Bernie*,[24] he cited no authority to support that view.

[15] ibid 150.
[16] Seymour (n 6) 165.
[17] Citing *Smith v Smith* (1745) 2 Atk 304; 26 ER 977.
[18] See **3.11** *et seq.*
[19] Seymour (n 6) 165.
[20] ibid 171, cites Lord Redesdale and Lord Manners in *Wellesley v Wellesley* (1828) 2 Bli NS 124; 4 ER 1078 as saying that the *parental* jurisdiction had been exercised for 150 years and 'more than a century' respectively. See similarly W MacPherson, *A Treatise on the Law Relating to Infants* (London: Maxwell and Son,1842), 102; J Chambers, *A Practical Treatise on the Jurisdiction of the High Court of Chancery over the Persons and Property of Infants* (London: Saunders and Benning, 1842), 11.
[21] *Wellesley v Beaufort* (1827) 2 Russ 1, 21; 38 ER 236, 243 (Lord Eldon).
[22] Seymour (n 6) 166–71.
[23] See **2.38** *et seq.*
[24] *Falkland v Bernie* (1696) 2 Vern 333; 23 ER 814.

Seymour suggests, indeed, that the Court of Chancery's 'parental' jurisdiction with respect to children was 'plucked from the air' in *Falkland*, then reinforced in later cases in a period when 'precedent yielded to the exercise of general discretion'.[25] Consequently, while the jurisdictions over children and incapacitous adults were both rhetorically tied to the Crown's *parens patriae* powers, the two likely had no real connection. Whereas the jurisdiction over adults was expressly delegated by the Crown, the parental jurisdiction over children was probably merely claimed by an assertive court at the end of the seventeenth century. Whether this justifies its current label as an 'inherent' jurisdiction is debatable, but having been exercised without challenge for well over 300 years it is reasonable to term it that.

1850–1950

2.12 As Seymour comments, 'doubts about the foundations of the *parens patriae* jurisdiction do not seem to have troubled later courts',[26] and by the middle of the nineteenth century, the *parens patriae* approach of the Court of Chancery was firmly established in wardship proceedings.[27]

2.13 By the latter part of the nineteenth century, the court no longer required a child to have property for there to be wardship.[28] In *Brown v Collins*, Kay J explained that the court's jurisdiction stemmed from the child being 'a British subject', and existed 'whether they have property or not'.[29]

2.14 While the marriage of a ward was a significant issue from earliest times,[30] the court took a particular interest in it from the mid-nineteenth century. The first edition of *Simpson on the Law of Infants* in 1875 devoted an entire chapter to the marriage of wards, detailing the 'requisite qualifications' of a 'fitting marriage'.[31] Wards were not permitted to marry without the court's consent, and those who facilitated such a marriage could face a custodial sentence.[32]

2.15 The Matrimonial Causes Act 1857, s 35 gave the Divorce Court the power to make children wards of court after divorce, though in practice this power was exercised only where 'substantial property' was involved.[33] By now, there were a

[25] Seymour (n 6) 172.
[26] ibid 173.
[27] *Re Spence* (1847) 2 Ph 247, 252; 41 ER 937, 938. See also Lord Cranworth LC in *Hope v Hope* (1854) 4 De GM & G 238, 344–5; 43 ER 534, 540–1.
[28] Seymour (n 6) 176, cites *Re McGrath (Infants)* [1893] 1 Ch 143 as showing caution about this issue right to the end of the century.
[29] *Brown v Collins* (1883) 25 ChD 56, 60.
[30] It was certainly addressed by the Court of Wards: Bell (n 12) 114.
[31] Simpson (n 1) ch 19.
[32] In *Re H's Settlement* [1909] 2 Ch 260, Warrington J committed the ward himself to prison for marrying without the court's consent.
[33] Cretney (n 7) 585.

number of procedural routes by which a child might become a ward of the court,[34] but none was entirely straightforward and all relied on there being some financial aspect to the case. In this period, the status of wardship appears to have always arisen as an aside: '[n]o child, even if in need of protection, could be made a ward by simple application to that effect.'[35] Nonetheless, by the start of the twentieth century, wardship 'had acquired all the characteristics that it now has save that because of the procedural restraints it was still only invoked in practice in connection with wealthy wards'.[36]

2.16 From at least the end of the nineteenth century,[37] wardship applications were determined in accordance with the welfare principle,[38] and this approach was put on a statutory footing by the Guardianship of Infants Act 1925. By now, the jurisdiction was said to be 'paternal',[39] or sometimes 'parental'.[40] Nevertheless, wardship was still thought 'generally difficult to exercise' if the child had no property.[41]

1950–1989

2.17 This period begins with the Law Reform (Miscellaneous Provisions) Act 1949, which aimed 'to alter the law with regard to making infants wards of court'.[42] Only one provision in the Act addressed wardship or the inherent jurisdiction. By s 9:

i. a child became a ward automatically when an application for wardship was made, and that wardship continued only for such period as the court rules provided unless it was confirmed by the court;
ii. other than for that initial period between an application being made and a hearing, a child could only become a ward by order of the court; and
iii. the court could terminate wardship by order to that effect.

2.18 Far from aiming to encourage wardship, the provision was an attempt to impose judicial oversight and stop children being made wards as an abuse of process. An 'odd anomaly' had arisen, whereby a person could ward a child simply

[34] Simpson (n 1) 223.
[35] Lowe and White (n 2) para 4.1.
[36] ibid para 1.6.
[37] The idea begins far earlier (Bell (n 12) ch 6), but it was in this period that the principle of the ward's welfare being the court's *paramount* interest rose to the fore.
[38] See, eg, *Re Callaghan* (1885) 28 Ch D 186 (CoA), 189.
[39] *R v Gyngall* [1893] 2 QB 232 (CoA), 238–9 (Lord Esher MR); see also *J v C* [1970] AC 668 (HL), 720 (Lord Upjohn).
[40] *Scott v Scott* [1913] AC 417 (HL), 437 (Viscount Haldane LC).
[41] B Bicknell, *The Law and Practice in Relation to Infants* (London: Solicitors' Law Stationery Society, 1928), 85. See *Re Agar-Ellis* (1883) 24 Ch 317 (CoA): *cf* 328 (Brett MR) and 332 (Cotton LJ).
[42] HC Deb, 28 January 1949, vol 460, col 1245.

by settling a minor sum of money on them – this could be done without the consent of the child's parent(s), and the status was automatic: the court could not prevent it happening, nor discharge the wardship once made.[43] Lord Merriman,[44] arguing in favour of the new provision, noted that the sums of money being used for this purpose had dropped from £5 (about £150 in today's money) to 2/6d (less than £5 in today's money), a situation he described as 'absolutely farcical and … liable to abuse in connection with the custody of children'.[45] The Act therefore aimed to prevent parents (and others) settling nominal sums on a child and then bringing proceedings superficially connected to that property but which were really about regulating the child's upbringing[46] – instead, a High Court judge would have to approve applications for wardship.[47]

2.19 The court retained the power to ward a child within existing proceedings, but the most straightforward route to wardship was now simply to issue an application under the new Act. Wardship commenced *automatically* on the application being issued, but the Rules provided that it terminated again 21 days later unless a High Court judge had ordered it to continue.[48] And section 9(3) gave the court, for the first time, the power to 'de-ward' a child, 'remov[ing] the hardships hitherto caused by the irrevocable nature of the writ'.[49]

2.20 Despite lawmakers' intentions to reduce the use of wardship, the effect was to enable a child 'to be made a ward solely for the purpose of protecting him', as opposed to administering property.[50] This new simplified procedure, and the simultaneous introduction of the Legal Aid and Advice Act 1949, 'opened the jurisdiction to a wider category of people'.[51]

2.21 Whether in response to pressures in relation to wardship or not, an important and much-cited decision of Lord Denning MR in 1968 made explicit that the inherent jurisdiction and wardship were not synonymous, and that the inherent jurisdiction could be exercised without a child being made a ward first. Lord Denning explained, in what became a classic statement of the law, that wardship was 'machinery' that is used 'as a matter of convenience' to operate the inherent jurisdiction:

> I think that [counsel] takes altogether too limited a view of the jurisdiction of the Court of Chancery. It derives from the right and duty of the Crown as *parens patriae* to take

[43] HL Deb, 28 July 1949, vol 164, col 670.
[44] Then President of the High Court's Probate, Divorce and Admiralty Division.
[45] HL Deb 28 July 1949, vol 164, col 671.
[46] Cretney (n 7) 585.
[47] HL Deb 28 July 1949, vol 164, col 670 (Lord Llewellin).
[48] RSC 1950, Order 54P, r 3. If a listing was provided during the 21-day period, the wardship extended until the hearing date even if outside 21 days from the application being issued. There is currently no equivalent time limitation: see **4.17**.
[49] O Kahn-Freud, 'Law Reform (Miscellaneous Provisions) Act 1949' (1950) 12 *MLR* 222, 225.
[50] Lowe and White (n 2) para 1.13.
[51] ibid para 1.13.

> care of those who are not able to take care of themselves. The Crown delegated this power to the Lord Chancellor, who exercised it in his Court of Chancery.[52] In the ordinary way he only exercised it when there was property to be applied for the infant: see *Wellesley v Beaufort (Duke of)*.[53] The child was usually made a ward of court, and thereafter no important step in the child's life could be taken without the court's consent. But that was only machinery. Even if there was no property and the child was not a ward of court, nevertheless the Court of Chancery had power to interfere for the protection of the infant by making whatever order might be appropriate. That was made clear by Lord Cottenham LC in *In re Spence*,[54] where the infants were not wards and there was no property. …
>
> This wide jurisdiction of the old Court of Chancery is now vested in the High Court of Justice and can be exercised by any judge of the High Court. As a matter of convenience, the jurisdiction is exercised by making the child a ward of court and putting it under the care of a judge of the Chancery Division. But that is only machinery. If a question arises as to the welfare of a child before any judge of the High Court, he can make such order as may be appropriate in the circumstances. He need not send the case over to a Chancery judge. Nor need he adjourn the case for the child to be made a ward of court.[55]

2.22 Lowe and White noted a 'steady increase' in the number of wardship applications from 1951 onwards, with a consequence that 'the scope of all the jurisdiction has developed almost beyond recognition from its feudal roots and even since 1949'.[56] Lowe and White also ascribe part of the cause of the increase in applications – from 74 in 1951 to 2,815 in 1985[57] – to the transfer of the wardship jurisdiction from the Chancery Division to the newly-created Family Division in 1970.[58] One consequence of this change was that the Family Division had District Registries, which led to 'increasing familiarity with wardship in the provinces',[59] and reduced the costs and inconvenience previously associated with a wardship application.[60]

2.23 The Family Law Reform Act 1969 added two powers to the court's wardship arsenal. By s 6, the court was empowered to order periodic payments for the maintenance of a ward, and s 7 enabled the court to commit a ward to the care of a local authority ('LA'). The Act also reduced the age to which the court could exercise its inherent jurisdiction from 21 to 18, in line with the change to

[52] *Cf* **2.11**: the claim that the power was 'delegated' from the Crown reflects the evolving narrative, but has limited historical support.

[53] *Wellesley v Beaufort (Duke of)* (1827) 2 Russ 1, 20, 21; 38 ER 236.

[54] *In re Spence* (1847) 2 Ph 247; 41 ER 937.

[55] *Re L (An Infant)* [1968] P 119 (CoA), 156. See also W Holdsworth, *History of English Law*, Vol VI (London: Methuen and Co, 1924), 648.

[56] Lowe and White (n 2) para 1.13.

[57] ibid para 10.

[58] Administration of Justice Act 1970.

[59] Lowe and White (n 2) para 1.13.

[60] *Re H (A Minor) (Wardship: Jurisdiction)* [1978] Fam 65 (CoA), 72 (Ormrod LJ).

the age of majority more generally. Cretney notes that 'contrary to expectations (or hopes) [the Act] had no effect on the increase in the number of applications to ward a child'.[61] Indeed, the express power to place wards in LA care likely fuelled the 'exponential' increase in the use of wardship proceedings.[62]

2.24 A significant shift towards the end of this period came from the House of Lords decisions in *A v Liverpool CC*[63] and *Re W (A Minor) (Wardship: Jurisdiction)*.[64] These cases clarified that the court could not use wardship to review LA decisions about children made under the LA's statutory powers,[65] and perhaps led to a tempering of wardship applications in at least some types of case.[66]

2.25 At the same time, it was becoming apparent that the law in relation to children in general, including wardship, was 'complicated, confusing and unclear'.[67] Regarding the inter-relationship between wardship and statutory provisions for child protection, for example, Ormrod LJ in 1978 noted that 'in the existing state of the law it is difficult to know where the limits [of the wardship jurisdiction] lie'.[68] There was a clear sense – expressly encouraged by the court[69] – that the wardship jurisdiction offered a (partial) solution to flaws in the statutory schemes, and LAs in particular were making extensive use of it.[70] This confused state of the law led to the Law Commission's work on children in the 1980s, which included a specific consultation on wardship.[71]

The Law Commission's Consultation on Wardship

2.26 The Law Commission's consultation considered the role of wardship in the context of a sophisticated statutory child law regime, in circumstances where substantial reform of child law generally was required. Amongst various proposals, one was that wardship should be abolished, with some of its key features

[61] Cretney (n 7) 588.

[62] N Lowe, 'Inherently Disposed to Protect Children: The Continuing Role of Wardship' in R Probert and C Barton (Eds), *Fifty Years in Family Law: Essays for Stephen Cretney* (Cambridge: Intersentia, 2012), 165; Cretney (n 7) 585, fn 125.

[63] *A v Liverpool CC* [1982] AC 363 (HL).

[64] *Re W (A Minor) (Wardship: Jurisdiction)* [1985] AC 791 (HL).

[65] See **3.53** *et seq*. *A v Liverpool CC* and *Re W* were seen as ground-breaking, though they reflected earlier similar decisions: see, eg, *Re Baker* [1962] Ch 201 (CoA), 223 (Pearson LJ); *Re M* [1961] Ch 328 (CoA), 341 (Lord Evershed MR).

[66] Lowe and White (n 2) paras 1.15–6.

[67] Law Commission, *Review of Child Law: Guardianship and Custody*, Law Com 172 (London: HMSO, 1988) ('Law Com 172'), paras 1.1 and 1.3.

[68] *Re H (A Minor) (Wardship: Jurisdiction)* [1978] Fam 65 (CoA), 72.

[69] See, eg, *Re D (A Minor) (Justices' Decision: Review)* [1977] Fam 159, 164 (Dunn J); *Re C (A Minor) (Justices' Decision: Review)* (1981) 2 FLR 62 (CoA); *Re LH (A Minor)* [1986] 2 FLR 306, 310 (Sheldon J); *Re R (A Minor) (Discharge of Care Order: Wardship)* [1987] 2 FLR 400 (CoA).

[70] Lowe and White (n 2) paras 1.14–15; Cretney (n 7) 589–91.

[71] Law Commission, *Review of Child Law: Wards of Court*, WP No 101 (London, HMSO, 1987).

incorporated within a new statutory code. This proposal received very little support,[72] and provoked strong resistance from the High Court judiciary.[73] High Court resistance to any restrictions on its wardship powers was not new, as former Law Commissioner Stephen Cretney recalled from a similar discussion as part of an earlier Law Commission project:

> We were told, in graphic language, that Carey Street [adjacent to the Royal Courts of Justice] would be rendered impassable by the bodies of the Judges of that division were we to fetter the wardship jurisdiction ...[74]

2.27 Mr Justice Sheldon wrote to the Law Commission, expressing views 'held also, I believe, by most, if not all, of the Family Division Judges', arguing against any reform of the court's wardship powers. His view was that 'an undefined and unlimited wardship jurisdiction is the most valuable weapon that the court has in its arsenal in dealing with the welfare of children'.[75] Hollings J wrote to express specific agreement with Sheldon J's letter,[76] while HHJ Callman (a long-time Deputy High Court Judge) considered the Commission's idea of abolishing wardship 'an academic and unrealistic approach [that is] far too restrictive and limiting'.[77] Booth J was the only High Court Judge to express any support for the Commission's proposals, and then only on the condition of 'the court having the full jurisdiction to act in the best interests of the child as the High Court can presently do in wardship'[78] – in other words, if wardship was to be abolished, the same unlimited powers must be provided under statute.

[72] John Hall was one of the few to favour this approach: Archives, letter dated 12 April 1987. Other academic comment was cautious, favouring the retention of the wardship jurisdiction to deal with lacunae in any new statutory scheme: see, eg, Martin Parry, Archives, letter dated 28 May 1987 and Andrew Bainham, Archives, letter dated 15 June 1987. Olive Stone expressed 'astonishment' that the Commission had even considered abolishing wardship: 'Recent legislation should be in force and under attack in the courts for not less than two decades, and preferably longer, before we can have confidence in its effectiveness': Archives, letter dated 6 May 1987.

[73] The Law Commission's record of 'Wardship Interviews with Judges' conducted on 1 July 1987 is marked in the National Archives as 'destroyed'; similar interviews about the wider custody consultation are 'closed until 01 January 2047'. Around 10 individual items within the Archives on the wardship consultation have been removed, marked as 'closed' until various dates between 2047 and 2090. Quite what could be so sensitive as to require being classified for up to 100 years is hard to imagine.

[74] Archives, letter dated 1 June 1987.

[75] Archives, letter dated 18 June 1987. Sheldon J wrote again a month later, to 'reinforce my plea ... that there should be no diminution of or interference with our wardship jurisdiction': Archives, letter dated 15 July 1987.

[76] Archives, letter dated 23 June 1987. Brenda Hoggett wrote back noting that the Law Commission's wardship proposals had 'certainly provoked a great deal of interest' and that 'I think that the view of the judiciary is pretty clear and unanimous': Archives, letter dated 25 June 1987.

[77] Archives, letter dated 29 July 1987. See similarly the Council of Her Majesty's Circuit Judges: Archives, letter dated 3 July 1987.

[78] Archives, undated submission to the Law Commission. Cf the statutory wardship powers in Australia and New Zealand: see **5.21** and **5.26** respectively.

2.28 Law Commissioner Brenda Hoggett's contemporaneous academic writing about the then-defunct inherent jurisdiction in relation to incapacitous adults (see below[79]) makes for an interesting comparison. Noting judicial calls for the 'speedy restitution' of the inherent jurisdiction over adults,[80] Hoggett wrote: 'some members of the judiciary may well be tempted to regard it as a natural right of which they have been wrongly deprived'.[81] Judicial reaction to the suggested abolition of wardship over children reveals a similar attitude.

2.29 While the Law Commission ultimately compromised and deferred a full consideration of wardship,[82] significant reforms were proposed and later adopted as part of the Children Act 1989 ('CA 1989'). One area that the Law Commission did not engage with, though – despite significant pressure from judicial[83] and other respondents[84] – was reform of *A v Liverpool CC*[85] and *Re W*,[86] which had imposed limitations on the High Court's power, in wardship, to interfere with other statutory bodies, such as LAs' decision-making in relation to children.[87] Indeed, the principles of those cases are reflected in various aspects of the CA 1989.

The Law Commission's Report and the Children Act 1989

2.30 Having decided against abolishing wardship, the Law Commission's final recommendation was to 'incorporate the most valuable features of wardship into … a new statutory scheme' which 'should reduce the need to resort to wardship proceedings save in the most unusual and complex cases'.[88] A particular way in which this aim was to be achieved was through *prohibited steps orders*, which

[79] See **2.39** *et seq*.
[80] *T v T* [1988] Fam 52, 68 (Wood J).
[81] B Hoggett, 'The Royal Prerogative in Relation to the Mentally Disordered: Resurrection, Resuscitation, or Rejection?' in M Freeman (Ed), *Medicine, Ethics and the Law* (London: UCL Press, 1988), 85.
[82] No further review ever took place.
[83] Hollings J wrote that 'the restrictions imposed by *A v Liverpool Corp* etc ought to be removed or modified': Archives, letter dated 23 June 1987. Sheldon J, pressing for the removal of the *A v Liverpool CC* restrictions on wardship, strikingly asked: 'Why … should the High Court not have the power, in effect, to interfere in any children's case if and whenever it considers that it would be proper to do so?': Archives, letter dated 15 July 1987 (and similarly on 18 June 1987). Hoggett replied to Sheldon J: 'Your suggestion that the High Court should be able, in effect, to interfere in any children's case if and whenever it considers that it would be proper to do so is a most interesting one': Archives, letter dated 17 July 1987.
[84] The Family Law Bar Association described *A v Liverpool CC* as 'the single biggest blot on our family law jurisprudence' that 'should be reversed by statute': Archives, undated submission to the Law Commission.
[85] [1982] AC 363 (HL); see **3.54–3.56**.
[86] [1985] AC 791 (HL); see **3.56**.
[87] Judges tried to side-step *A v Liverpool* in their judgments as well: see, eg, *D v X CC (No 1)* [1985] FLR 275 (Hollis J) and *D v X CC (No 2)* [1985] FLR 279 (Waite J); see M Hayes, 'Relatives, Care Proceedings and Wardship' [1984] *Fam Law* 234.
[88] Law Com 172, para 1.4.

would allow the court to 'spell out those matters which will have to be referred back to the court' rather than relying on 'the vague requirement in wardship that no "important step" may be taken'.[89] The Commission proposed expanding the range of people who could apply for private law orders, so that the benefits of wardship's standing rules – that anyone with a legitimate interest in the child can apply – would be extended to the new statutory scheme.[90] A further measure to disincentivise wardship applications was a specific power that, in any proceedings brought under the High Court's inherent jurisdiction, the court 'should be able to dispose of them by means of an order under the new [statutory] scheme'.[91]

2.31 The Commission's proposals were adopted and implemented by the CA 1989. Private law orders (*prohibited steps orders* and *specific issue orders*[92]) were modelled on wardship with the aim of ending the need for inherent jurisdiction proceedings in virtually all cases.[93] In child protection cases, specific limitations on the inherent jurisdiction were introduced by s 100 of the Act,[94] which:

- repealed the court's statutory power to use wardship to place a child in LA care;[95]
- imposed prohibitions on the court's ability to use the inherent jurisdiction to require a child to be accommodated by an LA;[96]
- prevented LAs from making any application under the High Court's inherent jurisdiction without leave. Leave could be granted only if the remedy sought was not one available to the LA under any statutory powers *and* if there was reasonable cause to think that the child would suffer significant harm if the inherent jurisdiction were not invoked.[97]

2.32 This dramatic re-writing of child law led to a marked change of attitude towards the inherent jurisdiction. The Court of Appeal in *Re T (Child: Representation)* in 1994 set the tone for the post-CA 1989 approach:

> The courts' undoubted discretion to allow wardship proceedings to go forward in a suitable case is subject to their clear duty, in loyalty to the scheme and purpose of the Children Act legislation, to permit recourse to wardship only when it becomes apparent to the judge in any particular case that the question which the court is determining in regard to the minor's upbringing or property cannot be resolved under the statutory procedures ...[98]

[89] Law Com 172, para 4.20.
[90] Law Com 172, paras 4.32 and 4.41.
[91] Law Com 172, para 4.35.
[92] CA 1989, s 8.
[93] Law Com 172, paras 4.18–4.20.
[94] See also **3.27** *et seq*, **9.5–9.6** and **15.5–15.7**.
[95] CA 1989, s 100(1).
[96] CA 1989, s 100(2).
[97] CA 1989, s 100(3)–(5).
[98] [1994] Fam 49 (CoA), 59–60 (Waite LJ).

2.33 For the better part of 20 years after the passage of the CA 1989, the court rarely invoked wardship or the inherent jurisdiction, making use of its new statutory powers and embodying the policy of the Act to 'reduce the need to resort to wardship proceedings save in the most unusual and complex cases'.[99] While Bainham initially suggested that there was 'a good chance that the independent wardship jurisdiction will outlive its usefulness and become redundant',[100] from the start the court suggested some continued role for wardship and the inherent jurisdiction. Shortly after the Act entered force, Waite LJ for example commented that '[i]t would be rash to start writing obituaries today for a jurisdiction which as survived with protean tenacity down the centuries'.[101]

2.34 Things started to change in 1999, with Singer J's decision in *Re KR (Abduction: Forcible Removal by Parents)*,[102] which James Munby later argued marked 'the re-invigoration of the inherent jurisdiction in relation to children'.[103] While the court had been using the inherent jurisdiction before, *Re KR* pushed the door open and gave the inherent jurisdiction over children a new lease of life. From being a subsidiary set of powers used only in exceptional circumstances, the inherent jurisdiction started to re-claim its former position as a go-to, almost default reaction to some types of case,[104] even when statutory remedies were available.

2.35 The change of approach is apparent from the Supreme Court's decision in *Re NY (Abduction: Inherent Jurisdiction)* in 2019.[105] Invited expressly to hold that the inherent jurisdiction should not be used in an international child abduction case where the CA 1989 remedy of a *specific issue order* would perform the same function,[106] the court declined. Lord Wilson held that 'Parliament … nowhere sought to preclude exercise of the inherent jurisdiction so as to make orders *equivalent* to those for which sections 8 and 10 of [the CA 1989] provide',[107] and that '[t]here is no law which precludes the commencement of an application under the inherent jurisdiction unless the issue "cannot" be resolved under the 1989 Act'.[108]

2.36 The important point for present purposes is the tone. Whereas in *Re T* in 1994, Waite LJ had stressed the need to use the CA 1989 unless the particular question '*cannot* be resolved under the statutory procedures',[109] by 2019 Lord Wilson

[99] Law Com 172, para 1.4.
[100] A Bainham, 'The Children Act 1989: The Future of Wardship' [1990] *Family Law* 270.
[101] *Re X (Wardship: Disclosure of Documents)* [1992] Fam 124 (CoA), 137.
[102] *Re KR (Abduction: Forcible Removal by Parents)* [1999] 2 FLR 542.
[103] J Munby, 'Whither the Inherent Jurisdiction? Part I' [2021] *Fam Law* 215, 221.
[104] In *AS v CPW* [2020] EWHC 1238 (Fam), [2020] 4 WLR 127, [31], Mostyn J refers to such applications as 'almost a reflex'.
[105] *Re NY (Abduction: Inherent Jurisdiction)* [2019] UKSC 49, [2019] 3 WLR 962.
[106] I acted as counsel for the appellant, with Mark Twomey QC and Alex Laing, instructed by Dawson Cornwell.
[107] *Re NY (Abduction: Inherent Jurisdiction)* [2019] UKSC 49, [2019] 3 WLR 962, [40] (emphasis added). On *Re NY*, see also **3.43–3.48**, **7.16**, **7.21–7.28** and **15.6–15.7**.
[108] ibid [44].
[109] *Re T (Child: Representation)* [1994] Fam 49 (CoA), 60 (emphasis added).

specifically disavowed that approach, instead permitting applicants to use either even when the court's powers were the same under the CA 1989.

2.37 As the remainder of this book will demonstrate, the court continues to use the inherent jurisdiction in a wide array of cases including, as I argue, when there are adequate statutory remedies available and in circumstances where the court's use of its inherent jurisdiction runs contrary to statutory limitations.

The Inherent Jurisdiction in Relation to Adults

2.38 In this section, I chart the history of the court's powers in relation to: (i) adults who lack mental capacity to make a relevant decision, and (ii) adults who have mental capacity, but who are categorised as 'vulnerable' because some external factor (another person, usually) is undermining their autonomy to make a relevant decision. The modern cases often elide these two categories and use the terms '(in)capacity' and 'vulnerability' interchangeably – doing so is 'a misleading conflation of two quite distinct things'.[110] Care is therefore needed because both the history and the modern law are very different for these two groups. In mapping this history, I draw on the work of Brenda Hoggett in 'The Royal Prerogative in Relation to the Mentally Disordered: Resurrection, Resuscitation or Rejection?' ('Hoggett'),[111] and James Munby in 'Protecting the Rights of Vulnerable and Incapacitous Adults – The Role of the Courts: An Example of Judicial Law Making' ('Munby (2014)')[112] and Parts I and II of 'Whither the Inherent Jurisdiction?' ('Munby (2021)').[113]

Incapacitous Adults

2.39 At the outset, it is necessary to address terminology. First, prior to the twentieth century, judges never referred to the court's jurisdiction in relation to incapacitous adults as an 'inherent jurisdiction'; as I will set out, the jurisdiction was delegated from the Crown, and was referred to almost exclusively as the (Royal) prerogative. Consequently, although the modern cases treat this area as part of 'the' inherent jurisdiction, historically the prerogative was quite separate from the court's jurisdiction in respect of children. Analogy with the children cases is therefore complicated and in many ways inapt.[114]

[110] J Munby, 'Whither the Inherent Jurisdiction? Part II' [2021] *Fam Law* 365, 370.
[111] In M Freeman, *Medicine, Ethics and the Law* (London: UCL Press, 1988).
[112] [2014] *CFLQ* 64.
[113] [2021] *Fam Law* 215 and 365 respectively.
[114] Hoggett (n 111) 88–9.

2.40 Second, there is a question mark over whether the jurisdiction in relation to incapacitous adults was part of the Crown's *parens patriae* powers. On the one hand, the jurisdiction in respect of incapacitous adults and the Crown's *parens patriae* powers appear to have different origins. On the other, Hoggett accepts that 'the rationale for the two could be the same',[115] and certainly by the nineteenth century the judges were referring to *parens patriae* in this context.[116] Whether this label was strictly accurate or not is therefore probably not crucial, since the two powers have long been equated in substance. I use the term *parens patriae* in this section.

2.41 Third, historically the law differentiated between 'idiots' (those who congenitally lacked mental capacity from birth) and 'lunatics' (those who lost capacity later in life). While there were overlaps, the law treated the two groups differently in important respects, and so I continue to use this language where it is necessary for clarity.

2.42 The Crown's involvement in the management of the lands of adults of unsound mind seems to have begun in the reign of Henry III (reigned 1216–72), and was first set out in statute by Edward II (reigned 1307–27).[117] Known as *de Praerogative Regis*, the Act entrusted the custody of idiots' person and property to the king, thereby giving the Crown a beneficial interest in their lands and vesting the profits of those lands in the king. The position was the same for lunatics, except the king could not profit from their lands and had to account for them.[118]

2.43 The state of being an idiot or a lunatic had to be evidenced 'by inquisition'. Initially conducted by *escheators* (local representatives of the Crown), these inquisitions were later passed to five Commissioners appointed under the Great Seal – but in either case, assessed by a jury until 1853,[119] and regulated throughout by statute.[120] According to Blackstone, juries rarely returned a verdict of idiocy,[121] and so, in practice, most people were treated as lunatics and the focus was on preserving and protecting the property of the person.[122]

2.44 While the Crown plainly had wide powers in relation to the person and property of mentally incapacitated people, there were important limitations that increased over time, and which Hoggett highlights as differentiating the position further from that in relation to children.[123] The most important was that the

[115] ibid 96.

[116] See, eg, *Ex p Cramner* (1806) 12 Ves Jun 445, 449; 33 ER 168, 170 (Lord Erskine); *Re Spence* (1847) 2 Ph 247, 252; 41 ER 937, 938.

[117] Edw II, c 9, *Prerogativa Regis* (1322).

[118] Hoggett (n 111) 89–90.

[119] Lunacy Regulation Act 1853.

[120] Hoggett (n 111) 91, citing H Theobald, *The Law Relating to Lunacy* (London: Stevens and Sons, 1924), 23 *et seq.*

[121] W Blackstone, *Commentaries on the Law of England*, 11th edn (Oxford: Clarendon Press, 1811), 303–5, cited by Hoggett (n 111) 90.

[122] Hoggett (n 111) 90.

[123] ibid 91.

court's jurisdiction relied on the individual first having been found to be an idiot or a lunatic at an inquisition, a process which 'appears to have been a *sine qua non* for the exercise of the Crown's powers'.[124]

2.45 The exercise of the Crown's prerogative powers over idiots and lunatics was delegated by each monarch by Royal Warrant to the Lord Chancellor *personally*,[125] and eventually by further delegation to the Chancery judges in the High Court.[126] The implication, at least, was that without such Warrant, the authority would revert to the monarch,[127] and the jurisdiction in relation to incapacitous adults was not inherent in *the court* at all:[128] Chancery judges were exercising delegated prerogative powers.

2.46 Parliament consolidated much of the existing legislation into the Lunacy Act 1890. The legislation, however, clearly assumed the continued existence of prerogative powers in some circumstances; *Re Sefton*, for instance, shows that the prerogative retained a residual role, allowing the court to address issues on which the Act was silent.[129]

2.47 The Mental Health Act 1959 led to a major change of practice. On its coming into force in 1960, the Royal Warrant issued by Elizabeth II when she took the throne in 1956 was revoked, so ending the judges' prerogative jurisdiction over incapacitous adults. While the expectation, presumably, was that these powers would no longer be needed, it created a serious lacuna in the law:

> The problem arose because, while the 1959 Act transferred the inherent *parens patriae* jurisdiction in relation to an incapacitated adult's financial affairs to the (old) Court of Protection, the corresponding jurisdiction in relation to such an adult's non-financial affairs was inadvertently abolished.[130]

2.48 Not until the passage of the Mental Capacity Act 2005 ('MCA 2005') was this situation addressed in legislation. Meanwhile, though, the High Court responded to concern about its inability to provide for the medical treatment of incapacitous adults who were not covered by the Mental Health Acts by invoking its declaratory powers.[131] The first step was in *T v T*:[132] Wood J called for

[124] ibid.

[125] *Ex p Lund* (1802) 6 Ves Jun 781; 31 ER 1306; *Beall v Smith* (1873) LR 9 ChApp 85, 92. See W Holdsworth, *History of English Law*, Vol 1 (London: Methuen and Co, 1922), 475.

[126] Hoggett (n 111) 92; Munby (2014) (n 112) 67.

[127] Presumably it would be exercised through Ministers as part of the prerogative, since the monarch cannot personally decide legal cases: *Prohibitions Del Roy* (1607) 12 Coke Rep 63; 77 ER 1342.

[128] Hoggett (n 111) 92.

[129] *Re Sefton* [1898] 2 Ch 378.

[130] Munby (2014) (n 112) 67. The use of 'inherent' in this passage, and throughout Munby's writing, is misleading: the label was never used historically since, as Hoggett showed, the jurisdiction was not *inherent*, but *delegated*. Query whether this is a deliberate choice by Munby, since the subsequent court activity that he led is far more easily justified if the jurisdiction is conceived as being inherent, something the court always had.

[131] N Lowe, 'The Limits of the Wardship Jurisdiction Part 1: Who Can Be Made a Ward of Court?' (1988) *J of Child Law* 6, 8.

[132] *T v T* [1988] Fam 52, 68.

the 'speedy restitution of this [previous] prerogative jurisdiction', but meanwhile made a novel use of the High Court's declaratory powers to declare future medical treatment of a woman lacking mental capacity to be lawful. The House of Lords in *Re F (Mental Patient: Sterilisation)* later endorsed the use of declarations,[133] largely based on the common law doctrine of necessity.[134]

2.49 *Re F* was, however, initially also a significant obstacle to any 'resurrection' of the inherent jurisdiction in relation to incapacitous adults. The House of Lords confirmed that, following the Mental Health Act 1959 and the revocation of the 1956 Royal Warrant on 1 November 1960, 'the *parens patriae* jurisdiction as related to persons of unsound mind no longer exists'.[135] The argument of James Munby QC that the *parens patriae* jurisdiction survived as a matter of common law was rejected,[136] and the Lords held specifically that the scope of declarations was far less wide-ranging than *parens patriae* had been – based, as they were, on the common law doctrine of necessity. Although Lord Goff suggested that, in the context of a sterilisation operation, he could 'see little, if any, practical difference between seeking the court's approval under the *parens patriae* jurisdiction and seeking a declaration as to the lawfulness of the operation',[137] Lord Brandon's leading judgment made the distinction clear, and held that 'if that [*parens patriae*] jurisdiction, *or something comparable with it*, is to be re-created, then it must be for the legislature and not for the courts to do the re-creating'.[138]

2.50 Initially, the cases that followed applied the limited approach to declarations set out by the Lords. It rapidly became apparent, however, that while making a declaration might resolve the statutory lacuna in relation to certain forms of medical treatment where the doctrine of necessity could be deployed, this solution was inadequate in other cases.[139] A declaration changes nothing; it merely states that something is or is not lawful. What the court wanted was the ability to make decisions about what was best for the person concerned in situations where several potential options might all be lawful.[140]

2.51 The court began to move away from *necessity* as the foundation for its power to make declarations, but the cases remained limited to determining the lawfulness of actions which might genuinely have been unlawful had the court not resolved the issue.[141] In *Re C (Mental Patient: Contact)*,[142] for example, the court made a declaration of what Eastham J held to be a common law right for the parents of a

[133] *Re F (Mental Patient: Sterilisation)* [1990] 2 AC 1 (HL).
[134] Munby (2014) (n 112) 68; Munby (2021) (n 133) 221–2.
[135] [1990] 2 AC 1 (HL), 57 (Lord Brandon); see also 70 (Lord Griffiths) and 71 (Lord Goff).
[136] ibid 71 (Lord Goff).
[137] ibid 83.
[138] ibid 63 (emphasis added).
[139] See, eg, *Cambridgeshire CC v R (An Adult)* [1995] 1 FLR 50 (Hale J); Munby (2014) (n 112) 69–70.
[140] Munby (2014) (n 112) 71–2.
[141] See, eg, *Re T (Adult: Refusal of Treatment)* [1993] Fam 95 (CoA).
[142] *Re C (Mental Patient: Contact)* [1993] 1 FLR 940.

mentally handicapped adult to have access to her. Because the declaration was said to reflect a *right* that the patient herself could have exercised but for her incapacity, Eastham J said that the declaration did not 'reintroduc[e] the *parens patriae* jurisdiction by the back door'.[143] That reasoning does not withstand much scrutiny – the patient might not have wished this 'right' to be exercised had she had capacity to decide.

2.52 A loosening of the court's language with respect to the test for invoking the inherent jurisdiction can also be seen in the Court of Appeal decision of *Re F (Adult: Court's Jurisdiction)*, describing declarations as 'a flexible remedy able to meet a variety of situations'.[144] However, the court there plainly did not see the scope of declarations as being equivalent to the previous *parens patriae* jurisdiction: Thorpe LJ's judgment opened by noting explicitly that that jurisdiction was not available,[145] and approved comments from Hale J that there was no satisfactory legal mechanism available such that 'it is to be hoped that Parliament will before too long turn its attention to the matter'.[146]

2.53 Subsequently the court dramatically changed its approach, in a process that Munby (extra-judicially) readily admits involved 'the invention by the judges of the Family Division … of a novel jurisdiction'.[147] While perhaps the early vestiges of this started in the 1990s,[148] the Human Rights Act 1998 was key in facilitating a shift away from the limitations of the declaratory jurisdiction.[149] As Munby says:

> The outcome was the re-discovery – in plain language … the invention – by the family judges of a full-blown welfare-based *parens patriae* jurisdiction in relation to incapacitous adults which, except in one respect (there is no power to make an adult a ward of court), is indistinguishable from the long established *parens patriae* jurisdiction in relation to children. A jurisdiction, moreover, which, truth be told, bears no relation to the declaratory jurisdiction as reinvigorated by the House of Lords in 1989.[150]

2.54 This 're-discovery' was an extraordinary legal development, contravening binding House of Lords authority and using (or mis-using) it as the basis for deciding the exact opposite. There are real echoes of Lord Denning[151] in Munby

[143] ibid 945.
[144] *Re F (Adult: Court's Jurisdiction)* [2001] Fam 38 (CoA), 50 (Butler-Sloss P).
[145] ibid 51.
[146] *Cambridgeshire CC v R (An Adult)* [1995] 1 FLR 50, 56.
[147] Munby (2014) (n 112) 64. There is a degree of coyness to this remark: Munby J was more or less single-handedly responsible for this development.
[148] See, eg, *Re G (Adult Patient: Publicity)* [1995] 2 FLR 528, 530 (Sir Stephen Brown P): the court's declaratory power 'is not strictly the exercise of a *parens patriae* jurisdiction but is similar to it'.
[149] Munby (2014) (n 112) 73. *Cf Re S (Adult Patient) (Inherent Jurisdiction: Family Life)* [2002] EWHC 2278 (Fam), [2003] 1 FLR 292 (Munby J).
[150] Munby (2021) (n 112) 225; see also Munby (2014) (n 112) 77.
[151] I think in particular of *Eves v Eves* [1975] 1 WLR 1338 (CoA). Lord Denning MR cited Lord Diplock's judgment in *Gissing v Gissing* [1971] AC 886 (HL) to say in relation to a family property dispute: 'Equity is not past the age of child bearing. One of her latest progeny is a constructive trust of

J's claim that the court had an inherent jurisdiction over incapacitous adults;[152] it was simply a re-writing of history and, as he later admitted, the invention of a new jurisdiction.

2.55 The position in relation to incapacitous adults moved on in 2007, when the MCA 2005 entered force. As I address later,[153] the court has held that the MCA 2005 does not oust the inherent jurisdiction in its entirety, so that it remains available alongside the Act when the statutory remedies are insufficient. However, in practice, the majority of cases are now addressed under the Act and the inherent jurisdiction has only a residual function.[154]

Capacitous but Vulnerable Adults

2.56 Striking as the re-invention of the inherent jurisdiction in relation to incapacitous adults was, the history of the law regarding adults who have capacity but who are deemed 'vulnerable' is even more extraordinary. In this section I focus on the development of the case law, but it is important to note that the judicial developments came after a detailed Law Commission report that proposed a legal framework in relation to vulnerable adults.[155] This was not taken forward by Parliament, either as part of the MCA 2005 or otherwise. I discuss the Law Commission's proposals in chapter fourteen.[156]

2.57 The authorities show no body of historical precedent for the idea that the court could exercise jurisdiction over someone who was not shown to be of unsound mind; the old law in relation to 'idiots' and 'lunatics' applied only where there was an assessment (by inquisition) that capacity was impaired. Hoggett identifies a handful of cases where there was suggestion of a jurisdiction over adults where neither idiocy nor lunacy was found,[157] but she describes these suggestions as being 'roundly taken to task' by contemporaneous writers.[158] Indeed, there was substantial judicial opposition to any claim of jurisdiction in such cases: Lord Lyndhurst LC described one such application as 'an irregularity'.[159]

a new model. Lord Diplock brought it into the world and we have nourished it.' *Gissing* had overturned numerous decisions (mostly of Lord Denning) that provided a remedy in such cases; using *Gissing* to support the creation of a new – but identical! – remedy bears analogy to Munby J's approach to *Re F*. But whereas Lord Denning ascribed his 'progeny' to equity, Munby claimed the 'progeny' of the inherent jurisdiction as his own personally: Munby (2021) (n 113) 367.

[152] *Re SA (Vulnerable Adult with Capacity: Marriage)* [2005] EWHC 2942 (Fam), [2006] 1 FLR 867, [37].

[153] See **13.4–13.9**.

[154] See **13.10** *et seq*.

[155] Law Commission, *Mental Incapacity*, Law Com 231, (London: HMSO, 1995).

[156] See **14.4–14.9**.

[157] Hoggett cites the obiter suggestion of Jessel MR in *Vane v Vane* (1876) LR 2 Ch 124.

[158] Hoggett (n 111) 92, citing H Pope, *The Law and Practice of Lunacy*, 2nd edn (London: Sweet and Maxwell 1890), 218 and Theobald (n 120) 275.

[159] *Ex p Ridgeway; in the matter of Crompton* (1828) 5 Russ 895; 38 ER 985; see also *Bishop of Exeter v Ward* (1833) 2 My & K 54; 39 ER 865 (Sir John Leach MR). See C Stebbings, 'Protecting the Property

2.58 More recently, in November 2003 Dame Elizabeth Butler-Sloss P expressly denied there being any inherent jurisdiction in relation to adults with capacity. In *Re A Local Authority (Inquiry: Restraint on Publication)*,[160] a local authority sought to publish a report that arose out of care proceedings; publication was opposed by a number of parties, including Ms A, described as 'the principal person involved'.[161] The President reviewed the authorities and concluded '[i]t is clear that the inherent jurisdiction of the High Court cannot be invoked to protect Ms A who is an adult and not under a disability'.[162] It is clear in context that being 'under a disability' meant lacking mental capacity.

2.59 Without any historical support, therefore, and with the President of the Family Division having denied that any such jurisdiction existed in November 2003, the court invented a new welfare-based jurisdiction in relation to vulnerable but capacitous adults. James Munby – whose role in developing the law on vulnerable adults is so extensive that his self-description as being 'a proud father' is entirely apt[163] – identifies the creation of the jurisdiction as having occurred during 'the bare year that separated the judgment on 10 December 2004 of Singer J in [*Re SK (An Adult) (Forced Marriage: Appropriate Relief)*] … and my judgment on 15 December 2005 in *Re SA (Vulnerable Adult with Capacity: Marriage)*'.[164]

2.60 *Re SA* remains the seminal authority in this area. It is significant that Munby J cited Butler-Sloss P's judgment in *Re A Local Authority*, but not the relevant passage.[165] The extensive passages that he did quote, setting out the inherent jurisdiction's flexibility,[166] come from the section of Butler-Sloss P's judgment headed 'Adults under a disability' – in other words, *incapacitous* adults. The case is therefore expressly not authority in support of Munby J's approach, and his use of it was misleading.

2.61 It is also worth noting the timing. By the time of these first cases in 2004–05, the scope of the new Mental Capacity Act was clear. The draft Bill was first published on 27 June 2003; the final version was introduced to Parliament on 17 June 2004 and gained Royal Assent on 7 April 2005. Singer J's decision in *Re SK* (heard 10 December 2004 and decided 3 February 2005) and Munby J's more far-reaching decision in *Re SA* (15 December 2005) both came in the immediate

of the Mentally Ill: The Judicial Solution in Nineteenth Century Lunacy Law' [2012] *CLJ* 384, 394 (the point appears more fully in the pre-publication version: ore.exeter.ac.uk/repository/handle/10036/4359, 15–16).

[160] *Re A Local Authority (Inquiry: Restraint on Publication)* [2003] EWHC 2746 (Fam), [2004] Fam 96.

[161] ibid [1].

[162] ibid [64] and [66].

[163] Munby (2021) (n 113) 367.

[164] ibid 365, citing *Re SK (An Adult) (Forced Marriage: Appropriate Relief)* [2004] EWHC 3202 (Fam), [2006] 1 WLR 81 and *Re SA (Vulnerable Adult with Capacity: Marriage)* [2005] EWHC 2942 (Fam), [2006] 1 FLR 867.

[165] See B Hewson, '"Neither Midwives nor Rainmakers": Why DL Is Wrong' [2013] *PL* 451, 457.

[166] [2003] EWHC 2746 (Fam), [2004] Fam 96, [96]–[97], quoted in *Re SA (Vulnerable Adult with Capacity: Marriage)* [2005] EWHC 2942 (Fam), [2006] 1 FLR 867, [41].

aftermath of the Act's finalisation, when it was clear that the Law Commission's proposals in relation to vulnerable but capacitous adults would not be included. The timing of this new judicial venture, just as Parliament did not take forward the Law Commission's proposals on vulnerable adults, gives the impression that the judges disapproved of the decision not to legislate and took matters into their own hands. It is hard to see this development as anything less than shocking.

2.62 Vulnerability in general has a longer history in the law, albeit not one much engaged with by the cases developing the inherent jurisdiction. For example, there is an established history of equitable interventions in contract law to protect vulnerable individuals against duress, unconscionable bargains and undue influence.[167] The 'vulnerability' of the weaker party is taken into account when considering whether to grant recission on the facts of the case, but duress, unconscionability or undue influence per se do not found a separate cause of action for protection in general terms – they act as a shield, not a sword. By contrast, the new inherent jurisdiction treats the person being coerced as a *subject* in proceedings brought by a third party, often as a pre-emptive protective action. The use of vulnerability as a basis for granting the High Court jurisdiction to take pro-active protective measures is therefore entirely novel.[168]

2.63 The lack of any meaningful history to this development goes a long way to explaining the current state of the law, as explored in chapter fourteen. Judgments in this area are confused and confusing, and there are few clear principles.

Conclusion

2.64 One of the curiosities of the inherent jurisdiction is its chameleon quality, its history written and re-written by the judges over the centuries to meet modern needs. While this is true regarding children, with the 're-invigoration' of the inherent jurisdiction starting in 1999 and developing rapidly from the mid-2000s, it is particularly evident in relation to adults. The court – led with vigour by Munby J – disregarded clear House of Lords authority concerning *incapacitous* adults to (re-)create a jurisdiction now said to be 'inherent' in the court, but which historically was delegated from the Crown and had been expressly withdrawn. In respect of so-called *vulnerable* adults, the court – again led by Munby J – conjured a jurisdiction out of the air, without even the cover of the murky history that shrouded the law on incapacitous adults. These dubious modern histories are important in understanding some of the challenges that arise in the operation of the inherent jurisdiction today.

[167] See, eg, *Earl of Aylesford v Morris* (1873) LR 8 Ch App 484; *Allcard v Skinner* (1887) 36 ChD 145; see generally E McKendrick, *Contract Law: Text, Cases, and Materials*, 10th edn (Oxford: OUP, 2022), chs 18–20.

[168] See D Lock, 'Decision-making, Mental Capacity and Undue Influence: Action by Public Bodies to Explore the Grey Areas between Capacity and Incapacity' [2015] *Judicial Review* 42, 43–4.

3

Fundamental Principles of the Inherent Jurisdiction

3.1 This chapter sets out the fundamental principles governing the inherent jurisdiction and its exercise by the court. It is necessary to keep in mind the three different parts of the inherent jurisdiction: (i) regarding children, (ii) regarding incapacitous adults, and (iii) regarding capacitous but vulnerable adults. I will outline the scope of the inherent jurisdiction, followed by the statutory and common law rules restricting its use. The history of the inherent jurisdiction regarding children is very different from that regarding both incapacitous and vulnerable adults.[1] However, particularly in respect of the principles that limit the scope and exercise of the inherent jurisdiction, there is sufficient overlap that they can be addressed together in this chapter. Consequently, while I will address incapacitous[2] and vulnerable[3] adults separately, the majority of what is said in relation to children applies to those situations as well.

3.2 For children, the starting point is that the inherent jurisdiction is a 'theoretically limitless' set of substantive powers that the court can exercise in relation to a child, which can (at least in principle) be used to determine absolutely any issue that might arise in connection with the child.[4] The same is true for *incapacitous* adults, though the availability of this jurisdiction is largely curtailed by the Mental Capacity Act 2005 ('MCA 2005'). The scope of the inherent jurisdiction in relation to *vulnerable* but capacitous adults is more complex. In all three cases, however, the inherent jurisdiction 'cannot be regarded as a lawless void permitting judges to do whatever we consider to be right for children or the vulnerable'.[5] Indeed, the restrictions are more significant – and tell us more about the inherent jurisdiction and its place in the modern law – than the headline 'theoretically limitless' rule.

3.3 When thinking about the fundamental principles in this chapter, it is worth bearing in mind the broad justifications that are presented for retaining

[1] See **ch 2**.
[2] See **3.18–3.19** and **3.31–3.33**.
[3] See **3.20–3.22** and **3.34**.
[4] *Re W (Consent to Medical Treatment)* [1993] 1 FLR 1 (CoA), 12 (Lord Donaldson MR); *Re X (Wardship: Jurisdiction)* [1975] Fam 47 (CoA), 57 (Lord Denning MR).
[5] *London Borough of Redbridge v A* [2015] EWHC 2140 (Fam), [2015] Fam 335, [36] (Hayden J).

the inherent jurisdiction at all.[6] The overarching argument is that the inherent jurisdiction is needed: (i) for children, 'as a means by which to provide protection for children whose welfare requires it',[7] (ii) for *incapacitous* adults likewise, and (iii) more narrowly in relation to vulnerable adults who, by definition, have capacity and therefore the right to their own autonomy, 'to protect and to facilitate their exercise of that autonomy'.[8]

The Scope of the Inherent Jurisdiction

3.4 The inherent jurisdiction is said to be 'theoretically limitless'.[9] Indeed, judges frequently comment that '[u]nder its inherent jurisdiction, the court may make any order or determine any issue in respect of a child'[10] – but subject to 'far-reaching limitations in principle on the exercise of this jurisdiction',[11] as set out later in this chapter.

3.5 The scope of the inherent jurisdiction is connected to Lord Donaldson MR's description of the common law as the 'great safety net which lies behind all statute law, and is capable of filling gaps left by that law, if and insofar as those gaps have to be filled in the interests of society as a whole'.[12] However, as Sir James Munby (sitting as a judge after his retirement) explained, extending this metaphor, 'the inherent jurisdiction is a safety net, not a springboard'.[13] As Sir James said: 'novelty alone does not demand a remedy. Any development of the inherent jurisdiction must be principled and determined by more than the length of the Chancellor's foot'.[14] Consequently, while 'the inherent jurisdiction … is a sufficiently flexible remedy to evolve in accordance with social needs and social values',[15] that does not mean that the scope of the court's powers is without limitation.

[6] See **1.19–1.21**.

[7] *Re T (Secure Accommodation)* [2021] UKSC 35, [2022] AC 723, [65].

[8] *FS v RS and JS* [2020] EWFC 63, [2020] 4 WLR 139, [114].

[9] See, eg, *Re W (Consent to Medical Treatment)* [1993] 1 FLR 1 (CoA), 12 (Lord Donaldson MR); *Re X (Wardship: Jurisdiction)* [1975] Fam 47 (CoA), 57 (Lord Denning MR), 60 (Roskill LJ) and 61 (Sir John Pennycuick). *Cf* N Lowe, 'The Limits of the Wardship Jurisdiction Part 2 – The Extent of the Court's Power Over a Ward' (1989) 1 *Journal of Child Law* 44, who queries the claim.

[10] *HB v A Local Authority (Local Government Association intervening)* [2017] EWHC 524 (Fam), [2017] 1 WLR 4289, [50] (MacDonald J).

[11] *Re X (Wardship: Jurisdiction)* [1975] Fam 47 (CoA), 61 (Sir John Pennycuick); but *cf* Lord Denning MR at 57 and Roskill LJ at 60: 'it is not necessary to consider here what, *if any*, limits there are to that jurisdiction' (my emphasis).

[12] *Re F (Mental Patient: Sterilisation)* [1990] 2 AC 1 (CoA), 13.

[13] *FS v RS and JS* [2020] EWFC 63, [2020] 4 WLR 139, [100].

[14] ibid [103].

[15] *Re SK (An Adult) (Forced Marriage: Appropriate Relief)* [2004] EWHC 3202 (Fam), [2006] 1 WLR 81, [8] (Singer J).

Children

3.6 In relation to children, most inherent jurisdiction applications relate to an aspect of the child's upbringing, so the court is mandated by s 1(1) of the Children Act 1989 ('CA 1989') to make the individual child's welfare its paramount consideration.[16] While not technically required to approach an inherent jurisdiction application in the same way as a Children Act case, the court generally follows the same practice. This will likely include, for example, consideration of the factors set out in the *welfare checklist* in s 1(3) of the CA 1989,[17] and addressing allegations of domestic abuse in line with the approach taken to child arrangements cases.[18]

3.7 Rare examples exist of issues decided under the inherent jurisdiction that are not about a child's upbringing, as that term is understood in the context of the CA 1989. There were previously more examples,[19] but one that remains is where a person seeks a determination of parentage in relation to a deceased putative parent. While the inherent jurisdiction in relation to genetic testing in general is ousted by the Family Law Reform Act 1969, s 20,[20] the legislation does not address the issue of testing in relation to a deceased person and therefore in *Anderson v Spencer* the inherent jurisdiction was used.[21] *Anderson* concerned an application by an adult, so no question of best interests would apply. However, even where the application relates to a child, the decision is not about their upbringing or the administration of their property, so the child's welfare is not the paramount consideration.[22] Another example is the use of the inherent jurisdiction to recognise a foreign adoption order.[23] These are exceptions, and the vast majority of applications engage the welfare principle.

Wardship

3.8 One significant manifestation of the inherent jurisdiction in relation to children is that any child under the age of 18 can be made a ward of court. There is no equivalent jurisdiction applicable to adults.[24]

[16] This was also so under the previous legislation; indeed, the wardship court adopted the welfare principle long before it was statutorily mandated: see, eg, *Re Callaghan* (1885) 28 Ch D 186 (CoA), 189.

[17] On the application of the checklist to inherent jurisdiction cases, see *Re NY (Abduction: Inherent Jurisdiction)* [2019] UKSC 49, [2019] 2 FLR 1247, [49].

[18] That is, following Practice Direction 12J – Child Arrangements and Contact Orders: Domestic Abuse and Harm; see *Re NY*, ibid [50].

[19] Such as restrictions on publicity regarding a child, now decided under HRA 1998: *Re S (A Child) (Identification: Restrictions on Publication)* [2004] UKHL 47, [2005] 1 AC 593. See **12.18** *et seq*.

[20] *Re O (Blood Tests: Constraint)* [2000] Fam 139 (Wall J). For the approach before the 1969 Act, see *S v McC; W v W* [1972] AC 24 (HL).

[21] *Anderson v Spencer* [2018] EWCA Civ 100, [2019] Fam 66.

[22] Best interests should remain a primary consideration in any application concerning a child: UN Convention on the Rights of the Child 1989, Art 3.

[23] See **11.5–11.8**.

[24] *N v A Clinical Commissioning Group* [2017] UKSC 22, [2017] AC 549, [24].

3.9 The status of a ward of court is 'unique among child jurisdictions'.[25] While in one sense wardship is merely 'machinery' that is 'convenient' to use when exercising the court's inherent jurisdiction over children,[26] it has substantial consequences – 'wardship confers on the ward a status to which the law attaches certain incidents',[27] placing the child under the court's 'cloak of protection'.[28] Historically, it was said that in wardship proceedings, '[t]he plaintiffs are not asserting any right; they are committing their child to the protection of the court'[29] – today, applicants generally are asserting a claim, seeking the court's assistance to protect the child *and* to achieve their particular objective.

3.10 As set out in more detail in chapter four,[30] a child is made a ward of court immediately and automatically from the moment when an application for wardship is lodged with the court;[31] that wardship then lasts until a first hearing, when the wardship is either confirmed or not.[32] If confirmed, wardship continues until the ward turns 18 unless the court orders the wardship's earlier termination. This immediate and continuing protection of the ward is the corollary of the court's having ultimate responsibility for the ward and special powers and control over both the ward's person and property.[33]

3.11 Practice Direction 12D – Inherent Jurisdiction (Including Wardship) Proceedings ('PD12D') states that the 'distinguishing characteristics' of wardship are that 'custody of a child who is a ward is vested in the court' and 'although day to day care and control of the ward is given to an individual or to a local authority, no important step can be taken in the child's life without the court's consent'.[34] However, the Practice Direction's claim that the day to day care and control of a child can be given to a local authority ('LA') is doubtful – doing so would be appear to conflict with statutory restrictions in CA 1989, s 100 (discussed below).[35]

3.12 There are two general and immediate consequences to wardship.[36] First, it is an automatic restriction that the ward may not be removed from

[25] N Lowe and R White, *Wards of Court*, 2nd edn, (London: Barry Rose, 1986), para 5.1 ('Lowe and White').

[26] *Re L (An Infant)* [1968] P 119 (CoA), 156 (Lord Denning MR).

[27] *Kelly v British Broadcasting Corporation* [2001] Fam 59 (Munby J), 71.

[28] *Re Z (A Minor) (Identification: Restrictions on Publication)* [1997] Fam 1 (CoA), 23.

[29] *In re B (JA) (An Infant)* [1965] 1 Ch 1112, 1117 (Cross J).

[30] See **4.16–4.22**.

[31] Senior Courts Act 1981, s 41(2). This rule is disapplied for children who are subject to a care order (s 41(2A)), consistently with the rule that the court cannot ward children who are in care: CA 1989, s 100(2)(c).

[32] FPR 2010, r 12.41.

[33] *Re E (SA)* [1984] 1 WLR 156 (HL), 159 (Lord Scarman).

[34] Para 1.3. For authority, see, eg, *Re W (An Infant)* [1964] Ch 202 (CoA), 210: 'in a wardship case the court retains the custody of the infant and only makes such orders in relation to that custody as may amount to a delegation of certain parts of its duties' (Ormrod LJ).

[35] See **3.27** *et seq*.

[36] Historically, a third consequence was that a ward could not be married without the court's consent. After the Marriage and Civil Partnership (Minimum Age) Act 2022, no one under 18 can now marry, so this restriction no longer applies. See also **12.2** *et seq* on preventing 'undesirable associations'.

the jurisdiction of England and Wales without the consent of the High Court ('the non-removal rule').[37]

3.13 The non-removal rule is amended if: (i) divorce, dissolution, nullity, annulment, or judicial / legal separation proceedings are underway elsewhere in the UK (ie, other than England and Wales), or (ii) the ward is habitually resident elsewhere in the UK. In such a case, the ward may be removed to that other part of the UK without the consent of the English High Court.[38] Lowe and White argued in 1986 that the uncertainty created by these alternative rules is 'not entirely satisfactory', and their suggestion that it would be better if the restriction were simply for non-removal from the entirety of the UK in all cases remains compelling.[39]

3.14 Breaching the non-removal rule is a contempt of court. The restriction applies to everyone, including the ward themselves, irrespective of whether they have notice of the wardship – though it is questionable whether contempt proceedings could be brought against anyone who was not aware of the wardship, and in reality it is likely that proper service with a sealed court order is a minimal requirement to commit for contempt.[40] Wardship also gives the court 'rights of custody', and so civil remedies for child abduction may also arise if the ward is removed outside the UK.[41]

3.15 While the non-removal rule is easily stated, the second consequence of wardship is more amorphous – 'When a child is made a ward no important step in the child's life can be taken without the court's consent'.[42] This 'no important step' rule flows from the court having taken ultimate responsibility for the child,[43] meaning that parental responsibility can be exercised only to the extent permitted by the court.[44] As a High Court Judge, Munby J once said, 'This is not some empty exhortation or mere platitude for, subject to proof of knowledge that the child in question is a ward of court, it is a contempt of court to undertake or facilitate any such step without the consent of the court.'[45]

[37] PD12D, para 4.1.

[38] Family Law Act 1986, s 38. If the other part of the UK is Scotland, wardship cannot apply after a child is 16. This provision was considered an interim measure (Lowe and White (n 25) para 5.2), but nearly 40 years later there is no indication that it will be amended.

[39] Lowe and White (n 25) para 5.2. As they say, that approach would be in line with the criminal law under the Child Abduction Act 1984.

[40] FPR 2010, r 37.4; see **15.13**.

[41] See **ch** 7.

[42] *Re S (Infants)* [1967] 1 WLR 396 (Cross J). 'This statement has been so often repeated that it can be confidently said to be an established principle': Lowe and White (n 25) para 5.6.

[43] *Re E (SA)* [1984] 1 WLR 156 (HL), 159 (Lord Scarman); Lowe and White (n 25) para 5.6.

[44] J Mitchell, 'Whatever Happened to Wardship? Part II' [2001] *Fam Law* 212, 213: wardship 'inhibits the exercise of parental responsibility by the ward's parents or anyone else'.

[45] *Kelly v British Broadcasting Corporation* [2001] Fam 59, 75, approved in *Re A Ward of Court (Wardship: Interview)* [2017] EWHC 1022 (Fam), [2017] Fam 369 (Munby P), [17].

3.16 Defining what constitutes an 'important step' is not straightforward.[46] While the overall scope of the rule is unclear, some examples can be given:

i. A ward cannot be adopted or placed for adoption without the permission of the court.[47]
ii. Substantial changes in relation to education, such as a change of school, should not be done without the court's approval. Less significant educational decisions (eg, whether the ward should travel to the neighbouring town for a school sports match) are unlikely to need approval, and can be made by the person(s) with day-to-day care of the ward.
iii. Significant medical treatment requires the court's approval, although presumably in a genuine emergency there will be no difficulty in providing medically-appropriate treatment and then informing the court afterwards. What constitutes 'significant' medical treatment is unclear – Munby J once gave examples of an abortion or a sterilisation operation,[48] but the list is likely rather broader. In other contexts, the court has suggested that giving a child standard immunisations is not 'significant'.[49]
iv. No one may change the ward's name without the court's permission.[50]
v. A ward may not be admitted to hospital under Part II of the Mental Health Act 1983 without the leave of the court, and various other aspects of care under that Act also require the court's leave.[51]
vi. A ward may not be placed in voluntary accommodation under s 20 of the CA 89,[52] or have their foster carers or place of residence while in voluntary accommodation changed,[53] without the court's permission.
vii. No application may be made on behalf of a ward to the Criminal Injuries Compensation Board without authorisation from the court.[54]

3.17 Conversely, the court has given examples of steps that *can* be taken without the court's permission. Unless otherwise ordered, it is permissible to change the

[46] *Cf* the equally amorphous category of 'important matters' about which holders of PR are supposed to agree in private law cases: see R George, S Thompson and J Miles, *Family Law: Text, Cases, and Materials*, 5th edn (Oxford: OUP, 2023), 705–11.

[47] *F v S (Adoption: Ward)* [1973] Fam 203 (CoA); *M v Warwickshire CC* [2007] EWCA Civ 1084, [2008] 1 WLR 991, [26(a)].

[48] *Kelly v British Broadcasting Corporation* [2001] Fam 59, 76.

[49] *Re H (Parental Responsibility: Vaccination)* [2020] EWCA Civ 664, [2021] Fam 133; see also **8.3.ii**.

[50] See, eg, *Re J (A Minor) (Change of Name)* [1993] 1 FLR 699 (Booth J); and obiter comments in *Kelly v British Broadcasting Corporation* [2001] Fam 59, 76 (Munby J).

[51] Mental Health Act 1983, s 33.

[52] Agreeing to s 20 requires a parent to delegate their PR to the LA, but under wardship PR is effectively suspended – the wardship court must therefore authorise the parent to exercise this aspect of their PR. Note that it must still be the parent placing the child in s 20 accommodation: if the court causes or requires it, it will violate CA 1989, s 100(2)(b). Conversely, it is said that a child *already in* s 20 accommodation can be made a ward: *Re E (Wardship Order: Child in Voluntary Accommodation)* [2012] EWCA Civ 1773, [2013] 2 FLR 63, but see **9.7–9.13**.

[53] *Re CB (A Minor)* [1981] 1 WLR 379 (CoA).

[54] PD12D, para 6. If this is really the rule, it seems anachronistic: *cf* **3.17**: the ward can bring an ECHR claim.

place of residence of a ward within England and Wales without the court's permission, though the court must be notified of the new address.[55] No permission is required for a media organisation to interview a ward of court, nor to publish that interview,[56] subject to the important constraints that apply in relation to court proceedings.[57] Likewise, no permission is required for the police to interview a ward,[58] nor for the ward to be called as a witness in any court proceedings.[59] Despite earlier authority the other way under previous legislation,[60] the police do not require the court's consent to issue a youth caution to a ward,[61] nor for a ward to be prosecuted.[62] No permission is required for a ward to bring a claim in the European Court of Human Rights.[63] Some of these examples link to broader principles around the appropriate limitations of the inherent jurisdiction generally: as set out below, the inherent jurisdiction (including by way of wardship) cannot impinge on the powers allocated by statute to other bodies,[64] and cannot be used to put a ward in a better position under the law than could be achieved by an assiduous parent exercising their parental responsibility.[65]

Incapacitous Adults

3.18 Despite the apparent set-back of the House of Lords decision in *Re F (Mental Patient: Sterilisation)* – which held that 'the *parens patriae* jurisdiction as related to persons of unsound mind no longer exists'[66] – the court subsequently 'invent[ed] … a corresponding jurisdiction in relation to incapacitous adults' equivalent to that which had always existed in relation to children.[67] Consequently, in theory, the court has 'a full-blown welfare-based *parens patriae*

[55] FPR 2010, r 12.39(3). If a passport, location or collection order is made (see **7.40–7.45**), the child must remain at their current address unless a move is permitted by the court, but this is a function of those orders and applies whether or not the child is a ward.

[56] *Kelly v British Broadcasting Corporation* [2001] Fam 59 (Munby J).

[57] Administration of Justice Act 1960, s 12; Contempt of Court Act 1981, s 2; Children Act 1989, s 97.

[58] *Re A Ward of Court (Wardship: Interview)* [2017] EWHC 1022 (Fam), [2017] Fam 369.

[59] *Re R (Wardship: Criminal Proceedings)* [1991] Fam 56 (CoA).

[60] See, eg, *Re A (A Minor) (Wardship: Police Caution)* [1989] Fam 103 (Cazalet J). Until 2012, parental *consent* was necessary before a child could be given a caution: see Home Office, *The Cautioning of Offenders*, Circular No 14/1985, cl 4. The law was amended by the Legal Aid, Sentencing and Punishment of Offenders Act 2012.

[61] Under the Crime and Disorder Act 1998, s 66ZA, an 'appropriate adult' must be present when a youth caution is issued, but no one is asked to consent to the caution. Since a parent could not resist the decision to administer a youth caution, if the wardship court were to do so it would violate the principle that the inherent jurisdiction cannot be used to put a child in a better position than they would be under the general law: see **3.61** *et seq*.

[62] See **3.58.ii**.

[63] *Re M (Petition to European Commission of Human Rights)* [1997] 1 FLR 755 (Johnson J).

[64] See **3.53** *et seq*.

[65] See **3.61** *et seq*.

[66] *Re F (Mental Patient: Sterilisation)* [1990] 2 AC 1 (HL), 57 (Lord Brandon); see **2.49**.

[67] J Munby, 'Whither the Inherent Jurisdiction? Part I' [2021] *Fam Law* 215, 221.

jurisdiction in relation to incapacitous adults which, except in one respect (there is no power to make an adult a ward of court), is indistinguishable from the long-established parens patriae jurisdiction in relation to children'.[68] While there is no wardship power over incapacitous adults,[69] the significance of this distinction is limited. Wardship, as noted, is merely a mechanism for exercising the inherent jurisdiction in relation to children, and the overall scope of the inherent jurisdiction appears equally wide.

3.19 However, despite this potentially vast scope of the inherent jurisdiction in relation to incapacitous adults, in reality the jurisdiction is rarely available, because the MCA 2005 renders it dormant and unusable in virtually all circumstances to which the Act applies.[70] However – somewhat surprisingly, given that the MCA was intended to be a comprehensive statutory code[71] – the inherent jurisdiction remains available alongside the Act in limited circumstances. Consequently, as detailed later, there remains a subsidiary, limited role for the inherent jurisdiction in relation to incapacitous adults.[72]

Capacitous but Vulnerable Adults

3.20 The inherent jurisdiction in relation to so-called 'vulnerable adults' was created during the course of 2004–05;[73] it has no history, and older cases actively rejected any suggestion that the court had jurisdiction over capacitous adults.[74] Consequently, while it uses the same name – *the inherent jurisdiction* – and it is presumably subject to the same limitations as set out below, the principles that apply appear quite different.

The Meaning of 'Vulnerable'

3.21 How do the cases define an adult who is 'vulnerable'? An adult here has mental capacity to make a relevant decision – they are capacitous, but vulnerable because they are (or are suspected of being) the victim of coercion or duress, or for some other reason are not in fact able to make a decision for themselves, even though in terms of mental capacity they could in principle do so. The inherent jurisdiction exists alongside the MCA 2005, 'targeted solely at those adults whose ability to make decisions for themselves has been compromised by matters other than those covered by the 2005 Act'.[75] Munby J in *Re SA (Vulnerable Adult with*

[68] ibid 225.
[69] *N v A Clinical Commissioning Group* [2017] UKSC 22, [2017] AC 549, [24].
[70] See further **3.31** and **ch 13**.
[71] See **13.5** *et seq*.
[72] See **ch 13**.
[73] J Munby, 'Whither the Inherent Jurisdiction? Part II' [2021] *Fam Law* 365, 365.
[74] See **2.56**.
[75] *Re L (Vulnerable Adults with Capacity: Court's Jurisdiction)* [2012] EWCA Civ 253, [2013] Fam 1, [53].

Capacity: Marriage) described the people within the court's jurisdiction in this way:

> the inherent jurisdiction can be exercised in relation to a vulnerable adult who, even if not incapacitated by mental disorder or mental illness, is, or is reasonably believed to be, either: (i) under constraint; or (ii) subject to coercion or undue influence; or (iii) for some other reason deprived of the capacity to make the relevant decision, or disabled from making a free choice, or incapacitated or disabled from giving or expressing real and genuine consent.[76]

3.22 The approach set out by Munby J was later approved by the Court of Appeal in *Re L (Vulnerable Adults with Capacity: Court's Jurisdiction).*[77] Because it covers people outside the scope of the MCA 2005, the inherent jurisdiction over vulnerable adults has been described by McFarlane LJ as 'a jurisdictional hinterland'.[78] I discuss the court's definition of vulnerability in chapter fourteen.[79]

The Court's Decision-Making Approach

3.23 Whereas the broad limits of the inherent jurisdiction in relation to children are clear enough, when it comes to vulnerable adults 'the "expanding empire of the law" as Lord Sumption referred to it recently, is in many respects still developing'.[80] There is no equivalent to the statutory welfare principle that applies in children cases, nor does the court claim a 'full-blown welfare based *parens patriae* jurisdiction' over vulnerable adults in the way it does in relation to incapacitous adults.[81] However, the authorities are less clear about what the court's approach should in fact be.

3.24 The earliest case explicitly concerning a capacitous but vulnerable adult related to a potential forced marriage.[82] *Re SK (An Adult) (Forced Marriage: Appropriate Relief)* was decided prior to the MCA 2005 and thus when the court's inherent jurisdiction in relation to *incapacitous* adults was still being

[76] *Re SA (Vulnerable Adult with Capacity: Marriage)* [2005] EWHC 2942 (Fam), [2006] 1 FLR 867, [77]. *Cf Ealing LBC v KS* [2008] EWHC 636 (Fam), [2008] 2 FLR 720, [148] (Sumner J).

[77] *Re L (Vulnerable Adults with Capacity: Court's Jurisdiction)* [2012] EWCA Civ 253, [2013] Fam 1 (Kay, McFarlane and Davis LJJ), upholding a decision of Theis J.

[78] ibid [1].

[79] See **14.22** *et seq.*

[80] *A Local Authority v CD* [2019] EWHC 2943 (Fam), [22] (Cobb J), alluding to Lord Sumption's first Reith Lecture, 'Law's Expanding Empire', 21 May 2019, available online at downloads.bbc.co.uk/radio4/reith2019/Reith_2019_Sumption_lecture_1.pdf (accessed 1 June 2024).

[81] Munby (n 67) 221.

[82] James Munby subsequently claimed *Re T (Adult: Refusal of Treatment)* [1993] Fam 95 (CoA) as a forebearer of these authorities, though he accepts (having been counsel in it) that the claim 'might … have surprised those involved in the earlier case – it certainly surprised me!': Munby (n 73) 366.

used. Singer J cited language from the incapacity context in relation to best interests, and went on:

> By analogy, … it is within the court's power … to make orders and to give directions designed to ascertain whether or not [the person] has been able to exercise her free will in decisions concerning her civil status and her country of residence.[83]

3.25 Following the enactment of the MCA 2005, Munby J used *Re SK* to underpin his more wide-ranging judgment in *Re SA*, discussed already in relation to the meaning of vulnerability. While much of the judgment draws on the court's powers in relation to *incapacitous* adults, the key passage shows a narrower approach to *vulnerable* adults:

> [T]he court has the power to make whatever orders and to give whatever directions are needed to ascertain the true wishes of a vulnerable adult or to ascertain whether a vulnerable adult is able to exercise her free will or is confined, controlled, coerced or under restraint.[84]

3.26 Various authorities that purport to relate to vulnerable adults lay claim to a wider set of powers, in effect a welfare jurisdiction to make whatever decision the court considers to be in the vulnerable person's best interests. However, on closer analysis, these cases are almost all examples of judges engaging in 'the misleading conflation of two quite distinct things', muddling the law between *incapacitous* versus *vulnerable* adults.[85] The principles applicable to *incapacitous* adults cannot simply be 'read across' to those adults who have capacity but who are vulnerable, and the court's frequent elision of the principles relating to incapacitous versus vulnerable adults makes much of the case law confusing. The purpose of the court's jurisdiction in relation to vulnerable adults is to protect a person who is mentally able to make a decision but whose autonomy is being infringed by the behaviour of someone else – the law is 'facilitative, rather than dictatorial', as McFarlane LJ put it.[86] The only principled approach therefore is to make short-term protective orders that enable the person to exercise their own autonomy and make whatever decision they wish, regardless of how ill-advised it may appear to be from the outside.[87] The extent to which the court in fact adheres to this approach is explored in chapter fourteen.

[83] *Re SK (An Adult) (Forced Marriage: Appropriate Relief)* [2004] EWHC 3202 (Fam), [2006] 1 WLR 81 (Singer J).

[84] *Re SA (Vulnerable Adult with Capacity: Marriage)* [2005] EWHC 2942 (Fam), [2006] 1 FLR 867, [94].

[85] Munby (n 73) 370.

[86] *Re L (Vulnerable Adults with Capacity: Court's Jurisdiction)* [2012] EWCA Civ 253, [2013] Fam 1, [67]. But *cf* at [65], focusing on 'protection' of the adult, which is also the rationale in *Re SA (Vulnerable Adult with Capacity: Marriage)* [2005] EWHC 2942 (Fam), [2006] 1 FLR 867, [37] (Munby J).

[87] See similarly L Pritchard-Jones, '"Palm Tree Justice": The Inherent Jurisdiction in Adult Welfare Cases' (2023) 86 *MLR* 1358, 1379 ('orders made should be those which facilitate the making of an autonomous decision') and K Heywood, 'Safeguarding Reproductive Health? The Inherent Jurisdiction,

Statutory Restrictions on the Inherent Jurisdiction

Children Cases

3.27 The inherent jurisdiction in relation to children is addressed in numerous statutes.[88] The main restrictions on the inherent jurisdiction are found in the CA 1989, in particular in s 100:[89]

> **100 Restrictions on use of wardship jurisdiction**
>
> (1) Section 7 of the Family Law Reform Act 1969 (which gives the High Court power to place a ward of court in the care, or under the supervision, of a local authority) shall cease to have effect.
>
> (2) No court shall exercise the High Court's inherent jurisdiction with respect to children—
>
> (a) so as to require a child to be placed in the care, or put under the supervision, of a local authority;
>
> (b) so as to require a child to be accommodated by or on behalf of a local authority;
>
> (c) so as to make a child who is the subject of a care order a ward of court; or
>
> (d) for the purpose of conferring on any local authority power to determine any question which has arisen, or which may arise, in connection with any aspect of parental responsibility for a child.
>
> (3) No application for any exercise of the court's inherent jurisdiction with respect to children may be made by a local authority unless the authority have obtained the leave of the court.
>
> (4) The court may only grant leave if it is satisfied that—
>
> (a) the result which the authority wish to achieve could not be achieved through the making of any order of a kind to which subsection (5) applies; and
>
> (b) there is reasonable cause to believe that if the court's inherent jurisdiction is not exercised with respect to the child he is likely to suffer significant harm.
>
> (5) This subsection applies to any order—
>
> (a) made otherwise than in the exercise of the court's inherent jurisdiction; and
>
> (b) which the local authority is entitled to apply for (assuming, in the case of any application which may only be made with leave, that leave is granted).

3.28 Sub-sections 1 and 2 can be read together. The former repeals earlier powers to use wardship to place a child in the care of (or under the supervision of) an LA. The latter restricts the court's use of its inherent jurisdiction in four specific ways that interrelate with the public law child protection powers in Part IV of the

Contraception and Metal Incapacity' (2011) 19 *Medical Law Review* 326, 331 ('the goal of [the inherent] jurisdiction is to safeguard decision making, rather than to safeguard well-being per se').

[88] See, eg, Senior Courts Act 1981, s 41, regulating the means by which a child becomes and ceases to be a ward.

[89] On the history of s 100, see **2.27–2.31**, and *Re T (Secure Accommodation)* [2021] UKSC 35, [2022] AC 723, [70]–[78] ('*Re T (Secure Accommodation)*').

CA 1989 and the family support provisions in Part III. The High Court is prohibited from invoking the inherent jurisdiction to place a child in the care of, or under the supervision of, or in accommodation provided by or on behalf of, an LA. The court cannot make a child a ward if they are the subject of a care order[90] – and, separately, if a child is already a ward of court, the making of a care order automatically discharges the wardship.[91] Finally, the court cannot use the inherent jurisdiction to confer authority or power on an LA to determine any issue that falls within the scope of parental responsibility ('PR') in relation to a child. These restrictions are all aimed at ensuring that the only way that an LA comes to have responsibility for a child, in terms of making decisions or having the child in their care, supervision or accommodation, is under the mechanisms of Parts III and IV of the CA 1989.[92]

3.29 Still aimed at ensuring the supremacy of the statutory powers, sub-sections (3) to (5) have a different focus: restricting the ability of LAs to make applications for inherent jurisdiction orders. First, the LA requires leave (no other applicant requires leave at all, even other state bodies). Leave can only be granted if there is no statutory order that the LA could seek (with leave, if required) to achieve the same result, *and* if there is 'reasonable cause' to believe that, if the inherent jurisdiction is not used, the child 'is likely to suffer significant harm'. This substantive 'significant harm' threshold is the same as in relation to public law care proceedings,[93] and is designed to ensure that LAs cannot circumvent the CA 1989's restrictions on their ability to seek compulsory intervention in family life.

3.30 While LAs are significantly restricted in their ability to invoke the inherent jurisdiction, s 100 is not an absolute bar to LA applications, nor was it intended to be.[94] Indeed, there will be times when an LA has no alternative but to make an application under the inherent jurisdiction because, somewhat ironically, there are circumstances in which the statutory remedies that might otherwise suffice are themselves barred by statute. This situation arises when a child is in LA care, which gives PR to the LA[95] but an issue to do with the child's upbringing arises that is too serious for the LA to determine by itself through exercising its own PR because it would violate the Article 8 rights of the parents and/or the child. Generally, disputes about the exercise of PR are resolved by making specific issue or prohibited steps orders under s 8 of the CA 1989 – but, when a care order is in force, the court may not make a specific issue or prohibited steps order.[96] This provision was likely intended to protect LAs by preventing parents or others from seeking to interfere

[90] CA 1989, s 100(2)(c); Senior Courts Act 1981, s 41(2A).

[91] CA 1989, s 91(4).

[92] *Re T (Secure Accommodation)* (n 89) [108] and [116].

[93] CA 1989, s 31; the need for 'reasonable cause' mirrors the test for an emergency protection order under s 44.

[94] See Lord Mackay LC introducing the Children Bill in the House of Lords: Hansard (HL Debates), 6 December 1988, col 493.

[95] CA 1989, s 33(3).

[96] ibid s 9(1).

with the LA's exercise of its PR when a care order is in force. However, as the court has become increasingly alert to the implications of Article 8, it has become at best 'ill-advised' for an LA to seek to rely on its own PR in more serious decisions about children's upbringing,[97] unless the underlying issue formed part of the reason why the care order was made in the first place. These might include decisions relating to significant medical treatment[98] or an application for British nationality,[99] for example. Consequently, barred from obtaining a specific issue order, the LA has no choice but to seek orders under the inherent jurisdiction.[100]

Incapacitous Adult Cases

3.31 As set out earlier,[101] the inherent jurisdiction in relation to incapacitous adults is almost entirely dormant because it has been superseded by the MCA 2005. The MCA therefore constitutes an almost complete limitation on the availability of the inherent jurisdiction for incapacitous adults.

3.32 The MCA applies where a person ('P') does not have capacity to make a relevant decision 'because of an impairment of, or a disturbance in the functioning of, the mind or brain',[102] and expressly assumes that P *does* have capacity unless shown otherwise.[103] Where P does not have capacity regarding the relevant issue, the MCA provides: (i) a range of possible orders that can be made,[104] and (ii) general principles applicable to such decisions, including that the decision must be in P's best interests and that consideration should be given to whether the purpose could be achieved in a way that is less restrictive of P's rights and freedom of action.[105]

3.33 Unlike the CA 1989, the MCA 2005 makes no express reference to the inherent jurisdiction.[106] Consequently, the impact of the Act on the inherent jurisdiction is better seen as an example of the common law principle that the inherent jurisdiction cannot be used to cut across a statutory scheme, which I address below.[107]

[97] *Re AB (Care Proceedings: Medical Treatment)* [2018] EWFC 3, [2018] 4 WLR 20, [24(iii)].

[98] *Re H (Parental Responsibility: Vaccination)* [2020] EWCA Civ 664, [2021] Fam 133, [64]–[65]; for critical comment, see R George, 'Parental Responsibility, Vaccinations, and the Role of the Court' (2020) 136 *LQR* 559.

[99] *Re Y (Children in Care: Change of Nationality)* [2020] EWCA Civ 1038, [2021] Fam 199; for critical commentary, see J Masson and D Prabhat, 'Allowing Appeals to Increase High Court Power' (2021) 43 *JSWFL* 327.

[100] See *Re C (Child in Care: Choice of Forename)* [2016] EWCA Civ 374, [2017] Fam 137. In the context of medical treatment, see **8.25** *et seq*; on LAs and child protection more generally, see **ch 9**.

[101] See **3.19**.

[102] MCA 2005, s 2(1).

[103] ibid ss 1(2) and 4.

[104] See, eg, MCA 2005, ss 4A, 15 and 16.

[105] MCA 2005, s 1(5) and (6).

[106] On the reasons why, see **13.4–13.6**.

[107] See **3.36**.

Vulnerable Adult Cases

3.34 The MCA 2005 applies only to *incapacitous* adults. Adults who are 'vulnerable', as defined, have capacity and are therefore outside the Act's remit. Consequently, the MCA does not affect the 'jurisdictional hinterland [that] exists outside its borders to deal with cases of "vulnerable adults" who fall outside that Act and which are determined under the inherent jurisdiction'.[108] Likewise, there is nothing in the Care Act 2014 that expressly deals with the inherent jurisdiction, and most of its provisions do not appear to impact the scope of the inherent jurisdiction. However, the abolition by that Act[109] of an LA's previous statutory power to apply to court to remove persons in need of care from their homes[110] is potentially significant. If a previous power to remove a person by court order has been expressly repealed, it is questionable whether the court can legitimately use its inherent jurisdiction to make the same order, though this is likely better seen as an example of the common law restrictions, to which I now turn.

Common Law Restrictions on the Inherent Jurisdiction[111]

3.35 I have noted the complex history and indeterminate relationship between the inherent jurisdiction and the Crown's prerogative power to protect its vulnerable subjects in chapter two. For present purposes, it can be assumed that the inherent jurisdiction has at least a sufficient link to that power that it is subject to general constitutional restrictions that apply to the exercise of the prerogative.[112] These have been established over the years in various contexts. As a preliminary point, it is generally the case that these common law principles have restricted the *use* or *exercise* of the inherent jurisdiction, rather than ousting its existence entirely.

No Cutting Across a Statutory Scheme

3.36 The first common law restriction on the inherent jurisdiction is an obligation, where the application of the inherent jurisdiction is contemplated, to

[108] *Re L (Vulnerable Adults with Capacity: Court's Jurisdiction)* [2012] EWCA Civ 253, [2013] Fam 1, [1]. See further **ch 14**.

[109] See s 46, discussed at **14.49**; see also **14.8** on the Care Act 2014 generally.

[110] National Assistance Act 1948, s 47.

[111] I gratefully acknowledge that parts of this section draw on the written submissions that I prepared with Mark Twomey QC and Alex Laing in *Re NY (Abduction: Inherent Jurisdiction)* [2019] UKSC 49, [2019] 2 FLR 1247.

[112] That these restrictions apply is uncontroversial. From a strict historical analysis, the picture is probably more nuanced, but in practice this is unlikely to matter.

ensure that it does not to cut across a statutory scheme. This principle has a rich history.[113]

The General Principle

3.37 The classic starting point is *Attorney-General v De Keyser's Royal Hotel Ltd*,[114] a case concerning the Crown's power to requisition property for use in war time. The power to requisition property for the defence of the realm generally fell under the prerogative, but the approach to it, including a requirement of compensation, was regulated by the Defence Act 1842. Following use of the claimant's hotel during the First World War, the government denied that compensation was payable, relying on the prerogative powers. The government's position was rejected. In the Court of Appeal, Sir Charles Swinfen Eady MR had said:

> Those powers which the executive exercises without Parliamentary authority are comprised under the comprehensive term of the prerogative. Where, however, Parliament has intervened and has provided by statute for powers, previously within the prerogative, being exercised in a particular manner and subject to the limitations and provisions contained in the statute, they can only be so exercised. Otherwise, what use would there be in imposing limitations, if the Crown could at its pleasure disregard them and fall back on prerogative?[115]

3.38 In the House of Lords, this passage was expressly adopted by Lord Atkinson[116] and by Lord Dunedin.[117] Lord Parmoor put the same conclusion in these words:

> The constitutional principle is that when the power of the Executive to interfere with the property or liberty of subjects has been placed under Parliamentary control, and directly regulated by statute, the Executive no longer derives its authority from the Royal Prerogative of the Crown but from Parliament, and that in exercising such authority the Executive is bound to observe the restrictions which Parliament has imposed in favour of the subject. … It would be an untenable proposition to suggest that Courts of law could disregard the protective restrictions imposed by statute law where they are applicable.[118]

[113] The principle is reaffirmed by *R (Miller) v Secretary of State for Exiting the European Union* [2017] UKSC 5, [2018] AC 61, [42]: 'it is not open to judges to apply or develop the common law in a way which is inconsistent with the law as laid down in or under statutes'. See also [48]: 'a prerogative power will be displaced in a field which becomes occupied by a corresponding power conferred or regulated by statute'.

[114] *Attorney-General v De Keyser's Royal Hotel Ltd* [1920] AC 508 (HL).

[115] *In re a Petition of Right of De Keyser's Royal Hotel Ltd* [1919] 2 Ch 197 (CoA), 216.

[116] *Attorney-General v De Keyser's Royal Hotel Ltd* [1920] AC 508 (HL), 538–9.

[117] ibid 526.

[118] ibid 575–6.

De Keyser obviously has no direct connection to family law, or the inherent jurisdiction as discussed in this book, but the general principle it established – the *De Keyser* principle – is important. Where there was previously a prerogative power, but Parliament has now addressed the same issue in legislation, it is impermissible to rely on the prerogative.

3.39 The same point was later made in the family law context by the House of Lords in *Richards v Richards*.[119] The case concerned what were then conventionally termed *ouster orders* under the Matrimonial Homes Act 1967,[120] and the relationship with the inherent jurisdiction power to issue injunctions. The court's general ability to use the inherent jurisdiction to issue injunctions is affirmed by statute,[121] and, prior to the passage of the 1967 Act, the inherent jurisdiction injunction was *the* way that an applicant could seek to regulate occupation of a former family home. In holding that this route was no longer permissible following the Matrimonial Homes Act, Lord Hailsham LC said:

> where, as here, Parliament has spelt out in considerable detail what must be done in a particular class of case, it is not open to litigants to bypass the special Act, nor to the courts to disregard its provisions by resorting to the earlier procedure, and thus choose to apply a different jurisprudence from that which the Act prescribes.[122]

3.40 This principle can also be seen in applications relating to children. For example, in *Re O (Blood Tests: Constraint)*,[123] Wall J denied the ongoing existence of any inherent jurisdiction to order scientific testing to determine paternity when the facts of the case fell within the statutory scheme established by the Family Law Reform Act 1969. Likewise, in *F v S (Wardship: Jurisdiction)*,[124] Ward J held that any inherent jurisdiction orders which related to 'custody orders', as defined in Part I of the Family Law Act 1986, could only be made where the jurisdictional rules of that Act were met.[125] More recently, Lieven J invoked the *De Keyser* principle in denying the availability of the inherent jurisdiction to revoke adoption orders in circumstances where the Adoption and Children Act 2002 provides a comprehensive statutory code.[126]

[119] *Richards v Richards* [1984] AC 174 (HL).

[120] The equivalent legislation today is by way of occupation orders under the FLA 1996, ss 33–40.

[121] Senior Courts Act 1981, s 37(1); and previously Supreme Court of Judicature (Consolidation) Act 1925, s 45.

[122] *Richards v Richards* [1984] AC 174 (HL), 199. See also *JK v A Local Health Board* [2019] EWHC 67 (Fam), [2020] COPLR 246, [57] (Lieven J): 'The inherent jurisdiction cannot be used to simply reverse the outcome under a statutory scheme, which deals with the very situation in issue, on the basis that the court disagrees with the statutory outcome.'

[123] *Re O (Blood Tests: Constraint)* [2000] Fam 139.

[124] *F v S (Wardship: Jurisdiction)* [1991] 2 FLR 349 (HC).

[125] Ward J explicitly invoked the *De Keyser* principle: ibid 355.

[126] *Re X and Y (Revocation of Adoption Orders)* [2024] EWHC 1059 (Fam); but *cf* **ch 11** and the approach of other cases to revocation of adoption.

No Cutting Across the Children Act 1989

3.41 While the general principle of not cutting across a statutory scheme is clear, the extent to which it is applied when it comes to the inter-connection between the inherent jurisdiction and the CA 1989 is more ambivalent. The starting point is the Law Commission's preparatory work that led to the CA 1989. The scope of the restrictions on the inherent jurisdiction was summarised by the Law Commission in this way:

> It is clear that the existence of statutory schemes does not oust the wardship jurisdiction. However, the court must now decline to exercise it in a way which conflicts with the statutory responsibilities of local authorities. Nor will the court allow individuals to use wardship as a disguised form of appeal against decisions of lower courts under the statutory schemes. This constitutes the major exception to the universal availability of wardship and to the welfare principle itself.[127]

3.42 Following the enactment of the CA 1989, the inter-relationship between that Act and the inherent jurisdiction was considered expressly by the Court of Appeal. In *Re T (Child: Representation)*,[128] Waite LJ said:

> The scheme of the Children Act is to establish a statutory code for both the private and public law field. It implements proposals in the Law Commission Paper No 172, of which a major objective was stated (para 4.35) to be the reduction of the need to resort to the wardship jurisdiction of the High Court. … The jurisdiction is not only circumscribed procedurally. The courts' undoubted discretion to allow wardship proceedings to go forward in a suitable case is subject to their clear duty, in loyalty to the scheme and purpose of the Children Act legislation, to permit recourse to wardship only when it becomes apparent to the judge in any particular case that the question which the court is determining in regard to the minor's upbringing or property cannot be resolved under … the Act in a way which secures the best interests of the child …[129]

3.43 This principle was previously reflected in the wording of para 1.1 of Practice Direction 12D which – until it was re-written following *Re NY (Abduction: Inherent Jurisdiction)*[130] – stated expressly that inherent jurisdiction proceedings 'should not be commenced unless it is clear that the issues concerning the child cannot be resolved under the Children Act 1989'. This wording was an accurate statement of the law, applying *Re T* and the *De Keyser* principle more generally. Given that starting point, it may be somewhat surprising that the Supreme Court in *Re NY* held that this wording in Practice Direction 12D 'goes too far'.[131]

[127] Law Commission, *Wards of Court*, WP No 101 (London: HMSO, 1987), para 2.33 (footnotes omitted). The reference to LA powers was in reference to *A v Liverpool City Council* [1982] AC 363 (HL), on which see **3.53** *et seq*; on the disguised appeals point, see, eg, *Re K (KJS)* [1966] 1 WLR 1241.

[128] *Re T (Child: Representation)* [1994] Fam 49 (CoA).

[129] ibid 282.

[130] *Re NY (Abduction: Inherent Jurisdiction)* [2019] UKSC 49, [2019] 2 FLR 1247 ('*Re NY*').

[131] ibid [44].

3.44 *Re NY* concerned child abduction. The appellant argued specifically that the court should not rely on its inherent jurisdiction when the same substantive remedy was available under the CA 1989 by making a specific issue order under s 8.[132] While a Practice Direction 'has no legislative force',[133] the previous wording of PD12D reflected established legal principles from *De Keyser* and, in the context of the CA 1989 specifically, *Re T*. Why, then, did Lord Wilson reject it in *Re NY*? The reasoning is less than clear.

3.45 Lord Wilson noted that the CA 1989 imposes clear limitations on the use of the inherent jurisdiction in relation to public law child protection cases,[134] but observed that there is no equivalent limitation in relation to private law children cases.[135] Lord Wilson referred to earlier decisions in the child abduction context, including at Supreme Court level,[136] which either used the inherent jurisdiction or stated expressly that the court could use either the inherent jurisdiction or the CA 1989.[137] The fact that this issue was not argued in any of those cases was not mentioned by Lord Wilson; nor did he mention Waite LJ's decision in *Re T*, though it was relied on by the appellant. The wording of PD12D was therefore disapproved by the court, despite being a fair reflection of the case law. Instead, Lord Wilson gave the following guidance:

> There is no law which precludes the commencement of an application under the inherent jurisdiction unless the issue 'cannot' be resolved under the 1989 Act. Some applications … can be commenced … as an application for the exercise of the inherent jurisdiction. But then, if the issue could have been determined under the 1989 Act as, for example, an application for a specific issue order, the policy reasons to which I have referred will need to be addressed. … The judge will need to be persuaded that, exceptionally, it was reasonable for the applicant to attempt to invoke the inherent jurisdiction. It may be that, for example, for reasons of urgency, of complexity or of the need for particular judicial expertise in the determination of a cross-border issue, the judge may be persuaded that the attempted invocation of the inherent jurisdiction was reasonable and that the application should proceed. Sometimes, however, she or he will decline to hear the application on the basis that the issue could satisfactorily be determined under the 1989 Act.[138]

3.46 The 'policy reasons' that Lord Wilson alludes to here are not prominent in his judgment. He is presumably referring to a single sentence four paragraphs earlier where he states that there are policy reasons why a claim should be dealt with by the lowest court with jurisdiction to hear it.[139]

[132] On child abduction, see **ch 7**; *Re NY* is discussed in that context at **7.21–7.28**.
[133] *U v Liverpool CC (Practice Note)* [2005] EWCA Civ 475, [2005] 1 WLR 2657, [48], quoted with approval in *Re NY* (n 130) [38].
[134] CA 1989, s 100; see **ch 9** and **15.5–15.7**.
[135] *Re NY* (n 130) [40].
[136] *A v A (Children: Habitual Residence)* [2013] UKSC 60, [2014] AC 1; *Re L (Custody: Habitual Residence)* [2013] UKSC 75, [2014] AC 1017.
[137] *A v A*, ibid [26]. See analysis at **7.23–7.24**.
[138] *Re NY* (n 130) [44].
[139] *Re NY* (n 130) [37].

3.47 While I do not take issue with that argument, it is not relevant in the context of *Re NY*. No one argues that child abduction cases are not appropriately allocated to High Court judges; but that aim can be achieved either by issuing proceedings under the inherent jurisdiction, or by allocating a CA 1989 application in the Family Court to be heard at High Court judge level (or be formally transferred to the High Court). This is a technical issue, not a practical or substantive one; the same judge, sitting in the same physical court at the Royal Courts of Justice, will hear the case either way. Consequently, the 'policy arguments' identified by Lord Wilson are irrelevant to abduction cases, and the same argument applies by analogy to the other issues that the court currently permits to be brought either under the inherent jurisdiction or the CA 1989.[140]

3.48 As to the rest of Lord Wilson's guidance, the three stated possible reasons why the inherent jurisdiction may be needed – 'for reasons of urgency, of complexity or of the need for particular judicial expertise in the determination of a cross-border issue' – are unpersuasive. Those criteria describe almost all international child abduction cases and, as Mostyn J has said, all three issues can all be addressed in an application for a specific issue order under the CA 1989, issued in the Family Court sitting at the Royal Courts of Justice and immediately allocated to a High Court judge.[141]

3.49 Lord Wilson's ambivalence about the application of the *De Keyser* principle to inherent jurisdiction cases in relation to children is not entirely new. For example, in *Re C (Detention: Medical Treatment)*,[142] Wall J accepted the following proposition of law put forward by James Munby QC as amicus curiae:

> the existence of a parallel statutory regime has never been treated as fettering the *parens patriae* jurisdiction save in those cases where the statute in question either ousts the jurisdiction altogether or specifically regulates or fetters the exercise of the jurisdiction. Examples relevant to the instant case are sections 25 and 100(2) and (3) of the Children Act 1989.[143]

3.50 This may be an overly loose definition, depending in what is meant by 'ousting' the jurisdiction. For example, it was at one time said that the inherent jurisdiction empowered the court to remove a person from property which they were legally entitled to occupy where such orders were necessary to protect a child who was a ward of court.[144] The Family Law Act 1996 does not say, in terms,

[140] For example, on medical treatment cases, see **ch 8**.

[141] *Re N (Abduction: Children Act or Hague Convention Proceedings)* [2020] EWFC 35, [2020] 2 FLR 575, [9].

[142] *Re C (Detention: Medical Treatment)* [1997] 2 FLR 180.

[143] ibid 190. See also *Re O (Blood Tests: Constraint)* [2000] Fam 139, 148 (Wall J). The inclusion of s 25 (secure accommodation) by Wall J is notable, given later developments using the inherent jurisdiction to authorise deprivation of liberty outside the CA 1989: see **3.51** and **ch 10**.

[144] *C v K (Inherent Powers: Exclusion Order)* [1996] 2 FLR 506 (Wall J).

that it is 'ousting' this inherent jurisdiction power, but given that it regulates in detail how and in what circumstances occupation orders may be made, it would be surprising to find that the inherent jurisdiction continued in parallel with the statutory scheme.[145] This result would also mean that a person could be removed from their property based solely on an assessment of the child's welfare under the inherent jurisdiction, even when the statutory criteria for an occupation order were not met.

3.51 The Supreme Court in *Re T (Secure Accommodation)* took a similarly narrow view of the CA 1989's provisions. The appellant child argued that, since s 25 of the Act made provision for 'secure accommodation orders' in specified circumstances, using the inherent jurisdiction to deprive the child of their liberty in other circumstances outside that statutory provision would be 'cutting across the statutory scheme'. However, Lady Black adopted a narrow definition of the term 'secure accommodation' as meaning only accommodation that can 'be said to be *designed* for the purpose of restricting liberty', which in practice, she held, is likely only to include 'secure accommodation units of the sort approved by the Secretary of State as secure children's homes'.[146] By limiting the definition of 'secure accommodation' so substantially, Lady Black was able to say that any other placement – even though it might have the *effect* of depriving a child of their liberty – fell outside the statutory scheme: 'where the placement is not "secure accommodation", there can be no question of the use of the inherent jurisdiction cutting across the statutory scheme in section 25'.[147]

3.52 Consequently, while the court has no difficulty *in principle* with accepting that the *De Keyser* rule applies to children cases,[148] *in practice* the court often limits its application. While this is never stated, the implication is that the court's understandable concern for the welfare of children, and its general adherence to the idea that the inherent jurisdiction is there to provide protection when needed, takes clear precedence over the constitutional principle of *De Keyser*. In *Re T (Secure Accommodation)*, for example, the core problem is that there are simply far too few placements classified as 'secure accommodation' available for the number of children and young people who need them. The court has no ability to create resources, nor to compel the Secretary of State to provide more placements that comply with the statutory requirements. It is therefore easy to see why, faced with

[145] *Cf Re T (A Child: One Parent Killed by other Parent)* [2011] EWHC 1185 (Fam), [2012] 1 FLR 472, [81]: HHJ Bellamy (obiter) suggests that the reasoning in *C v K* 'remain[s] applicable to filling any gaps arising in the protection afforded by Part IV to the Family Law Act 1996 and in particular cover[s] the making of an exclusion zone as well as the making of an occupation/ouster order'. Sir Andrew McFarlane P made similar obiter comments in *Re Al M (Non-Molestation Application)* [2020] EWHC 3305 (Fam), [2022] 2 FLR 179. This approach may be doubtful, given *Richards v Richards* [1984] AC 174 (HL), which was not cited in either case; see **3.39**.

[146] *Re T (Secure Accommodation)* (n 89) [138].

[147] ibid. *Cf* Wall J's view of s 25, quoted at **3.49**.

[148] See, eg, *Re T (Secure Accommodation)* (n 89) [127].

highly vulnerable children and no other option, the court declines to accept limitations on its inherent jurisdiction. It is problematic, though – the court effectively allows pragmatism to override constitutional principle. And while few might take issue with that approach in the context of the protection of children, the precedent is not without danger. First, as explored throughout this book, the court is not well placed to make significant policy decisions,[149] and so the 'pragmatic' solutions that it reaches are often problematic. More fundamentally, if the principles can be disregarded here – when the effect is to deprive the subject child of their liberty, albeit in the name of protection – what is to stop them being disregarded in other contexts where there might be less universal agreement about the validity of the cause?

The Rule in *A v Liverpool CC*

3.53 The second common law restriction on the inherent jurisdiction is the rule in *A v Liverpool CC*:[150] where Parliament has entrusted an issue to another statutory body, the High Court cannot use the inherent jurisdiction to interfere with decisions made by that body when exercising its statutory powers.

3.54 In *Liverpool*, the LA obtained a care order under the Children and Young Persons Act 1969 and placed the child with foster carers. While they initially facilitated weekly contact with the child's mother, after three months this was reduced to monthly supervised contact: the LA did not consider that return to the mother's care was likely and therefore did not consider substantial contact to be in the child's interests. The mother sought orders in wardship to address contact, and in due course to grant her care and control of the child. Balcombe J refused the application, but granted the mother leave for a leap-frog appeal to the House of Lords.[151] The House of Lords dismissed the appeal, upholding the earlier authority and reinforcing the limitations of the exercise of wardship as against LAs.[152]

3.55 The principle in *A v Liverpool CC* is not about whether the High Court's inherent jurisdiction continues to exist or not in relation to these issues – it does – but rather about the *exercise* of those powers. Woolf LJ later explained it in this way:

> The true position is that the [inherent] jurisdiction remains but that the court must limit the exercise of its jurisdiction so as to avoid coming into conflict with the exercise by the local authority of its statutory powers and duties. … Furthermore, notwithstanding the statutory code, there is no reason whatever why the court should refrain from

[149] See the general point at **1.22–1.27**.
[150] *A v Liverpool CC* [1982] AC 363 (HL).
[151] The judge was bound by *Re M* [1961] Ch 328 (CoA) and other authorities, though *cf Re H* [1978] Fam 65 (CoA).
[152] [1982] AC 363 (HL).

> exercising its jurisdiction when it is desirable for it to do so in order to assist a local education authority to perform its statutory duties. It is only if the effect of exercising its powers would be to create a conflict between the role of the court and the role of the education authority, or the risk of such conflict, that the court should decline to intervene.[153]

3.56 *A v Liverpool CC* was not well received.[154] Stephen Cretney called it 'controversial';[155] Michael Freeman described it as 'replete with unsubstantiated assertions, inaccuracies, errors in logical reasoning' and as displaying 'a shoddiness of approach'.[156] While Nigel Lowe thought that there were reasons to support the outcome reached, those reasons were 'not adverted to by their Lordships' and there were 'puzzling aspect[s] to the *Liverpool* case'.[157] Nonetheless, the rule has stuck,[158] further reinforced by the House of Lords in *Re W (A Minor) (Wardship: Jurisdiction)*,[159] in which Lord Scarman concluded:

> to use the wardship jurisdiction to supervise or review the merits of local authority decisions taken pursuant to their duties and within their powers under the care legislation is to offend one of the basic rules of our law, namely the obedience of our courts to the enacted will of Parliament.[160]

3.57 The *Liverpool* case preceded the enactment of the CA 1989, which altered some aspects of the relationship between the court and LAs regarding children in care. Those changes prompted James Munby QC as counsel in *Re A (Minors) (Residence Orders: Leave to Apply)* to describe the Act as having 'eroded the underlying principle of *A v Liverpool City Council*'.[161] Balcombe LJ largely agreed, describing the suggestion that the court required 'exceptional circumstances' to interfere with an LA's decisions about a child in care as a fallacy, because *A v Liverpool* was decided before the CA 1989.[162] Balcombe LJ held that the court's express ability under s 9(1) of the CA 1989 to make what is now termed a 'live with' order determining the child's living arrangements while the child is in care 'represents a fundamental change in the law',[163] illustrating that the court could make orders that might 'interfere' with the LA's decision-making in respect of children in care. However, this example is unconvincing, given that if the court exercises that power, the care order is automatically terminated.[164] Far from

[153] *Re D (A Minor)* [1987] 1 WLR 1400 (CoA), 1413.
[154] See also **2.29**.
[155] S Cretney, *Principles of Family Law*, 4th edn (London: Sweet and Maxwell, 1984), 562.
[156] M Freeman, 'Controlling Local Authorities in Child Care Cases' (1982) 146 *Justice of the Peace* 188.
[157] N Lowe, 'To Review or Not to Review?' (1982) 45 *MLR* 96, 98 and 99.
[158] Later commentators were less critical: see, eg, M Hayes, 'The Proper Role of Courts in Child Care Cases' [1996] *CFLQ* 210; C Smith, 'Judicial Power and Local Authority Discretion – The Contested Frontier' [1997] *CFLQ* 243.
[159] *Re W (A Minor) (Wardship: Jurisdiction)* [1985] AC 791 (HL).
[160] ibid 802.
[161] *Re A (Minors) (Residence Orders: Leave to Apply)* [1992] Fam 182 (CoA), 187.
[162] ibid 193.
[163] ibid. The Law Commission had rejected entreaties to reverse the *A v Liverpool CC* rule: see **2.29**.
[164] CA 1989, s 91(1).

allowing the court to *regulate* the LA's exercise of its power over children in care, s 9(1) merely allows it to terminate that power entirely. In the ways relevant to the *Liverpool* principle, therefore, the CA 1989 reflects no new approach.

3.58 Regardless, the principle established in *A v Liverpool CC* in relation to children in care remains of general application, as can be seen from decisions beyond the child protection context.[165] For example, while it may not be an exhaustive list, it is clearly established that the inherent jurisdiction and wardship should not be used to review or interfere with:

i. immigration decisions of the Home Office or the Immigration and Asylum Tribunal in relation to a child or any relative of the child.[166] This general principle includes the sub-principle 'that the use of the court's jurisdiction merely to attempt to influence the Secretary of State by obtaining findings of fact or expressions of opinion on matters which are for his decision is an abuse of process'.[167]
ii. investigations or decisions of the police, security services, Crown Prosecution Service[168] or any other body with investigatory, enforcement or regulatory powers in relation to a child,[169] nor with the decision whether a child can be called as a witness in a criminal (or other) trial.[170]
iii. decisions by another court of competent jurisdiction concerning the child or incapacitous / vulnerable adult, such as a Crown Court determining what (if any) reporting restrictions to impose in relation to a criminal trial involving a ward of court, whether as defendant or as a witness.[171]
iv. decisions of prison authorities, such as the appropriate type of penal accommodation in a particular case,[172] or in relation to a child living with the mother in a prison mother-and-baby unit.[173]

[165] See the summary by Munby P in *Re A Ward of Court (Wardship: Interview)* [2017] EWHC 1022 (Fam), [2017] Fam 369, [9]–[16] (hereafter, '*Re a Ward of Court*').

[166] *Re Mohamed Arif (An Infant)* [1968] Ch 643 (CoA); *Re A (A Minor) (Wardship: Immigration)* [1992] 1 FLR 427 (CoA); *Re A (Female Genital Mutilation: Asylum)* [2019] EWHC 2475 (Fam), [2020] 1 FLR 253 (McFarlane P). Cf *Re F (A Minor) (Immigration: Wardship)* [1990] Fam 125 (CoA): in exceptional circumstances, possible to ward a child while an immigration decision is pending if other circumstances require the court's protection, providing it is clear that the wardship is not to influence the immigration question.

[167] *R v Secretary of State for the Home Department, Ex p T* [1995] 1 FLR 293 (CoA), 298.

[168] *Re K (Minors) (Wardship: Criminal Proceedings)* [1988] Fam 1, 11 (Waterhouse J): 'the responsibility for deciding whether or not a prosecution shall be initiated rests with the prosecuting authority and … it would be a constitutional impropriety for this court to intervene'.

[169] *Re A Ward of Court* (n 165): no requirement for court permission before police interview a ward, though the person responsible for the ward should notify the court at the earliest opportunity.

[170] *Re R (Wardship: Criminal Proceedings)* [1991] Fam 56 (CoA).

[171] *Re R (Wardship: Restrictions on Publication)* [1994] Fam 354 (CoA): the Crown Court has statutory powers under Children and Young Persons Act 1933, s 39.

[172] *R (R) v Shetty (Responsible Medical Officer)* [2003] EWHC 3022 (Admin) (Munby J): a dispute in relation to an adult with significant mental health problems regarding transfer within the prison system can be addressed only by judicial review. See also *Re Mohamed Arif (An Infant)* [1968] Ch 643 (CoA), 662: 'it could not be contended that the judge would have any jurisdiction to order that a criminal ward be transferred from place of detention A to place of detention B'.

[173] *CF v Secretary of State for the Home Department* [2004] EWHC 111 (Fam), [2004] 2 FLR 517 (Munby J).

v. decisions of the probation service following the release of a prisoner.[174]
vi. decisions of education authorities in relation to the schooling of, or other educational questions concerning, a child.[175]
vii. decisions of adoption agencies in the exercise of their statutory duties.[176]
viii. decisions relating to child soldiers taken by the Secretary of State for Defence (and presumably their delegate, such as the soldier's commanding officer for the time being).[177]
ix. decisions of public authorities which involve balancing the competing needs of the general population (or a section of it), or allocating resources between competing needs of different individuals, such as medical treatment decisions which turn on resourcing,[178] or housing authority decisions about the allocation of public housing.[179] Indeed, the principle extends beyond public bodies: the court cannot use the inherent jurisdiction to compel private bodies to act in particular ways either.[180]

3.59 This list of limitations flows into the further principle, discussed next, that wardship and the inherent jurisdiction cannot be used to offer a child any generally advantageous position as compared to another child who is not the subject of court orders. While the examples listed mostly relate to children, particularly wards of court, the same principles apply in relation to incapacitous or vulnerable adults.[181]

3.60 One of the consequences of this principle is that the High Court must take care not to appear to place undue pressure on other bodies. It is not uncommon, for example, in cases concerning child abduction or transnational marriage abandonment[182] for a child or parent to require a visa or passport to enable them to return to the UK, whether during or following the completion of court proceedings. The court needs to be careful not to appear to be interfering with Home Office processes or decision-making, but it can be appropriate to inform the Secretary of State about the position in the court proceedings.

[174] *R (ZX) v Secretary of State for Justice* [2017] EWCA Civ 155, [2017] 4 WLR 106, a decision in relation to an adult prisoner; the application to children cases is confirmed in *Re A Ward of Court* (n 165) [13].

[175] *Re B (Infants)* [1962] Ch 201 (CoA): a local education authority had duties and enforcement powers under (then) the Education Act 1944, and should not seek to use wardship in place of those powers.

[176] *Re W (A Minor) (Adoption Agency: Wardship)* [1990] Fam 156 (Brown P).

[177] *Re JS (A Minor) (Wardship: Boy Soldier)* [1990] Fam 182 (Hollis J).

[178] *Re J (Wardship: Medical Treatment)* [1991] Fam 33 (CoA). See further **3.61–3.63**.

[179] *Holmes-Moorhouse v Richmond upon Thames LBC* [2009] UKHL 7, [2009] 1 WLR 413, decided under the CA 1989, but applicable to the inherent jurisdiction: *Re A Ward of Court* (n 165) [13].

[180] See **3.63**.

[181] Munby (n 67) 216, citing in relation to adults cases like *E (by her litigation friend, the Official Solicitor) v Channel Four, News International and St Helens BC* [2005] EWHC 1144 (Fam), [2005] 2 FLR 913.

[182] That is, where one spouse stands the other in a foreign country, usually their original home country, as a way of terminating the relationship and pushing them out of the family. Such acts are a recognised form of domestic abuse: Practice Direction 12J – Child Arrangements and Contact Orders: Domestic Abuse and Harm, para 2B.

Inherent Jurisdiction and Wardship Cannot Put a Person in a Better Position under the General Law

3.61 The third common law restriction on other inherent jurisdiction is the principle that wardship cannot be used to place wards of court in a generally better position than other children. The same principle extends to the inherent jurisdiction more broadly, including in relation to adults, but the origins are in wardship and, in particular, in the idea of the ward having a special status under the High Court's protection.[183] The historic descriptors of the wardship jurisdiction as 'parental' or 'paternal' in nature are relevant here;[184] the court's powers are used to take decisions that diligent parents might take, not to conjure up rights or benefits that other children cannot access. Wardship is to offer protection, not a general improvement in the child's situation under the law.

3.62 Millett LJ once explained this principle in this way:

> the wardship court has no power to exempt its ward from the general law, or to obtain for its ward rights and privileges not generally available to children who are not wards of court; … the wardship court can seek to achieve for its ward all that wise parents or guardians acting in concert and exclusively in the interests of the child could achieve, but no more.[185]

This principle is applied, for example, in the context of medical treatment. As Lord Donaldson MR once said: 'as to the considerations which should determine such an allocation [of medical resources] … the fact that the child is or is not a ward of court is a total irrelevance'.[186]

3.63 This principle extends to private bodies as well, and to uses of the inherent jurisdiction outside wardship. For example, the court cannot use its inherent jurisdiction to compel a private school against their wishes to give a place to a child, whether or not that child is a ward of court.[187] Munby J expressed the point in this way:

> the court exercising its private law powers under the inherent jurisdiction can no more compel an unwilling public authority than it can a private organisation or other outside party to provide care and attention to a child (even if the child is a ward of court) or to an incompetent adult.[188]

[183] See **3.9**.

[184] See, eg, *Scott v Scott* [1913] AC 417 (HL), 437 (Viscount Haldane LC) and 462 (Lord Atkinson).

[185] *Re R (Wardship: Restrictions on Publication)* [1994] Fam 354 (CoA), 271. See similarly *Re F (A Minor) (Publication of Information)* [1977] Fam 58 (CoA), 86 (Lord Denning MR).

[186] *Re J (Wardship: Medical Treatment)* [1991] Fam 33 (CoA), 41–2. See also *Re J (Child in Care: Medical Treatment)* [1993] Fam 15 (CoA).

[187] *Re C (A Minor) (Wardship: Jurisdiction)* [1991] 2 FLR 168 (CoA). The same applies to state schools: *X County Council v DW* [2005] EWHC 162 (Fam), [2005] 2 FLR 508 (Munby J).

[188] *A v A Health Authority; Re J (A Child); R (S) v Secretary of State for the Home Department)* [2002] EWHC 18 (Fam/QB), [2002] Fam 213, [53].

Elsewhere, regarding an application by an adult for financial orders against his parents, Sir James Munby has described 'the fundamental principle that the inherent jurisdiction cannot be used to compel an unwilling third party to provide money or services'.[189]

Conclusion

3.64 This chapter has set out the fundamental principles governing the inherent jurisdiction, including its scope in relation to children and both incapacitous and vulnerable adults, and the statutory and common law rules restricting its exercise by the court. As can already be seen, the general principles in relation to children are clear, and the approach to *incapacitous* adults – in so far as it survives the MCA 2005 – appears to mirror that in relation to children (other than wardship). However, the principles regarding capacitous but *vulnerable* adults are far less well established. The court often uses the language of capacity and vulnerability interchangeably, though they are entirely different concepts, and the justification for the court's involvement in each category of case is very different. That difference of justification ought also to flow through into different principles applicable to the court's substantive approach – though, as we will see in chapters thirteen and fourteen, it is not always apparent that this is true in practice.

3.65 Moreover, while the common law *restrictions* on the use of the inherent jurisdiction are well established, there is a clear ambivalence about applying them in relation to children and incapacitous or vulnerable adults. As will be explored throughout this book, the court has consistently used its inherent jurisdiction to ensure the protection of the individual, even when doing so requires core constitutional principles to become blurred. While this 'protective imperative' may be understandable in individual cases, it creates significant rule of law challenges: it is hard to say with certainty when the court will interfere at all and, if it does, what principles it will apply in doing so.

3.66 The next chapter will address the procedural requirements of inherent jurisdiction applications, some of which have significant effects on the substance of what can be ordered by the court. I have not said anything in this chapter about my argument that the inherent jurisdiction is over-used. Having set that claim out in the introduction, I shall return to it in Part II of the book.

[189] *FS v RS and JS* [2020] EWFC 63, [2020] 4 WLR 139, [123]. On financial support for wards of court, see **12.16**.

4

Procedure in Children Cases

4.1 This chapter addresses the practical and procedural aspects of inherent jurisdiction and wardship applications in children cases. Many of the same principles apply to cases involving incapacitous and vulnerable adults, but I address those cases separately.[1]

How to Apply

4.2 Applications are made by way of Form C66, regardless of the remedy sought. The form has space to set out, in summary, the orders sought and why it is necessary to use the inherent jurisdiction.

4.3 All inherent jurisdiction applications must be made in the High Court.[2] The Family Court cannot exercise the inherent jurisdiction to make substantive orders, though s 31E(1) of the Matrimonial and Family Proceedings Act 1984 does allow the Family Court 'to use the High Court's inherent jurisdiction to make incidental or supplemental orders to give effect to decisions which are within its own jurisdiction'.[3] Consequently, the Family Court can do things like make an interlocutory injunction, issue a bench warrant or activate a port alert to support a prohibited steps order that prevents a child's removal from the country. However, s 31E 'does not give power to the Family Court to make a Tipstaff order',[4] nor to make or discharge a wardship order,[5] nor to make other substantive orders under the inherent jurisdiction. Any application in relation to these issues requires a case to be transferred to the High Court.

4.4 The High Court can make orders under the inherent jurisdiction of its own motion, without an application, within existing proceedings;[6] this includes the

[1] See **chs 13** and **14**.

[2] Family Procedure Rules 2010 (FPR 2010), r 12.36(1); President's Guidance, *Jurisdiction of the Family Court: Allocation of Cases within the Family Court to High Court Judge Level and Transfer of Cases from the Family Court to the High Court* (24 May 2021), Sch, Pt A.

[3] *A v B (Port Alert)* [2021] EWHC 1716 (Fam), [2021] 4 WLR 108, [34]; *Re K (Children) (Powers of the Family Court)* [2024] EWCA Civ 2, [2024] 4 WLR 9.

[4] *A v B*, ibid [34]; on Tipstaff orders, see **7.40–7.46**.

[5] FPR 2010, r 12.36(2).

[6] *Re NY (Abduction: Inherent Jurisdiction)* [2019] UKSC 49, [2019] 2 FLR 1247, [54].

power to ward a child.[7] There is no indication of what, if any, limitations there are on when the High Court can invoke its inherent jurisdiction of its own motion. The range of situations in which the High Court can do so must be wider than the equivalent power of the court to make orders without an application under the Children Act 1989 ('CA 1989'),[8] since in *Re NY (Abduction: Inherent Jurisdiction)* the Supreme Court approved the use of the inherent jurisdiction in proceedings that started under the 1980 Hague Convention on the Civil Aspects of International Child Abduction, which is not within the list of situations set out in s 8(4) of the CA 1989. Surely the inherent jurisdiction could be invoked in any children proceedings in the High Court, and probably in any 'family' case, broadly defined.

Who Can Apply?

4.5 Anyone with a 'genuine interest' in the child's welfare can apply under the inherent jurisdiction.[9] If the court considers that the application is not genuinely motivated by an interest in the child's welfare, it can be struck out as an abuse of process.[10] In practice, a wide variety of applicants seek to invoke the inherent jurisdiction, including parents, hospital trusts and (subject to obtaining the court's permission[11]) local authorities; there are also examples of applications by siblings,[12] by lawyers acting on behalf of a child but not on specific instructions,[13] by psychologists,[14] and by children's rights charities.[15]

4.6 A child can also apply on their own behalf.[16] In such a case, the Family Procedure Rules purport to limit such applications to 'wardship proceedings only',

[7] FPR 2010, r 4.3(1). See *Re A (Custody Decision After Maltese Non-Return Order)* [2006] EWFC 3397 (Fam), [2007] 1 FLR 1923, [117] (Singer J); *Re S (Brussels II Revised: Enforcement of Contact Order)* [2008] 2 FLR 1358, [47] (Roderic Wood J); *Re K (Children with Disabilities: Wardship)* [2011] EWHC 4031 (Fam), [2012] 2 FLR 745, [39]–[40] (Hedley J). Earlier authority held that there was no power to make a child a ward except by application: see, eg, *Re AW (Adoption Application)* [1993] 1 FLR 62, 78–79 (Bracewell J).

[8] CA 1989, s 10(1)(b), which applies to 'family proceedings' as defined in s 8(4).

[9] FPR 2010, r 12.3. This is a long-established rule: see, eg, *Startin v Bartholomew* (1843) 6 Beav 143, 49 ER 779.

[10] *Re Dunhill* (1967) 111 Sol Jo 113: a nightclub owner sought to have one of his models warded for publicity purposes. See also Practice Direction (Wardship Applications) [1967] 1 WLR 623 (Cross J); *Re O (Wardship: Adopted Child)* [1978] Fam 196 (CoA), 207 (Ormrod LJ, recording that there was no dispute that the court had this power).

[11] See **4.7** *et seq.*

[12] *Re KR (Abduction: Forcible Removal by Parents)* [1999] 2 FLR 542 (Singer J).

[13] See, by analogy, *Re SK (An Adult) (Forced Marriage: Appropriate Relief)* [2004] EWHC 3202 (Fam), [2006] 1 WLR 81 (Singer J).

[14] *Re D (Wardship: Sterilisation)* [1976] Fam 185 (Heilbron J).

[15] *Article 39 v Secretary of State for the Home Department* [2023] EWHC 1398 (Fam), [2023] 4 WLR 58.

[16] Law Commission, *Review of Child Law: Guardianship and Custody*, Law Com 172 (London: HMSO, 1988), para 4.44. See, eg, *PK v Mr and Mrs K* [2015] EWHC 2316 (Fam), [2016] 2 FLR 576, [10] (Pauffley J): the child 'became a ward of court as the result of her own application'.

rather than wider inherent jurisdiction applications.[17] It is unclear why the child should necessarily be required to bring wardship proceedings specifically. No other applicant is so limited and, in general, the court disfavours wardship being used when it is not necessary.[18] As a matter of principle, the mere fact that the child is the applicant for inherent jurisdiction orders does not justify the use of wardship, which may be inappropriate or disproportionate to the facts. It is also doubtful that this approach is applied in practice. For instance, in *Re JS (Disposal of Body)*,[19] the inherent jurisdiction application was made by 14-year-old JS herself; she was never made a ward. Consequently, if the Family Procedure Rules purport to hold that applications by the child concerned must invoke wardship, they do not reflect High Court practice and are probably ultra vires.

Applications by Local Authorities

4.7 If a local authority ('LA') seeks to apply for orders under the inherent jurisdiction, it must overcome significant hurdles that do not apply to any other applicant (including other corporate applicants such as hospital trusts or charities). The LA, uniquely, must satisfy the leave requirements of CA 1989, s 100(3), by meeting the criteria set out in s 100(4):

> The court may only grant leave if it is satisfied that—
> (a) the result which the authority wish to achieve could not be achieved through the making of any order of a kind to which subsection (5) applies; and
> (b) there is reasonable cause to believe that if the court's inherent jurisdiction is not exercised with respect to the child he is likely to suffer significant harm.

Subsection (5) requires consideration of whether the LA can achieve the same outcome by making another application, not under the inherent jurisdiction, for which it is entitled to apply (assuming that leave is granted if required).

4.8 In other words, the LA can apply for inherent jurisdiction orders *only*: (i) if there is reasonable cause to believe that the child will suffer significant harm if those orders are not made, and (ii) the LA cannot adequately protect the child by applying for any other orders that are available to it, such as a care order under CA 1989, s 31 or an emergency protection order under s 44. So long as a child is not already in LA care,[20] the LA can also apply for specific issue or

[17] FPR 2010, r 12.3.
[18] See, eg, *AS v CPW* [2020] EWHC 1238 (Fam), [2020] 4 WLR 127 (Mostyn J), [30]–[32], criticising the approach where 'wardship is sought almost as a reflex', and challenging applicants for wardship to ask: 'what does wardship add to the invocation of the inherent jurisdiction and/or statutory jurisdiction. The answer is, in many cases, nothing.'
[19] *Re JS (Disposal of Body)* [2016] EWHC 2859 (Fam), [2017] 4 WLR 1. I represented JS; there was no application for wardship, nor was it ordered by the court at any stage.
[20] CA 1989, s 9(1).

prohibited steps orders under CA 1989,[21] so leave should not be granted under s 100 if one of these orders would suffice. The detail of this issue is discussed in chapter three.[22]

Respondents to Applications

4.9 In most applications, the respondents will be the parents of the child (or the other parent, where the applicant is a parent), or the child's guardian if applicable.[23] The court can make 'any other person who has an interest in or relationship to the child' a respondent.[24]

4.10 The child can be joined as a party to inherent jurisdiction proceedings following the standard provisions of Part 16 of the FPR 2010 and the guidance in Practice Direction 16A – Representation of Children. However, the FPR 2010 make special provision for wardship proceedings when there is no suitable adult respondent whom the applicant can name.[25] In such a case, the child can potentially be named as respondent if there is no other suitable person, but this may be done only with the court's permission following a *without notice* hearing for the court to determine whether the matter should remain one-sided or proceed with the child as respondent.[26]

4.11 Where the application concerns a child having formed (or seeking to form) 'an association, considered to be undesirable, with another person', that person should not be made a party to the proceedings.[27] Rather, there should be a specific application within the proceedings for an injunction or committal against that person, and they should be made respondent to that application only. Any *without notice* injunction against that person should be made for 'a few days only' before the matter is brought back to court, having given the respondent time to obtain representation. The respondent should not be provided with the papers from the full application, but only those relating to the injunction or committal application.

[21] *Re R (Blood Transfusion)* [1993] 2 FLR 757. Booth J refused leave under s 100: 'The result which the local authority wishes to achieve, namely, the court's authorisation for the use of blood products, can clearly be achieved by the means of [a specific issue] order.'

[22] See **3.27–3.30**.

[23] FPR 2010, r 12.3.

[24] ibid r 12.3.

[25] FPR 2010, s 12.37 is drafted so as to imply that a child can be made a party to wardship proceedings *only* if there is no other suitable respondent. That is not how the Rules are applied in practice and, as with the Rules concerning applications by children (see **4.5**), if this is the intended meaning then the r 12.37 is probably ultra vires.

[26] FPR 2010, r.12.37(2).

[27] Practice Direction 12D, para 3.1. On 'undesirable association' cases, see **12.2** *et seq*.

Which Children Can Be Made the Subject of an Application?

4.12 As discussed previously,[28] the phrase 'the inherent jurisdiction' is used in two different senses:

(i) the *specific sense*, more helpfully termed the court's *nationality-based jurisdiction*, which is a claim for the court to be able to exercise jurisdiction over a British child who is not habitually resident nor physically present in England and Wales; and
(ii) the *general sense*, which is an umbrella term for the 'theoretically limitless' substantive orders that the court can make about children over whom it has 'jurisdiction' (in the sense of the authority to make any orders at all).

Calling both these terms 'the inherent jurisdiction' leads to significant confusion in the case law.[29] To reduce confusion, I address the *specific sense* of the court's nationality-based jurisdiction in chapter six, along with the general rules for when the court has power to make orders at all. This section relates to the circumstances in which the court can make use of the inherent jurisdiction in the *general sense*, meaning the court's substantive powers.

Inherent Jurisdiction Applications Generally

4.13 An application for an inherent jurisdiction order can, in principle, be made in relation to any child over whom the court has 'jurisdiction', in the sense of the court having authority or power to determine the dispute or resolve the issue. I term this *authority-jurisdiction*, to reduce confusion with 'the inherent jurisdiction'.

4.14 The orders that can be made under the inherent jurisdiction are limited by the *authority-jurisdiction* rules of the Family Law Act 1986 ('FLA 1986'). If the inherent jurisdiction application concerns 'care of a child … or provides for contact with, or the education of, a child', the court must find *authority-jurisdiction*

[28] See **1.9**.

[29] For example, some cases wrongly suggest that the inherent jurisdiction in the *general sense* is not available when the 1996 Hague Convention applies to a case, when they should limit themselves to saying that the *specific sense* of the court's nationality-based jurisdiction cannot be invoked in such a case: see *Re NY (Abduction: Inherent Jurisdiction)* [2019] EWCA Civ 1065, [46] (rev'd on other grounds, [2019] UKSC 49, [2019] 2 FLR 1247) and *Re I-L (1996 Hague Child Protection Convention: Inherent Jurisdiction)* [2019] EWCA Civ 1956. Likewise, it is wrong to say that the inherent jurisdiction in the *general sense* 'should be approached with caution and circumspection' – that is a limitation applicable to the invocation of nationality-based jurisdiction: see *Z v V (Children Act 1989 and Senior Courts Act 1981)* [2024] EWHC 365 (Fam), [20(iv)] (Peel J). On the nationality-based jurisdiction, see **ch 6**.

within the terms of the FLA 1986 itself. In short, for those types of order, *authority-jurisdiction* must be found either:

(i) **if the 1996 Hague Convention applies,**[30] under that Convention – that is, primarily based on habitual residence under Article 5, or alternatively on one of the Convention's secondary bases for *authority-jurisdiction* under Articles 6–12; or
(ii) **if the 1996 Hague Convention does not apply**, under ss 2A or 3 of the FLA 1986 – meaning on the basis of: (a) the child being habitually resident in England and Wales, (b) the child being physically present in England and Wales, and not habitually resident in Scotland or Northern Ireland, or (c) the child's parents being involved in continuing matrimonial or civil partnership proceedings in England.

Inherent jurisdiction orders that are not about the care of the child, contact or education are outside the *authority-jurisdictional* limitations of the 1986 Act,[31] and so can (if appropriate) be made when the court relies on its nationality-based jurisdiction, discussed in chapter six.

4.15 An exception to this general rule is that a child who is a member of a household where a parent is entitled to diplomatic immunity cannot be made a ward of court[32] or be made subject to other inherent jurisdiction orders unless the child also has British nationality.[33]

Wardship Applications

4.16 There are special features relating to an application to make a child a ward of the court.[34] Most notably, it is the making of the *application* itself that initially makes the child a ward of the court.[35] Consequently, wardship comes into effect immediately upon an application to make a child a ward being lodged with the High Court.[36] The only exception is where a care order is already in force with

[30] On which, see *Re T (Jurisdiction: Matrimonial Proceedings)* [2023] EWCA Civ 285, [2023] 1 WLR 2362, [101]–[104].

[31] See, eg, *A v A (Children: Habitual Residence)* [2013] UKSC 60, [2014] AC 1: a 'bare return order' requiring a child to be returned to this country after a wrongful removal or retention does not fall within s 1(1)(d).

[32] *Re C* [1959] Ch 363 (Harman J).

[33] Diplomatic Privileges Act 1964, s 2. It will still not be possible to make the parent a respondent, but the child could be named as respondent with the court's permission: FPR 2010, r 12.37.

[34] On the effects of wardship, see **3.8–3.17**.

[35] Senior Courts Act 1981, s 41(2).

[36] *Cf Article 39 v Secretary of State for the Home Department* [2023] EWHC 1398 (Fam), [2023] 4 WLR 58. The charity *Article 39* applied in wardship regarding a number of missing asylum-seeking children, the identities of whom were unknown to the charity, though they were known to the respondent Home Office. Lieven J refused the application, but did not address the question of how s 41(2) of the Senior Courts Act 1981 applied to these facts. I was junior counsel for the applicant.

respect to the child.[37] This rule avoids an applicant circumventing the restriction in s 100(2)(c) of the CA 1989, whereby the High Court is prohibited from 'mak[ing] a child who is the subject of a care order a ward of court'.

4.17 A child who has become a ward automatically on the making of an application ceases to be one only 'at the end of such period as may be prescribed unless an order has been made in accordance with the application'.[38] Previously, court rules prescribed the period in question as being 21 days from the date of the application.[39] Some sources state this still to be the law,[40] but nowhere in the Family Procedure Rules or the Practice Directions currently in force is any time limit provided. Indeed, FPR 2010, s 12.41 states that when a child becomes a ward automatically under this provision, they only 'cease to be a ward *on the determination of the application* unless the court orders that the child be made a ward of court'.[41] The Red Book guidance to this provision merely says, surely correctly, that it is 'essential to ensure that at the first opportunity [after the application is issued] a direction hearing is applied for and an order is sought'.[42] If, at the first hearing, the court does not make an order continuing the wardship, the wardship terminates automatically; but there is no specific timeframe within which that first hearing must take place.

4.18 The court may question why wardship is being used in a particular case. Even when use of the inherent jurisdiction more generally can be explained, applicants may need to justify what wardship adds in practical terms.[43]

4.19 On receipt of a wardship application, the Family Procedure Rules provide that the court must record the child's name in the 'Register of Wards'[44] – but in reality, this Register seems not to exist.[45] Clearly the court ought to keep a clear record of the children over whom it has taken custody, and be able to answer straightforward questions like how many children are wards at any time. The failure to do this is a significant problem, contributing to the family justice system's 'data black holes',[46] where it is impossible to know what is happening in the court.

[37] Senior Courts Act 1981, s 42(2A). A care order means an order pursuant to s 31(1) CA 1989, or an interim care order: see ss 31(11) and 105.

[38] Senior Courts Act 1981, s 41(2).

[39] RSC, O90, r 4.

[40] See, eg, childlawadvice.org.uk/information-pages/wardship (accessed 1 June 2024); www.kabirfamilylaw.co.uk/wardship-of-the-court (accessed 1 June 2024). L Buckley-Thomson, 'What Place Does Wardship Have in Modern Family Proceedings?' (2013), online at www.familylawweek.co.uk/articles/what-place-does-wardship-have-in-modern-family-proceedings (accessed 1 June 2024), cites FPR 2010, r 12.41 in support, but the rule says nothing about any 21-day limit.

[41] Emphasis added.

[42] C Prest, *The Family Court Practice* (London: LexisNexis, 2023), 1706.

[43] *AS v CPW* [2020] EWHC 1238 (Fam), [2020] 4 WLR 127, [31]–[32] (Mostyn J); *A v B (Port Alert)* [2021] EWHC 1716 (Fam), [2021] 4 WLR 108, [8] (Mostyn J); *Z v V (Children Act 1989 and Senior Courts Act 1981)* [2024] EWHC 365 (Fam), [33] (Peel J). On the effects of wardship, see **3.8–3.17**.

[44] FPR 2010, r 12.38.

[45] See **1.3**.

[46] House of Lords Select Committee, *Children and Families Act 2014: A Failure of Implementation*, HL 100 (London: TSO, 2022), para 126.

4.20 Every respondent (other than the child themselves, if applicable) must provide the court with: (i) their own address, and (ii) either the present whereabouts of the child or, if the respondent does not know where the child is, an answer to that effect.[47] The child's whereabouts means the child's address, the person(s) with whom the child is living, and any other information about where the child may be found.[48] If a ward's address or whereabouts subsequently changes during the pendency of the wardship, the court must also be informed.[49] A solicitor can be compelled to reveal the ward's location even if that information comes from confidential and privileged instructions.[50]

4.21 Wardship can be discharged by the High Court on application or of the court's own motion.[51] Wardship also terminates automatically if the ward is made the subject of a care order (including an interim care order).[52] This is a logical consequence of the rules prohibiting the High Court from placing a ward of court in the care of or under the supervision of an LA or from making a child who is the subject of a care order a ward of court;[53] the two statuses are mutually exclusive, and the statutory care order takes precedence.

4.22 The fact that a child has been made a ward does not necessitate the substantive proceedings that follow remaining in the High Court, though only the High Court has the power to order that the wardship be discharged.[54] Practice Direction 12D sets out types of wardship case that will normally be retained in the High Court:[55]

(a) those in which an officer of the Cafcass High Court Team or the Official Solicitor is or becomes the litigation friend or children's guardian of the ward or a party to the proceedings;
(b) those in which a local authority is or becomes a party;
(c) those in which an application for paternity testing is made;
(d) those in which there is a dispute about medical treatment;
(e) those in which an application is opposed on the grounds of lack of jurisdiction;
(f) those in which there is a substantial foreign element;
(g) those in which there is an opposed application for leave to take the child permanently out of the jurisdiction or where there is an application for temporary removal of a child from the jurisdiction and it is opposed on the ground that the child may not be duly returned.

In reality, it is rare for wardship cases to be transferred to the Family Court.[56]

[47] FPR 2010, r 12.39(1).
[48] ibid s 12.39(4).
[49] ibid r 12.39(3).
[50] *Ramsbotham v Senior* (1869) FLR Rep 591 (Malins VC); *Re L (A Child); Re Oddin* [2016] EWCA Civ 173, [2017] 1 FLR 1135, [38].
[51] Senior Courts Act 1981, s 41(3).
[52] CA 1989, s 91(4).
[53] ibid s 100(1) and (2)(c).
[54] FPR 2010, r 12.36(2). Presumably the Family Court has jurisdiction to make a care order that terminates the wardship automatically under CA 1989, s 91(4).
[55] PD12D, para 2.3.
[56] An example might be where wardship was used in complex private law proceedings, but that use of wardship in the first place is dubious: see **12.11–12.15**.

Unborn Children

4.23 No orders can be made under the inherent jurisdiction (including in wardship) prior to the birth of the subject child.[57] In *Re F (In Utero)*,[58] an LA was concerned about the mental health and nomadic existence of a pregnant woman, and whether she would attend appropriate medical appointments. The LA's application for the foetus to be made a ward of court was refused on the basis that there was no jurisdiction over an unborn child. In the Court of Appeal, May LJ noted that, if the power existed, he would have made the orders sought; but in upholding the decision of the trial judge, the Court of Appeal held that 'the court has no jurisdiction to ward an unborn child'.[59] May LJ's reasons included the inevitable conflict of interest between the unborn child and the mother in such a case; the practical inability to enforce orders in relation to the foetus against the mother; and the wording of s 41 of the Senior Courts Act 1981 which, in referring to 'minors', by implication applies only to 'a person, in the sense that he or she has been born'.[60] Balcombe LJ found the statutory interpretation point unconvincing,[61] but came to the same conclusion as May LJ based on arguments from first principles.

4.24 However, although there is no jurisdiction in relation to an unborn child under the inherent jurisdiction, the court can make anticipatory orders or declarations in advance of a child's birth that will take effect immediately on birth. The starting point is Munby J's decision in *Re D (Emergency Protection Order: Future Harm)*.[62] The case concerned an application made during a pregnant mother's labour. The background was particularly extreme: the mother was serving a prison sentence for blindfolding, gagging and threatening to kill her older daughter during supervised contact. She manifested suicidal ideation, stated that her children were better off dead than in LA care, and spoke of being 'reunited in death' with her children. The LA was granted a *without notice* declaration under the inherent jurisdiction that it was lawful to remove the newborn child from the mother immediately after birth, without prior warning. In considering the scope of the court's powers, Munby J said:

> The fact that the child is as yet unborn means that I cannot exercise jurisdiction under the Children Act 1989; it means that I cannot exercise jurisdiction in wardship. But it does not prevent me … exercising jurisdiction under the general law to declare the conduct of the local authority either compliant or, as the case may be, non-compliant

[57] The New Zealand court takes the opposite view: see **5.31**. On jurisdiction in relation to a deceased child, see **12.21–12.23**.

[58] *Re F (In Utero)* [1988] Fam 122 (CoA).

[59] ibid 138.

[60] ibid 138.

[61] ibid 142–3.

[62] *Re D (Emergency Protection Order: Future Harm)* [2009] EWHC 446 (Fam), [2009] 2 FLR 313; *Kettering General Hospital NHS Trust v C* [2023] EWFC 12 (Hayden J).

> with Art 8. Any contrary view would lead to this absurdity, that in circumstances where … it would be perfectly lawful for a local authority not to engage a parent in its decision-making process between the moment of birth and the subsequent intervention by [an emergency protection order under CA 1989, s 44], and for the court to grant appropriate declaratory relief to that effect, it would not be possible for the court to declare it to be lawful for the local authority to adopt precisely the same approach in the period leading up to birth. That would be absurd and would tend to frustrate the very need to protect the child which is implicit in the Strasbourg jurisprudence.[63]

In considering such an application, Munby J stressed that orders would be made only in 'highly exceptional and rare cases', where the approach was 'not merely appropriate, it is imperatively demanded in the interests of the safety – the physical safety – in the period immediately following the birth of the as yet unborn child'.[64] Any attempt to lower the threshold for this pre-birth intervention has been resisted by the court.[65]

Applications to Set Aside Inherent Jurisdiction Orders

4.25 Since 2020,[66] the Family Procedure Rules have provided expressly that a party may apply to set aside any order, declaration or judgment made under the inherent jurisdiction in cases 'where no error of the court is alleged'.[67] This provision was introduced to address the uncertainty about whether the High Court[68] could set aside its own orders.[69]

4.26 Any application for the High Court to set aside an inherent jurisdiction order is made under the procedure set out in Part 18 of the Family Procedure Rules.[70] Where possible, the matter should be heard by the same judge who made the order being reviewed. The rule applies to any inherent jurisdiction order, declaration or judgment, including those made by consent.[71]

4.27 This process is categorically different from an appeal. Whereas an appeal is, of its nature, a claim that the original decision was 'wrong' (or procedurally unjust),[72] the set-aside application 'should only be made where no error of the

[63] ibid [12].
[64] ibid [25].
[65] See, eg, *Re DM (Unborn Child)* [2014] EWHC 3119 (Fam), [29] (Hayden J); *X County Council v M* [2014] EWHC 2262 (Fam), 142 BMLR 196, [15] (Keehan J). In *X County Council*, the issue was limited to not disclosing the LA's care plan for immediate removal of the then-unborn child to the mother.
[66] SI 2020/135.
[67] FPR 2010, r 12.42A.
[68] The Family Court has power to do so under s 31F(6) of the Matrimonial and Family Proceedings Act 1984.
[69] The court held that it had this power prior to the rule change: *Re W (Abduction: Setting Aside Return Order)* [2018] EWCA Civ 1904, [2018] 4 WLR 149, [66].
[70] PD12D, para 8.1.
[71] ibid para 8.5.
[72] CPR 1998, r 52.21(3).

court is alleged'.[73] There are no strict rules about the circumstances that may lead to an application to set aside an inherent jurisdiction order, but a non-exhaustive list of issues is provided in Practice Direction 12D:[74]

> The grounds may include: (i) fraud; (ii) material non-disclosure; (iii) certain limited types of mistake; (iv) a fundamental change in circumstances which undermines the basis on which the order was made; and (v) the welfare of the child requires it.

It is important to see each of these five exemplars as separate. For example, '[t]here is no basis in the rules for … aligning the welfare ground with the change-of-circumstances ground'.[75]

4.28 This power is equivalent to the Family Court's power to rescind its own orders under s 31E(6) of the Matrimonial and Family Proceedings Act 1984. The guidance in relation to that provision therefore applies by analogy to the inherent jurisdiction power to set aside orders.[76]

Conclusion

4.29 This chapter addresses procedural issues in relation to children, though (other than in respect of wardship) most of it applies by analogy also to cases concerning adults. Chapter five addresses an overview of the approaches to inherent jurisdiction in a number of other common law countries, highlighting similarities and differences from the English approach, after which in Part II of the book I turn to consider the application of the inherent jurisdiction to specific areas of the law.

[73] PD12D, [8.4].
[74] ibid [8.4].
[75] *Re S (Inherent Jurisdiction: Setting Aside Return Order)* [2021] EWCA Civ 1223, [2022] Fam 237, [48].
[76] See *Re A and B (Rescission of Order: Change of Circumstances)* [2021] EWFC 76, [2022] 1 FLR 1143, esp [39] (Cobb J), approved in *Cazalet v Abu-Zalaf* [2023] EWCA Civ 1065, [24].

5

The Inherent Jurisdiction in Other Common Law States

5.1 The English High Court is not alone; courts in other states also make use of an inherent jurisdiction (though often referred to by different terminology) in relation to children and incapacitous[1] adults. This chapter sets out a brief overview of the approaches in five other common law states: Scotland, Ireland, Canada, Australia, and New Zealand. It is not my purpose to provide a comprehensive analysis of the inherent jurisdiction in these states, but rather to draw broad comparisons and to set my analysis of the English position in broader context. Comparisons, however, need to be made with care, remaining 'alive to subtle differences' that exist in local contexts.[2] The main point to emphasise is the rarity of the court's recourse to the inherent jurisdiction in other common law states, which raises questions about whether the English court is justified in using its inherent jurisdiction as often as it does.

Scotland

5.2 The Court of Session in Scotland has an inherent jurisdiction over children, generally termed the *nobile officium*, and sometimes referred to as a *parens patriae* jurisdiction. Stephen Thomson suggests that the terms perhaps have only 'a degree of relation' to one another,[3] but the frequent convergence of the two ideas can be seen in the observations of Lord Robertson in *Beagley v Beagley*:

> [t]here is an inherent power in the Court of Session to exercise in its *nobile officium*, as *parens patriae* jurisdiction over all children within the realm, and an application by anyone able to demonstrate an interest may bring a petition to the *nobile officium* if the interests of a child is involved or threatened.[4]

[1] Other than in Canada (see **5.16**), there does not appear to be much consideration of the inherent jurisdiction in relation to capacitous but vulnerable adults.

[2] G Lindsay, 'Children: The Parens Patriae, and Supervisory, Jurisdiction of the Supreme Court of NSW', *Child Representation Conference* (Terrigal NSW, 18 November 2017), [27], online at supreme-court.nsw.gov.au/documents/Publications/Speeches/2017-Speeches/Lindsay_20171117.pdf.

[3] S Thomson, *The Nobile Officium: The Extraordinary Equitable Jurisdiction of the Supreme Courts of Scotland* (Edinburgh: Edinburgh University Press, 2015), 118.

[4] *Beagley v Beagley* 1984 SC (HL) 69, 83. *Beagley* was upheld by the House of Lords on appeal. Lord Templeman (ibid 94) described the *nobile officium* as 'an inherent broad equitable jurisdiction', but no member of the House of Lords equated it expressly with *parens patriae*.

Historically, the *nobile officium* was the way in which child custody disputes were resolved in Scotland,[5] but more recent authorities view it as performing a primarily supportive role, filling legislative gaps.

5.3 Thomson notes that the scope of the *nobile officium* 'is, in principle, open-ended'.[6] However, in practice there are substantial limits on its exercise,[7] such that he also describes the *nobile officium* as a 'residual, exceptional mechanism for marginal cases'.[8] For example, the *nobile officium* cannot be used to seek orders when statutory remedies are available (even if the petitioner finds those remedies undesirable for some reason),[9] to make orders that are in conflict with statutory provisions,[10] or to interfere with decisions entrusted to another statutory body.[11]

5.4 Unlike the inherent jurisdiction in England, which is in daily use by the High Court, the Scottish court rarely uses the *nobile officium*.[12] Almost all recent invocations of the *nobile officium* in relation to children arise from cases with English roots,[13] in the context of the deprivation of liberty ('DOL') of high-risk vulnerable children.[14] Due to a significant shortage of suitable secure accommodation placements in England and Wales, some judges looked to Scotland. While the English court retains primary responsibility for children placed by them in Scotland,[15] the child's physical presence in Scotland requires the Scottish court's involvement – but no statutory provisions existed to address this cross-border situation.[16] In the absence of statutory powers, the Scottish court invoked the *nobile officium*. However – in contrast to the English position, where the inherent jurisdiction is the accepted legal remedy in DOL cases – the court stressed that it was 'expecting that

[5] *McArthur v McArthur* 1955 SC 414, 416 (Lord Justice-Clerk Thomson); see Thomson (n 3) 121.

[6] Thomson (n 3) 126.

[7] For a summary, though not in the context of decisions about children in particular, see *Laws of Scotland: Stair Memorial Encyclopaedia*, para 431.

[8] Thomson (n 3) 126. See similarly the *Laws of Scotland: Stair Memorial Encyclopaedia*, para 243, which terms the *nobile officium* 'the extraordinary equitable power which rests in the court to make such order as it thinks appropriate to cure a potential injustice where no ordinary remedy can be invoked'.

[9] See *Petition of SU* [2021] CSIH 65.

[10] *D v Grampion RC* 1995 SC (HL) 1, 7 (Lord Jauncey); *Humphries v X and Y* 1982 SC 79, 83-4 (Lord President Emslie); see Thomson (n 3) 122–4.

[11] *Beagley v Beagley* 1984 SC (HL) 69; the English decision of *A v Liverpool CC* [1982] AC 363 (HL) was cited in argument but not in the judgments, despite the principle being applied being identical: see **3.55** *et seq*.

[12] Thomson (n 3) writing in 2015, references no case more recent than 1997 in his chapter, and most authorities he cites are from the middle of the 20th century or earlier.

[13] In *Petition for the Exercise of the Nobile Officium by the London Borough of Lambeth and Medway Council* [2021] CSIH 59, Lord Menzies noted that there had been 22 such applications.

[14] See **ch 10**.

[15] *Cumbria CC v X* 2017 SC 451, [40] (Lord Drummond Young).

[16] Lord Menzies describes this as a 'statutory lacuna': *Petition for the Exercise of the Nobile Officium by the London Borough of Lambeth and Medway Council* [2021] CSIH 59, [3]; see similarly *Re X and Y (Jurisdiction: Secure Accommodation)* [2016] EWHC 2271 (Fam), [2017] Fam 80 (Munby P): 'serious lacunae in the law'.

the necessary legislation will now be addressed, and once in force these petitions will be superseded'.[17] The Cross-Border Placements (Effect of Deprivation of Liberty Orders) (Scotland) Regulations 2022 followed,[18] which implemented a system to authorise children's DOL in Scotland following orders made in England, Wales or Northern Ireland.

Ireland

5.5 Ireland has retained *parens patriae* jurisdiction in relation to children and adults who lack capacity.[19] Unlike the position in England, the Irish court had the power to make both children and adults wards of court,[20] but the power over adults was repealed by the Assisted Decision-Making (Capacity) Act 2015, which entered force in 2023.[21] Whether the court will hold that the 2015 Act entirely removes the inherent jurisdiction over incapacitous adults remains to be seen, but the new legislation does not affect the law in relation to children.

5.6 As in England, no significant step can be taken in respect of a ward without the court's consent.[22] In 2020 and 2021, minors under the age of 18 accounted for only around five per cent of wardship cases – just 15 cases in 2021 and 21 in 2022.[23] According to the Irish court website, the most common reason for a child being warded is that they have been given a financial award for personal injuries and the funds require management.[24] Only a tiny number of wardships commenced for welfare reasons.

5.7 Historically, wardship was exercisable only in relation to a child for welfare reasons when there was some significant concern with the parents' conduct which, in effect, imposed a high threshold before the court would intervene.[25] This may explain the relatively limited use of wardship for children in Ireland compared with England.

5.8 The inherent jurisdiction is broader than wardship,[26] although, the Irish court is consistent in saying that the inherent jurisdiction should 'be used sparingly, and

[17] *City of Wolverhampton Council v Lord Advocate and Advocate General* [2021] CSIH 69, [18] (Lady Paton).
[18] SI 2022/225. Note also the Children (Care and Justice) (Scotland) Act 2024, which received Royal Assent as this book was going to press.
[19] The jurisdiction is preserved by the Courts (Supplemental Provisions) Act 1961, s 9. On the history of the Irish legislation, see *Re A Ward of Court (Withholding Medical Treatment) (No 2)* [1996] 2 IR 79 (SC), 102–107 (Hamilton CJ).
[20] For adults, under the Lunacy Regulation (Ireland) Act 1871.
[21] See **5.9**.
[22] See, eg, *Re A Ward of Court (Withholding Medical Treatment) (No 2)* [1996] 2 IR 79 (SC), 117.
[23] Courts Service, *Annual Report 2022* (Dublin: Office of the Courts Service, 2023), 80.
[24] See www.courts.ie/wardship-minors (accessed 1 June 2024).
[25] See, eg, *Re Kindersley* [1944] IR 111, 130–131.
[26] *AM v Health Service Executive* [2019] IESC 3 (SC), [90].

only as a "backstop" when statutes do not govern the situation'.[27] Joan Donnelly describes the approach as showing 'utmost restraint'.[28]

5.9 Until the commencement of the Assisted Decision-Making (Capacity) Act 2015 in April 2023, the Irish law dealt with incapacitous adults by way of making them adult wards of court.[29] The new Decision Support Service has taken over this function, and existing adult wardships are being reviewed with a view to being discharged by 2026. The Act transfers jurisdiction over incapacitous adults to the Circuit Court, with only limited decisions in relation to organ donation, withdrawal of life-sustaining treatment and questions about advance decisions to refuse treatment in relation to pregnancy reserved to the High Court.[30] The Irish court has never exercised inherent jurisdiction in relation to vulnerable but capacitous adults.[31]

Canada

5.10 Canada's superior courts inherited their inherent jurisdictions from the English court. Various pieces of statutory reform have expressly stated that the court's *parens patriae* jurisdiction (as it is often termed in the Canadian context) remains available.[32] That statement is subject to the general principles, familiar from the English context: (i) that the *parens patriae* jurisdiction can be used only when there is no available statutory remedy,[33] and (ii) that the jurisdiction cannot be used to interfere with decisions entrusted to other statutory bodies.[34] Decisions under the inherent jurisdiction are determined according to the best interests test.[35]

5.11 The general principles of the *parens patriae* jurisdiction in Canada are discussed in the Supreme Court of Canada's decision in *Re Eve*.[36] The case concerned

[27] ibid [91]. In *DG v Eastern Health Board* [1997] IESC 7, [1997] 3 IR 511 (SC), the Supreme Court held that the inherent jurisdiction could be used to authorise DOL outside a statutory scheme; however, the European Court of Human Rights found this to breach Art 5: see **10.30–10.36**.

[28] J Donnelly, 'Inherent Jurisdiction and Inherent Powers of Irish Courts' (2009) 9 *Judicial Studies Institute Journal* 122, 132.

[29] On reasons why young adults were made wards, see Child Law Project, 'Ten Young People Before Wards List in High Court' (2022), online at www.childlawproject.ie/latest-volume/ten-young-people-before-wards-list-in-high-court (accessed 1 June 2024); G Gulati et al, 'The Inherent Jurisdiction of the Irish High Court: Interface with Psychiatry' (2020) 69 *International Journal of Law and Psychiatry* 101533.

[30] Assisted Decision-Making (Capacity) Act 2015, ss 4 and 85(6)(b).

[31] Gulati et al (n 29). In *Health Service Executive v JB (No 2)* [2016] IEHC 575, the court confirmed that the inherent jurisdiction cannot be used to authorise a DOL for a capacitous adult even when, absent a DOL, the person was likely to relapse and thereby later lose capacity.

[32] See, eg, Children's Law Reform Act (Ontaria) 1990, s 69.

[33] *Beson v Director of Child Welfare (NFLD)* [1982] 2 SCR 716 (SCC); *CG v Catholic Children's Aid Society of Hamilton-Wentworth* [1998] OR (3d) 334 (Ontario CoA).

[34] *Bhajan v Bhajan* (2010) 104 OR (3d) 368 (Ontario CoA).

[35] *Re Eve* [1986] 2 SCR 388 (SCC) ('*Re Eve*').

[36] ibid confirmed in *BJT v JD* [2022] SCC 24.

an application by the mother for a non-therapeutic sterilisation of her mentally handicapped daughter. LaForest J, giving the judgment of the Supreme Court, gave a detailed analysis of the inherent jurisdiction, but declined to exercise it on the facts. Later cases, stressing the caution required before considering invoking *parens patriae*, frequently emphasise that the court did not actually exercise it in *Re Eve*.[37]

5.12 *Re Eve* held that '[e]ven where there is legislation in the area, the courts will continue to use the *parens patriae* jurisdiction to deal with uncontemplated situations where it appears necessary to do so for the protection of those who fall within its ambit'.[38] LaForest J said:

> the situations under which it can be exercised are legion … and the categories under which the jurisdiction can be exercised are never closed … The courts will not readily assume that it has been removed by legislation where a necessity arises to protect a person who cannot protect himself.[39]

5.13 Subsequently, the court has cautioned that while *parens patriae* can be used to supplement and support a statutory scheme, it cannot be used inconsistently with legislation. In *Director of Children and Family Services v MK and CJO*,[40] the trial judge had used *parens patriae* to attach conditions to an order placing a child in state care, where the statute made no provision for such conditions. The Manitoba Court of Appeal removed those conditions, holding them to be inconsistent with the statutory scheme and an inappropriate attempt to control the welfare authority's decision-making about a child in care.[41]

5.14 Although the Canadian court has been clear that it cannot use *parens patriae* when a statutory remedy is available, it has nevertheless been creative. For example, in *AA v BB*,[42] an application was brought by the same-sex partner of a child's mother for a declaration of parentage at a time when Ontario legislation did not allow the applicant to be recognised as the child's legal mother. The Ontario Court of Appeal held that this was a legislative gap arising from changing social circumstances which could be filled using *parens patriae*; the declaration of parentage was granted. Unlike in *Director of Children and Family Services v MK and CJO*, the gap that was being filled in *AA v BB* was said to be in accordance with the general principles of the Act, and therefore it was appropriate for *parens patriae* to be invoked even though the outcome was not covered by the statute. The legislation was later amended, such that *parens patriae* is no longer needed in similar cases.

[37] See, eg, *AB v Bragg Communication* [2011] NSJ No 113, [58] (Nova Scotia CoA).
[38] *Re Eve* (n 35) [42].
[39] ibid [74]–[75].
[40] *Director of Children and Family Services v MK and CJO* [2023] MBCA 98 (Manitoba CoA). See similarly *JU v Alberta (Regional Director of Child Welfare)* [2001] ABCA 125 (Alberta CoA); *Re NVRD (A Child)* [2019] SKQB 302 (Saskatchewan HC).
[41] ibid [74]–[75].
[42] *AA v BB* (2007) 83 OR (3d) 561 (Ontario CoA).

5.15 The Canadian court has generally held that it can exercise jurisdiction over Canadian children abroad on the basis of nationality, where doing so is necessary to protect them. In *Yassin v Loubani*,[43] the British Columbia Court of Appeal upheld orders founded on nationality-based jurisdiction, which required that Canadian children who were present and habitually resident in Saudi Arabia be brought to Canada. The same approach was taken by Harvison Young J in the Ontario Superior Court in *Johnson v Athimootil*.[44] Having found no jurisdiction under the statutory test, the judge held that she could exercise jurisdiction based on the children's Canadian nationality and order their return from Saudi Arabia.[45] The continued existence of a nationality-based jurisdiction was confirmed by the Ontario Court of Appeal in *Dovigi v Razi*,[46] although the court declined to exercise it on the facts. There is substantial similarity between this approach and that taken in England.[47]

5.16 Canada also has a *parens patriae* jurisdiction over *incapacitous* adults.[48] There also seem to be examples of *parens patriae* being used in relation to *capacitous* adults – though unlike the English cases, at least some of these seem to be on the application of the vulnerable person.[49]

Australia

5.17 The position in Australia is complicated by the division of powers between the Federal courts and the courts of the States and Territories.[50] Both have powers that are relevant, so I take them separately.

[43] *Yassin v Loubani* [2006] BCJ No 2928 (British Columbia CoA). Leave to appeal to the Supreme Court of Canada was refused: [2007] SCCA No 19.

[44] [2007] OJ No 3788 (Ontario Superior Court).

[45] *Johnson v Athimootil* Cf *Zaman v Khan* [2009] OJ No 1171 (Ontario Superior Court): with reference to *Hope v Hope* (1854) 4 De GM & G 238; 43 ER 534 (HL) as authority for nationality-based jurisdiction, Bielby J held that 'the *Hope* decision … is not the law in Ontario' because '[t]he jurisdictional considerations of the 21st century are much different than in the 19th century'. *Zaman* appears to be an outlier, inconsistent with the later Ontario Court of Appeal decision in *Dovigi*, below.

[46] *Dovigi v Razi* [2012] ONCA 361, 110 OR (3d) 593.

[47] See **ch 6**.

[48] M Hall, 'The Vulnerability Jurisdiction: Equity, Parens Patriae, and the Inherent Jurisdiction of the Court' (2016) 2 *Canadian Journal of Comparative and Contemporary Law* 185. Unlike Hall, I think that the Canadian references to 'inherent jurisdiction' are likely synonymous with *parens patriae* and that, as in England, the latter term has gradually given way to the former: *cf LM and RBW v Director General of Child, Family and Community Services* [2015] BCSC 2261 (British Columbia, Macintosh J), [14]: '… the parens patriae jurisdiction is an inherent jurisdiction …'.

[49] See, eg, *ATC v NS* [2014] ABQB 132 (Edmonton HC): applicant granted a restraining order against her former partner when the statutory criteria of the Protection Against Family Violence Act 2000 were not met. *Cf RP v RV* [2012] ABQB 353 (Calgary HC): application for an injunction by a mother on behalf of her 13-year-old son against his father, a situation where the child was ineligible for statutory protection.

[50] Western Australia is an exception: the Family Court of Western Australia exercises both State and Federal jurisdiction.

States and Territories

5.18 The Supreme Courts of the States and Territories have *parens patriae* jurisdiction inherited from the English High Court,[51] including wardship powers; this jurisdiction is sometimes referred to as the inherent jurisdiction or the protective jurisdiction. Historically,[52] this power was thought to have been 'never much used' by the State Supreme Courts,[53] and the advent of Federal family law under the Family Law Act 1975 (Cth) led to the view that use of these powers would become 'even more rare'.[54]

5.19 Private child law in Australia is a Commonwealth matter, and in that context 'there seems little scope now for any residual wardship jurisdiction in the states'.[55] The same is true in relation to 'matrimonial causes' cases, and applications regarding child maintenance and the determination of the parentage of children, which are also vested in the Federal courts.[56] However, in public law child protection cases, and other cases where State or Territory legislation is engaged, the courts retain their wardship and inherent jurisdiction powers.[57]

5.20 Wardship has the same consequences as in English law: parental powers are vested in the court, and no significant step can be taken in the child's life without the court's consent, and the court will exercise a welfare jurisdiction over its ward.[58] The power of the State courts in the exercise of their inherent jurisdiction maps directly with their English counterparts, with frequent reference to historic and more recent English authorities to support that position.[59] The High Court of Australia has said that the limitations of the courts' power in their inherent jurisdictions are not defined.[60]

The Federal Family Court

5.21 The Federal Family Court of Australia is a statutory court, and so 'its jurisdiction – its authority to decide – must be defined in accordance with ss 75,

[51] See, eg, New South Wales Act 1823, s 9.
[52] See Lindsay (n 2).
[53] H Finlay, *Family Law in Australia*, 2nd edn (Sydney: Butterworths, 1979), 178.
[54] ibid.
[55] G Monahan and L Young, *Family Law in Australia*, 6th edn (Sydney: LexisNexis Butterworths, 2006), 74.
[56] On matrimonial causes cases, see *Fountain v Alexander* [1982] HCA 16, (1982) 150 CLR 615.
[57] See, eg, *DG of Children's Services v Y* [1999] NSWSC 644, [95] (Austin J).
[58] See, eg, *Re Jules* [2008] NSWSC 1193, (2008) 40 Fam LR 122. See also Lindsay (n 2) 26–32.
[59] See, eg, *Fountain v Alexander* [1982] HCA 16, (1982) 150 CLR 615, 633 (Mason J), citing *Hope v Hope* (1854) 4 De GM & G 328; 43 ER 534, *Re McGrath (Infants)* [1893] 1 Ch 143 and *Re X (A Minor)* [1975] Fam 47.
[60] *Secretary, Department of Health and Community Services v JWB (Marion's Case)* [1992] HCA 15, (1992) 175 CLR 218, 258.

76 and 77 of the Constitution'.[61] There being no statutory provision granting the Federal Family Court inherent or *parens patriae* jurisdiction, it does not have such powers.[62] There is, however, a statutory power that gives the court powers that are largely akin to inherent jurisdiction powers under s 67ZC of the Family Law Act 1975 (Cth):

> **S 67ZC: Orders relating to welfare of children**
>
> (1) In addition to the jurisdiction that a court has under this Part in relation to children, the court also has jurisdiction to make orders relating to the welfare of children.
>
> (2) In deciding whether to make an order under subsection (1) in relation to a child, a court must regard the best interests of the child as the paramount consideration.

The High Court has described this provision as 'similar to the parens patriae jurisdiction, without the formal incidents of one of the aspects of that jurisdiction, the jurisdiction to make a child a ward of court',[63] which fits with the intentions behind the legislation.[64]

5.22 The scope of s 67ZC has been subject to considerable judicial attention, not least because of its constitutional implications. Two immediate limitations can be noted. The first is the general restriction imposed by s 67ZK of the Family Law Act, forbidding the Family Court of Australia from using this power (other than in relation to child maintenance) for any child who is the subject of State child protection measures. Second, due to the historical basis of the Federal Government's jurisdiction over children, s 67ZC is limited to the children of married parents.[65]

5.23 More general limitations bear similarity to the English position. The most notable is the rule that s 67ZC cannot be used to interfere with other statutory agencies or those exercising prerogative powers affecting children.[66] Like the English court's approach to the inherent jurisdiction, s 67ZC gives the court powers that go beyond what a parent can do in the exercise of their parental responsibility.

[61] *Minister for Immigration and Multicultural and Indigenous Affairs v B* [2004] HCA 20, (2004) 219 CLR 365, [6]. Between 1987 and 1999, the Family Court of Australia was vested with the powers of the State courts and so could exercise their inherent jurisdictions: Jurisdiction of Court (Cross-Vesting) Act 1987. However, this legislation was ruled unconstitutional: *Re Wakim, Ex p McNally* [1999] HCA 27, (1999) 198 CLR 511.

[62] The Family Court of Western Australia is an exception: as a combined State and Federal court exercising both jurisdictions, it does have inherent jurisdiction.

[63] *Secretary, Department of Health and Community Services v JWB (Marion's Case)* [1992] HCA 15, (1992) 175 CLR 218.

[64] Watson Committee Report, *Wardship, Guardianship, Custody, Access, Change of Name* (Canberra: Australian Government, 1982).

[65] A Dickey, *Family Law*, 6th edn (Sydney: Lawbook Co, 2014), 262.

[66] *Minister for Immigration and Multicultural and Indigenous Affairs v B* [2004] HCA 20, (2004) 219 CLR 365 (immigration authorities); *Department for Health and Human Services v Ray* [2010] FamCAFC 258, (2010) 247 FLR 455 (State child protection authorities).

The discussion of this issue arose in relation to the sterilisation of a child in *Marion's Case*,[67] where a majority of the High Court of Australia held that sterilisation could not be authorised by parents and that the matter required court approval.[68] However, as in England, the list of 'important issues' which fall outside the scope of parental responsibility, and which therefore require court approval under its wider powers, has not expanded beyond the issue of sterilisation.[69]

New Zealand

5.24 In New Zealand, family work is predominantly done in the specialist Family Court. The New Zealand Family Court is a statutory court, established by the Family Court Act 1980 – as such, it has no inherent jurisdiction.

5.25 Family disputes can also be heard in the High Court when appropriate, though in practice an application under the inherent jurisdiction is usually the reason for doing so.[70] The High Court inherited all the powers held by the English High Court at the time it was founded, including inherent jurisdiction and wardship powers.[71] The inherent jurisdiction is framed broadly as a protective power designed 'to take care of those who are not able to take care of themselves'.[72]

5.26 Resort to the High Court's inherent jurisdiction and wardship is very limited, largely because there is a *statutory* jurisdiction equivalent to wardship, exercisable in both the Family Court and the High Court.[73] This power, termed *Guardianship of the Court* (but often referred to as wardship), is in s 34(2) of the Care of Children Act 2004:

> The court has the same rights and powers in respect of the person and property of the child as the High Court had in relation to wards of court … except that the court may not—
>
> (a) direct any child who is of or over the age of 16 years to live with any person unless the circumstances are exceptional; or

[67] *Secretary, Department of Health and Community Services v JWB (Marion's Case)* [1992] HCA 15, (1992) 106 ALR 385.

[68] Note the strong dissents from Brennan, Deane and McHugh JJ who considered that parents were able to authorise the sterilisation of a minor when that procedure was medically justified.

[69] For a time, decisions concerning gender affirming treatment for transgender children was on the list in Australia, but was removed again by *Re Kelvin* [2017] FamFAFC 258.

[70] *Director-General of Social Welfare v B (No 2)* (1988) 4 FRNZ 98 (HC).

[71] Supreme Court Act 1841, affirmed by Judicature Act 1908, s 16 and Senior Courts Act 2016, ss 6(4) and 12(a).

[72] *Pallin v Department of Social Welfare* [1983] NZLR 266 (CoA), 272 (Cooke J).

[73] From 1991, this was a 'partial' wardship power under ss 9A–9C of the Guardianship Act 1968, as amended by the Guardianship Amendment (No 2) Act 1991. From 1998, this became a 'full' wardship jurisdiction under ss 10A–10E of the 1968 Act, as amended by the Guardianship Amendment Act 1998. The powers are now in ss 30–35 of the Care of Children Act 2004.

(b) commit for contempt of court a child or the child's spouse for marrying without the court's consent while the child is under the guardianship of the court.

5.27 Because the effect of using this power is to suspend parents' parental responsibility (termed 'guardianship' in New Zealand law), the court has said that there is a 'threshold level of protection from inappropriate conduct that must be established to invoke the protective wardship jurisdiction'.[74] Some uses of the statutory wardship scheme are familiar from the English context, such as in relation to disputes about medical treatment[75] or to support child protection services,[76] though typically these powers are used only where there is likely to be an on-going issue requiring court involvement.[77] The New Zealand court also uses its statutory wardship in situations where the English court would typically not use the inherent jurisdiction, such as to review the actions of the child protection service Oranga Tamariki,[78] in high conflict private law parenting disputes,[79] and in relation to adoption orders.[80]

5.28 While the existence of statutory wardship may explain its limited use, the inherent jurisdiction still exists,[81] and is occasionally used to respond to situations where statutory wardship is not available[82] or is considered inappropriate. Heath J has explained the residual role of the inherent jurisdiction in this way:

> The inherent jurisdiction of the High Court is available to deal adequately with questions that are not the subject of specific legal rules. The jurisdiction can be exercised only in circumstances that fall within its proper scope and when there is no conflict with statutory or regulatory provisions.[83]

5.29 The inter-relationship between this inherent jurisdiction and statutory wardship is unclear. The court has given the statutory scheme a wide interpretation,

[74] *Hawthorne v Cox* [2008] 1 NZLR 409 (HC), [88]. Heath J suggested that this amounted to a requirement of 'imminent danger' to the child, but whether that test applies more broadly is unclear.

[75] See, eg, the high profile case of *Te Whatu Ora, Health New Zealand, Te Toka Tumai v C and S* [2022] NZHC 3283; see also M Henaghan, B Atkin, S Burnhill and A Chapman, *Family Law in New Zealand*, 21st edn (Wellington: LexisNexis, 2023), 436–449.

[76] See, eg, *Chief Executive of Oranga Tamariki v Grechan* [2020] NZFC 11494; see also M Henaghan et al (n 75) 435–436.

[77] *Re Norma* [1992] NZFLR 445 (HC).

[78] This role is consistent with the Oranga Tamariki / Children and Young People's Well-Being Act 1989, s 117(2) which automatically discharges orders giving guardianship (parental responsibility) for a child to social services if the child is placed under statutory wardship. There do not appear to be recent reported cases using this power; the authorities cited in M Henaghan et al (n 75) 433–436, date mostly from the 1980s, with one or two examples from the late 1990s.

[79] See, eg, *RAGB v LMB* [2013] NZFC 455 (FC, Judge Murfitt). See also Heneghan et al (n 75) 427–431. In England, *cf* **12.11–12.16**.

[80] Heneghan et al (n 75) pp 432–433.

[81] Care of Children Act 2004, s 13(2).

[82] The Family Court can only invoke s 34(2) *on application*, whereas the High Court can use its inherent jurisdiction of its own motion: *R v R* [2003] NZFLR 200, [19] (Gendall J).

[83] *Re JSB (A Child)* [2010] NZLR 236, [49] (Heath J, citations omitted); see also *Re X* (1990) 7 FRNZ 216, 222; *Re Lee* [2017] NZHC 3263, [29] *et seq*.

and consequently the High Court has held that 'the parens patriae jurisdiction … has been largely (if not totally) subsumed' by s 34(2) of the Care of Children Act 2004.[84]

5.30 Similarly to the English approach, the inherent jurisdiction can be used in international child abduction cases,[85] though unlike in England this is not generally the default response to abductions that are not covered by the 1980 Hague Convention.[86] The New Zealand High Court does not claim a nationality-based jurisdiction in relation to New Zealand national children, but perhaps because the jurisdictional rules under the Care of Children Act 2004, s 126 are so wide that this would not be necessary. The court has jurisdiction under s 126 if the child is physically present in New Zealand or 'if the child, a person against whom an order is sought, or the applicant, is, when the application is made, domiciled or resident in New Zealand'.

5.31 One area where the New Zealand court has taken a different approach to its English counterpart is the role of the inherent jurisdiction at the start and end of life. The New Zealand court has held that both the statutory scheme and the inherent jurisdiction can be invoked in relation to children *in utero*.[87] By contrast, while the court has held that there is no statutory jurisdiction after a child's death,[88] Heath J held that the inherent jurisdiction could be invoked to determine what should happen to the body of a deceased child.[89]

5.32 The New Zealand court also appears to retain an inherent jurisdiction in relation to adults. There is an extensive statutory scheme exercised by the Family Court over adults who either wholly or partially lack capacity to understand the nature or consequences of issues relating to their personal care or welfare, or to adults who understand those issues but are wholly unable to communicate decisions in respect of them.[90] However, the High Court has held that the inherent jurisdiction remains available as a 'complementary' scheme 'when justice requires it' and when the statutory provisions do not provide an adequate remedy.[91] Katz J held that '[t]o the extent that issues may arise which fall outside the scope of

[84] *Re An Unborn Child* [2003] NZFLR 344, [36]–[37] (Heath J). The judge commented that it was 'difficult to speculate' on circumstances where the inherent jurisdiction would still be needed, but that 'it would be foolish to rule out the need for such a residual jurisdiction'.

[85] See, eg, *H v J* [1997] NZFLR 307 (HC); *SS v HKM (Court Guardianship)* [2010] NZFLR 949 (HC).

[86] The court also uses its general statutory powers under the Care of Children Act 2004 (eg, *AND v MMN* (FC Christchurch, FAM-2011-009-000341) (Judge E Smith)) and orders for habeas corpus (eg, *Jayamohan v Jayamohan* [1995] NZFLR 913 (HC); *Re G* [1997] 2 NZLR 201 (HC); *Kaufusi v Klavenes* (HC Auckland, CIV-2010-404-005635) (Hansen J)).

[87] *Re An Unborn Child* [2003] NZFLR 344 (Heath J); *cf* the obiter view to the contrary in *Re Ulutau* (1988) 4 FRNZ 512 (Tipping J).

[88] *Watene v Vercoe* [1996] NZFLR 193 (FC, Judge Callaghan).

[89] *Re JSB (A Child)* [2010] NZLR 236 (HC).

[90] Protection of Personal and Property Rights Act 1988, s 6(1).

[91] *Carrington v Carrington* [2014] NZHC 869, [2014] NZFLR 571 (Katz J).

the [Protection of Personal and Property Rights Act], the High Court will be able to intervene to protect the vulnerable, utilising its inherent parens patriae jurisdiction'.[92]

Conclusion

5.33 This chapter has set out the approach of five other common law jurisdictions to their courts' inherent jurisdictions. The very fact that the courts in these countries retain residual, non-statutory powers is significant – it shows a role claimed by the judges (and accepted or, at least, not specifically over-ruled by policy-makers) in protecting children and, at least in some jurisdictions, certain categories of adult. It shows a commonality of approach to permitting legal protection, and in some cases legal development, in areas that have previously not been foreseen. The challenge is in finding the balance between what is an unforeseen gap in protection, and what is a deliberate policy decision to limit the scope of the law – a recurrent theme of this book.

5.34 A further notable aspect of the general existence of these powers is that some countries with statutory courts (New Zealand and Australia's Federal Family Court) have *statutory* provisions giving those courts wide-ranging powers *equivalent* to the inherent jurisdiction. This approach is an obvious parliamentary endorsement of the principle of such powers existing, and of their utility. On one level, the statutory basis of those powers reduces the constitutional difficulties with the courts' approach: after all, their respective parliaments have expressly given them this power. On the other hand, from a rule of law perspective, a broad, undefined power for judges to do what they think is best, specifically beyond their enumerated powers, still raises questions about the appropriateness of judicial intervention in children's and families' lives.

5.35 As to the application of these inherent jurisdictions, there are some commonalities of approach. One example is a general recognition that the inherent jurisdiction must give way to statutory provisions, with judges cautioning that the inherent jurisdiction can be used only to supplement, rather than subvert, legislative schemes. Indeed, while the principle enunciated is largely the same, the courts of the other jurisdictions considered here might appear more faithful to it in practice than is the English court.

5.36 However, there are also some marked differences of approach. For example, the other jurisdictions looked at here more commonly accept that the inherent jurisdiction can legitimately be used to review or interfere with decisions of

[92] ibid [60]. See also *JMG v CCS Disability Action (Wellington Branch Inc)* [2012] NZFLR 369 (HC, Miller J); *Dawson v Keesing* (HC Auckland CIV-2004-2735, 5 April 2006) (Priestley J).

other bodies entrusted with the care of children.[93] The Irish court has, until very recently, had the power to make adults wards of court – and while that is technically very different from the English position, there is some interesting overlap with the English court's increasingly common view that it will use its inherent jurisdiction in relation to adults, potentially on a long-term basis, which might be viewed as wardship in all but name.[94] The Canadian courts are the only ones that share the English view on a nationality-based jurisdiction.[95]

5.37 The main point for my purposes is that, in all these jurisdictions, resort to the inherent jurisdiction is rare, and appears reserved for genuinely unforeseen cases. This approach stands in contrast to the English position. The English court has expressly declined to state that cases can be brought under the inherent jurisdiction only when no statutory remedy is available[96] and, as we will see throughout the book, the inherent jurisdiction is routinely used for child abduction,[97] medical treatment of children,[98] child protection,[99] and both incapacitous[100] and capacitous (but 'vulnerable') adults.[101] The fact that the courts in other common law jurisdictions do not see the need to invoke their inherent jurisdiction in most of these situations – and certainly not with the frequency of the English court – raises questions about the English approach.

[93] Note the view of the respondents to the Law Commission in 1987–88, seeking to persuade it to recommend the reinstatement of this power to the English High Court: see **2.29**.

[94] See **ch 14**.

[95] New Zealand's jurisdictional rules are so broad that this question likely never arises there.

[96] *Re NY (Abduction: Inherent Jurisdiction)* [2019] UKSC 49, [2019] 3 WLR 962, [44]; see **3.43–3.48**.

[97] See **ch 7**.

[98] See **ch 8**.

[99] See **chs 9** and **10**.

[100] See **ch 13**.

[101] See **ch 14**.

PART II

Specific Applications

6

The Court's Nationality-Based Jurisdiction Over Children

6.1 Most of this book is about the court's substantive powers under its inherent jurisdiction to make orders, usually based on the welfare principle, about a child's life (or, in the case of chapters thirteen and fourteen, about an adult's life[1]). I call this *the general sense* in which the term 'the inherent jurisdiction' is used.[2] Used in the general sense, the inherent jurisdiction represents substantive powers akin to those within s 8 of the Children Act 1989 ('CA 1989'), for example. This chapter is about a different, *specific sense* of the inherent jurisdiction.[3] Used in this specific sense, the inherent jurisdiction determines whether the court has authority to deal with the dispute or issue in the first place – it is a source of what is normally termed 'jurisdiction', but which I term *authority-jurisdiction* for clarity in a book about the inherent jurisdiction.

6.2 In general, when deciding whether the court can make substantive, *general sense* inherent jurisdiction orders, the issue of authority-jurisdiction – the court's authority to make orders at all in relation to the particular child – is determined on ordinary principles. In the same way that the court must determine whether it has authority-jurisdiction before making orders under (for example) the CA 1989, the analytical framework starts with Part I of the Family law Act 1986 ('FLA 1986'), and will usually be answered by reference to the Hague Convention on Jurisdiction, etc 1996 ('HC 1996').[4] However, there is a 'residual' basis for authority-jurisdiction that exists – the *specific sense* of the inherent jurisdiction – where the court claims authority to make orders about a child who does not meet the statutory or Convention rules for conferring authority-jurisdiction. Instead, the claim to authority-jurisdiction is based on the child's British nationality. For this reason, it was termed 'nationality-based jurisdiction' by Lord Hughes in

[1] This chapter focuses on children. On incapacitous adults, see **13.21–13.24**; on capacitous but vulnerable adults, see **14.66–14.68**.

[2] See further **1.9**.

[3] On the importance of not confusing these two different senses of 'the inherent jurisdiction', see Black LJ in *Re J (1996 Hague Convention) (Morocco)* [2015] EWCA Civ 329, [2015] 2 FLR 513, [75].

[4] The usual bases for authority-jurisdiction in children cases are habitual residence or physical presence, whether under the Hague Convention 1996 or the FLA 1986, though in some situations the Convention provides others: see N Lowe and M Nicholls, *The 1996 Hague Convention on the Protection of Children* (Bristol: Family Law, 2012), ch 3.

A v A (Children: Habitual Residence) ('*A v A*'),[5] and by Lady Hale and Lord Toulson in their joint judgment in *Re B (Habitual Residence: Inherent Jurisdiction)* ('*Re B*').[6] I am using that terminology here because it more accurately reflects what the court is claiming, but also to avoid the confusion of using the term 'the inherent jurisdiction' to describe the two quite separate elements.

6.3 If the court exercises nationality-based jurisdiction (the inherent jurisdiction in the specific sense), it will then make orders using its inherent jurisdiction in the general sense – but the inherent jurisdiction powers in the general sense can also be used when the court has *authority-jurisdiction* on other, more standard bases. This chapter is about the narrow sense of the inherent jurisdiction, the claim to having jurisdiction over a child based on their British nationality.

The Scope of the Nationality-Based Jurisdiction

6.4 The starting point – subject to major limitations, as below – is that the court theoretically has potential to invoke nationality-based jurisdiction in relation to any child who is a British national whether in this country or abroad,[7] or indeed to any non-British child who owes allegiance to the British crown. Ordinarily, allegiance in this context is determined by nationality, but can theoretically be shown in other ways, such as by travelling on a British passport,[8] or (at least historically) by being resident or even just physically present in England and Wales.[9]

6.5 The authorities draw a distinction about the nature of the *authority-jurisdiction* that is conferred on the court when it is based on nationality alone, emphasising that the purpose of the court's involvement is *protective*, as distinct from exercising the wider *custodial* powers of the inherent jurisdiction in the general sense.[10]

[5] *A v A (Children: Habitual Residence)* [2013] UKSC 60, [2014] AC 1 ('*A v A*'), [70(v)].

[6] *Re B (Habitual Residence: Inherent Jurisdiction)* [2016] UKSC 4, [2016] AC 606 ('*Re B*'), [61].

[7] See, eg, *Hope v Hope* (1854) 4 De GM & G 328, 344–5; 43 ER 534, 540–1 (HL) and *Harben v Harben* [1957] 1 WLR 261 (HC).

[8] *Re P (GE) (An Infant)* [1965] Ch 568 (CoA), 585, 589 and 593. See *Joyce v DPP* [1946] AC 347 (HL), 369. William Joyce ('Lord Haw-Haw') was executed for treason for acts done during World War II while in possession of a British passport, despite its being obtained based on a false basis and Joyce not in fact being a British subject. As Lord Jowett LC explained, 'the possession of a passport by one who is not a British subject gives him rights and imposes upon the sovereign obligations which would otherwise not be given or imposed'.

[9] See Law Commission, *Custody of Children: Jurisdiction and Enforcement within the United Kingdom*, Law Com 138, (London: HMSO, 1984), para 2.9, and the authorities cited therein. Whether in the modern age it can meaningfully be said that anyone physically present in England and Wales, for that reason alone, 'owes allegiance' to the British Crown is rather doubtful. However, it is unlikely to matter in practical terms because any child physically present in this country will be subject to the English court's jurisdiction *at least* to the extent of making urgent protective orders (HC 1996, Arts 11 and 12; FLA 1986, s 2(3)(b)) and potentially for full jurisdiction subject to *forum conveniens* arguments (FLA 1986, s 3(1)(b)).

[10] See, eg, *C v D* [2023] EWHC 1251 (Fam), [54] (MacDonald J), summarising the authorities as showing that 'this court does retain a protective (as distinct from custodial) jurisdiction in respect

This differentiation appears also to be the basis of the Law Commissions' decision,[11] in what became the Family Law Act 1986 ('FLA 1986'), to compartmentalise inherent jurisdiction orders that deal with a child's care, contact or education from other orders. *Authority-jurisdiction* over care, contact and education can be conferred only under the Act and, consequently, the court cannot make orders about the child's care, contact or education when invoking its nationality-based jurisdiction. If nationality-based jurisdiction is invoked, the court is limited to *other* protective orders, which might include requiring the child to be returned to this country,[12] or ordering an investigation into the child's circumstances.[13] Curiously, *wardship* is said to be available when the court is exercising its nationality-based jurisdiction.[14]

6.6 The nationality-based jurisdiction is remarkable. It arose (and perhaps continues) from 'a process marked by benevolent opportunism';[15] and while the origin of the jurisdiction is ancient,[16] the authorities developed their modern scope in the second half of the nineteenth century,[17] at the height of the age of Empire and British imperialism. The continuation of this jurisdiction today is certainly an anomaly,[18] and there is a respectable view that it is indeed 'exorbitant'.[19] Nonetheless, its continued existence is well established,[20] and it has been deployed to provide protection to children abroad who might otherwise have had no recourse to meaningful assistance.

The Existence of the Nationality-Based Jurisdiction

6.7 The authorities start with the House of Lords decision in *Hope v Hope* in 1854, when Lord Cranworth LC explained the rationale for the nationality-based jurisdiction in this way:

> The jurisdiction of this court … with regard to the custody of infants rests upon this ground, that it is the interest of the state and of the Sovereign that children should

of [the child] based on her status as a British national'. On the questionable utility of these terms, see **1.15–1.18**.

[11] Law Commission (n 9) para 1.25.

[12] *A v A* (n 5) [28] (Lady Hale).

[13] *Re B* (n 6) [86] (Lord Sumption).

[14] *A v A* (n 5) [28] (Lady Hale) and [70(iv)] (Lord Hughes). Since the very nature of wardship is that the child's *custody* is vested in the court (see **3.11–3.17**), wardship would appear to be the archetypal custodial order – but the authorities say otherwise.

[15] J Seymour, 'Parens Patriae and Wardship Powers: Their Nature and Origin' (1994) 14 *OJLS* 159, 188.

[16] See **ch 2**.

[17] See, eg, *Hope v Hope* (1854) 4 De GM & G 328; 43 ER 534 and *Re Willoughby* (1885) 30 Ch D 324.

[18] Of the other countries summarised in this book, only Canada claims nationality-based jurisdiction: see **5.15**.

[19] *Re B* (n 6) [87] (Lord Sumption). In 1988, Nigel Lowe called for its abolition, describing it as 'dated and inappropriate' and 'anachronistic': 'The Limits of the Wardship Jurisdiction Part 1: Who Can Be Made a Ward of Court?' (1988) 1 *Journal of Child Law* 6, 9.

[20] See **6.9**.

> be properly brought up and educated; and according to the principle of our law, the Sovereign, as parens patriae, is bound to look to the maintenance and education (as far as it has the means of judging) of all his subjects. … [O]ne of the incidents of a British born subject is, that he or she is entitled to the protection of the Crown, as parens patriae.[21]

Being 'entitled to the protection of the Crown' is an important part of the rationale for the nationality-based jurisdiction, and continues to underpin judicial thinking in this area.

6.8 In drawing together the threads of the authorities in 1965,[22] the Court of Appeal in *Re P (GE) (An Infant)* was clear about the on-going existence of the nationality-based jurisdiction.[23] Pearson LJ said:

> It is clear from the authorities that the English court has, by delegation from the Sovereign, jurisdiction to make a wardship order whenever the Sovereign as parens patriae has a quasi-parental relationship towards the infant. The infant owes a duty of allegiance and has a corresponding right to protection and therefore may be made a ward of court: *Hope v Hope*. Subsequent cases confirm that that is the basis of the jurisdiction.
>
> An infant of British nationality, whether he is in or outside this country, owes a duty of allegiance to the Sovereign and so is entitled to protection, and the English court has jurisdiction to make him a ward of court.[24]

Similarly, Lord Denning MR said that the English court 'always retains jurisdiction over a British subject wherever he may be, though it will only exercise it abroad where the circumstances clearly warrant it'.[25] Again, the idea of a 'right of protection' is clear in the court's thinking, while Lord Denning's note of caution about invoking the jurisdiction only in limited circumstances also continues to resonate in the modern cases.

6.9 The continued existence of this jurisdictional basis was confirmed by Lady Hale in *A v A (Children: Habitual Residence)* in 2013. She concluded that 'there is no doubt that the jurisdiction exists, in so far as it has not been taken away by the provisions of the 1986 [Family Law] Act'.[26] The FLA 1986 (and through it the HC 1996) present significant restrictions on the availability of the nationality-based jurisdiction, but the principle of its existence is not in doubt.

[21] *Hope v Hope* (1854) 4 De GM & G 328, 344–5; 43 ER 534, 540–1.

[22] These include *Re Willoughby* (1885) 30 Ch D 324; *Re Liddell's Settlement Trusts* [1936] Ch 365; *Harris v Harris* [1949] 2 All ER 318; *R v Sandbach Justices, ex p Smith* [1951] 1 KB 62; *Harben v Harben* [1957] 1 WLR 261 (HC).

[23] *Re P (GE) (An Infant)* [1965] Ch 568 (CoA). *Re P* is often cited as authority in relation to the court's nationality-based jurisdiction, but the court's comments on this issue were obiter: jurisdiction was established based on the child's 'ordinary residence' in this country at the time of the application (though he was physically in Israel after being abducted). The court seemed to accept the appellant's invitation that 'all that is sought in these proceedings is a general definition of the jurisdiction in wardship' – which sounds like a lot to ask.

[24] ibid 587.

[25] ibid 582.

[26] *A v A* (n 5) [63].

Restrictions Arising from the FLA 1986 and the Hague Convention 1996

6.10 While the court can theoretically invoke nationality-based jurisdiction in any case concerning a British (or British-allegiant) child, there are limitations based on both the FLA 1986 and the HC 1996. These rules impose hard limitations on when the nationality-based jurisdiction is even theoretically available.

6.11 It is difficult to see how the FLA 1986's jurisdictional framework could have been drafted in a less clear or straightforward manner. Its provisions are 'somewhat opaque'[27] and 'extremely difficult to unravel',[28] its jurisdictional mechanisms 'difficult and complicated'.[29] The FLA has also been subject to numerous amendments, not all of which have been incorporated satisfactorily.[30] Nonetheless, it is the jurisdictional framework that applies.

6.12 The FLA 1986 addresses the authority-jurisdiction of the English court to make any order which falls within the Act's scope, those orders being terms termed 'Part I orders'.[31] Section 1 of the Act provides, as far as relevant:

> **1. Orders to which Part I applies**
>
> (1) Subject to the following provisions of this section, in this Part "Part I order" means—
>
> (a) a section 8 order made by a court in England and Wales under the Children Act 1989, other than an order varying or discharging such an order;
>
> ...
>
> (d) an order made by a court in England and Wales in the exercise of the inherent jurisdiction of the High Court with respect to children—
>
> (i) so far as it gives care of a child to any person or provides for contact with, or the education of, a child;[32] but
>
> (ii) excluding an order varying or revoking such an order.

These are sometimes termed respectively 's 1(1)(a) orders' and 's 1(1)(d) orders'.

6.13 The court can make any Part I order only when the authority-jurisdiction rules of the FLA are satisfied. The rules themselves are not straightforward, and are

[27] *Re B (A Child: Court's Jurisdiction)* [2004] EWCA Civ 681, [2004] 2 FLR 741, [12] (Wall LJ).

[28] *Re S (A Child: Abduction)* [2002] EWCA Civ 1941, [2003] 1 FLR 1008, [28] (Thorpe LJ).

[29] N Lowe, 'The Family Law Act 1986: A Critique' [2002] *Fam Law* 39, 54.

[30] For passing comment on this 'odd' situation, see *Re S (A Child) (Jurisdiction)* [2022] EWHC 1720, [13] (McFarlane P); in *A v A* (n 5) [19], Lady Hale suggested that an omission from the wording of s 3 'appears to be an oversight.'

[31] FLA 1986, s 1(1).

[32] The list of issues covered – care, contact and education – reflects the Law Commissions' view that it was 'straightforward' to include these issues in what it originally termed 'custody orders' (what are now termed 'Part I orders') as being 'those which affect the person but not the property of a child': Law Commissions (n 9) para 1.23. Given this purpose, the issues chosen appear overly narrow, excluding for example medical treatment, which is plainly about the child's person rather than property.

different as between s 1(1)(a) orders and s 1(1)(d) orders. For all s 1(1)(a) and 1(1)(d) orders, the starting point is the HC 1996.[33]

The Hague Convention 1996

6.14 If the HC 1996 applies,[34] it provides a complete code for determining authority-jurisdiction. In other words, authority-jurisdiction can only be based on one of the Convention's provisions; if the Convention does not confer authority-jurisdiction, there is no scope for continuing to search for it elsewhere.[35] Consequently, if the HC 1996 applies, it is not possible to invoke the nationality-based jurisdiction, as there is no route within the Convention's rules that allows for domestic law to be asserted as an alternative basis of authority-jurisdiction.[36]

6.15 Because nationality-based jurisdiction is only relevant if the child in question is physically outside the UK,[37] the HC 1996's role in international cases is particularly important. In a dispute between two states which are both Convention signatories, the Convention applies and determines the issue of which state has authority-jurisdiction. In such a case, there is no scope for relying on the English court's nationality-based jurisdiction.[38] It is only when the second state in question is not a Convention signatory that nationality-based jurisdiction is even potentially applicable. If a child has been removed from England and Wales to a non-Convention state, but is still habitually resident here at the date when substantive orders are made, the court has authority-jurisdiction *under the Convention*[39] – the nationality-based jurisdiction is both unnecessary and unavailable.[40] Similarly, a child who is habitually resident in a non-Convention state but is physically present in England and Wales is subject to the court's authority-jurisdiction under the Convention[41] – again nationality-based jurisdiction is both unnecessary and unavailable. The relevant case is therefore when a child is physically present and

[33] FLA 1986, s 2(1)(a) and 2(3)(a).

[34] For detail on the Convention, see Lowe and Nicholls (n 4).

[35] *Re J (1996 Hague Convention) (Morocco)* [2015] EWCA Civ 329, [2015] 2 FLR 513, [74] (rev'd on other grounds [2015] UKSC 70, [2016] AC 1291).

[36] ibid. The position was different under the previously-applicable EU Regulation.

[37] See n 9.

[38] *Re J (1996 Hague Convention) (Morocco)* [2015] EWCA Civ 329, [2016] AC 1291, [74].

[39] *Hackney LBC v P (Jurisdiction: 1996 Hague Child Protection Convention)* [2023] EWCA Civ 1213, [2024] 1 FLR 1139, [125(iii)].

[40] This does *not* mean that substantive orders under the inherent jurisdiction in the *general sense* are unavailable. Those substantive orders are part of English law and can be deployed when authority-jurisdiction is founded under the Convention. Suggestions to the contrary are confusing the two different senses of 'the inherent jurisdiction': see, eg, *Re NY (Abduction: Inherent Jurisdiction)* [2019] EWCA Civ 1065, [46] (rev'd on other grounds, [2019] UKSC 49, [2019] 2 FLR 1247) and *Re I-L (1996 Hague Child Protection Convention: Inherent Jurisdiction)* [2019] EWCA Civ 1956, [2020] 1 FLR 656.

[41] *Hackney LBC v P (Jurisdiction: 1996 Hague Child Protection Convention)* [2023] EWCA Civ 1213, [2024] 1 FLR 1139, [109].

habitually resident in a non-Convention state at the date when substantive orders are made. Here, the Convention simply does not apply.[42] The intellectual enquiry then turns to the provisions of the FLA 1986.[43]

Part I of the FLA 1986

6.16 The analysis in this section assumes that the HC 1996 does not apply, as set out above. Here, the approach under the FLA 1986 differs between 's 1(1)(a) orders' – being orders under CA 1989, s 8 other than orders varying or discharging those orders – and 's 1(1)(d) orders' – being inherent jurisdiction orders relating to the care of a child or arrangements for their contact or education, again other than orders varying or discharging those orders. The court has authority-jurisdiction to make a s 1(1)(a) order if *either*: (i) 'the question of making the order arises in or in connection with matrimonial proceedings or civil partnership proceedings and the condition in section 2A of this Act is satisfied',[44] *or* (ii) 'the condition in section 3 of this Act is satisfied'. By contrast, the court has authority-jurisdiction to make a s 1(1)(d) order if *either*: (i) 'the condition in section 3 of this Act is satisfied', *or* (ii) 'the child concerned is present in England and Wales on the relevant date and the court considers that the immediate exercise of its powers is necessary for his protection', even if the child is habitually resident in another part of the UK.

6.17 The condition in s 3, which applies to both ss 1(1)(a) and 1(1)(d), itself has two alternative elements. Either: (i) the child is habitually resident in England and Wales at the date of the initiation of the proceedings, or (ii) the child is physically present in England and Wales at the date of the initiation of the proceedings and is not habitually resident in any other part of the UK.

6.18 The effect of this is that s 1(1)(d) orders are *not* available in connection with matrimonial or civil partnership proceedings, but *are* available whenever the child is physically present in England and Wales if orders are required immediately for the child's protection, irrespective of habitual residence any other court within the UK. So, in the event that a child is: (i) habitually resident in Scotland or Northern Ireland, (ii) physically present in England and Wales, (iii) when there are no connected matrimonial proceedings, and (iv) requires immediate protection, the court *cannot* make a s 8 order, but *can* make orders under the inherent jurisdiction.[45] The court can also make public law child protection orders if appropriate, which are

[42] ibid [105].

[43] *Re A (Habitual Residence: 1996 Hague Child Protection Convention)* [2023] EWCA Civ 659, [2023] 2 FLR 1247 [65].

[44] This provision is of wide application: see *Re T (Children) (Jurisdiction: Matrimonial Proceedings)* [2023] EWCA Civ 285.

[45] This rule is an anachronism. The Law Commissions' reason for recommending it was simply that they were continuing existing practice, whereby 'In England and Wales …., the existing jurisdiction

not governed by the FLA 1986 at all, and where the basis of jurisdiction at common law appears to be either habitual residence or physical presence.[46]

6.19 From all of this, it follows that when an order under the inherent jurisdiction falls within s 1(1)(d) of the FLA, by dealing with the care, contact or education of a child, the court can *only* make such an order if it has authority-jurisdiction under the FLA's internal scheme. The same applies to s 8 orders under the CA 1989, which is covered by FLA 1986, s 1(1)(a).[47] In such a case, there is no scope for using the nationality-based jurisdiction.

6.20 By contrast, however, as long as the Convention is not engaged, the FLA 1986 is applicable only to those inherent jurisdiction orders within s 1(1)(d) (care, contact, education). Any inherent jurisdiction orders *not* caught by s 1(1)(d) are therefore in theory available when the court relies on its nationality-based jurisdiction, subject to the limitations on the *exercise* of the nationality-based jurisdiction discussed below. There is no defined list of matters that might be within the scope of the inherent jurisdiction but which are not connected with care, contact or education, but potential issues might include:

i. orders requiring the return of an abducted child;[48]
ii. orders relating to children who have been abandoned abroad with their parent as part of a 'stranding' case;[49]
iii. orders in relation to the provision of information about a child, such as their whereabouts or well-being;[50]
iv. orders in relation to medical treatment of a child;
v. orders about the child's religious upbringing (in so far as not connected to education);
vi. orders permitting or vetoing the issue of a British passport for the child;
vii. orders to revoke an earlier adoption;[51] and
viii. orders in relation to a child born to a surrogate overseas where the intended parents require legal authority in relation to an aspect of parental

to deal with emergency cases … is exercised by the High Court in wardship': Law Commission (n 9) para 4.20. Given that wardship was meant to be substantially reduced by the 1989 reforms, the rule should have been re-thought following the enactment of the CA 1989.

[46] See *Re R (Care Orders: Jurisdiction)* [1995] 1 FLR 711 (Singer J) and *Re M (A Minor) (Care Orders: Jurisdiction)* [1997] Fam 67 (Hale J), cited with apparent approval in *Hackney LBC v P (Jurisdiction: 1996 Hague Child Protection Convention)* [2023] EWCA Civ 1213, [2024] 1 FLR 1139, [67].

[47] For the avoidance of doubt, the court cannot invoke the nationality-based jurisdiction and then make orders under s 8 of the CA 1989: see *Re B* (n 6) [85]; *Re NY (Abduction: Inherent Jurisdiction)* [2019] UKSC 49, [2019] 2 FLR 1247, [42]. However, there does not seem to be a *jurisdictional* limitation on the court making other statutory orders, such as appointing a guardian under CA 1989, s 5 or making an order giving parental responsibility under CA 1989, s 4/4ZA – only orders under CA 1989, s 8 are regulated by the FLA 1986.

[48] *A v A* (n 5) [27].

[49] See, eg, *W v W (Transnational Abandonment)* [2021] EWHC 3411 (Fam) (Peel J).

[50] *F v S (Wardship: Jurisdiction)* [1991] 2 FLR 349 (Ward J).

[51] See **ch 11**.

responsibility pending the making of a *parental order* under s 54 or 54A of the Human Fertilisation and Embryology Act 2008 ('HFEA 2008').[52]

Overarching all these examples, it is permissible to make a child a ward of court.[53]

Exercising the Nationality-Based Jurisdiction

Determining when the Jurisdiction is Available

6.21 The court is clear that resort to the nationality-based jurisdiction is permissible only where there is no other legal basis for a claim of authority-jurisdiction. Because of the need to avoid any risk that invoking the nationality-based jurisdiction will act to 'circumvent the statutory limits upon the jurisdiction of [the] court',[54] a significant body of authority exists on the circumstances in which it will be appropriate for the court to invoke authority-jurisdiction on the basis of nationality alone. In general, the court is reluctant to use its nationality-based jurisdiction, and has expressed caution about it in numerous cases, sometimes in strong language.

6.22 One classic expression of the court's hesitation to allow the nationality-based jurisdiction to be invoked too readily is seen in Thorpe LJ's judgment in *Al Habtoor v Fotheringham* in 2001, when he said that the court should be 'extremely circumspect in assuming any jurisdiction in relation to children physically present in some other jurisdiction founded only on the basis of nationality'.[55] McFarlane LJ later referred to cases which would justify the use of the inherent jurisdiction in this way as being 'at the very extreme end of the spectrum'.[56] Sir James Munby P also endorsed this approach in *Re M (Wardship: Jurisdiction and Powers)*,[57] but noted that the use of the nationality-based jurisdiction was 'surely unproblematic' where a child was at risk of harm that would engage Articles 2 or 3 of the ECHR.

[52] When the child is in this country, an interim child arrangements order ('CAO') is usually made to grant PR to the intended parents. A CAO is a s 8 order, so that will not be possible when the child is born abroad and not yet physically in this country, but interim orders could be required in some cases, eg, in relation to a medical operation.

[53] *A v A* (n 5) [28].

[54] *Y v I* [2009] EWHC 1378 (Fam), [35(b)]; see also *Re H (Jurisdiction)* [2014] EWCA Civ 1101, [2015] 1 FLR 1132, [54]; *Re B* (n 6) [85] (Lord Sumption, dissenting).

[55] *Al Habtoor v Fotheringham* [2001] EWCA Civ 186, [2001] 1 FLR 951, [42]. This approach was hardly new. In *Harris v Harris* [1949] 2 All ER 318 (DC), 322, Lord Merriman P described it as 'the rarest possible thing … to make a custody order in respect of a child who is out of the jurisdiction', while in *R v Sandbach Justices, Ex p Smith* [1951] 1 KB 62 (DC), 67, Lord Goddard CJ said that making such an order 'would be very unusual … and in many cases a most undesirable thing'.

[56] *Re N (Abduction: Appeal)* [2012] EWCA Civ 1086, [2013] 1 FLR 457, [29].

[57] *Re M (Wardship: Jurisdiction and Powers)* [2015] EWHC 1433 (Fam), [2016] 1 FLR 1055, [32].

6.23 Thorpe LJ's phrase, 'extreme circumspection', appeared to be endorsed by the Supreme Court in *A v A* in 2013, though Lady Hale added that 'all must depend on the circumstances of the particular case'.[58] Lord Hughes, dissenting on other issues, agreed that 'this nationality based jurisdiction should be exercised with great caution in a case where the habitual residence of the child in England is not established'.[59]

6.24 The issue returned to the Supreme Court in *Re B (Habitual Residence: Inherent Jurisdiction)* in 2016,[60] though the majority resolved the appeal on the basis of the child's habitual residence and so the discussion of the nationality-based jurisdiction was obiter (though fully argued before the court). The court split 3:2 on the approach to the nationality-based jurisdiction; Lady Hale and Lords Wilson and Toulson took a more expansive approach, while Lords Sumption and Clarke were more restrictive.

6.25 The majority rejected the suggestion that the nationality-jurisdiction required any particular factual circumstances to exist before it could be invoked. The joint judgment of Lady Hale and Lord Toulson (with which Lord Wilson agreed) said:

> It is, however, one thing to approach the use of the jurisdiction with great caution or circumspection. It is another thing to conclude that the circumstances justifying its use must always be "dire and exceptional"[61] or "at the very extreme end of the spectrum".[62] There are three main reasons for caution when deciding whether to exercise the jurisdiction: first, that to do so may conflict with the jurisdictional scheme applicable between the countries in question; second, that it may result in conflicting decisions in those two countries; and third, that it may result in unenforceable orders. …
>
> … The very object of the international framework is to protect the best interests of the child … Considerations of comity cannot be divorced from that objective. If the court were to consider that the exercise of its [nationality-based] inherent jurisdiction were necessary to avoid [the child's] welfare being beyond all judicial oversight …, we do not see that its exercise would conflict with the principle of comity or should be trammelled by some *a priori* classification of cases according to their extremity.[63]

6.26 By contrast, Lord Sumption (with whom Lord Clarke agreed) dissented, arguing that the exercise of the nationality-based jurisdiction should, indeed, be

[58] *A v A* (n 5) [65].

[59] ibid [70(iv)–(v)]. This was a curious remark, though, because if the child's habitual residence was established in England, there would be no need to consider nationality-based jurisdiction.

[60] For commentary, see D Williams, M Gration and M Wright, 'Habitual Residence and the 'Parens Patriae' Jurisdiction after Re B [2016] UKSC 4' [2016] *International Family Law* 239.

[61] Alluding to *Re B (Forced Marriage: Wardship: Jurisdiction)* [2008] EWHC 1436 (Fam), [2008] 2 FLR 1624, [10] (Hogg J).

[62] Alluding to *Re N (Abduction: Appeal)* [2012] EWCA Civ 1086, [2013] 1 FLR 457, [29] (McFarlane LJ).

[63] *Re B* (n 6) [59], [61] and [62]. It was suggested that this approach would 'relax the shackles a little and … permit a more adventurous use of "parens patriae" where it may be necessary in order to protect a child and where the risk of jurisdictional conflict is either non-existent or minimal': Williams, Gration and Wright (n 60) 245.

considered exceptional.[64] He noted in general that the continued existence of the nationality-based jurisdiction was 'something of an anomaly', and argued that its use was, in practice, reserved for two categories of case, both broadly speaking 'protective'.

> The first comprises abduction cases before the enactment of a statutory jurisdiction to deal with them. The second comprises cases where the child is in need of protection against some personal danger, for example where she has been removed for the purpose of undergoing a forced marriage or female genital mutilation. All of the modern cases fall into this last category.[65]

6.27 Within Lord Sumption's second category – protection against personal danger – examples are readily identifiable and include:

i. *Re B; RB v FB and MA (Forced Marriage: Wardship: Jurisdiction)*:[66] a 15-year-old girl who was, by descent, a British national and had a British passport, but who was born and raised in Pakistan and who had never visited England, approached the High Commission in Islamabad seeking consular assistance following what she said was a forced marriage. The girl had a half-brother in Scotland who was willing to accommodate her. Hogg J concluded that 'in these very dire circumstances the tentacles of this court should stretch towards Pakistan to rescue this child from the circumstances she found herself in'.[67]
ii. *A v A (Return Order on the Basis of British Nationality)*:[68] this was the remitted hearing following the Supreme Court appeal in *A v A*, in which Parker J accepted that it would 'only be in the rarest possible cases' that the court would rely on its nationality-based jurisdiction. The child in that case was a British national, but born in Pakistan and had never been to England – though the reason was that her mother had been detained against her will in Pakistan by the father while pregnant. The judge ordered that the child be brought to England, using the nationality-based jurisdiction.
iii. *Re K and D (Wardship: Without Notice Return Order)*:[69] two children aged 15 and 13 had been taken from England to Northern Cyprus by their mother. The mother herself was arrested while in the Republic of Cyprus with the children, but the younger child absconded and returned himself to Northern Cyprus, where he was placed in a children's home. The local authority in

[64] *Re B* (n 6) [85].
[65] ibid [82].
[66] *RB v FB and MA (Forced Marriage: Wardship: Jurisdiction)* [2008] EWHC 1436 (Fam), [2008] 2 FLR 1624.
[67] ibid [9]. In *Re N (Abduction: Appeal)* [2012] EWCA Civ 1086, [2013] 1 FLR 457, [28], McFarlane LJ pointedly made 'no observation one way or the other as to the legality of the approach taken by Hogg J', but the decision was noted without demur by Lady Hale in *A v A* (n 5) [62].
[68] *A v A (Return Order on the Basis of British Nationality)* [2013] EWHC 3298 (Fam), [2014] 2 FLR 244.
[69] *Re K and D (Wardship: Without Notice Return Order)* [2017] EWHC 153 (Fam), [2017] 2 FLR 901.

England was granted permission to invoke the inherent jurisdiction,[70] and MacDonald J subsequently invoked the nationality-based jurisdiction – he warded the younger child and ordered her returned to England.

6.28 Turning to Lord Sumption's first category (child abduction), it is unclear which 'statutory jurisdiction' in relation to abduction cases he means, but there are numerous modern examples of the nationality-based jurisdiction being used in response to child abduction. A particular difficulty that Lord Sumption identified with the application in *Re B* was that the applicant sought not only the return order, but also 'contact and shared residence' orders – these s 8 orders can only be made when the FLA 1986 authority-jurisdiction rules are met, which they were not in *Re B*. Consequently, although the *return order* might not cut across the statutory regime for when the court has authority-jurisdiction, Lord Sumption was concerned that the return order was merely a stalking horse for a substantive child arrangements application:

> The real object of exercising [the nationality-based jurisdiction] would be to bring the child within the jurisdiction of the English courts (i) so that the court could exercise the wider statutory powers which it is prevented by statute from exercising while she is in Pakistan, and (ii) so that they could do so on different and perhaps better principles than those which would apply in a Court of family jurisdiction in Pakistan.[71]

6.29 While I agree with Lord Sumption's analysis, the difficulty is that the effects are entirely arbitrary. Take the example of a child abducted from this country and taken to Country X, which is not a signatory of the HC 1996. The parent in this country for whatever reason does not bring an application before the English court until the point where the child has become habitually resident in Country X. The only available basis for engaging the English court is therefore to seek to invoke the nationality-based jurisdiction. Here is where the arbitrariness arises:

i. In Case A, the child was already the subject of a child arrangements order under s 8 of the CA 1989 at the time of her removal to Country X (the substantive content of the order is irrelevant). The applicant is free to seek to invoke the nationality-based jurisdiction seeking the child's return, and also seek to vary or enforce the existing s 8 order (eg, to ensure that the child should live with that parent on their return from Country X), and will not violate the FLA 1986's rules about when the court has authority-jurisdiction to make s 8 orders.
ii. Conversely, in Case B, no existing child arrangements order was in force at the time of the child's removal, but in fact the child was living with the applicant before being abducted. Now, although the applicant can seek to invoke

[70] CA 1989, s 100.

[71] ibid [85]. See similarly *F v S (Wardship: Jurisdiction)* [1991] 2 FLR 349 (Ward J), 356 (rev'd on other grounds [1993] 2 FLR 686 (CoA)): 'a devious entry to the court by the back door where Parliament has so firmly shut the front door to custody orders being made in these circumstances'.

the nationality-based jurisdiction to get the child returned, they risk being criticised because the 'real object' of the return order is, in fact, to ensure that the child returns to live with the applicant. Since achieving that outcome will require the court later to make a s 8 child arrangements order, the applicant is seeking to use the nationality-based jurisdiction to bring the child here so that the court can then make a s 8 order – precisely what it is prohibited from doing by the FLA 1986.

Yet these two cases are materially the same – the existence of the child arrangements order is irrelevant. In Case A, the child arrangements order could have been for the applicant to see the child for contact one afternoon a week, yet that parent is legally in a far better position than the parent in Case B who had the child living with them but never needed a court order to confirm that reality.

6.30 Moylan LJ has attempted to limit the effect of these arbitrary distinctions by emphasising that 'there may well not be a bright line between an order which conflicts with the limitations imposed by the 1986 Act and one which does not'.[72] Moylan LJ has also highlighted the need to consider the *substance* of the application, considering not only what is written on the C66 application form, but also in the statement(s) filed in support.[73] However, the FLA 1986's rules mean that an applicant must be careful, because in child abduction there will be cases where they will want to get *within* the FLA 1986 scheme, and other cases where they will need specifically to get *outside* it:

i. An application brought reasonably quickly, such that the child is (likely to be) habitually resident within England and Wales at the time of the application will positively want to seek a child arrangements order or inherent jurisdiction orders in relation to care, contact or education, so as to fall within s 1(1)(a) or 1(1)(d) of the Act. This grants the court authority-jurisdiction based on the child's habitual residence.
ii. Conversely, if habitual residence is more likely to be in Country X, the applicant will need to *avoid* seeking orders relating to child arrangements (other than to vary or discharge existing orders), because the aim must then be to permit the court to invoke its nationality-based jurisdiction, which relies on the FLA 1986 scheme *not* being engaged (nor must the applicant look like they are trying to get a s 8 order by the back door).

This leaves the problematic case where the issue of habitual residence is simply unclear – which is not infrequent. The success of an application will turn on whether the applicant successfully predicts the issue of habitual residence, or

[72] *Re M (Exercise of Inherent Jurisdiction)* [2020] EWCA Civ 922, [2021] Fam 163, [137], discussed generally at **6.32**.

[73] *Re A (Habitual Residence: 1996 Hague Child Protection Convention)* [2023] EWCA Civ 659, [2023] 2 FLR 1247, [62].

whether statements have been written so as to allow the judge to 'interpret' what has been sought in line with the outcome that the court seeks to find.

6.31 These permutations are entirely unsatisfactory, and demonstrate an urgent need for the court's general authority-jurisdiction rules under the FLA 1986 to be overhauled. They are complex and unclear, and they produce arbitrary results that are intellectually incoherent and, more importantly, that actively disable the court from engaging quickly and definitively in response to urgent child welfare cases.

Determining when to Exercise the Jurisdiction

6.32 The Court of Appeal has given detailed guidance on the appropriate circumstances in which the nationality-based jurisdiction should be exercised in *Re M (Exercise of Inherent Jurisdiction)* ('*Re M*'),[74] and again in *Re S (Inherent Jurisdiction: Setting Aside Return Order)* ('*Re S*').[75]

6.33 In *Re M*, Moylan LJ's conclusion was that there was a 'substantive threshold' for an applicant to cross; 'the need to use great caution must have some substantive content'.[76] Rejecting the idea that the three 'reasons for caution' identified in *Re B*[77] constituted the 'substantive test', Moylan LJ proposed that:

> there must be circumstances which are sufficiently compelling to require or make it necessary that the court should exercise its protective jurisdiction. If the circumstances are sufficiently compelling then the exercise of the jurisdiction can be justified as being required or necessary …[78]

6.34 In *Re S*, Baker LJ endorsed this approach, while noting that the court's 'first and foremost' assessment was 'what orders are required to secure the children's welfare'.[79] That is not to say, however, that the court invokes the nationality-based jurisdiction merely based on the child's welfare.[80] The 'substantive threshold' that the Court of Appeal identified in *Re M* must be met: as Baker LJ put it in *Re S*, the court must conduct 'an assessment of the circumstances to establish whether … they are sufficiently compelling to require the court to exercise its protective [nationality-based] jurisdiction'.[81] If that threshold is met, the court proceeds to

[74] *Re M (Exercise of Inherent Jurisdiction)* ('*Re M*') [2020] EWCA Civ 922, [2021] Fam 163.

[75] *Re S (Inherent Jurisdiction: Setting Aside Return Order)* ('*Re S*') [2021] EWCA Civ 1223, [2022] Fam 237. See also the helpful summary in *K v H (Exercise of Jurisdiction Based on Nationality)* [2021] EWHC 1918 (Fam), [2022] 1 FLR 1171, [35] (MacDonald J).

[76] ibid [106].

[77] See **6.25**, viz. 'first, that to do so may conflict with the jurisdictional scheme applicable between the countries in question; second, that it may result in conflicting decisions in those two countries; and third, that it may result in unenforceable orders'.

[78] *Re M* (n 74) [105].

[79] *Re S* (n 75) [51].

[80] *SS v MCP (No 2)* [2021] EWHC 2898 (Fam), [2021] 4 WLR 140, [23] (Mostyn J).

[81] *Re S* (n 75) [52].

consider what orders it will make, based on the child's welfare before then assessing the enforceability of orders.

6.35 While there is limited authority on the question of when the court will consider the substantive threshold to be met, it appears to require some kind of peril for the child in question.[82] The nationality-based jurisdiction that the court is exercising is expressly *protective*, but the mere fact that a child abroad needs some kind of protection is not in itself enough: 'the exercise of the [nationality-based] jurisdiction is to be confined to those cases in which there are circumstances sufficiently compelling to make it *necessary* to protect the children'.[83] Munby P suggested that cases where a child's rights under Article 2 (right to life) or 3 (right to freedom from torture or inhuman or degrading treatment) of the ECHR were engaged would be 'surely unproblematic' as examples where the court could rely on its nationality-based jurisdiction.[84] Consequently, the court has used the jurisdiction in relation to the so-called radicalisation cases,[85] as a response to transnational spousal abandonment,[86] and as a measure against FGM and forced marriage.[87]

6.36 By contrast, cases where children are abducted and retained away from their primary carer have struggled to get the court to engage the nationality-based jurisdiction:[88] 'even given the added factors that the children are thereby deprived of a connection with part of their mixed heritage and that the mother finds contact with them difficult, is not sufficiently compelling'.[89] The court therefore appears to have taken a restrictive view on the harm that it sees arising from child abduction cases,[90] which has therefore substantively restricted the scope for the use of the nationality-based jurisdiction in one of the most likely areas where a child might need the court's help. Ironically, international child law in general gives the state of

[82] *SS v MCP (No 2)* [2021] EWHC 2898 (Fam), [2021] 4 WLR 140, [28].

[83] *GC v AS (No 2)* [2022] EWHC 310 (Fam), [2022] 2 FLR 756, [29] (Poole J); see similarly *Re K and D (Wardship: Without Notice Return Order)* [2017] EWHC 153 (Fam), [2017] 2 FLR 901, [33] (MacDonald J).

[84] *Re M (Wardship: Jurisdiction and Powers)* [2015] EWHC 1433 (Fam), [2016] 1 FLR 1055, [32].

[85] ibid.

[86] See obiter remarks in *W v W (Transnational Abandonment)* [2021] EWHC 3411 (Fam), [6] (Peel J) and *Re JKL (Transnational Abandonment: Interim Order)* [2020] EWHC 2509 (Fam), [101] (DHCJ Harrison QC). In both cases, jurisdiction was determined based on habitual residence.

[87] *Re KR (Abduction: Forcible Removal by Parents)* [1999] 2 FLR 542 (Singer J).

[88] For a recent example where nationality-based jurisdiction was invoked, see *KH v BM* [2023] EWHC 3194 (Fam) (DHCJ Gollop KC) – though query whether the decision violates the FLA 1986 restrictions, since the express purpose of the application was to seek orders relating to child care arrangements.

[89] *GC v AS (No 2)* [2022] EWHC 310 (Fam), [2022] 2 FLR 756, [30]. *Cf V v N (Exercise of Jurisdiction Based on Nationality)* [2021] EWHC 3109 (Fam): two children had been left with grandparents in Pakistan while both parents were in this country – the court exercised its nationality-based jurisdiction and ordered their return, the evidence showing their carer in Pakistan was unwell and the children were expressing suicidal ideation.

[90] On the harms of child abduction, see, eg, M Freeman, *Parental Child Abduction: The Long-Term Effects* (London: International Centre for Family Law, Policy and Practice, 2016).

former habitual residence on-going authority-jurisdiction over the child after an abduction[91] – so if the English court claimed nationality-based jurisdiction over British children who had been abducted from England abroad, the effect would be to mirror other aspects of international child law. It is unclear why the court has taken such a narrow approach to child abduction – it is certainly an unfortunate effect of the current approach to the nationality-based jurisdiction.

Conclusion

6.37 Though it clearly still exists, the nationality-based jurisdiction is very substantially restricted in its scope. Its role is limited in two key respects. First, the nationality-based jurisdiction can be invoked only when the rules of the FLA 1986 permit it. Those rules are cumbersome and in some important respects arbitrary in terms of what is and is not included within the scheme. The second key limitation is that the case law makes clear that there is a significant substantive threshold to be met before the court will accept that it should permit the nationality-based jurisdiction to be invoked. Consequently, while the nationality-based jurisdiction remains in the background, the limitations on its use mean that its practical scope is very limited. A child will, in most cases, need to be facing an immediate or serious peril before the court will be persuaded that it is necessary for it to intervene to make protective orders.

6.38 On one level, that approach is defensible and may reflect sound policy. It is also notable that, Canada aside, the other states explored in this book do not have an equivalent nationality-based jurisdiction over their children.[92] However, the rules of when the court does and does not have authority to make decisions over a child should be clear and set by Parliament. The rules currently imposed by the FLA 1986 are clearly unsatisfactory, but the court's guidance on when the nationality-based jurisdiction is available is equally opaque. This is an example of the court not being a good vehicle for making policy.[93] There are significant and complex variables that need to be weighed in the balance to decide the circumstances under which it might be appropriate for the English court to make decisions about a child who is neither habitually resident nor physically present here. The court is not well placed to conduct that exercise, and this area of law would benefit substantially from a full review, such as could be done by the Law Commission.

[91] See, eg, HC 1996, Art 7.
[92] See **ch 5**.
[93] See generally **1.22–1.27**.

7

Child Abduction

7.1 The unilateral removal of a child from one geographic location to another without the consent of everyone entitled to give or refuse it, or permission from the court, is usually termed child abduction.[1] Historically, wardship and the inherent jurisdiction were *the* remedies for child abduction.[2] However, various developments in international and domestic law have substantially changed the legal landscape.

7.2 This chapter is not about the legal approach to child abduction generally.[3] My focus is on the uses of the court's inherent jurisdiction in this area – when is it used, why, and to what extent this is justifiable. I argue that while the inherent jurisdiction can offer singularly potent responses to short-term issues, like locating an abducted child, the primary issue of ordering their return can almost always be addressed using the powers available under the Children Act 1989 ('CA 1989'). Child abduction is therefore a core example of the court making unnecessary use of its inherent jurisdiction.

7.3 It is worth recalling that the term 'the inherent jurisdiction' is used in two senses:

i. the *general sense*, meaning the substantive orders that the court can make, akin to orders under CA 1989, s 8; and
ii. the *specific sense*, meaning the court's nationality-based jurisdiction, addressed in chapter six.

Both can be relevant in child abduction cases, but the focus in this chapter is on the use of the inherent jurisdiction in the *general sense*. When I refer here to the *specific sense*, I call it the nationality-based jurisdiction.

The Court's Authority-Jurisdiction in Child Abduction Cases

7.4 In an international abduction case, whether *incoming* from another country or *outgoing* from England and Wales, the court needs to consider the basis on

[1] Terms like 'snatching' and 'kidnapping' were used in the past, but are rarely seen today.
[2] N Lowe and R White, *Wards of Court*, 2nd edn, (London: Barry Rose, 1986), ch 17.
[3] The go-to text is N Lowe and M Nicholls, *International Movement of Children: Law, Practice and Procedure*, 2nd edn (Bristol: Family Law, 2016) ('Lowe and Nicholls'), chs 15–26, though note the effects of Brexit in some respects.

which it has authority to make orders about the child. Generally, this concept is termed 'jurisdiction', but throughout this book I term it *authority-jurisdiction* to reduce confusion with the inherent jurisdiction.

7.5 In most cases, the rules on authority-jurisdiction come from the Family Law Act 1986 ('FLA 1986'). As set out in detail in chapter six,[4] the FLA 1986 provides the rules for authority-jurisdiction in relation to any child if the order sought is:

i. an order under CA 1989, s 8 (other than an order to vary or discharge such an order);[5] or
ii. an order under the *general sense* of the inherent jurisdiction, if that order addresses the child's care, contact or education (again other than an order to vary or discharge such an order).[6]

In these cases, authority-jurisdiction must come from the FLA 1986, usually meaning that the child must be either habitually resident in England and Wales or physically present here.[7]

7.6 By contrast, inherent jurisdiction orders outside the three listed issues (care, contact or education) are not governed by the FLA 1986 at all. The court can consequently make those orders regardless of whether it has authority-jurisdiction under the Act's rules or not.

7.7 In particular, such orders are available when the court invokes its nationality-based jurisdiction.[8] The court is entitled to do so if a British national child is: (i) physically outside England and Wales, (ii) not habitually resident in England and Wales, and (iii) in a situation of sufficient peril that the English court considers it justifiable to make orders about the child despite the normal rules of authority-jurisdiction not being met.[9] If the court does invoke its nationality-based jurisdiction,[10] the substantive orders it makes must be under the inherent jurisdiction (in the general sense), and must not be about the child's care, contact or education (other than to vary or discharge existing orders).[11] A 'bare return order' requiring the child to be brought back to this country is permissible,[12] but caution is required to ensure that such an order is not a back door route designed to allow the court to make one of the proscribed orders later.[13]

[4] See **6.16–6.20**.
[5] FLA 1986, s 1(1)(a).
[6] ibid s 1(1)(d).
[7] ibid s 3.
[8] Nationality-based jurisdiction is a form of authority-jurisdiction.
[9] See **6.32–6.36**.
[10] This can be difficult to do: see **6.36**.
[11] See **6.20**.
[12] *A v A (Children: Habitual Residence)* [2013] UKSC 60, [2014] AC 1 ('*A v A*').
[13] *Re B (Habitual Residence: Inherent Jurisdiction)* [2016] UKSC 4, [2016] AC 606, [85]; see **6.28–6.29**.

The Scope of Child Abduction

7.8 The essential element of child abduction is the unilateral removal of a child from one location to another without the consent of one or more persons who are entitled to give or refuse such consent (and without court permission). Typically, an abduction case involves the movement of a child across an international or jurisdictional border – the legal remedies are the same whether the abduction is *incoming* or *outgoing*,[14] and these international cases are the focus of this chapter. A child can also be abducted within England and Wales,[15] and I address this more briefly.

7.9 Assuming that the court has authority-jurisdiction, the legal remedies that may be available vary depending on where an abduction is from and to:

i. **Abduction within England and Wales** will almost certainly be dealt with under the CA 1989. An applicant can try to prevent an abduction before it happens by applying for a prohibited steps order; once the abduction has happened, the remedy is to seek a specific issue order to have the child returned.
ii. **Abduction between different parts of the UK** will usually be addressed with statutory remedies in the 'home' state from which the child has been abducted – in England and Wales, under the CA 1989. The relevant orders are then recognised and enforced in the other relevant part of the UK under the FLA 1986. Curiously, if the child is abducted *to* England and Wales from Scotland or Northern Ireland, and so is physically present there but habitually resident elsewhere in the UK, the English court can *only* make orders under the inherent jurisdiction.[16]
iii. **International abductions between the UK and another state where a relevant international instrument applies** are addressed under the relevant international legal mechanisms. Key provisions include: (a) the Hague Convention on the Civil Aspects of International Child Abduction 1980 ('HC 1980'),[17] (b) the Hague Convention on Jurisdiction, Applicable Law, Recognition, Enforcement and Co-operation in Respect of Parental Responsibility and Measures for the Protection of Children 1996 ('HC 1996'),[18]

[14] *Re N (Abduction: Children Act or Hague Convention Proceedings)* [2020] EWFC 35, [2020] 2 FLR 575, [3] (Mostyn J).

[15] The phrase 'domestic abduction' is used in the inaptly named *Re R (Internal Relocation: Appeal)* [2016] EWCA Civ 1016, [2017] 2 FLR 921 (Black LJ), but *cf* the equally inaptly named *BB v CC (Residence Order)* [2018] EWFC B78 (Moor J), [5].

[16] See **6.18**; as noted there, this rule is an anachronism stemming from failure to amend the FLA 1986.

[17] HC 1980 currently has 103 contracting states, but 21 are not yet accepted as signatories by the UK, meaning that the Convention is not in force between the UK and those states: www.hcch.net/en/publications-and-studies/details4/?pid=3282&dtid=36 (accessed 1 June 2024).

[18] HC 1996 currently has 54 contracting states, though four are yet to bring it into force. Unlike HC 1980, signatories do not have to be 'accepted' by other states before the Convention comes into force.

and (c) the little-used European Convention on Recognition and Enforcement of Decisions Concerning Custody of Children and on Restoration of Custody of Children 1980 ('the European Convention').[19] HC 1980 and the European Convention provide their own bespoke remedies for child abduction, though domestic legal powers can sometimes still be used, either to supplement Convention-specific powers,[20] or as a concurrent application.[21] By contrast, HC 1996 addresses abduction indirectly, primarily by allocating jurisdiction between states and facilitating recognition and enforcement of orders.[22] The substantive orders made when HC 1996 applies are domestic English orders, as discussed in this chapter.

iv. **International abductions where no relevant international law is applicable between the UK and the relevant other state** are the cases where wardship and the inherent jurisdiction are most likely to be used – though my argument challenges the default use of these remedies, suggesting that CA 1989 orders should be preferred.

Return Orders

7.10 The principal order in response to child abduction is termed a *return order*. It is an order directed to a named individual requiring them to cause or effect the return of the named child(ren) from their current location to their previous place of residence. Such an order is called a *return order* regardless of whether it is made under one of the specialist international instruments, the CA 1989, or the inherent jurisdiction. My focus in this chapter is only on these last two legal remedies – the CA 1989 and the inherent jurisdiction – which are used either when HC 1980 does not apply or when there is reason to bring a concurrent application.[23]

7.11 Under the inherent jurisdiction, the court can make a return order as part of the broad suite of substantive orders that can be made about a child. Under the CA 1989, the order would normally be a specific issue order, but it could also be a child arrangements order concerning the person with whom a child is to live coupled with directions or conditions about that order pursuant to s 11(7) of the Act. Whichever legal mechanism is used, the actual orders would be worded

[19] See, eg, *AA v TT (Recognition and Enforcement)* [2014] EWHC 3488 (Fam), [2015] 2 FLR 1; *Re S (A Minor) (Custody: Habitual Residence)* [1998] AC 750 (HL), 769–772; *Re S (Abduction: European Convention)* [1996] 1 FLR 660 (HC); *Re G (Foreign Contact Order: Enforcement)* [2003] EWCA Civ 1607, [2004] 1 WLR 521.

[20] HC 1980, Art 18: courts can use any other powers that they have, separate from the Convention itself, to order a child's return.

[21] R George and J Netto, 'Concurrent Convention and Non-Convention Cases: Child Abduction in England and Wales' (2023) 12 *Laws* 70.

[22] HC 1996, esp Arts 7 and 23.

[23] George and Netto (n 21).

identically – the only difference is that the order under the inherent jurisdiction is headed 'under the Senior Courts Act 1981',[24] rather than 'under the Children Act 1989'.

7.12 In *Re NY (Abduction: Inherent Jurisdiction)*, Lord Wilson specifically held that the two kinds of return order – made under the CA 1989 or the inherent jurisdiction – are 'equivalent'.[25] The first step in questioning the court's recourse to the inherent jurisdiction is therefore to establish whether that claim is correct.

The Legal Approach to Return Orders

7.13 An application for a return order under either the CA 1989 or the inherent jurisdiction will be adjudicated in the same way. The court's decision is a welfare determination, based on the child's best interests as the court's paramount consideration.[26] The court will consider the *welfare checklist* factors[27] and the guidance on private law cases concerning domestic abuse allegations as appropriate.[28] Built on the 'classic' observations of Buckley LJ in *Re L (Minors) (Wardship: Jurisdiction)*,[29] the modern law is set out by the House of Lords in *Re J (Custody Rights: Jurisdiction)*[30] ('*Re J*') and the Supreme Court in *Re NY*. Notably, *Re J* was an application under the CA 1989, while *Re NY* was an inherent jurisdiction case, reinforcing the conclusion that the substantive approach is the same under both legal routes. It is helpful to set out that approach here.

7.14 *Re J* emphasises that the court, in considering any application for a return order, is focused on the individual child's welfare.[31] Within that general approach, though, 'the court does have power, in accordance with the welfare principle, to order the immediate return of a child to a foreign jurisdiction without conducting a full investigation of the merits'.[32] The approach is properly summarised as 'a return order made after a summary welfare determination'.[33]

[24] The reference is presumably to Senior Courts Act 1981, s 19. Often what is actually written – wrongly – is 'Under the inherent jurisdiction': see *Re HJ (Transfer of Proceedings)* [2013] EWHC 1867 (Fam), [2014] 1 FLR 430 (Munby P).

[25] *Re NY (Abduction: Inherent Jurisdiction)* [2019] UKSC 49, [2019] 2 FLR 1247, [40] ('*Re NY*'). Together with Mark Twomey QC and Alex Laing, instructed by Anne-Marie Hutchinson and James Netto, I acted for the appellant in this appeal.

[26] CA 1989, s 1(1).

[27] ibid s 1(3).

[28] *Re NY* (n 25) [50].

[29] *Re L (Minors) (Wardship: Jurisdiction)* [1974] 1 WLR 250 (CoA).

[30] *Re J (Custody Rights: Jurisdiction)* [2005] UKHL 40, [2006] 1 AC 80.

[31] ibid [22], [25] and [31].

[32] ibid [26].

[33] *Re A and B (Children) (Summary Return: Non-Convention State)* [2022] EWCA Civ 1664, [2023] 1 FLR 1229, [3] (Moylan LJ).

7.15 The key points from Lady Hale's 'definitive statement of the law' in *Re J* were summarised by Cobb J in *J v J (Return to Non-Hague Convention Country)* as follows:[34]

i) '… any court which is determining any question with respect to the upbringing of a child has had a statutory duty to regard the welfare of the child as its paramount consideration' [18];
ii) 'There is no warrant […] for the principles of the Hague Convention [1980] to be extended to countries which are not parties to it' [22];
iii) '… in all non-Convention cases, the courts […] must act in accordance with the welfare of the individual child. If they do decide to return the child, that is because it is in his best interests to do so, not because the welfare principle has been superseded by some other consideration.' [25];
iv) '… the court does have power, in accordance with the welfare principle, to order the immediate return of a child to a foreign jurisdiction without conducting a full investigation of the merits. […]' [26];
v) 'Summary return should not be the automatic reaction to any and every unauthorised taking or keeping a child from his home country. On the other hand, summary return may very well be in the best interests of the individual child' [28];
vi) '… focus has to be on the individual child in the particular circumstances of the case' [29];
vii) '… the judge may find it convenient to start from the proposition that it is likely to be better for a child to return to his home country for any disputes about his future to be decided there. A case against his doing so has to be made. But the weight to be given to that proposition will vary enormously from case to case. What may be best for him in the long run may be different from what will be best for him in the short run. It should not be assumed […] that allowing a child to remain here while his future is decided here inevitably means that he will remain here for ever' [32];
viii) 'One important variable … is the degree of connection of the child with each country. This is […] to ask in a common sense way with which country the child has the closer connection. What is his 'home' country? Factors such as his nationality, where he has lived for most of his life, his first language, his race or ethnicity, his religion, his culture, and his education so far will all come into this' [33];
ix) 'Another closely related factor will be the length of time he has spent in each country. Uprooting a child from one environment and bringing him to a completely unfamiliar one, especially if this has been done clandestinely, may well not be in his best interests' [34];
x) 'In a case where the choice lies between deciding the question here or deciding it in a foreign country, differences between the legal systems cannot be irrelevant. But their relevance will depend upon the facts of the individual case. If there is a genuine issue between the parents as to whether it is in the best interests of the child to live in this country or elsewhere, it must be relevant whether that issue is capable of being tried in the courts of the country to which he is to be returned' [39];
xi) 'The effect of the decision upon the child's primary carer must also be relevant, although again not decisive.' [40]

[34] *J v J (Return to Non-Hague Convention Country)* [2021] EWHC 2412 (Fam), [37]; internal references are to *Re J* (n 30); ellipses are from *J v J*, except where marked with square brackets.

7.16 *Re J* is supplemented by eight questions posed by Lord Wilson in *Re NY*. Lord Wilson highlights factors to which the court is likely to give 'some consideration',[35] again helpfully summarised by Cobb J in *J v J*:[36]

i) The court needs to consider whether the evidence before it is sufficiently up to date to enable it then to make the summary order [56];
ii) The court ought to consider the evidence and decide what if any findings it should make in order for the court to justify the summary order (esp. in relation to the child's habitual residence) [57];
iii) In order sufficiently to identify what the child's welfare required for the purposes of a summary order, an inquiry should be conducted into any or all of the aspects of welfare specified in section 1(3) of the 1989 Act; a decision has to be taken on the individual facts as to how extensive that inquiry should be [58];
iv) In a case where domestic abuse is alleged, the court should consider whether in the light of Practice Direction 12J, an inquiry should be conducted into the disputed allegations made by one party of domestic abuse and, if so, how extensive that inquiry should be [59];
v) The court should consider whether it would be right to determine the summary return on the basis of welfare without at least rudimentary evidence about basic living arrangements for the child and carer [60];
vi) The court should consider whether it would benefit from oral evidence [61] and if so to what extent;
vii) The court should consider whether to obtain a Cafcass report [62]: 'and, if so, upon what aspects and to what extent';
viii) The court should consider whether it needs to make a comparison of the respective judicial systems in the competing countries – having regard to the speed with which the courts will be able to resolve matters, and whether there is an effective relocation jurisdiction in the other court [63].

7.17 The legal approach to return orders made under the CA 1989 and the inherent jurisdiction is therefore 'equivalent', as Lord Wilson says. It is possible to identify minor procedural differences, but they are inconsequential:

i. The application form is different – applications for s 8 orders are made on Form C100, whereas inherent jurisdiction applications are made on Form C66.
ii. There are different rules about standing to make an application – the rules for s 8 applications are set out in CA 1989, s 10,[37] whereas the only rule for applications under the inherent jurisdiction is that the applicant has a 'genuine interest' in the child's welfare.[38] Anyone with a genuine interest regarding a child who has been or is at risk of being abducted would face no difficulty on either route.

[35] *Re NY* (n 25) [55].
[36] [2021] EWHC 2412 (Fam), [38]; internal references are to *Re NY* (n 25).
[37] See *Re B (Paternal Grandmother: Joinder as Party)* [2012] EWCA Civ 737, [2012] 2 FLR 1358.
[38] See **4.5**.

iii. Ordinarily, s 8 orders cannot be made past the child's 16th birthday because of CA 1989, s 9(7) and so it might be thought that the inherent jurisdiction (applicable until the child's 18th birthday) would be more suitable for older children. However, s 8 orders are available for children aged 16 and 17 if 'the circumstance of the case are exceptional',[39] which would surely include child abduction.[40] In any case, if s 9(7) were an obstacle, it would be contrary to the spirit of that provision for the exact same order then to be made under the inherent jurisdiction – the inherent jurisdiction should not be used to cut across a statutory scheme.[41]

iv. Any s 8 application can be issued only in the Family Court,[42] whereas an inherent jurisdiction application can be issued only in the High Court.[43] However, this difference is meaningless in practice, because the High Court and the Family Court both sit at the Royal Courts of Justice, and a CA 1989 application can be allocated immediately to High Court judge level.[44]

v. The welfare checklist[45] and some guidance about the court's approach[46] are *technically* mandatory only in relation to CA 1989 applications – but the Supreme Court has held that they must also be used when relevant to an inherent jurisdiction application.[47] These lists reflect the modern understanding of factors relevant to a child's welfare, which is the paramount consideration whether under the CA 1989 or the inherent jurisdiction.

7.18 There is one important exception to this general conclusion that return orders under the CA 1989 and the inherent jurisdiction are equivalent. This is where:

i. a British child is taken or retained abroad;
ii. the other state is not a signatory of HC 1996;[48]
iii. the child becomes habitually resident in the foreign state *prior to* any application being made to the English court;[49] and

[39] CA 1989, s 9(7).

[40] There is little authority on the meaning of this sub-section, but Peter Jackson J suggested that the intention was to allow orders to be made where a child required 'additional protection': *Re C (Older Children: Relocation)* [2015] EWCA Civ 1298, [2016] 2 FLR 1159.

[41] See **3.36** *et seq*.

[42] FPR 2010, r 5.4(1).

[43] ibid r 12.36(1).

[44] *Re NY* (n 25) [37].

[45] CA 1989, s 1(3).

[46] Such as Practice Direction 12J, *Child Arrangements and Contact Orders: Domestic Abuse and Harm*.

[47] *Re NY* (n 25) [50].

[48] If HC 1996 applies, Art 7 will give the English court on-going authority-jurisdiction as the state of *former* habitual residence in most cases after an abduction.

[49] If the application is made while the child remains habitually resident here, the court has authority-jurisdiction under FLA 1986: see *Re A (Habitual Residence: 1996 Hague Child Protection Convention)* [2023] EWCA Civ 659, [2023] 2 FLR 1247.

iv. there are 'circumstances which are sufficiently compelling to require or make it necessary that the court should exercise its protective jurisdiction',[50] ie, its nationality-based jurisdiction.[51]

In this situation, if the court considers that a return order should be made in the child's best interests, it can make that order *only* under the inherent jurisdiction. Because the FLA 1986's rules on authority-jurisdiction have not been met,[52] orders under s 8 are not available – but, as the Supreme Court held in *A v A*, a return order under the inherent jurisdiction is.[53]

7.19 This exception to the equivalence of return orders under the CA 1989 and the inherent jurisdiction arises because of the particular rules of authority-jurisdiction under the FLA 1986. It is something of an anachronism, and shows the court finding a technical loophole to circumvent the FLA's rules and allow it to protect British children in situations of particular peril. Although applicants in child abduction cases have often struggled to persuade the court to invoke the nationality-based jurisdiction or make return orders on the particular facts of their cases,[54] this use of the inherent jurisdiction has a particular purpose and justification.

7.20 The existence of this exceptional sub-category of child abduction case does not undermine the general argument that, in the vast majority of cases, the CA 1989 and the inherent jurisdiction are technically available and, as outlined, the legal approach to them is identical. The question then is whether, apart from this exceptional case, both remedies *should* be available.

Analysis

7.21 Applying the general principles governing the inherent jurisdiction, the starting point ought to be that if Parliament has created a legislative power that is equivalent to an inherent jurisdiction power, the legislation effectively 'ousts' the inherent jurisdiction.[55] On that basis, since (aside from the exceptional case) the two legal mechanisms for making return orders are 'equivalent', the CA 1989 should be used and the inherent jurisdiction should become unavailable. However, to the contrary, the Supreme Court has expressly kept open the option of using the inherent jurisdiction in these cases.[56] Why did the court take that view?

[50] *Re M (Exercise of Inherent Jurisdiction)* [2020] EWCA Civ 922, [2021] Fam 163, [105].
[51] See **ch 6**.
[52] See **7.5**.
[53] *A v A* (n 12).
[54] See **6.36**.
[55] See **3.36** *et seq.*
[56] *Re NY* (n 25).

7.22 Lord Wilson's first point in favour of keeping open the possibility of an inherent jurisdiction application was that, although *Re J* was an application for a specific issue order, Lady Hale had suggested that both remedies were available in child abduction cases. However, the only remark that Lady Hale made about that point in *Re J*, which was not the subject of argument, was that the welfare principle under s 1 of the CA 1989 applies 'in any proceedings where the court has jurisdiction to determine a question concerning a child's upbringing, whether on an application for an order under the 1989 Act itself, as in this case, or in the inherent jurisdiction'.[57] This point does not take the argument very far.

7.23 A more pertinent example was Lord Wilson's reference to Lady Hale's comments in *A v A*. The issue in that case was the basis on which the English court had authority-jurisdiction in relation to a child abroad, in particular how it should determine the child's place of habitual residence. On the basis that the FLA 1986's rules about authority-jurisdiction were met, Lady Hale said:

> So, assuming for the moment that an order to return or bring a child to this [country] falls within the definition of a specific issue order, the judge might have made such an order even though this was not what the mother applied for. But that is not what he did. *There are many orders relating to children which may be made either under the Children Act 1989 or under the inherent jurisdiction of the High Court*…[58]

7.24 On its face, this final sentence appears to confirm that the court can use its inherent jurisdiction even when an order under the CA 1989 would achieve the same thing. However, the comment must be seen in context. The original application in *A v A* was under the inherent jurisdiction, and counsel argued that the order made by the trial judge must, therefore, have been an inherent jurisdiction order. Rejecting that argument, Lady Hale noted that the court can make orders under the CA 1989 even when the application has been made under the inherent jurisdiction,[59] and then made the quoted comment. So, Lady Hale's remark was made in the context of determining what had actually happened at first instance, and was not any argument of principle. Moreover, because of the existence of the exceptional case identified earlier, where the inherent jurisdiction is indeed required in the child abduction context,[60] it is correct that a return order can be made under either legal mechanism. Lady Hale's comment should not be read, however, to mean that the two can always be used *interchangeably*.[61] Seen in context, therefore, *A v A* is weak support for Lord Wilson's argument, not least because the point was not argued in that case whereas it was put squarely in *Re NY*.

[57] *Re J* (n 30) [18].
[58] *A v A* (n 12) [26] (emphasis added).
[59] CA 1989, ss 10(1)(b) and 8(3)(a).
[60] See **7.18–7.19**.
[61] The example then given by Lady Hale of medical treatment for a child being authorised under either the inherent jurisdiction or the CA 1989 suggests that she intended to make a more general remark – but the point was not argued. On reasons why the inherent jurisdiction is not needed in medical cases, see **ch 8**.

7.25 Lord Wilson similarly quoted from the Supreme Court's abduction case of *Re L (Custody: Habitual Residence)*,[62] which also involved a return order being made under the inherent jurisdiction. As Lord Wilson said:

> In that the child was habitually resident in England, there is no doubt that his return to Texas could equally have been made the subject of a specific issue order. But it was not made the subject of such an order; and it was never suggested that it should have been so made.[63]

But that is exactly the point – no one made the argument, so the fact that the Supreme Court upheld orders made under the inherent jurisdiction says nothing as a matter of principle about whether that was the appropriate legal mechanism to make the return order or not.

7.26 Lord Wilson then went on to reject the suggestion that the inherent jurisdiction should not be used for the reason that the relevant Practice Direction, then in force, said so. Prior to *Re NY*, Practice Direction 12D said that inherent jurisdiction proceedings 'should not be commenced unless it is clear that the issues concerning the child cannot be resolved under the Children Act 1989'.[64] Lord Wilson held this provision to be too widely stated;[65] but he did not engage with the long-standing Court of Appeal authority that underpinned the Practice Direction,[66] relied on by the appellant. He noted that the CA 1989 had limited the use of the inherent jurisdiction in relation to placing children in the care of local authorities,[67] but argued that there was no other statutory limitation on the use of the inherent jurisdiction. This argument is to ignore entirely the *De Keyser* principle: '[w]here … Parliament has intervened and has provided by statute powers, previously within the prerogative, … they can only be so exercised'.[68] That principle was reflected in the earlier Court of Appeal authority, and undermines Lord Wilson's assertion that there was 'no law which precludes commencement of an application under the inherent jurisdiction unless the issue "cannot" be resolved under the 1989 Act'.[69]

7.27 Having rejected the argument that the *De Keyser* principle applied to this situation, Lord Wilson nevertheless went on to suggest limitations to using the inherent jurisdiction to make return orders. He said that there were 'strong reasons of policy' why all cases should be heard at the lowest level of court which has jurisdiction to hear them,[70] and said that applicants would need to be able to address this

[62] *Re L (Custody: Habitual Residence)* [2013] UKSC 75, [2014] AC 1017.
[63] *Re NY* (n 25) [43].
[64] Practice Direction 12D – Inherent Jurisdiction (Including Wardship) Proceedings, para 1.1. Since December 2021, the PD has reflected *Re NY* (n 25) [44], quoted at **7.28**.
[65] *Re NY* (n 25) [44].
[66] *Re T (Child: Representation)* [1994] Fam 49 (CoA); see **3.42**.
[67] *Re NY* (n 25) [40], citing CA 1989, s 100(2).
[68] *In a Petition of Right of De Keyser's Royal Hotel Ltd* [1919] 2 CH 197 (CoA), 216, approved *Attorney-General v De Keyser's Royal Hotel Ltd* [1920] AC 508 (HL); see **3.37–3.38**.
[69] *Re NY* (n 25) [44].
[70] ibid [37].

issue if they were seeking to invoke the inherent jurisdiction.[71] It is unclear what this argument has to do with the issues in the case. There was no suggestion that international child abduction cases should not be heard by High Court judges – but that can be done regardless of which legal remedy is sought.[72]

7.28 Further – and confusingly – having rejected the argument of principle that the CA 1989 should be used in preference to the inherent jurisdiction, Lord Wilson then held that use of the inherent jurisdiction should be 'exceptional'.[73] He does not explain where this test comes from or why it should be the case, but gave three examples of reasons that might justify use of the inherent jurisdiction:

> It may be that, for example, for reasons of urgency, of complexity or of the need for particular judicial expertise in the determination of a cross-border issue, the judge may be persuaded that the attempted invocation of the inherent jurisdiction was reasonable and that the application should proceed. Sometimes, however, she or he will decline to hear the application on the basis that the issue could satisfactorily be determined under the 1989 Act.[74]

7.29 There are several difficulties with this approach. First, there is no reason for the court to 'decline to hear the application' as such: the judge can make the appropriate orders under the CA 1989, even though the application was under the inherent jurisdiction.[75] More substantially, the three reasons given by Lord Wilson – urgency, complexity, need for judicial expertise – describe almost every international child abduction case;[76] far from being 'exceptional', they are the norm. And, as Mostyn J has said, Lord Wilson's concerns 'can be fully accommodated by allocating the matter upwards within the Family Court, if necessary to High Court judge level'.[77]

7.30 Despite Lord Wilson's suggestion that applications under the inherent jurisdiction should be made only 'exceptionally', and Mostyn J's later comment that it was 'hard to conceive of circumstances where [using the inherent jurisdiction] would be justified',[78] in reality applications are still routinely brought under the inherent jurisdiction, and are rarely made under the CA 1989.[79]

[71] ibid [44].

[72] See **7.17.iv**.

[73] *Re NY* (n 25) [44].

[74] ibid. The same wording is now found in Practice Direction 12D, *Inherent Jurisdiction (Including Wardship) Proceedings*, para 1.1.

[75] CA 1989, ss 10(1)(b) and 8(3)(a). This was the clear intention: Law Commission, *Review of Child Law: Guardianship and Custody*, Law Com 172 (London: HMSO, 1988) para 4.35; see **2.30**.

[76] R George and A Laing, 'Return Orders and the Inherent Jurisdiction after Re NY' [2020] *Fam Law* 271, 275.

[77] *Re N (Abduction: Children Act or Hague Convention Proceedings)* [2020] EWFC 35, [2020] 2 FLR 575, [9].

[78] ibid.

[79] There were at least 36 abduction cases reported on Bailii where the application was brought under the inherent jurisdiction in 2020–22, the three years following *Re NY*, versus one relying on the CA 1989.

7.31 Lord Wilson's reluctance in *Re NY* to prevent applications being brought under the inherent jurisdiction contrasts with his proposed approach to child abduction cases in *Re B (A Child) (Reunite International Child Abduction Centre and others intervening)* three years earlier:

> Were the court's eventual conclusion to be that it was in [the child's] interests to return to England … its order could include consequential provision under section 11(7)(d) of the 1989 Act for the respondent to return her, or cause her to be returned, to England for such purposes.

This suggestion is, in my view, quite right. The court can make entirely adequate orders under s 8 of the CA 1989, supplemented as required by conditions or directions as to how that orders should be implemented under s 11(7). In other words, the court can – and therefore should – use its statutory powers, which are entirely adequate to this situation.

7.32 One feature that may influence practice – though one not mentioned in *Re NY* – is that inherent jurisdiction proceedings appear to be treated differently for legal aid purposes from CA 1989 cases. In inherent jurisdiction proceedings, legal aid is available to both parties on a means and merits basis, without any other threshold for eligibility. While the Legal Aid Agency (LAA) guidance states that applications for specific issue and prohibited steps orders relating to child abduction (both incoming and outgoing) are 'generally within scope' for legal aid without evidence of domestic abuse or child abuse,[80] practitioners' experience is that legal aid is available more quickly and with fewer complications if the application is made for wardship or otherwise under the inherent jurisdiction. An LAA application takes around three to four weeks to process; abduction cases cannot wait that long, so solicitors rely on 'delegated functions', allowing them to self-certify a case pending LAA review. This can be done for either inherent jurisdiction or CA 1989 abduction applications, but practitioners find more difficulty in getting approval for CA 1989 cases, with the risk that they will not be paid (and that they will be liable for the fees of counsel whom they have instructed).[81] It is clearly inappropriate for legal aid rules to be a factor determining the legal approach taken, particularly when the Supreme Court has said that the inherent jurisdiction should be used only 'exceptionally'.

7.33 Before leaving this subject, it is worth comparing the approach to return orders in cases of domestic child abduction. The legal approach is the same as for international cases, by analogy with *Re J*.[82] The court can make return orders when a child is abducted elsewhere within the UK,[83] and will undertake welfare enquiries

[80] Legal Aid Agency, *Scope of Family Proceedings Under LASPO* (January 2021).

[81] Thanks to James Netto, Partner at the International Family Law Group for help on this point.

[82] *Re R (Internal Relocation: Appeal)* [2016] EWCA Civ 1016, [217] 2 FLR 921.

[83] *Re R (Children: Peremptory Return)* [2011] EWCA Civ 558, [2011] 2 FLR 863. As in the case name, in the domestic abduction context these are sometimes termed 'peremptory return orders', which appears simply to mean that the court can, in the right circumstances, make the order based on a very summary assessment of welfare.

that are proportionate to the issues in the case, including conducting a fact-finding hearing prior to making a return order if necessary.[84] However, in these cases the remedy sought is usually: (i) in the local Family Court, and (ii) for a s 8 order under CA 1989.[85] There are fewer complications in relation to foreign law, international enforcement, and so on, which explains why domestic cases can be properly dealt with in the local Family Court. What is less obvious is why CA 1989 remedies are accepted as being entirely adequate in the domestic abduction context, yet for international cases the statutory remedies are considered inadequate.

7.34 My argument, as throughout this book, is that where there is an equivalent statutory remedy available the inherent jurisdiction should not be used.[86] No explanation has been given as to why a specific issue order is inadequate in the vast majority of international child abduction cases,[87] and Lord Wilson expressly held the two remedies to be 'equivalent'[88] – so there is no reason to use the inherent jurisdiction. Lord Wilson's three suggested justifications for using of the inherent jurisdiction – urgency, complexity, need for judicial expertise in cross-border issues – are unpersuasive, and can all be addressed by a specific issue order application being immediately allocated to a High Court judge.[89] Return orders following child abduction are therefore a core example of the court unnecessarily and inappropriately relying on its inherent jurisdiction when it has available to it an entirely adequate statutory remedy.

Other Uses of the Inherent Jurisdiction in Child Abduction Cases

7.35 I now turn to consider supplemental issues that can arise in child abduction cases. I will assess whether the available statutory remedies to address these issues are adequate, and if not whether the court's recourse to the inherent jurisdiction is appropriate. I start with the use of wardship in the abduction context.

Wardship

7.36 Mostyn J once noted that, when lawyers are faced with child abduction, 'wardship is sought almost as a reflex'.[90] The *theoretical* benefit of wardship in

[84] *BB v CC (Residence Order)* [2018] EWFC B78.
[85] The exception is abductions from Scotland or Northern Ireland to England and Wales: see **7.9.ii**.
[86] See generally **3.36** *et seq*.
[87] See the exception at **7.18–7.19**.
[88] *Re NY* (n 25) [40].
[89] *Re N (Abduction: Children Act or Hague Convention Proceedings)* [2020] EWFC 35, [2020] 2 FLR 575, [9] (Mostyn J).
[90] *AS v CPW* [2020] EWHC 1238 (Fam), [2020] 4 WLR 127, [31].

placing the child under the High Court's 'cloak of protection' is easily identified[91] – but specifying in practical terms what wardship actually does for a child in an abduction case is more difficult.[92]

7.37 There are two features of wardship – as distinct from more general powers under the inherent jurisdiction – that are of potential importance in *preventing* child abduction before it takes place.[93] First, its immediacy: a child becomes a ward immediately upon issue of a wardship application, whether or not any court hearing takes place at that time.[94] Second, once a child is a ward, no person may remove them from the jurisdiction of England and Wales[95] without the leave of a High Court judge. However, it would be unusual to rely on the mere status of wardship alone. Alongside the wardship application, the court usually makes a *passport order*, requiring the passports of the child (and a relevant adult respondent) to be seized.[96] This order, and the port alert that flows from it, are the practical tools to stop an abduction, rather than the status of wardship, and there is no need to make a child a ward before obtaining a passport order. Moreover, if actual seizure of passports by the Tipstaff is not required, a port alert can be made by the Family Court in support of a prohibited steps order under CA 1989, s 8 preventing the removal of a child from the country.[97] Wardship therefore adds nothing to the making of either a passport order or a prohibited steps order coupled with a port alert.[98]

7.38 The fact that a child was made a ward prior to their abduction can also be useful *after the event* if the child is taken or retained abroad. If the person objecting to the child's removal does not have 'rights of custody' for the purposes of an HC 1980 application, wardship gives an unambiguous basis for an application to be brought in the other state under that Convention. This is because *the English court* has rights of custody over its ward,[99] which have been breached by the child's removal or retention. Alternatively, in the case of a state not party to HC 1980, the existence of wardship prior to the abduction can be helpful in demonstrating to some foreign courts that the English court is fully seized of proceedings concerning the child's welfare.

[91] *Re Z (A Minor) (Identification: Restrictions on Publication)* [1997] Fam 1 (CoA), 23.

[92] *Z v V (Children Act 1989 and Senior Courts Act 1981)* [2024] EWHC 365 (Fam), [20(viii)] and [33] (Peel J).

[93] See **3.8–3.17**.

[94] Senior Courts Act 1981, s 41(2). In practice, most applications are brought immediately before a judge, including out-of-hours if necessary: see Practice Direction 12E – Urgent Business. See further **4.16** *et seq*.

[95] There are limited exceptions to this rule, whereby the restriction becomes non-removal from the UK, rather than from England and Wales, under FLA 1986, s 38: see **3.13**.

[96] See **7.42–7.43**.

[97] *A v B (Port Alert)* [2021] EWHC 1716 (Fam), [2021] 4 WLR 108 (Mostyn J).

[98] See *Z v V (Children Act 1989 and Senior Courts Act 1981)* [2024] EWHC 365 (Fam), [33] (Peel J).

[99] *Re H (Abduction: Rights of Custody)* [2000] 2 AC 291 (HL); Lowe and Nicholls (n 3) paras 19.95–19.98.

7.39 Mostyn J has said that anyone seeking to make a child a ward of court 'need[s] to ask: what does wardship add to the invocation of the inherent and/or statutory jurisdiction? The answer is, in many cases, nothing'.[100] There are countries, such as Pakistan and India, that recognise the idea of wardship and give weight to that status in their domestic law. In these cases, there may be significant legal benefit in using wardship, even post-removal. Also, in cases where the practical steps to seeking a child's return are as much diplomatic as legal, being able to say that the child is under the protection of the English High Court may add weight to the case. Otherwise, the legal benefits of warding a child post-removal are less apparent. That is not to say that the court should not act – but using *wardship* in most cases adds nothing.

Tipstaff Orders

7.40 The Tipstaff holds an ancient office traceable to at least 1377,[101] and is the High Court's enforcement officer, with jurisdiction throughout England and Wales. The Tipstaff (or his deputies) can give effect to orders directly, or can instruct the police to take action on his behalf. The Tipstaff has power to arrest someone he reasonably believes is in breach of an order and who has been served with a copy of that order, or who is aware of the order and its content; he can make forced entry to property if necessary.[102]

7.41 There are three particular orders relevant to child abduction, known collectively as *Tipstaff orders*: (i) passport orders, (ii) location orders, and (iii) collection orders. As the Tipstaff is the *High Court's* enforcement officer, these orders are within the exclusive purview of the High Court and cannot be made except using the inherent jurisdiction. Applications are made in consultation with the Tipstaff,[103] almost invariably on a *without notice* basis.[104]

7.42 A *passport order* directs the Tipstaff to seize passports, ID cards or any other travel document of the respondent to the proceedings, the named child(ren), and any other person named in the order. The Tipstaff will arrest a person who does not provide the documents required unless he is satisfied with the explanation given

[100] *AS v CPW* [2020] EWHC 1238 (Fam), [2020] 4 WLR 127, [32].

[101] See A Betts, 'The Tipstaff' (1918) 30 *Juridical Review* 342: the name relates to the truncheon or baton originally carried by the holder of the office, 'a wooden staff with horn at either end' according to a 1392 account, and by 1691 described (rather less excitingly) as 'a painted staff'. The Tipstaff retains a ceremonial staff.

[102] Practice Direction 12D – Inherent Jurisdiction (Including Wardship) Proceedings, para 7.2. *Re HM (Vulnerable Adult: Abduction)* [2010] EWHC 870 Fam, [2010] 2 FLR 1057, [38], cited with approval in *Re B (Wrongful Removal: Orders Against Non-Parties)* [2014] EWCA Civ 843, [2015] Fam 209, [15].

[103] Practice Guidance: *Case Management and Mediation of International Child Abduction Proceedings* (2023), para 2.3.

[104] ibid paras 2.1–2.5; *Re A (Return to Sweden)* [2016] EWCA Civ 572, [2016] 4 WLR 111, [55].

for their whereabouts; the respondent is then brought before a High Court judge. The order requires that the child(ren) named in the order not be moved from the address at which they are presently residing, and the Tipstaff will put a port alert into effect immediately that the order is made. A port alert places the named individuals on a 'stop list' at all UK ports and airports, preventing them from leaving the country and requiring their documents to be seized if they attempt to enter or leave the UK.

7.43 A passport order is only required if there is evidence that the respondent presents a risk (usually a flight risk) if 'tipped off' about the court proceedings before their documents are held. Absent such risk, it is nevertheless possible to make an order requiring the individual to surrender their passport to the court or 'with some suitable custodian, for example the tipstaff or a solicitor who has given the court an appropriate undertaking'.[105]

7.44 A *location order* has all the same effects as a passport order (so it is not possible to have both), used if a child's whereabouts are unknown. The Tipstaff has various powers to search for a child, including to force entry to property if necessary. Location orders are usually supported by disclosure orders, seeking information from public or private organisations, or occasionally from private individuals, to give information to assist the Tipstaff in locating the child.[106]

7.45 A *collection order* also has the same effects as a passport order, but additionally instructs the Tipstaff to take physical custody of a child and deliver them to a named person – that may include a local authority,[107] but will most commonly be one of the child's parents. Given the potential for the execution of collection orders to cause the child distress, the court is cautious about making them;[108] they are usually used to restore the status quo ante of care arrangements when a child has recently been summarily removed from their primary carer by the respondent and may be at immediate risk in the respondent's care.

7.46 Some of these powers have statutory equivalents, although they have significant limitations which mean that Tipstaff orders are invariably used in child abduction cases.

i. There is a statutory power to order the disclosure of information to help determine a child's whereabouts,[109] which can perform some of the functions of a location order. However, when the child is located, the immediate

[105] *Re B (Wrongful Removal: Orders Against Non-Parties)* [2014] EWCA civ 843, [2015] Fam 209, [16]. The Tipstaff should not be asked to take documents in cases where he has no prior involvement.

[106] *Re HM (Vulnerable Adult: Abduction)* [2010] EWHC 870 (Fam), [2010] 2 FLR 1057, [36], approved *Re B (Wrongful Removal: Orders against Non-Parties)* [2014] EWCA Civ 843, [2015] Fam 209.

[107] *Re A (Return to Sweden)* [2016] EWCA Civ 572, [2016] 4 WLR 111, [45]; *Justice for Families Ltd v Secretary of State for Justice* [2014] EWCA Civ 1477, [2015] 2 FLR 321.

[108] *Re J (Children: Ex Parte Orders)* [1997] 1 FLR 606 (Hale J), 609.

[109] FLA 1986, s 33.

safeguarding provisions of a location order are not in place (such as the port alert and the requirement that the child not be removed from the place they are living at the time they are located).

ii. The court has a statutory power to order the 'recovery' of a child, requiring the police to 'take charge of the child and deliver him to the person concerned'.[110] However, this remedy is available only when an existing order that required the child to be given up to 'the person concerned' has not been obeyed. This is an important statutory power for many cases, but it does not allow the court to make immediate protective orders that may be necessary in some abduction cases. The other advantage of the Tipstaff collection order is that the child can be delivered to anyone named in the order. This power is particularly important in an international abduction case where the applicant may not be in this country, thus allowing the child to be removed and accommodated safely pending court determination of appropriate next steps.

iii. The court has a statutory power to order the surrender of *UK-issued* passports on which *a child* can travel.[111] However, this provision requires an existing order to be in force preventing the removal of the child from the UK and, in any case, it does not allow the court to seize any non-UK passport, nor any passport of an adult, thus severely limiting the utility of the remedy in international child abduction cases.

Consequently, while these statutory powers are not insignificant, they fail to offer the extent of the protections available under the inherent jurisdiction. In responding to child abduction cases, these wider inherent jurisdiction powers are highly valuable, and the currently available statutory alternatives are inadequate – though it could be said that the court is ignoring the parliamentary-imposed limitations on its powers by making equivalent orders in a wider range of circumstances under its inherent jurisdiction.[112]

Locating a Child

7.47 When a child's location is unknown following an abduction, an applicant can consult with the Tipstaff and seek a location order. As the Tipstaff's jurisdiction runs throughout England and Wales, if a child is missing outside that territory, the assistance available from the Tipstaff will be limited. In these cases, there is often little that the English court can do, though if there are family members or others in this country who may have information or influence, the court can make orders against them.

[110] ibid s 34.
[111] ibid s 37.
[112] *Cf* **3.36** *et seq.*

7.48 Another remedy available in extreme cases where a parent cannot otherwise be located, and where they either cannot be contacted or they refuse to engage, is to seek a freezing order against their assets, if they have any in the UK. Freezing orders are part of the High Court's broader inherent jurisdiction, not specific to children;[113] they are usually used to ensure that legal rights are protected and judgments honoured,[114] but can be deployed in response to child abduction in some circumstances. This remedy was referred to in passing by Munby LJ in a Court of Protection case in the High Court:

> [The court has] powers to seize or block an abducting parent's (access to) funds. The court can make a freezing order to restrain the abducting parent's recourse to his assets and, where the parent has acted in breach of the court's order or breach of an undertaking and is thus in contempt, the court can also make a sequestration order … Moreover, the court has power to direct that the sequestered funds be used to fund litigation brought in a foreign court with a view to securing the return to this jurisdiction of the abducted child ….[115]

7.49 The circumstances that will justify an application of this nature will be highly unusual, and it is unsatisfactory that the only reported authority on the point comes from obiter comments in the context of the court's powers to protect vulnerable adults. Munby LJ sets out a two-stage process:

(i) A freezing order per se is available without the parent being in breach of any existing order, the freezing order being used to stop the on-going abduction.
(ii) If, separately, the respondent is also proved to be in breach of an order and so in contempt of court, the court can also order the sequestration of the frozen assets, for example to give the applicant parent access to funds to enable them to bring legal proceedings in another state to secure the child's return.

7.50 There are no known reported cases where freezing orders have been used as a means of locating a missing child prior to welfare-based orders for the child's return having been made. However, in an unreported case,[116] the High Court made such an order when a father was on the run with two children following a violent abduction from their mother. Using bank disclosure, he was tracked across numerous countries; with the principal source of funds located in a UK bank account, the court made a freezing order to cut off the father's ability to fund the continuing abduction. The father subsequently agreed to the children being returned to England.

[113] See **1.12**.
[114] *Mareva Compania Naviera SA v International Bulkcarriers SA* [1975] 2 Lloyd's Rep 509, [1980] 1 All ER 213 (CoA).
[115] *Re HM (Vulnerable Adult: Abduction)* [2010] EWHC 870 (Fam), [2010] 2 FLR 1057, [39], citing *Richardson v Richardson* [1989] Fam 95 and *Mir v Mir* [1992] Fam 79.
[116] *Re W (Abduction: Freezing Order)*, unreported, 1 December 2021. I acted for the applicant, instructed by James Netto of the International Family Law Group.

7.51 This use of the inherent jurisdiction takes an existing remedy and applies it to a novel situation, and appears compatible with the general principles governing the appropriate functions of the judiciary[117] – an 'extension of existing laws and principles' as distinct from 'legislat[ing] in a new field'.[118] The orders made are also short-term, responding to particularly egregious abductions, and therefore a proportionate response that fits within the general strong anti-abduction policy adopted at domestic and international level.

Conclusion

7.52 The legal approach to child abduction is currently settled. The statutory remedies available with respect to *supplementary* issues that arise in child abduction cases are inadequate, and the additional powers of the inherent jurisdiction are both valuable and necessary. The Tipstaff's services are an essential weapon in the court's arsenal, allowing children to be located and their position secured pending proper court determination. While not required in every child abduction case, for those where there is a serious risk of onward abduction or where a child may disappear, a location or passport order is vital. Likewise, in the rare situation where a child has been taken by someone who is an immediate risk to the child, the power to have that child removed by the Tipstaff under a collection order is a potent protective tool. While these remedies go beyond the powers that Parliament has provided, they generally go 'with the grain'[119] – to use a term from human rights law – of the statutory powers and can be seen in the context of a concerted policy effort, both domestically and internationally, to tackle child abduction quickly and effectively.

7.53 By contrast, it is unclear why the court continues to entertain applications for return orders almost invariably under the inherent jurisdiction. There is no justification for the inherent jurisdiction (and often wardship) being used as the standard legal basis for making a return order.[120] No authority has identified any shortcoming in the remedies available under the CA 1989, yet it is difficult to locate any recent reported cases where international abduction was addressed using a specific issue order.[121] As noted earlier, *domestic* child abduction is addressed using the mechanisms in the CA 1989. Return orders in international child abduction cases are therefore a significant example of the court invoking its inherent jurisdiction unnecessarily, as a matter of routine, when available statutory remedies could achieve the same result.

[117] See **1.22–1.27**.

[118] *Malone v Metropolitan Police Comr* [1979] Ch 344, 372–3 (Megarry V-C).

[119] *Ghaidan v Godin-Mendoza* [2004] UKHL 30, [2004] 2 AC 557, [33]; see **1.22–1.27**.

[120] Again, note the exceptional case at **7.18–7.19**.

[121] Other than *Re J* itself, see also *Re S (Minors) (Abduction)* [1994] 1 FLR 297 (CoA) and *Re M (Abduction: Peremptory Return Order)* [1996] 1 FLR 478 (CoA). The only recent case I am aware of is *Re A and B (Rescission of Order: Change of Circumstances)* [2021] EWFC 76, [2022] 1 FLR 1143 (Cobb J), an application to set aside a specific issue order, the original application for that SIO having been made by a litigant in person.

8

Medical Decision-Making about Children[1]

8.1 As the default holders of parental responsibility ('PR'),[2] parents are charged with making decisions about their children's upbringing. The scope of PR[3] includes authorising or refusing to authorise medical treatment.[4] However, 'the law regards the upbringing of children not as a matter of exclusive parental rights, to be defended unless forfeited, but as a collaborative responsibility in which parents take the leading role'.[5] Though it has been a matter of debate in recent years,[6] the court is clear that is has authority to intervene in any case where an application is made by an interested party, and the court will not defer to parents but rather make an independent decision about what is in the best interests of the child concerned.[7]

8.2 My aim in this chapter is not to consider the correct approach for the law to take when there is a dispute about what form of treatment, if any, a child should receive. As throughout the book, my interest is in the court's use of its wardship and inherent jurisdiction powers in this area, and whether that approach is justified or not.

[1] Parts of this chapter were previously published as 'The Legal Basis of the Court's Jurisdiction to Authorise Medical Treatment of Children', in I Goold, J Herring and C Auckland (eds), *Parental Rights, Best Interests and Significant Harms* (Oxford: Hart Publishing, 2019).

[2] Children Act 1989 (CA 1989), s 3. See further J Bridgeman, 'Beyond Best Interests: A Question of Professional Conscience?' in I Goold, J Herring and C Auckland (eds), *Parental Rights, Best Interests and Significant Harms* (Oxford: Hart Publishing, 2019). All statutory references are to the Children Act unless otherwise stated.

[3] PR is defined in s 3 only in broad terms, but it is well established that its scope includes medical decision-making: see, eg, S Gilmore, 'The Limits of Parental Responsibility' in R Probert, S Gilmore and J Herring (eds), *Responsible Parents and Parental Responsibility* (Oxford: Hart Publishing, 2014).

[4] Neither parents, patients, nor the court have the power to require a doctor to provide treatment which they do not consider medically appropriate: *Aintree University Hospitals NHS Foundation Trust v James* [2013] UKSC 67, [2014] AC 591, [18]; *An NHS Trust v Y* [2018] UKSC 46, [2019] AC 978, [92].

[5] R Taylor, 'Parental Decisions and Court Jurisdiction: Best Interests or Significant Harm?' [2020] *CFLQ* 141, 156.

[6] The argument that the court should require a threshold of 'significant harm' before it could intervene to override parents' decisions was pursued strongly, but roundly rejected, in *Yates v Great Ormond Street Hospital for Children NHS Foundation Trust* [2017] EWCA Civ 410, [2018] 4 WLR 5. For discussion, see Taylor, ibid.

[7] *Yates*, ibid.

The General Legal Position on the Medical Treatment of Children

8.3 Without consent, no doctor can provide treatment without putting him or herself at legal risk.[8] Generally, in the exercise of their PR, it is parents who provide or refuse that consent in relation to a child. In most situations, the consent of one PR holder is sufficient,[9] though if parents are separated then there is a somewhat un-delineated group of 'important decisions' where parents either need to agree or seek a court decision.[10] Three situations complicate that general case:

i. Where there is a genuine emergency, and it is not possible to contact the parents in the available time – here, the law allows a doctor to provide life-saving treatment without any consent on the basis of 'necessity'.[11]
ii. Where a local authority ('LA') has a care or interim care order in respect of a child, the LA thereby gains PR over the child.[12] Although the LA must consult with the parents and seek to reach agreement where possible,[13] there will be circumstances in which, if necessary, the LA can make medical decisions for the child in the exercise of its PR.[14] However, unless the issue of the parents' approach to healthcare was part of the basis for the making of the care order, the LA is likely to need to make a court application even though it has PR if the medical issue is 'serious' or 'grave' – failure to do so will constitute an unlawful interference with the Article 8 rights of the parents (and potentially of the child).[15] Conversely, routine medical decisions, including giving childhood vaccinations, can be authorised by the LA without a court application.[16]
iii. If the child has sufficient maturity to be considered *Gillick*-competent by the treating clinician,[17] the child can give consent to treatment. If the child

[8] Criminal and tortious consequences would follow, in addition to the repercussions at a professional level.

[9] CA 1989, s 2(7).

[10] See R George, S Thompson and J Miles, *Family Law: Text, Cases, and Materials*, 5th edn (Oxford: OUP, 2023), 705–11. The court resolves these private law cases by making a specific issue order or prohibited steps order under CA 1989, s 8 – the inherent jurisdiction is never used.

[11] *Re R (Wardship: Consent to Treatment)* [1992] Fam 11 (CoA).

[12] CA 1989, s 33(3). A child in voluntary accommodation under CA 1989, s 20 is in a different position: although PR has been *delegated* to the LA, they cannot exercise it to override any decision by the actual holder of PR.

[13] CA 1989, s 22(4) and (5); see Taylor (n 5).

[14] See also **8.28** *et seq* and **9.15** *et seq*. LAs should not seek a care order for a child on the basis of concerns around the child's medical treatment, unless there are other significant concerns about the parenting being given to the child: *Re E (A Child)* [2018] EWCA Civ 550, [2019] 1 WLR 594, [107].

[15] *Re H (Parental Responsibility: Vaccination)* [2020] EWCA Civ 664, [2021] Fam 133, [81].

[16] The parents could apply to injunct the LA, but will usually struggle to persuade the court to make that order: ibid [102].

[17] *Gillick v West Norfolk and Wisbech AHA* [1986] AC 112 (HL), 174; *R (Bell) v Tavistock and Portman NHS Foundation Trust* [2021] EWCA Civ 1363, [2022] 1 FLR 69, [55].

does not wish to make the decision, the parent retains their PR and can make the decision, but – contrary to earlier obiter comments from Lord Donaldson MR[18] – the parent cannot override the competent child's decision to refuse consent.[19]

8.4 Both in the general case and in these specific examples, situations arise where the approach favoured by the medical professionals differs from that favoured by the child's parents and/or the child themselves. Where the parent or child seeks treatment which the doctor does not consider appropriate, the only choice is to seek another doctor as no doctor can be required to provide treatment against their medical opinion[20] – and even if another doctor will provide treatment, the original doctor could seek court declarations as to whether that treatment was in the child's best interests.[21] Conversely, if the parent opposes treatment that the doctor thinks is in the child's best interests, the doctor will require a court order before treatment can be given.

8.5 In practice, medical professionals seek to reach agreement with parents (or *Gillick*-competent children, when applicable), and 'doctors rarely make applications for court interventions unless they think the child will be harmed'.[22] However, there are cases where a dispute cannot be avoided and the court acts as arbiter, determining on the evidence available whether a particular treatment is in the child's best interests and therefore lawful or not. With one or two notable exceptions,[23] the court almost invariably concludes that treatment which is proposed by medical professionals should be authorised.[24]

8.6 After some vacillation on the question,[25] the court has concluded that there is no special category of medical treatment decisions which holders of PR cannot decide, if they are in agreement with each other and with the child's

[18] *Re R (Wardship: Consent to Treatment)* [1992] Fam 11 (CoA). Though obiter, these comments were long treated as an accurate statement of the law.

[19] *AB v CD, The Tavistock and Portman NHS Foundation Trust* [2021] EWHC 741 (Fam), 179 BMLR 139, [60], [67]–[69].

[20] *Aintree University Hospitals NHS Foundation Trust v James* [2013] UKSC 67, [2014] AC 591, [18].

[21] The court can back any such determination with injunctions if necessary: *Yates v Great Ormond Street Hospital for Children NHS Foundation Trust* [2017] EWCA Civ 410, [2018] 4 WLR 5, [117].

[22] I Goold, C Auckland and J Herring, 'Medical Decision-Making on Behalf of Children in England and Welsh Law: A Child-Centred Best Interests Approach' in I Goold, C Auckland and J Herring (eds), *Medical Decision-Making on Behalf of Young Children: A Comparative Perspective* (Oxford: Hart Publishing, 2020), 126.

[23] *Re T (Wardship: Medical Treatment)* [1997] 1 WLR 242 (CoA); *Raqeeb v Barts NHS Foundation Trust* [2019] EWHC 2530 (Fam), [2020] 1 FLR 1298.

[24] J Bridgeman, 'The provision of Healthcare to Young and Dependent Children: The Principles, Concepts, and Utility of the Children Act 1989' (2017) 25 *Medical Law Review* 363, 375.

[25] See, eg, *Re D (Wardship: Sterilisation)* [1976] Fam 185 (Heilbron J) and *Re B (Wardship: Sterilisation)* [1988] AC 199 (HL); the majority in *Re B* thought that a court application prior to having a child sterilised was 'a matter of good practice' rather than a legal requirement. *Cf* the position in Australia: see **5.23**.

treating clinicians.[26] As Lieven J has explained, 'Parents can be asked by doctors to make the most serious of all decisions about the medical treatment on behalf of their children',[27] including experimental treatments or end-of-life decisions if necessary. Consequently, only where there is a dispute (between holders of PR, or between them and the medical team) will the court be involved, though in unusual cases an application can be brought to ensure that the steps taken are fully appropriate.[28]

8.7 As noted, the court is clear that it has authority to deal with disputes about medical treatment,[29] and that the court makes an independent decision based on its own assessment of the child's best interests: 'The starting point – and the finishing point too – must always be the judge's own independent assessment of the balance of advantage or disadvantage of the particular medical step under consideration.'[30] But what is the legal mechanism for the court's decisions? As with other issues concerning children discussed in this book, the principal contenders are the inherent jurisdiction and s 8 of the Children Act 1989 ('CA 1989').

The Inherent Jurisdiction in Relation to Medical Treatment

8.8 There are three aspects of the High Court's inherent jurisdiction that can be relevant to a decision about medical treatment.

8.9 First, the court can use its general *parens patriae*-type inherent jurisdiction powers to make determinations about a child's best interests. One way in which this can happen, though perhaps used less frequently than in the past, is for the child to be made a ward of court. In placing the child under the court's protection, wardship puts the court in the position of the child's parent, and the court's parental powers displace those of the parents (and anyone else who holds PR) – no significant decision may be made in relation to the child's life without the court's consent.[31] The court then acts as the judicial 'reasonable parent' in assessing the child's welfare or best interests.[32]

[26] *AB v CD, The Tavistock and Portman NHS Foundation Trust* [2021] EWHC 741 (Fam), 179 BMLR 139, [116] *et seq*. In the context of an incapacitous adult, see *An NHS Trust v Y* [2018] UKSC 46, [2019] AC 978, [102]; the situation there is legally more complicated because no one holds the equivalent of PR over an adult, yet the court also reaches the conclusion that there is no requirement to apply to court when all relevant individuals and the treating clinicians are in agreement.

[27] ibid [43].

[28] See, eg, *Pennine Care NHS Foundation Trust v T* [2022] EWHC 515 (Fam).

[29] *Yates v Great Ormond Street Hospital for Children NHS Foundation Trust* [2017] EWCA Civ 410, [2018] 4 WLR 5.

[30] *Re T (Wardship: Medical Treatment)* [1997] 1 WLR 242 (CoA), 254.

[31] See **3.15–3.17**.

[32] *J v C* [1970] AC 688 (HL).

8.10 Second, the inherent jurisdiction can be used to make declarations of lawfulness.[33] Such a declaration states that a previous or proposed course of medical treatment would, or would not, be lawful. The declaration changes nothing: '[a]ll that the court is being asked to do is to declare that, had a course of action been taken without resort to the court, it would have been lawful anyway'.[34]

8.11 Third, the inherent jurisdiction can be used to grant injunctive relief. The purpose of such an injunction is generally to preserve the status quo pending determination of the main issues, such as by preventing the removal of a patient from the hospital.[35]

Orders under the Children Act

8.12 The CA 1989 provides a number of remedies that are potentially available where a decision has to be made about a child's medical treatment. These are familiar from earlier chapters of this book.

8.13 The starting point of the Act is that it places the primary responsibility for the upbringing of children on the holders of PR, which is usually vested in both legal parents. In the event of a dispute about how aspects of PR should be exercised, the CA 1989 provides various orders that the court can make in private law disputes between parents or others concerned with the child's upbringing, in effect allowing the court to regulate how PR is exercised.

8.14 The orders that regulate such disputes are found in s 8 – they are generically termed 'section 8 orders', and the two relevant ones are defined in the Act as follows:

> 'a prohibited steps order' means an order that no step which could be taken by a parent in meeting his parental responsibility for a child, and which is of a kind specified in the order, shall be taken by any person without the consent of the court;
>
> 'a specific issue order' means an order giving directions for the purpose of determining a specific question which has arisen, or which may arise, in connection with any aspect of parental responsibility for a child.

[33] While declarations of lawfulness are invariably said to be made under the inherent jurisdiction, that is doubtful: *Chapman v Michaelson* [1909] 1 Ch 238 (CoA), 243. The power to make a declaration in support of another substantive remedy appears to be part of the inherent jurisdiction. However, the jurisdiction to grant a declaration *where no consequential remedy was sought* was granted to the Court of Chancery by s 50 of the Court of Chancery Procedure Act 1850, and extended to all divisions of the newly created High Court by Judicature Act 1873, s 24. Its continued existence is reflected in r 40.20 of the Civil Procedure Rules 1998.

[34] *Re F (Mental Patient: Sterilisation)* [1990] 2 AC 1 (CoA), 20 (Lord Donaldson MR) and similarly at 42 (Butler-Sloss LJ). See also *R (Burke) v General Medical Council* [2005] EWCA Civ 1003, [80], approved by *An NHS Trust v Y* [2018] UKSC 46, [2019] AC 978, [31]. Declarations are more commonly used in connection with the treatment of adults (see **2.48–2.52** on the historical reasons why), but can be sought regarding children: see, eg, *Re J (Transgender: Puberty Blocker and Hormone Replacement Therapy)* [2024] EWHC 922 (Fam) (McFarlane P). But on the need to do so, see **8.31** *et seq*.

[35] See, eg, *Re S (Hospital Patient: Court's Jurisdiction)* [1995] Fam 26, 35–36 (Hale J).

In effect, a *prohibited steps order* ('PSO') determines that a course of action, which a parent could have taken in the exercise of their PR, shall not be done (for example, a baby boy shall not be circumcised[36]), whereas a *specific issue order* ('SIO') provides that something which a parent could have done as an exercise of their PR shall be done (for example, a child shall receive an immunisation[37]). The scope of s 8 orders is important to note – they determine issues about PR, and so do not enable the court to order third parties to take positive steps which go beyond what a parent could authorise or require. In determining these cases, the court applies the welfare principle.[38]

8.15 CA 1989, s 9 contains important restrictions on the making of s 8 orders. Section 9(1) prevents the making of SIOs or PSOs in respect of a child who is in LA care under a care order or interim care order. Section 9(6) and (7) prevent the making of any s 8 order after the child has reached the age of 16, or which continues in effect after the child is 16, unless the circumstances are exceptional.

8.16 Finally, in order to be able to apply for any s 8 order, the applicant either needs to be an 'entitled' applicant, or to obtain leave from the court to bring an application. In relation to PSOs and SIOs, 'entitled' applicants are set out in s 10(4). It is a limited list, comprising only the child's parents, any guardian of the child, a step-parent with PR, and anyone with whom the child lives under a child arrangements order. Anyone else requires the court's permission to apply for an SIO or PSO. If the applicant is the child themselves (or an application brought on their behalf), the provisions for leave are set out in s 10(8); for anyone else, the relevant provisions are in s 10(9):

> [T]he court shall, in deciding whether or not to grant leave, have particular regard to—
> (a) the nature of the proposed application for the section 8 order;
> (b) the applicant's connection with the child;
> (c) any risk there might be of that proposed application disrupting the child's life to such an extent that he would be harmed by it; and
> (d) where the child is being looked after by a local authority—
>   (i) the authority's plans for the child's future; and
>   (ii) the wishes and feelings of the child's parents.

8.17 This provision does not impose a 'test', but rather identifies some factors relevant to whether leave should be given; other relevant factors can also be considered.[39] It is clear that (amongst others) NHS trusts[40] and LAs[41] can apply

[36] See, eg, *Re J (Child's Religious Upbringing and Circumcision)* [2000] 1 FLR 571 (CoA).
[37] See, eg, *Re C (Welfare of Child: Immunisation)* [2003] EWHC 1376 (Fam), [2003] 2 FLR 1054 (Sumner J).
[38] CA 1989, s 1(1).
[39] *Re B (Paternal Grandmother: Joinder as Party)* [2012] EWCA Civ 737, [2012] 2 FLR 1358.
[40] This issue is not controversial; see, eg, *Raqeeb v Barts NHS Foundation Trust* [2019] EWHC 2530 (Fam), [2020] 1 FLR 1298, [3].
[41] *Re R (A Minor) (Blood Transfusion)* [1993] 2 FLR 757 (Booth J).

for leave and, where they have a legitimate interest in the subject-matter of the application, the leave stage is unlikely to be problematic.

The Scope of the Children Act in Medical Cases

8.18 As Stephen Gilmore has noted, the statutory history of SIOs and PSOs reveals limited information.[42] However, one point of relevance comes from Lord Mackay LC at the Children Bill's Second Reading, when he said:

> if there is a dispute about a particular matter – for example, where the child should go to school, or *whether he should have a serious medical operation* – the court can make a specific issue order settling the matter.[43]

8.19 From the wording of the Act, the principal limitation on the scope of an SIO is that there is a 'question' relating to an aspect of PR;[44] similarly, a PSO is limited to steps 'which could be taken by a parent' in the exercise of PR. The scope of PR itself is wide,[45] and as a general proposition clearly includes consenting to the medical treatment of a child.

8.20 Where a court order is required – because there is a dispute, or where the medical team consider that the proposed treatment is in some sense controversial such that court approval is desirable[46] – a section 8 order can be used to authorise the medical treatment.[47] Inevitably, it was not long after the CA 1989 came into force that the issue arose. In *Re R (A Minor) (Blood Transfusion)*,[48] Booth J was faced with an application brought by an LA in respect of a young girl who was considered by her treating clinicians to require blood transfusions; her parents were Jehovah's Witnesses and opposed the transfusions on religious grounds. Other than in relation to this aspect of medical treatment, there was no dispute with the parents' care of their daughter.

8.21 *Re R* stands for the proposition that an SIO can be made to address the issue of contested medical treatment of a child, as between the parents and a third party (here, an LA). As Booth J put it:

> I am in no doubt that the application is well-founded under s 8 of the Act. The result which the local authority wishes to achieve, namely, the court's authorisation for the use of blood products, can clearly be achieved by the means of such an order. There

[42] S Gilmore, 'The Nature, Scope, and Use of the Specific Issue Order' [2004] *CFLQ* 367.
[43] Hansard, *Lords Debates*, vol 502, col 491 (6 December 1988), emphasis added. See also J Mackay, 'Perceptions of the Children Bill and Beyond' (1989) 139 *NLJ* 505, 506.
[44] Gilmore (n 42).
[45] See generally George, Thompson and Miles (n 10) 679–82.
[46] See **8.6**.
[47] See Gilmore (n 42) 380 and the cases cited therein.
[48] [1993] 2 FLR 757 (Booth J).

> is no need for the court otherwise to intervene to safeguard the little girl, so that I am satisfied that it is unnecessary and inappropriate for the court to exercise its inherent jurisdiction.[49]

Similarly, in *Re HG (Specific Issue Order: Sterilisation)*,[50] the High Court made a specific issue order relating to the sterilisation of a 17-year-old girl. The court has also made PSOs preventing a child from undergoing surgery or receiving blood transfusions.[51]

8.22 All the above decisions stem from High Court rulings in the immediate aftermath of the implementation of the Children Act. Despite being reported, those cases then disappear into history and are not cited in the later authorities, though they are referenced in some texts as examples of the uses of specific issue orders.[52] This begs the question: why, after the court initially held s 8 orders to be adequate to address medical treatment disputes, do later cases revert to using the inherent jurisdiction?

8.23 There is virtually no discussion of this issue in the case law. The only substantial engagement with these authorities came in *Re JM (A Child) (Medical Treatment)* ('*Re JM*'),[53] where Mostyn J held that an application under s 8 was the appropriate way for such cases to be addressed.[54] My argument is that where the court uses its inherent jurisdiction to make the primary orders which authorise (or forbid) medical treatment of children, it is doing so unnecessarily – the Children Act allows such orders to be made, and therefore the Act should be used.

Potential Limitations of s 8 Orders

8.24 *Re JM* and the early 1990s cases cited above represent a small minority of the decisions in this area; Mostyn J's decision clearly came as a surprise to some, and was controversial. For example, the leading family law text for practitioners, the *Family Court Practice 2017*, gave *Re JM* rather short shrift, saying that the approach set out by Mostyn J was 'not supported by authority':[55]

> In most serious medical treatment cases a declaration is sought that the treatment proposed is in the best interests of the child and for authorisation for the treatment to be given or withdrawn. This can only be granted by the High Court. Where a child

[49] ibid 760. See also the consent order made in *Re MM (Medical Treatment)* [2000] 1 FLR 224 (Black J).

[50] *Re HG (Specific Issue Order: Sterilisation)* [1993] 1 FLR 587 (DHCJ Singer QC).

[51] *Re S (A Minor) (Medical Treatment)* [1993] 1 FLR 376 (Thorpe J). *Cf Re W (A Minor) (Medical Treatment: Court's Jurisdiction)* [1993] Fam 64 (CoA).

[52] See, eg, R White, P Carr and N Lowe, *The Children Act in Practice* 3rd edn (Oxford: Butterworths, 2002), 164.

[53] *Re JM (A Child) (Medical Treatment)* [2015] EWHC 2832 (Fam), [2016] 2 FLR 235 ('*Re JM*').

[54] ibid [24].

[55] A Cleary, *The Family Court Practice 2017* (Bristol: Jordan Publishing, 2017), 1546. The passage does not appear in later editions, with *Re JM* excised entirely from 2018 onwards.

is in care, the local authority cannot apply for a specific issue order. The nature of the issues that arise is not within the scope of a s 8 order. It also does not take into account: the delay that this procedure would entail; the need for the child's interests to be independently considered by being made a party to the proceedings and for the child to be represented; the hurdles that would have to be overcome to obtain legal funding and representation for the child; and the fact that the case would have to be dealt with by a judge of the Family Division, thus requiring a transfer to the High Court.

Leaving the declaration point to one side for a moment, it is convenient to consider the other criticisms first.

Children under a Care Order

8.25 Where a child is the subject of a care order, s 9(1) of the CA 1989 prevents the court from making an SIO or PSO. The basis for this limitation is best explained as a matter of policy.[56] A care or interim care order gives PR for that child to the LA. There are limitations on some aspects of the LA's PR,[57] and it is required to consult with the parents and agree as much as possible[58] – but ultimately, except in decisions about contact,[59] the LA can 'trump' the PR of the parents on most issues.[60] This is a statutory reflection of the general principle of *A v Liverpool CC*[61] – the court cannot interfere with the way in which other public bodies exercise their statutory responsibilities (other than by judicial review). When the court makes a care or interim care order, the day-to-day decision-making about the child is ultimately being given to the LA, albeit with limitations. The effect of s 9(1) is to protect the LA from interference by the parents or the court in the exercise of those statutory functions, with the LA generally entrusted with decision-making about children placed under a care order.

8.26 In the context of serious medical decisions, however, that has not been the approach taken in recent caselaw – Munby P has suggested that the LA would be unwise to rely on its PR to override parental decisions about significant medical treatment.[62] The reason why the LA cannot – or, at least, should not – use its PR to sanction serious medical treatment under a care order is two-fold.[63] First, the Article 8 rights to respect for private and family life of the child and of the parents militate against a state body being able to make significant decisions for the child

[56] See Law Commission, *Review of Child Law: Guardianship and Custody*. Law Com 172 (London: HMSO, 1988), para 4.52.

[57] CA 1989, s 33(6) and (7).

[58] ibid s 22(4) and (5).

[59] ibid s 34(3).

[60] ibid s 33(3)(b).

[61] *A v Liverpool CC* [1982] AC 363 (HL); see **3.53** *et seq*.

[62] *Re AB (Care Proceedings: Medical Treatment)* [2018] EWFC 3, [2018] 4 WLR 20, [24(iii)].

[63] *Re C (Child in Care: Choice of Forename)* [2016] EWCA Civ 374, [2017] Fam 137, [76].

without court oversight. While it is clear that the LA can make everyday decisions about children's medical care, such as arranging standard immunisations,[64] the developing understanding of Article 8 has changed the position for 'serious' or 'grave' medical decisions. Second, in a case where there was scope for reasonable disagreement about the proposed course of treatment, the parents' only recourse would be to seek discharge of the care order. That might not be appropriate, but there would be no other way within the ambit of the Children Act for the LA's decision to be challenged.[65]

8.27 Consequently, if the LA's PR cannot be used to authorise the treatment but s 9(1) prevents the making of an SIO, the court may have to fall back on the inherent jurisdiction.[66] The same applies when it is the parent who wants their child to have a medical procedure but the LA disagrees; when a care order is in force, the court cannot make an SIO irrespective of which party applies, so the issue can be resolved only under the inherent jurisdiction.[67]

8.28 The same reasoning does not apply, however, where an LA becomes concerned about a need for vaccination or medical treatment of a child who is *not* in care – in this type of case, there is no reason why a s 8 order cannot be used.[68] To establish this point, it is necessary to address the obiter comments of the Court of Appeal in *Re H (Parental Responsibility: Vaccination)*.[69] The Court of Appeal suggested that the LA cannot make a court application of any kind regarding routine medical care of a child who is not already in care. The court concluded that the inherent jurisdiction cannot be invoked in such cases because the LA will not be able to meet the s 100 requirement of showing that there was reasonable cause to think that the child was likely to suffer significant harm if the inherent jurisdiction was not invoked.[70] However, as I argue in detail later,[71] that is the answer to the wrong question. The LA has no need to resort to the inherent jurisdiction when a child is not in care – it can apply for a s 8 order. The LA would need permission to make such an application,[72] but there is no threshold of significant harm before permission can be granted, and an LA is able to bring such an application.[73]

[64] *Re H (Parental Responsibility: Vaccination)* [2020] EWCA Civ 664, [2021] Fam 133. See **8.3.ii**.

[65] It might be possible for injunctive relief under s 8 of the Human Rights Act 1998 to be sought: see, by analogy, *Re DE (A Child)* [2014] EWFC 6, [2015] Fam 145.

[66] For an example of a health authority seeking inherent jurisdiction orders in relation to children subject to interim care orders, see *A Local Authority v MC* [2017] EWHC 370 (Fam). No mention is made of s 9(1), so it is unclear whether this was a considered decision to use the inherent jurisdiction or just the default response.

[67] See, eg, *Re P (Circumcision: Child in Care)* [2021] EWHC 1616 (Fam), [2022] 4 WLR 53; *Re C (Looked After Child: Covid-19 Vaccination)* [2021] EWHC 2993 (Fam), [2022] 2 FLR 194.

[68] This would include a child in voluntary accommodation under CA 1989, s 20.

[69] *Re H (Parental Responsibility: Vaccination)* [2020] EWCA Civ 664, [2021] Fam 133.

[70] See **3.27–3.30**.

[71] See **9.31–9.36**; see also R George, 'Parental Responsibility, Vaccination, and the Role of the State' (2020) 136 LQR 559.

[72] CA 1989, s 10(9).

[73] *Re R (A Minor) (Blood Transfusion)* [1993] 2 FLR 757 (Booth J).

Consequently, *Re H* is right that the inherent jurisdiction cannot be used, but it is wrong to suggest that the LA therefore has no remedy. A s 8 order can be sought, and indeed the fact that they can make that application disapplies the LA's ability to seek an inherent jurisdiction order regardless of the significant harm issue.[74]

Other Criticisms of *Re JM*

8.29 Returning to the criticisms of *Re JM* made in the *Family Court Practice*,[75] the issue of legal aid funding is a real one. In general, it is far easier to obtain legal aid for wardship or inherent jurisdiction applications than for a general private law dispute. Other than in international abduction cases, the guidance following LASPO 2012 requires a private law applicant either: (i) to show that they have been the victim of domestic abuse, or (ii) to seek what is termed 'exceptional case funding',[76] which is difficult to do.[77] The answer to this is for the Legal Aid Agency ('LAA') to change its guidance; there is no logic in granting funding for an application made under the inherent jurisdiction and denying funding for an identical application under the CA 1989, especially when the latter is the more appropriate legal approach. As a matter of principle, the LAA's flawed funding model should not affect how the law itself is used, though in practice this financial reality will be determinative for many applicants.

8.30 The other criticisms made by the *Family Court Practice* are ill-founded. First, although a s 8 application can be issued only in the Family Court, it can be made to the Urgent Applications judge sitting at the Royal Courts of Justice if the issue involved is appropriate High Court judge-level business. In other words, it can be heard immediately by a High Court judge sitting in the Family Court[78] – so there is no reason for delay. Nor is there any reason that the case requires the High Court, rather than the Family Court; but if it does, transfer is a technicality, not a practical obstacle. Second, making a child a party to proceedings is governed by the same rules and principles whether under the CA 1989 or the inherent jurisdiction.[79] Third, the claim that the issue is 'not within the scope of a s 8 order' is simply wrong. As already seen, even the most serious medical treatment issues are within the scope of PR, and therefore within the scope of a s 8 order.[80]

[74] CA 1989, s 100(5)(b) prohibits the use of the inherent jurisdiction to seek any order 'which the local authority is entitled to apply for (assuming, in the case of any application which may only be made with leave, that leave is granted)'.

[75] See **8.24**.

[76] LASPOA 2012, s 10.

[77] In 2013–14, only nine cases nationally were granted ECF from 819 applications. Since 2015–16, after a successful judicial review, between 100 and 200 cases receive ECF per year: MoJ, *Legal Aid Statistics Quarterly* (March 2024), Table 8.2.

[78] *Re N (Abduction: Children Act or Hague Convention Proceedings)* [2020] EWFC 35, [2020] 2 FLR 575 (Mostyn J).

[79] FPR 2010 r 16.2 and Practice Direction 16A.

[80] See **8.18** *et seq*.

The Need for Declarations

8.31 So far, my argument is that (except in the case of a child already in LA care, and leaving aside the practical obstacle of the legal aid rules), recourse to the inherent jurisdiction is not required. Returning now to the *Family Court Practice*, the most compelling argument is that a declaration may be needed, and only the High Court can make one. In *Re JM*, Mostyn J acknowledges this point:

> it is questionable whether the Family Court has the power to grant final declaratory relief, which may well be the principal relief (or a component of such relief) which is sought. This is because CPR r 40.20, whereby the court is given explicit power to make 'binding declarations whether or not any other remedy is claimed' is not replicated in the FPR (although, strangely, there is a power in FPR 2010, r 20.2(1)(b) to make an interim declaration). In a serious medical case the declaratory relief sought may concern the authorisation of a deprivation of liberty. That cannot be ordered within a specific issue direction.[81]

The answer for Mostyn J was that an applicant should seek *both* an order under s 8 *and* a declaration under the inherent jurisdiction. But are declarations needed at all?

Declarations Generally

8.32 As noted previously, the nature of a declaration under the inherent jurisdiction is, in one sense, straightforward – it *declares* a person's legal rights or status, or it declares whether a course of action, past or proposed, was or would be lawful. However, it does nothing to *change* the legal position.[82]

8.33 High Court declarations have at least three functions.[83] One is to determine the substantive issue – for instance, to declare whether it is or is not in a child's best interests for treatment to be given. That kind of declaration seems to encompass exactly the territory which can be addressed with a s 8 order, by the court determining whether a particular step in the exercise of PR should be taken or not taken, in the child's best interests. Second, the court may be asked to make declarations as to a child's lack of capacity. However, it is unclear that this is required for a child under the age of 16: the law presumes that the child is not competent to make such decisions; it is for clinicians, not the court, to assess *Gillick* competence;[84] and in any case, even when the child is competent the court has long asserted its

[81] *Re JM* (n 53) [26].
[82] See **8.10**.
[83] See generally *An NHS Trust v Y* [2018] UKSC 46, [2019] AC 978 discussing declarations in the context of an adult patient in a persistent vegetative state.
[84] *Bell v Tavistock and Portman NHS Foundation Trust* [2021] EWCA Civ 1363, [2022] 1 FLR 69, [80].

right to override the child's decision.[85] A final potential use of the declaration is to authorise a deprivation of liberty of a child.[86]

8.34 In the context of medical decision-making, relating to children *and* adults, the sole criterion in determining whether the court grants a declaration is the best interests of the patient, taken in their widest sense.[87] That, of course, is also the sole criterion for determining whether to make a specific issue or prohibited steps order,[88] and in that context also must be interpreted in its widest sense.[89] The intellectual process and the considerations relevant to the granting of a declaration and the making of a s 8 order appear, therefore, to be the same. The question is whether a High Court declaration adds anything different.

8.35 In general, the answer is no. The use of declarations in medical cases arose in relation to *adults*,[90] in response to the court's lack of power to make *orders* about incapacitous adults' medical treatment.[91] Doctors required certainty that treatment would not expose them to criminal or civil liability, and the declaration of lawfulness answered this problem. However, in relation to *incapacitous adults*, the court can now make orders under the Mental Capacity Act 2005 ('MCA 2005'), as medical treatment is well within the scope of a 'personal welfare decision' under that Act – and in relation to *children*, an order under s 8 of the CA 1989 performs the same function as a declaration, stating that the doctor is permitted to provide the relevant treatment. In relation to the actual treatment, therefore, there is no need for declarations.

Declarations in Relation to Deprivation of Liberty

8.36 The more specific suggested need for declarations is that the medical treatment may also involve a deprivation of liberty ('DOL') requiring court authorisation. A DOL for the purposes of Article 5 ECHR has three limbs or elements,[92] summarised by the Supreme Court as follows:

> (a) the objective component of confinement in a particular restricted place for a not negligible length of time; (b) the subjective component of lack of valid consent; and (c) the attribution of responsibility to the state.[93]

[85] *Re R (Wardship: Consent to Treatment)* [1992] Fam 11 (CoA).
[86] On deprivation of liberty under the inherent jurisdiction, see **ch 10**.
[87] See, eg, *Re F (Mental Patient: Sterilisation)* [1990] 2 AC 1 (HL), 56 (Lord Brandon) and 79 (Lord Goff).
[88] Children Act 1989, s 1(1).
[89] *Re G (Education: Religious Upbringing)* [2012] EWCA Civ 1233, [2013] 1 FLR 677.
[90] See *Re F (Mental Patient: Sterilisation)* [1990] 2 AC 1 (HL).
[91] See **2.47** *et seq.*
[92] *Storck v Germany* (2005) 43 EHRR 6.
[93] *P (by his Litigation Friend, the Official Solicitor) v Cheshire West and Chester Council* [2014] UKSC 19, [2014] AC 896, [37].

There are two questions. First, when does Article 5 become engaged in the medical treatment context? And second, is a declaration required to authorise the DOL if Article 5 is engaged?

8.37 With a younger child,[94] DOL for Article 5 purposes appears to arise only where the parents (or, if *Gillick* competent, the child) are not only in dispute with the hospital about the proposed course of treatment, but in fact do not consent to the child remaining in the hospital's care at all.

8.38 Where the parents consent to their child remaining in hospital (even if they dispute the course of treatment to be given), this will not amount to DOL for two reasons. First, with younger children, it is commonplace for them to have their movement highly curtailed and to be closely supervised. Whether this is at home, in childcare, or at a hospital makes little difference, and does not usually amount to 'confinement' within component 1 of *Storck*. And second, the child's position is properly regulated by the parents' exercise of their PR. So long as there is parental consent to the child remaining in hospital, there is no breach of Article 5 ECHR because components 2 and 3 of *Storck* are not satisfied.[95] (If a child is in LA care, the LA may not use its PR to authorise the deprivation of liberty; parental consent might still suffice, but ordinarily a court order will be required in such circumstances.[96])

8.39 The case law appears to start to draw a significant distinction in early adolescence, at 11 or 12 years of age.[97] However, even a child over this age is unlikely to be 'confined' for the purposes of *Storck* component 1 if their 'confinement' is in a hospital as a result of a medical condition that would require anyone to be hospitalised.[98] Consequently, whereas Mostyn J suggests that applications of this nature will normally include an application for a declaration authorising a DOL, in the majority of cases that would be unnecessary. The issue seems to arise only in relation to older children where both they and the holders of PR object to them remaining at the hospital.

8.40 On the second question of whether a declaration is required in those cases where a DOL arises, it is still unclear why the court cannot use the CA 1989.

[94] *Re D (Residence Order: Deprivation of Liberty)* [2019] UKSC 42, [2019] 1 WLR 5403.

[95] *P (by his Litigation Friend, the Official Solicitor) v Cheshire West and Chester Council* [2014] UKSC 19, [2014] AC 896, [54] (Lady Hale) and [72] (Lord Neuberger P); *Re D (A Child) (Deprivation of Liberty)* [2015] EWHC 922 (Fam), [2016] 1 FLR 142, [55]–[57], approved by *Re D (A Child) (Residence Order: Deprivation of Liberty)* [2017] EWCA Civ 1695, [103].

[96] *Re AB (A Child) (Deprivation of Liberty: Consent)* [2015] EWHC 3125 (Fam), [2016] 1 WLR 1160, [29], approved by *Re D (A Child) (Residence Order: Deprivation of Liberty)* [2017] EWCA Civ 1695, [109]–[112]; *cf Re J (Local Authority Consent to Deprivation of Liberty)* [2024] EWHC 1690 (Fam) (Lieven J).

[97] *Re A-F (Children)* [2018] EWHC 138 (Fam), [43].

[98] *R (Ferreira) v HM Coroner for Inner South London* [2017] EWCA Civ 31, [88]–[90], citing *Austin v UK* (2012) 55 EHRR 359, [59]; *Evans and James v Alder Hey Children's NHS Foundation Trust (No 2)* [2018] EWCA Civ 805, [60]–[62]; the same point is made in *Re Alfie Evans (No 2)*, 20 April 2018, [12] (reported refusal of Permission to Appeal to the Supreme Court).

The fact that the parents *could* give valid consent to authorise the DOL suggests that the issue falls within the ambit of PR. If that is so, a s 8 specific issue order can be used to direct that the child should receive the relevant medical treatment, and that this may include a DOL. In my view, both aspects of that order are within the scope of s 8 itself, but that is certainly so when considered along with s 11(7) of the CA 1989. That sub-section provides that a s 8 order may, amongst other things, 'contain directions about how it is to be carried into effect' or 'make such incidental, supplemental or consequential provisions as the court thinks fit'.[99] This language is clearly wide enough to allow the court to authorise a DOL for the purpose of receiving specified medical treatment.[100] Consequently, if a DOL does arise, it can be resolved by the making of orders under the CA 1989, and there is no need for High Court declarations.

8.41 However, even if this conclusion is wrong, the solution proposed by Mostyn J in *Re JM* is available. The fact that, in a small minority of cases, a declaration regarding DOL might be needed alongside a medical treatment decision, does not justify making the *principal decision* about the treatment itself under the inherent jurisdiction. The solution is for the court to determine the main issue under the CA 1989, and (if necessary) use its inherent jurisdiction to make the supplemental declaration. This is plainly not the approach being adopted in the majority of cases, where the inherent jurisdiction is almost invariably used to authorise medical treatment that could just as well be determined as a s 8 application.[101]

Conclusion

8.42 This chapter has focused on the use of the inherent jurisdiction in relation to medical treatment. Practice Direction 12D, *Inherent Jurisdiction (Including Wardship) Proceedings* identifies 'orders relating to medical treatment' as one of the common uses of the inherent jurisdiction[102] – which, as a statement of fact, is undeniably true.[103] However, it is unclear why this is the case. Just as a parent can

[99] CA 1989, s 11(7)(a) and (d) respectively.

[100] *Cf* the view, for which no authority is cited, that the inherent jurisdiction is required, in *Re A-F (Children)* [2018] EWHC 138 (Fam), [26] (Munby P).

[101] For recent examples unnecessarily using the inherent jurisdiction, see, eg, *Birmingham Women's and Children's NHS Foundation Trust v J* [2022] EWHC 2229 (Fam), [2023] 1 FLR 458 (Hayden J); *Wirral BC v RT and NT* [2022] EWCA Civ 1869 (Fam) (MacDonald J); *Royal National Orthopaedic Hospital v ZY* [2022] EWHC 1328 (Fam), 190 BMLR 115 (MacDonald J); *Great Ormond Street Hospital NHS Trust v A* [2021] EWHC 1517 (Fam) (Arbuthnot J).

[102] Para 1.2(c).

[103] Of 410 wardship and inherent jurisdiction cases reported on Bailii from 2013 to 2022, medical treatment cases accounted for 55 decisions (13 per cent); only public law / deprivation of liberty (104 cases, 25 per cent) and abduction (83 cases, 20 per cent) accounted for more.

authorise any medical treatment in the exercise of their PR, whether it is a trivial or a life-and-death decision,[104] so too the court's statutory powers under the CA 1989 can resolve any dispute about the medical treatment of a child.

8.43 Jo Bridgeman reaches the same conclusion in her compelling analysis of this issue.[105] She addresses in detail how CA 1989 orders can be used to reach the required outcomes in medical treatment cases, and concludes that this approach would involve far less interference with the general exercise by parents of their PR.[106] This is particularly true if the child is made a ward of court, since doing so suspends the parents' PR entirely and requires any important steps in the child's life to be approved by the court.[107] The court's default resort to its inherent jurisdiction in medical treatment cases has stopped judges from utilising the full scope of s 8 orders in this context.[108] The remedies in the Children Act are clear; they are prescribed by Parliament as the appropriate remedies for dealing with issues about PR; and they come with specific guidance about how they should be applied, not least the mandate to consider the factors set out in the *welfare checklist*.[109]

8.44 Medical treatment is therefore another example of my main thesis in this book – the court uses its inherent jurisdiction in cases where there is no inadequacy in the available statutory remedies, and therefore where doing so is inappropriate. Parliament has laid down the legal framework, and it is unclear why the court refuses to use those remedies, instead relying on its amorphous and unenumerated inherent jurisdiction.

[104] See **8.6**.
[105] Bridgeman (n 24).
[106] ibid 392.
[107] See **3.11–3.17**.
[108] Bridgeman (n 24) 396.
[109] CA 1989, s 1(3).

9

Child Protection

9.1 The protection of children from abuse and neglect, and the provision of services designed to assist families (including avoiding abuse and neglect), are addressed by a detailed statutory scheme found primarily in Parts III, IV and V of the Children Act 1989 ('CA 1989'). Parts IV and V involve various forms of compulsory intervention, including powers to remove children from their families – temporarily or permanently. This chapter is about the use of the inherent jurisdiction alongside this extensive statutory scheme.

9.2 As I will set out in the opening section, the CA 1989 child protection system was not intended to be a comprehensive legislative scheme that excluded the inherent jurisdiction, though the Act does contain significant limitations on the use of the inherent jurisdiction. The issues in this chapter reveal a mixture of justified and concerning uses of the inherent jurisdiction, and – unsurprisingly given the context of child protection – the court's *protective imperative* is a driving factor. A central issue is the use of secure accommodation and the deprivation of liberty of vulnerable children and young people for their own protection, which I address separately in the next chapter.

The Scheme of the CA 1989

9.3 The history of the CA 1989 is well documented.[1] A particular concern of policymakers in the 1980s was to curtail the use of wardship and the inherent jurisdiction as vehicles for child protection. Prior to the CA 1989, local authorities ('LAs') made 'increasing use of wardship', and child protection cases were 'the outstanding feature' driving use of the inherent jurisdiction at this time.[2] The court actively encouraged applications in wardship to supplement perceived inadequacies in child protection legislation – the statutory schemes were thought cumbersome and technical, leaving children at undue risk.[3] As the Law Commission noted,

[1] See, eg, J Eekelaar and R Dingwall, *The Reform of Child Care Law* (London: Routledge, 1990).
[2] Law Commission, *Wards of Court*, WP No 101 (London: HMSO, 1987), para 3.30 ('Law Com WP 101').
[3] See **2.25**.

while some cases were using wardship to fill gaps in the 'complicated, confusing and unclear' statutory scheme,[4] in other 'more borderline' cases wardship was used 'where the [local] authority might use the statutory procedures but choose instead to use wardship'.[5] This was partly a matter of litigation convenience, but LAs were also, with the complicity of the court, side-stepping legislative restrictions on their powers to intervene in family life.

9.4 It is not my purpose to set out the detail of the CA 1989's scheme on services for children and families or child protection.[6] The key issues that are relevant to understanding the intersection of the inherent jurisdiction with the statutory scheme are these:

i. **Voluntary accommodation:** Children can be placed in LA accommodation on a voluntary basis by parents.[7] The parents' parental responsibility ('PR') is *delegated* to the LA to the extent that they choose to do so,[8] but the LA does not acquire PR for the child, the child is not 'in care', and the parents can end the accommodation at any time.
ii. **Children in care:** Children come into LA care when a court makes a care order, interim care order or emergency protection order.[9] The threshold for making a full care order is that the child is suffering or is likely to suffer significant harm as a result of: (a) the care being provided to them, not being what would be reasonable to expect a parent to provide; or (b) the child being beyond parental control. If threshold is met, the court decides what (if any) order to make using the welfare principle, informed by Article 8 ECHR.
iii. **Parental responsibility for local authorities:** When a care order or interim care order is made, the LA obtains PR for the child. The CA 1989 imposes express limitations on the LA's PR,[10] and the parents' views must be considered when making decisions about the child[11] – but if necessary, the LA can override the parents and make decisions regarding children in care.[12]
iv. **Availability of s 8 orders in relation to aspects of parental responsibility:** Other than when restricted by s 9(1) (see next), the court can make *prohibited steps* or *specific issue* orders under s 8 to address any aspect of PR. LAs are never automatically 'entitled' to apply for s 8 orders but they can seek

[4] Law Commission, *Review of Child Law: Guardianship and Custody*, Law Com 172 (London: HMSO, 1988) ('Law Com 172'), paras 1.1 and 1.3.
[5] Law Com WP 101 (n 2) para 3.35.
[6] See R George, S Thompson and J Miles, *Family Law: Text, Cases, and Materials*, 5th edn (Oxford: OUP, 2023), ch 12.
[7] CA 1989, s 20.
[8] *Williams v Hackney LBC* [2018] UKSC 37, [2019] AC 421, [39].
[9] CA 1989, ss 31, 38 and 44 respectively.
[10] See **9.16** *et seq*.
[11] CA 1989, s 22(4) and (5).
[12] CA 1989, s 33(3)(b). Decisions about contact between parents and children in care can be made by the court under s 34.

permission to bring an application.[13] The test for permission is straightforward and, unlike in relation to applications for care orders, there is no threshold requiring an LA to demonstrate actual or likely significant harm before leave can be granted.

v. **The s 9(1) restriction on making s 8 orders for children in care:** Reflecting the fact that the CA 1989 primarily entrusts decision-making about children in care to the LA (see (iii) above),[14] s 9(1) of the CA 1989 prohibits the court from making a *prohibited steps* or *specific issue* order in respect of such children.

9.5 While the CA 1989 did not exclude wardship or the inherent jurisdiction entirely in child protection cases, it was intended to reduce LAs' resort to the inherent jurisdiction to 'the most unusual and complex cases'.[15] The major restrictions are found in s 100, which is set out and analysed in chapter three.[16] In summary, the section has a number of significant effects on use of the inherent jurisdiction:

i. The court is prevented from placing a child in the care of an LA, or in accommodation provided by or on behalf of an LA, nor can a child be put under LA supervision.
ii. The court cannot make any child who is subject of a care order a ward of court, nor grant to an LA the power to determine any aspect of PR in relation to a child.
iii. LAs must obtain leave before they can seek any inherent jurisdiction order, and leave can be granted only if: (a) the outcome that the LA seeks cannot be achieved by way of any other, non-inherent jurisdiction order that the LA is able to seek, and (b) there is reasonable cause to think that the child will suffer significant harm if the inherent jurisdiction is not used.

9.6 This provision therefore places substantial restrictions on both the court and the LA. It is designed to ensure the supremacy of the statutory powers in the CA 1989 and with them the procedural and substantive protections to parents, children and LAs themselves that the Act imposes. Similarly, wardship is impermissible when a child is in care: making a care order automatically discharges wardship,[17] and wardship is unavailable for a child already in care.[18] Again, these provisions ensure the primacy of the statutory scheme. Against this legislative background, I turn to the court's uses of the inherent jurisdiction in child protection cases.

[13] CA 1989, s 10(9). See *Re R (A Minor) (Blood Transfusion)* [1993] 2 FLR 757 (Booth J).
[14] Law Com 172 (n 4) para 4.52.
[15] ibid para 1.4; see also Law Com WP 101 (n 2) paras 3.37–38.
[16] See **3.27–3.30**.
[17] CA 1989, s 91(4).
[18] ibid s 100(2)(c); Senior Courts Act 1981, s 41(2A).

Children in Voluntary Accommodation

9.7 The first example arises when a child is accommodated by an LA voluntarily with the parents' agreement under CA 1989, s 20. In *Re E (Wardship Order: Child in Voluntary Accommodation)*,[19] the trial judge thought that wardship, in conjunction with a voluntary s 20 arrangement, would be a more beneficial long-term solution for the child than a care order:

> I believe that in this case wardship has more to offer than a care order. It would make both the local authority and the parents accountable to the court. It would enable the court to oblige the local authority to keep the court and the parents informed about its progress in arranging therapy and about the progress of therapy once begun. It would enable the court to ensure that the parents receive the information proposed under the care plan.[20]

Despite this, he refused to order wardship because he thought it incompatible with the s 100(2)(b) restriction on using the inherent jurisdiction to require a child to be accommodated by an LA. However, in the Court of Appeal, Thorpe LJ held that there was nothing to stop the court warding a child if LA accommodation was being provided under s 20, and that s 100 did not prevent this outcome when the parents agreed to the voluntary accommodation.

9.8 *Re E* has been interpreted as 'establish[ing] an ancillary use of wardship to support arrangements for a child's care that have been agreed, and are not the subject of a court order'.[21] But although the decision may be right as a strict matter of statutory interpretation, it is problematic for three reasons.

9.9 First, it is unclear how the status of wardship sits alongside the core principle of s 20 accommodation that the parent(s) can remove the child from the accommodation at any time.[22] Section 20 accommodation involves the parent voluntarily and for the time being *delegating* their PR to the LA[23] – a decision the parent can un-do at any time. Wardship, by contrast, is imposed by the court and can only be removed by court order; it requires court approval for any significant change regarding the ward's upbringing; and it requires the court to determine the child's 'custody' and 'care and control'.[24] The two statuses therefore appear fundamentally incompatible, exemplified by the obvious problem that arises if the parents want to end the s 20 accommodation and the court refuses to permit the parents to change the ward's place of residence based on its assessment of the ward's welfare needs.

[19] *Re E (Wardship Order: Child in Voluntary Accommodation)* [2012] EWCA Civ 1773, [2013] 2 FLR 63.
[20] ibid [3], quoting HHJ Bellamy.
[21] *Re M (Jurisdiction: Wardship)* [2016] EWCA Civ 937, [2017] 2 FLR 153, [34].
[22] *Williams v Hackney LBC* [2018] UKSC 37, [2019] AC 421, [44].
[23] ibid [39].
[24] See **3.8–3.17**.

9.10 Second, the rationale for using wardship in *Re E* undermines the CA 1989's legal framework and the respective role of the court and the LA. The Act requires the court to decide whether to make a care order or not – but if it does, the child who is then in care becomes primarily the responsibility of the LA. The LA is *not* accountable to the court for its implementation of the care plan: '[t]he court retains no supervisory role'.[25] Consequently, the LA is *not* required to keep the court informed about a child in care (though it is required to keep the parents updated, since they retain PR when a care order is in force). This separation of the roles of the court and of the LA has been described by McFarlane P as a 'cardinal principle' of child protection law.[26] *Re E* uses wardship to create a hybrid status where a child is de facto in LA care – but not under a care order – and the court obtains oversight of the LA that the CA 1989 specifically excludes.

9.11 Finally, the decision challenges the House of Lords decisions in *A v Liverpool CC*[27] and *Re W (A Minor) (Wardship: Jurisdiction)*,[28] that the court cannot use wardship to review LA decisions taken under their statutory powers.[29] *Re E* side-steps those restrictions by preventing the LA from obtaining its statutory powers in the first place – by proceeding under s 20 rather than under a care order – while still requiring the LA to treat the child as they would have done under a care order (hence the reference to the care plan).

9.12 *Re E* has been applied in few reported cases.[30] In *Re A (Wardship: 17-Year-Old: Section 20 Accommodation)*,[31] the child was accommodated under s 20, but often absconded and was involved in gang-related activity. He was assisting with police investigations and was at risk of reprisal. The LA's application for wardship was granted: Williams J held that wardship assisted the allocated social worker by giving the court responsibility for the child in the absence of any active parental involvement – the father was estranged and the mother abroad – and allowed the LA to seek court assistance in meeting their statutory responsibilities.

9.13 *Re A* shows that wardship can be used when a child is in s 20 accommodation without circumventing statutory restrictions. Despite concerns about the application of this principle in *Re E* itself, it does seem that the general idea that wardship and s 20 accommodation can be compatible is right. However, wardship

[25] *Re S (Care Order: Implementation of Care Plan)* [2002] UKHL 10, [2002] 2 AC 291, [25].
[26] *Re T–S (Children: Care Proceedings)* [2019] EWCA Civ 742, [2019] 4 WLR 71, [35].
[27] *A v Liverpool CC* [1982] AC 363 (HL).
[28] *Re W (A Minor) (Wardship: Jurisdiction)* [1985] AC 791 (HL).
[29] See **3.53** *et seq.*
[30] See also *Re K (Children with Disabilities: Wardship)* [2011] EWHC 4031 (Fam), [2012] 2 FLR 745 (Hedley J), decided before *Re E* but on the same principles; *Re Y (Risk of Young Person Travelling to Join IS) (No 2)* [2015] EWHC 2099 (Fam), [2016] 2 FLR 229 (Hayden J); *Leicester CC v AB* [2018] EWHC 1960 (Fam), [2019] 1 FLR 344 (Keehan J). *Cf Re V (Limits on Exercise of Inherent Jurisdiction)* [2024] EWHC 133 (Fam) (Cusworth J).
[31] *Re A (Wardship: 17-Year-Old: Section 20 Accommodation)* [2018] EWHC 1121 (Fam), [2019] 1 FLR 105 (Williams J).

must be used appropriately, such as in *Re A*, where the parents are effectively absent and the LA is seeking support via wardship. It must not be used to circumvent the LA's duties and powers under a care order, or to reduce the protections afforded to families by either s 20 itself or by a care order.

Children after Care Proceedings

9.14 Somewhat akin to *Re E*, the court's use of wardship in *Re W and X (Wardship: Relatives Rejected as Foster Carers)* is questionable.[32] The threshold for care proceedings was met, but the LA wanted to place the children with grandparents who had previously been negatively assessed as foster carers – which meant that, had the children been placed there, the LA would have been obliged by regulations then in force to remove them immediately. Declining to make a care order, Hedley J warded the children and placed them in the care of the grandparents, also making child arrangements orders under CA 1989, s 8. While the statutory provisions were later amended to remove this particular problem, the Court of Appeal nonetheless approved the principle in *Re T (A Child) (Placement Order)*.[33] There are two concerns about the use of wardship here. First, private law orders are always available at the conclusion of care proceedings if they best meet the child's welfare, and it is unclear what wardship added to the s 8 orders made under the CA 1989. Second, insofar as wardship was being used to circumvent the statutory restrictions, it was inappropriate. The judge claimed that this was a lacuna, but preventing people who have been negatively assessed by the LA from becoming LA foster carers (even for family members) seems an entirely legitimate policy aim for Parliament to have adopted – the decision was not 'with the grain' of the legislation, but undermined it.

Children in Local Authority Care

9.15 The general policy of the CA 1989 is that when a child is *in care*, two core principles apply: (i) the LA has PR for the child and gets to determine, as far as it is necessary to do so, the extent to which the parents can exercise their own PR;[34] and (ii) in making decisions about a child, the LA should consult with the child's parents, as well as with the child.[35] Both aspects raise issues that have engaged the inherent jurisdiction.

[32] *Re W and X (Wardship: Relatives Rejected as Foster Carers)* [2003] EWHC 2206 (Fam), [2004] 1 FLR 415 (Hedley J).

[33] *Re T (A Child) (Placement Order)* [2018] EWCA Civ 650, [2018] 2 FLR 926, [54].

[34] CA 1989, s 33(3) and (4).

[35] CA 1989, s 22(4) and (5).

Decisions where the Local Authority Cannot Use its Parental Responsibility

9.16 When a care order is made, the LA obtains PR for the child – but in two categories of case, the LA's PR is restricted.

Restrictions under the CA 1989

9.17 The first category arises from the CA 1989 itself. By s 33(6), there are three things that the LA is *prohibited* from doing: (i) causing the child to be brought up in a different religion, (ii) agreeing to, or refusing to agree to, the making of an adoption order, and (iii) appointing a guardian. By contrast, and the focus of my discussion, there are also *qualified* limitations in s 33(7). Subject to the details in s 33(8) that are not relevant here, s 33(7) provides:

> While a care order is in force with respect to a child, no person may—
>
> (a) cause the child to be known by a new surname; or
>
> (b) remove him from the United Kingdom,
>
> without either the written consent of every person who has parental responsibility for the child *or the leave of the court*. (emphasis added)

9.18 Curiously, though, the CA 1989 appears to provide no mechanism for the leave referred to in s 33(7) to be granted. Normally, a dispute about an aspect of PR is resolved by the court making a *specific issue* or *prohibited steps* order.[36] However, s 9(1) specifically prevents the court from making either of those orders in respect of a child in LA care.[37] Section 9(1) protects the LA from any interference by parents (or the court) seeking to use private law remedies to undermine the LA's decision-making, but it also does not permit such an order even if the LA brings the application. How, then, can leave to do the actions listed in s 33(7) be granted?

9.19 One possibility is if s 33(7) itself provides a power to grant leave.[38] While that power is not apparent from the wording of the sub-section, some courts have taken the view that the analogous private law provisions in s 13 of the CA 1989 (which address the same two issues as s 33(7) for private law cases) contain a power to grant leave.[39] I have previously argued that s 13 contains no such power, and that the relevant leave should be granted using a s 8 order.[40] I stand by that

[36] CA 1989, s 8.

[37] When a child is *not* in care, an LA can obtain leave under s 10(9) to bring an application for a s 8 order: see *Re R (A Minor) (Blood Transfusion)* [1993] 2 FLR 757 (Booth J). See further **9.31** *et seq*.

[38] See, eg, *Re S (Change of Surname)* [1999] 1 FLR 672 (CoA).

[39] In that context, see, eg, *Re B (Change of Surname)* [1996] 1 FLR 791 (CoA) and *Payne v Payne* [2001] EWCA Civ 166, [2001] 1 FLR 1052.

[40] R George, 'Changing Names, Changing Places: Rethinking s 13 of the Children Act 1989' [2008] *Fam Law* 1121, supported by *Re C (Older Children: Relocation)* [2015] EWCA Civ 1298, [2016] 2 FLR 1159, [59] (Peter Jackson J).

argument in the private law context. However, if s 33(7) contains no power to grant leave, it leads to the unlikely conclusion that the Act requires permission to be granted but provides no mechanism by which that can be done – bearing in mind the court cannot make a s 8 order with respect to a child in LA care. If there is no statutory mechanism, the inherent jurisdiction would be needed. That would mean that applications are reserved to the High Court, and the LA would need to meet the 'significant harm' threshold in s 100(4)(b) before being able to bring an application.[41] Neither of these consequences seems necessary or proportionate to the issues within s 33(7) – more sensible for the application to have no 'significant harm' threshold, and to be heard in the Family Court (along with all other aspects of care proceedings). Despite the potential inconsistency with s 13, I therefore conclude that leave should be granted under s 33(7) itself,[42] and that no recourse to the inherent jurisdiction is required in these cases.

Restrictions Arising from Article 8 of the ECHR

9.20 The second category of case where the LA cannot rely on its own PR arises not from the CA 1989, but from how jurisprudence on Article 8 of the ECHR has developed in recent years. The CA 1989 clearly envisages that, other than in relation to the issues specified in s 33(6) and (7), the LA will simply, where necessary, make decisions about children in care using its PR acquired under the care order. However, the court has increasingly held that parents' Article 8 rights require the LA to bring some issues to the court if the parents disagree with the LA's proposals.[43]

9.21 There is no bright-line rule about the circumstances in which this will apply, but there seem to be two characteristics: (i) the issue was not part of the reason why the care order was originally made, and (ii) the issue is sufficiently significant to require court involvement.

9.22 The first characteristic is straightforward. If the *reason* for the child being in care includes, for example, that the parents make healthcare decisions that put the child at risk of harm, the LA can take further decisions about healthcare without returning to court. But if a child is in care for other reasons and a significant healthcare dispute arises between the LA and the parents, the matter may require court involvement.

[41] If one parent with PR (but not the other) supported the LA's position in relation to change of surname or relocation, that parent could bring the application without s 100 being engaged.

[42] King LJ has suggested that s 33(7) provides 'a procedural route to the court' in respect of the issues specified: *Re C (Child in Care: Choice of Forename)* [2016] EWCA Civ 374, [2017] Fam 137, [78]. She also suggested making an order 'by way of a general "catch all" within the Act': ibid [76(ii)]. It is unclear what that means.

[43] See, eg, *Re AB (Care Proceedings: Medical Treatment)* [2018] EWFC 3, [2018] 4 WLR 20, [24(iii)] (Munby P).

9.23 The second characteristic enters the same ambiguous territory of 'significant decisions' seen in private law disputes between holders of PR.[44] It is 'a small category of cases',[45] involving 'decisions [that] are of such magnitude that it would be wrong for a local authority to use its power under s 33(3)(b) of the Children Act 1989 to override the wishes or views of a parent without sanction by the court'.[46] It does not include routine vaccination,[47] but it does include: a 'serious' or 'grave' medical decision;[48] the selection (or changing) of a child's forename;[49] and the making of an application for British citizenship.[50] For different reasons, it also includes deprivation of the child's liberty, addressed in the next chapter.

9.24 In these cases, as King LJ explained in *Re C (Child in Care: Choice of Forename)*,[51] the issues in question are all within the scope of PR, and therefore give the LA the technical power to determine the issues if doing so against the views of the parents is necessary.[52] However, doing so would involve a 'comprehensive invasion of the [parents'] article 8 rights',[53] which a court application is required to avoid. Because the court cannot make specific issue or prohibited steps orders about a child in care,[54] the only available remedy is the inherent jurisdiction – and consequently, the LA will be able to make the application only if the child would be at risk of significant harm if the inherent jurisdiction were not invoked.[55]

9.25 The court's analysis here is unassailable. The Act, as written, envisages the LA exercising its own PR without outside interference in relation to children in its care, and so bars the only statutory remedy that would otherwise be available to challenge LA decision-making – a s 8 order. However, the modern understanding of Article 8 ECHR means that court applications are now necessary in some cases – beyond what is listed in s 33(6) and (7)[56] – and the only way that this can be done is under the inherent jurisdiction.[57] This can be seen as an anomaly, with developments in Article 8 jurisprudence creating a lacuna in the CA 1989 that did not exist when it was passed. While the outcome is justified by the need for

[44] See J Eekelaar, 'Do Parents have a Duty to Consult?' (1998) 114 *LQR* 337.
[45] *Re C (Child in Care: Choice of Forename)* [2016] EWCA Civ 374, [2017] Fam 137, [104].
[46] *Manchester CC v P* [2023] EWHC 133 (Fam), [42] (MacDonald J).
[47] *Re H (Parental Responsibility: Vaccination)* [2020] EWCA Civ 664, [2021] Fam 133.
[48] ibid [81].
[49] *Re C (Child in Care: Choice of Forename)* [2016] EWCA Civ 374, [2017] Fam 137; *Re C (Change of Forename: Child in Care)* [2023] EWHC 2813 (Fam) (Cobb J). Changing the child's surname is governed by s 33(7).
[50] *Re Y (Children in Care: Change of Nationality)* [2020] EWCA Civ 1038, [2021] Fam 199; see J Masson and D Prabhat, 'Allowing Appeals to Increase High Court Power' (2021) 43 *JSWFL* 327.
[51] *Re C (Child in Care: Choice of Forename)* [2016] EWCA Civ 374, [2017] Fam 137.
[52] CA 1989, s 33(4).
[53] *Re C* (n 49) [76(i)].
[54] CA 1989, s 9(1).
[55] If someone other than an LA sought to bring such an application in relation to a child in care – a grandparent concerned about the choice of name being given, for example – they would not need to meet the 'significant harm' threshold. On children *not* in care, see **9.31** *et seq*.
[56] See **9.17**.
[57] Wardship is not available when the child is subject to a care order: CA 1989, ss 91(4) and 100(2)(c).

the court to evaluate interferences with Article 8 rights, this approach has again shifted the balance of power between the court and the LA regarding children in care. The 'cardinal principle' – that 'a local authority and the Family Court have different spheres of responsibility with respect to the making of orders, on the one hand, and, on the other hand, the determination of the care plan to be followed for a child once an order has been made'[58] – is further undermined by these cases. Further, the core principle of *A v Liverpool CC*[59] says that the court may not interfere with the statutory duties delegated to LAs;[60] yet that seems to be exactly what is happening here. While the aim may be laudable – the protection of Article 8 rights – the consequence is that the inherent jurisdiction is used to increase the court's ability to interfere with LA decision-making about children in their care.[61]

Consultation with Parents by the Local Authority

9.26 The court has held that it can use the inherent jurisdiction to override or disapply various statutory provisions that require the LA to consult with and provide information to parents during care proceedings (or adoption proceedings arising after care proceedings) and when a child is looked after by an LA.

9.27 In England,[62] by s 22(4) of the CA 1989, the LA must 'so far as is reasonably practicable' consult with the parents of any child in care before making any decision about that child. Secondary legislation also requires the LA to seek the parents' views before conducting any review of the wellbeing of any child in care.[63] Further, when a child is 'looked after' (which includes children in care), the LA 'shall take such steps as are reasonably practicable' to keep the child's parent and any other holder of PR informed of where the child is being accommodated.[64] There is no statutory power to disapply any of these requirements – the only exception is reasonable practicability,[65] not desirability.

9.28 The authorities start with obiter remarks of Charles J in 1999, suggesting that an LA might apply for declaratory relief against these statutory duties – duties that he thought 'not mandatory' such that non-compliance would be 'treated as an irregularity'.[66] This approach was later applied by Coleridge J,[67] who focused on the

[58] *Re T-S (Children: Care Proceedings)* [2019] EWCA Civ 742, [2019] 4 WLR 71, [35].
[59] *A v Liverpool CC* (n 25).
[60] See **3.53** *et seq*.
[61] Note the title of Masson and Prabhat (n 46): 'Allowing Appeals to Increase High Court Power'.
[62] In Wales, see the Social Services and Well-being (Wales) Act 2014 (SSWB(W)A 2014), s 6(4).
[63] Arrangements for Placement of Children by Voluntary Organisations and Others (England) Regulations 2011 (SI 2011/582), r 23(1)(b).
[64] CA 1989, Sch 2, para 15(2).
[65] For example, the LA is unable to contact the parents after reasonable attempts.
[66] *Re P (Children Act 1989, ss 22 and 26: Local Authority Compliance)* [2000] 2 FLR 910, 923.
[67] *Re C (Care: Consultation with Parents Not in Child's Best Interests)* [2005] EWHC 3390 (Fam), [2006] 2 FLR 787.

merits of the application – which he wrongly considered was governed by s 1 of the CA 1989 and thus approached on the erroneous basis that the child's best interests were paramount.[68] Neither Charles J nor Coleridge J considered how the inherent jurisdiction, whether by declaratory relief or otherwise, can absolve an LA of statutory duties. Nonetheless, this approach was endorsed by *Re O (A Child) (Care Proceedings: Issues Resolution Hearing)*.[69] In adopting the reasoning of the earlier cases, Hayden J (sitting in the Court of Appeal) held that 'a local authority may only be absolved from its duty to consult and to provide information to a parent in "exceptional circumstances"'.[70] Hayden J noted that the inherent jurisdiction can be used to 'authorise actions which fall outside statutory obligation or may, again as here, be *directly contrary to it*'.[71] This striking observation did not trigger any question of whether the inherent jurisdiction can legitimately be used for that purpose.

9.29 These authorities have been applied in several recent High Court cases. The focus is on the 'significant harm' requirement in s 100 that must be met before the LA can make an application under the inherent jurisdiction,[72] followed by consideration of whether the case is sufficiently 'exceptional' to justify the proposed steps.

9.30 It is easy to see why High Court judges were keen to exclude the fathers from being consulted about their children in these cases; they involved facts such as the father raping and sexually abusing the children,[73] or murdering the children's mother or other care-giver.[74] However, Parliament has imposed duties on LAs regarding children in their care, and has not provided any mechanism to disapply those duties. As a matter of constitutional principle, the High Court's inherent jurisdiction cannot override statutory duties.[75] The court in these cases is using its declaratory powers – but a declaration cannot change the legal position, it merely announces what is already the law.[76] In these cases, the court is purportedly using its 'declaratory' power to disapply legislative requirements. However well-meaning and intuitively understandable on the facts of the cases, doing so goes beyond the court's appropriate boundaries; if nothing else, it is a striking example of the

[68] An application to disapply the duty to consult is not a decision about the child's upbringing, even though the issues about which the LA was meant to consult are, and so s 1 of the CA 1989 is inapplicable. *Cf* by analogy *Re B (Paternal Grandmother: Joinder as Party)* [2012] EWCA Civ 737, [2012] 2 FLR 1358, [36].

[69] *Re O (A Child) (Care Proceedings: Issues Resolution Hearing)* [2015] EWCA Civ 1169, [2016] 1 WLR 512.

[70] ibid [28].

[71] ibid [24] (emphasis added).

[72] See, eg, *Re X and Y (Children)* [2018] EWHC 451 (Fam), [2018] 2 FLR 947, [55] (Knowles J); *A Local Authority v X* [2019] EWHC 2166 (Fam), [2020] 4 WLR 14, [59] (Theis J); *A Local Authority v F* [2022] EWFC 127, [2023] 1 FLR 1014 (Knowles J).

[73] *Re C* (n 67); *A Local Authority v X* (n 72).

[74] *Re X and Y (Children)* (n 72); *A Local Authority v F* (n 72).

[75] See generally **1.22–1.27**.

[76] *Re F (Mental Patient: Sterilisation)* [1990] 2 AC 1 (CoA), 20 (Lord Donaldson MR) and 42 (Butler-Sloss LJ).

inherent jurisdiction directly cutting across a statutory scheme – by purporting to disapply it. A less concerning approach would be to make declarations as to what *extent* of consultation was required and in respect of which issues, on the particular facts of the cases, to meet the statutory requirements – but simply to say that the statute can be disregarded is an inappropriate power for the court to grant itself.

Local Authorities and Children not in their Care

9.31 In general, LAs are not parties[77] to litigation concerning children unless those children are the subject of care or adoption proceedings or are in LA care. But there are exceptions.

9.32 One example[78] where the inherent jurisdiction may be relevant to an LA is in cases with an international element, such as parents seeking to avoid impending care proceedings by removing a child abroad,[79] or the so-called 'radicalisation cases' where parents are seeking to take, or have taken, their children abroad to join radical groups.[80] These cases are not my concern; the same issues arise as in child abduction generally.[81]

9.33 My focus here arises from comments in *Re H (Parental Responsibility: Vaccination).*[82] *Re H* held that when an LA has a care order for a child, the benefits of the child receiving standard childhood vaccinations are so clear,[83] and the issue of vaccination so insignificant,[84] that the LA is entitled to authorise vaccination even over the explicit objection of the parents, without risk of any breach of ECHR Article 8 rights.[85] However, in obiter comments, King LJ also considered what power the LA might have to arrange vaccination of a child who was *not* the subject of a care order. Here, the LA was said to have no basis for making *any* application to challenge the parents' decision not to vaccinate their child.

[77] The LA may be involved in other ways, such as preparing a welfare report in private law proceedings.

[78] Another example is the court's use of the inherent jurisdiction to make advance declarations concerning an unborn child that take effect immediately on the child's birth, when the child is at serious risk immediately from birth: see **4.24**.

[79] See, eg, *Manchester CC v D (Application for Permission to Withdraw Proceedings after Abduction)* [2021] EWHC 1191 (Fam), [2022] 1 FLR 490 (MacDonald J), and the publicity concerning children removed to Pakistan following the killing of their sibling: L Tickle and H Summers, 'Siblings of Sara Sharif, Found Dead at her Father's Home, Are Made Wards of Court', *The Guardian*, 24 December 2023. On the value of wardship in the Sharif case, see **7.39**.

[80] See the cases cited in the *President's Guidance on Radicalisation Cases in the Family Courts* (8 October 2015).

[81] See **ch 7**.

[82] *Re H (Parental Responsibility: Vaccination)* [2020] EWCA Civ 664, [2021] Fam 133 ('*Re H*'). See also R George, 'Parental Responsibility, Vaccination, and the Role of the Court' (2021) 136 *LQR* 559.

[83] *Re H* (n 82) [55].

[84] ibid [85].

[85] ibid [98].

9.34 The court's argument is constructed in this way. By itself and without any other concerns, a failure to arrange vaccination does not amount to significant harm, and so cannot justify the LA bringing care proceedings.[86] Without a care order, the LA has no PR for the child, and thus cannot itself authorise the child's vaccination – even though, if it happened to have a care order already, it could use its PR to do so.

9.35 King LJ then suggests that the LA cannot obtain orders for vaccination *at all* if the child is not subject to a care order, because an application under the inherent jurisdiction will fail the s 100(4) 'significant harm' threshold: if failure to vaccinate does not amount to significant harm in care proceedings, so too it will not overcome s 100(4)(b).[87]

9.36 That logic is impeccable – but the court is asking the wrong question, premised on the need to invoke the inherent jurisdiction rather than making a statutory order. There is no reason to turn to the inherent jurisdiction when the child is not in LA care, because the s 9(1) restriction on making s 8 orders is not engaged. The LA can apply for a specific issue or prohibited steps order without needing to meet any threshold of significant harm; they merely have to meet the same test under s 10(9) of the CA 1989 as any other non-entitled applicant seeking a private law order.[88] The court's focus on its inherent jurisdiction has caused it to lose sight of the more obvious and appropriate statutory remedy – a s 8 order.

Conclusion

9.37 Regulating the relationship between the court and the LA, and balancing the interests of parents, children and the state in the child protection context, is at the heart of the CA 1989. Unsurprisingly, the court's *protective imperative* plays a large role in its use of the inherent jurisdiction in child protection cases, but the effects are remarkable. The court has circumvented – and even purportedly *disapplied* – express statutory requirements. It has used the inherent jurisdiction to shift the balance of power and responsibility between itself and the LA, seemingly in breach of the *A v Liverpool CC* rule (though explained on the basis of respect for Article 8 rights). But it has also used its inherent jurisdiction to place unjustified restrictions on LAs, preventing them from accessing suitable statutory remedies to help children who are not in care. The overall effect of the court's use of its inherent jurisdiction in the child protection context is therefore both constitutionally concerning and internally incoherent.

[86] ibid [90]. This assumption is questionable, given the serious harms against which vaccination provides protection: see *Re SL (Permission to Vaccinate)* [2017] EWHC 125 (Fam), [2017] 4 WLR 53 (MacDonald J).

[87] *Re H* (n 82) [90].

[88] *Re R (A Minor) (Blood Transfusion)* [1993] 2 FLR 757 (Booth J).

10

Secure Accommodation and Deprivation of Liberty of Children

10.1 A significant and controversial use of the inherent jurisdiction in recent years has been in *secure accommodation* or *deprivation of liberty* ('DOL') cases. In these cases, a child (usually a teenager[1]) is thought to be at such high risk – usually from self-harm linked to trauma and mental health concerns, but sometimes from external factors like sexual exploitation or gang involvement[2] – that the only way to keep them safe is to place severe restrictions on their movement and confine them to a particular property (or sometimes an institutional setting like a hospital). Two legal mechanisms are available. First, there is a statutory power under the Children Act 1989 ('CA 1989'), s 25 – or for placements in Wales, under s 119 of the Social Services and Well-being (Wales) Act 2014 ('SSWB(W)A 2014')[3] – to order 'secure accommodation' when certain statutory criteria are met. Alternatively, exercising the inherent jurisdiction, the High Court can permit DOL outside the statutory scheme.

10.2 Facilities for s 25 are registered, regulated and authorised by the Secretary of State.[4] By contrast, those used under the inherent jurisdiction are often called 'bespoke', implying specially created, dedicated facilities – but in reality 'some of the country's most vulnerable teenagers are being housed [under the inherent jurisdiction] in accommodation that is barely fit for human habitation'.[5] Placements are in flats, hostels, caravans, barges and even tents – certainly not specialist facilities.[6] Sir James Munby P described the situation as a 'disgraceful and utterly shaming lack of proper provision'.[7]

10.3 This is not a small problem. In the year July 2022–June 2023, 1,389 applications for DOL were made to the court in relation to 1,249 separate children under

[1] Around 10% of children subject to deprivation of liberty are aged 12 or under: A Roe, *Children Subject to Deprivation of Liberty Orders* (London: Nuffield Family Justice Observatory, 2023), 13.

[2] ibid 20.

[3] For the purposes of this chapter, there is no material difference between the two statutes (though they are not identical in all respects); in general I refer to s 25, but the same points apply to both.

[4] On these terms, see **10.6**.

[5] Children's Commissioner, *Unregulated: Children in Care Living in Semi-Independent Accommodation* (London: CCE, 2020), 26.

[6] ibid 5.

[7] *Re X (A Child) (No 3)* [2017] EWHC 2036 (Fam), [2018] 1 FLR 1054, [37].

the inherent jurisdiction,[8] in addition to 217 applications under CA 1989, s 25.[9] There is significant regional variation in applications to deprive children of their liberty, from 15 per 100,000 in the East of England (East Anglia) to 40 per 100,000 in the North-West.[10]

10.4 The discomfort of many judges in making these orders is palpable, including in the Supreme Court decision of *Re T (Secure Accommodation)*.[11] Lady Black noted her 'profound anxiety' and stressed that 'judges and others have been drawing attention to the dangerous inadequacy of this aspect of the child care system for years'.[12] Lord Stephens referred to 'the enduring well-known scandal of the disgraceful and utterly shaming lack of proper provision for children who require approved secure accommodation'.[13] The accommodation being used in the absence of approved placements is shockingly inadequate yet hugely expensive,[14] and comes with no meaningful oversight.[15] And, although the Supreme Court says that the inherent jurisdiction should be used only on a short-term basis,[16] in reality it forms the backbone of the state's response to the needs of a group of highly vulnerable children.

The Legal Framework

10.5 The CA 1989 addresses secure accommodation for England[17] in s 25:

Use of accommodation for restricting liberty

(1) Subject to the following provisions of this section, a child who is being looked after by a local authority in England or Wales may not be placed, and, if placed,

[8] Roe (n 1) 7. The number continues at the same rate: MoJ, *Family Court Statistics Quarterly* (March 2024), Table 22.
[9] MoJ, ibid Table 3.
[10] Roe (n 1) 10.
[11] *Re T (Secure Accommodation)* [2021] UKSC 35, [2022] AC 723 ('*Re T*'). I acted for the appellant, along with Mark Twomey KC, Alex Laing and Rachel Cooper, in the Supreme Court. I gratefully acknowledge that parts of my analysis draw from submissions co-written with those colleagues.
[12] ibid [141].
[13] ibid [166].
[14] Placements frequently cost £1m a year per child: H Pidd, 'Councils in England and Wales Pay £1m a Year to House Child in Private Care Home', *The Guardian*, 28 August 2022; see also T Wall, 'Hundreds of Vulnerable Children Sent to Illegal and Unregulated Care Homes in England', *The Observer*, 13 April 2024.
[15] See concerns in *Re A (No Approved Secure Accommodation Available: Deprivation of Liberty)* [2017] EWHC 2458 (Fam), [2018] 1 FLR 621, [6] (Holman J). Although the LA is obviously involved, most placements are provided by private sector organisations, often with no experience of working in this area; see Children's Commission (n 5) and Pidd (n 14).
[16] *Re T* (n 11) [142] (Lady Black) and [178] (Lord Stephens).
[17] The criteria for accommodation in Wales under SSWB(W)A 2014, s 119(1) are materially the same.

may not be kept, in accommodation in England or Scotland[18] provided for the purpose of restricting liberty ("secure accommodation") unless it appears—

(a) that—

(i) he has a history of absconding and is likely to abscond from any other description of accommodation; and

(ii) if he absconds, he is likely to suffer significant harm; or

(b) that if he is kept in any other description of accommodation he is likely to injure himself or other persons.

10.6 Accommodation can be used as secure accommodation under s 25 only if it is *authorised* for use as such by the Secretary of State.[19] These authorised placements are also termed *statutory placements*. As accommodation provided 'wholly or mainly' for the purpose of providing care or accommodation for children, statutory placements are 'children's homes' and must be *registered* as such.[20] In addition to the standard regulatory requirements applicable to all children's homes,[21] statutory placements are also *regulated* in additional ways, including: (i) time limitations on how long any period of court authorisation can last,[22] and (ii) a requirement for at least three persons to be appointed by the LA to review the continuation of secure accommodation.[23] A child under the age of 13 can be placed in s 25 accommodation only with the specific approval of the Secretary of State or, in Wales, the Welsh Ministers.[24]

10.7 There are two reasons why s 25 may not apply when secure accommodation is considered appropriate. The less common problem is that the criteria in s 25(1) themselves are not met – for example, 'absconding' in limb (a) requires an intention not to return[25] – but most children in need of this kind of support will meet the alternative test in sub-paragraph (b) of being likely to injure themselves or another if not kept in secure accommodation.[26] More commonly, the chronic and severe shortage of authorised places means that even when the statutory criteria are met, it is often not possible to place a child in s 25 secure accommodation because there is simply none available.

10.8 Alongside this statutory scheme – and largely due to the shortage of authorised placements – the court says it can use the inherent jurisdiction to

[18] Confusingly, if the *placement* is in Wales, the SSWB(W)A 2014 applies; but even if the LA and court are in Wales, if the *placement* is in England or Scotland, the CA 1989 applies.

[19] Children (Secure Accommodation) Regulations 1991 (SI 1991/1505), r 3 ('CSAR 1991'); in Wales, see Children (Secure Accommodation) (Wales) Regulations 2015 (SI 2015/1988), r 8 ('CSA(W)R 2015'). Secure accommodation in Scotland is approved by the Scottish Ministers.

[20] Care Standards Act 2000, s 11.

[21] See, eg, Children's Home (England) Regulations 2015 (SI 2015/541).

[22] CSAR 1991 (n 19) rr 11–12; CSA(W)R 2015 (n 19) rr 2 and 7.

[23] CSAR 1991 (n 19) r 15; CSA(W)R 2015 (n 19) r 10.

[24] CSAR 1991 (n 19) r 4; CSA(W)R 2015 (n 19) r 13.

[25] *Re W (Secure Accommodation Order)* [2016] EWCA Civ 804, [2016] 4 WLR 159, [21].

[26] 'Injure' is not defined in the CA 1989, but the OED defines injury as including hurt, loss, harm, detriment or damage.

permit children's DOL in non-statutory placements. Such placements are still required to be *registered* as children's homes (though in fact many are not[27]), and ought therefore to be subject to the same standard regulatory requirements as ordinary children's homes – but they are not *authorised* by the Secretary of State, nor subject to the additional regulations applicable to statutory secure accommodation. While the Supreme Court in *Re T* approved the use of these non-statutory placements, the issue remains controversial, and the Justices' arguments are problematic. I argue that the court has adopted an approach that relies on the protective imperative to such an extent that it has disregarded fundamental legal principles.

Re T (Secure Accommodation)

10.9 The young person in *Re T (Secure Accommodation)* lived in Wales, and was originally the subject of a care order. The LA obtained inherent jurisdiction orders authorising them to deprive T of her liberty in two 'bespoke' placements. The first was neither registered as a children's home nor authorised by the Secretary of State; the second was registered but not authorised. T appealed against the orders, arguing that the use of the inherent jurisdiction for this purpose was unlawful, but the Supreme Court dismissed her appeal.

Cutting Across a Statutory Scheme

10.10 One of the fundamental principles of the inherent jurisdiction is that it cannot be used to 'cut across' a statutory scheme, as set out in *Attorney-General v De Keyser's Royal Hotel Ltd*.[28] I suggested in chapter three, however, that the application of this principle to children cases is somewhat ambivalent.[29] *Re T (Secure Accommodation)* reflects this ambivalence, with the court adopting an artificially narrow approach to the CA 1989's scope in order to permit it to continue using its inherent jurisdiction.

10.11 The legislation defines 'secure accommodation' as 'accommodation … provided for the purpose of restricting liberty' – and a child looked after by an LA 'may not be placed, and, if placed, may not be kept, in' secure accommodation, so defined, unless the s 25 criteria are met.[30] There may be circumstances in which a child needs to be deprived of their liberty in a placement outside this

[27] Wall (n 14).
[28] *Attorney-General v De Keyser's Royal Hotel Ltd* [1920] AC 508 (HL). See **3.33** *et seq*.
[29] See **3.41** *et seq* and, regarding *Re T* (n 11) in particular, **3.51**.
[30] CA 1989, s 25(1).

definition, such as a hospital, where s 25 will not apply,[31] but that was not the issue in *Re T*.

10.12 T was being accommodated in 'bespoke' placements, the entire purpose of which was to contain her for her own safety. On any ordinary use of language, it was 'accommodation … provided for the purpose of restricting liberty' within the meaning of s 25. This straightforward approach to defining secure accommodation gains some support from obiter views expressed earlier by Lady Black in *Re D (Residence Order: Deprivation of Liberty)* in 2019,[32] suggesting that the focus needed to be on the accommodation itself, rather than on the care regime to which the child was subjected. In *Re D*, Lady Black held that s 25 was 'concerned with accommodation which has the features necessary to safeguard a child with a history of absconding who is likely to abscond from *any* other description of accommodation or to prevent injury where the child in question would be likely to injure himself or others if kept in *any* other description of accommodation'.[33] Lady Black commended the earlier approach of Wall J, 'to count within the definition of secure accommodation [a placement that is] "designed for or having as its primary purpose" the restriction of liberty'.[34]

10.13 However, in *Re T*, Lady Black defined secure accommodation more narrowly. Addressing Wall J's test for secure accommodation, she held that placements were only 'designed for' the restriction of liberty if they were 'secure children's homes, *designed and developed* as such'.[35] Further, in determining whether accommodation met that test, Lady Black referred to the typical characteristics of statutory secure accommodation – things like: secure vehicle arrival areas; high walls; reinforced windows; and CCTV covering all public areas.[36] She argued that accommodation must have these qualities for restriction of liberty to be its 'primary purpose'. Having taken that view – focusing on the physical characteristics of the accommodation and the building's design and development, rather than the purpose of the placement or the effect on the child – it followed that only rarely will there be *secure accommodation*, within the statutory meaning, that meets the 'primary purpose test' unless the building was *designed* for the restriction of liberty.[37] Lady Black concluded her analysis of this issue by saying:

> the Secretary of State is correct in saying that accommodation outside a purpose-built unit, which may well be part of a highly specialised therapeutic care package specifically

[31] See, eg, *Re C (Detention: Medical Treatment)* [1997] 2 FLR 180 (Wall J). For an argument to reform s 25, see M Jones, 'Deprivation of a Child's Liberty: Section 25 and the Need for Legislative Reform' [2017] *Family Law* 645.

[32] *Re D (Residence Order: Deprivation of Liberty)* [2019] UKSC 42, [2019] 1 WLR 5403, [103].

[33] ibid [114] (original emphasis).

[34] ibid [115], citing *Re C (Detention: Medical Treatment)* [1997] 2 FLR 180. Lady Black also commended this approach in *Re T* (n 11) [133].

[35] *Re T* (n 11) [134] (emphasis added).

[36] ibid [136].

[37] ibid [138].

designed for the individual child, will usually have as its primary purpose the provision of care and/or treatment for the child, rather than preventing the child absconding or causing harm to him or herself or others. This will therefore limit the class of placements that can properly be termed 'secure accommodation' within section 25. And where the placement is not 'secure accommodation', there can be no question of the use of the inherent jurisdiction cutting across the statutory scheme in section 25.[38]

10.14 This argument is problematic in a number of ways. First, in trying to avoid an unduly wide definition of s 25 accommodation,[39] the court adopted a remarkably narrow one. Section 25 is plainly designed to prevent children being subject to DOL unless the statutory criteria are met. The court has introduced the 'designed for and primary purpose' test – in itself a substantial gloss on the statute – but worse, has interpreted that test as meaning that accommodation must meet specific, but arbitrary, factual criteria before it can be 'secure accommodation'. Had the court taken the more straightforward approach of simply asking whether the *intended* and *actual effect* of the child's placement was a DOL, a far wider range of situations would be included. By excluding what are, in fact, the vast majority of DOL placements from s 25,[40] the court entirely undermined the safeguards in the statutory scheme.

10.15 Second, Lady Black's conclusion that the inherent jurisdiction is not being used to 'cut across' the statutory scheme – because the CA 1989 covers only the limited set of situations that she has defined as falling within s 25 – is flawed. Not only does Lady Black's argument rely on an artificially narrow interpretation of s 25, it misapplies the *De Keyser* principle.[41] A statutory scheme regulates not only what falls within its scope, but also where the law draws the line – in this case, about which children can be deprived of their liberty for their own safety.[42] If Parliament has set out a system under which a child can be securely accommodated only when specific criteria are met, the *De Keyser* principle forbids the court then using its inherent jurisdiction to make DOL orders in a wider array of circumstances. In so doing, the court cut across the statutory scheme.

Criminal Restrictions

10.16 If the court was not persuaded that using the inherent jurisdiction to authorise a child's DOL outside s 25 cut across a general statutory scheme, more specific prohibitions might have given the court reason to rethink. In *Re T (Secure Accommodation)*, one of the properties in which T was accommodated was never registered as a children's home, and thus the operators of the accommodation

[38] ibid [138].
[39] ibid [132].
[40] See **10.3**.
[41] *Attorney-General v De Keyser's Royal Hotel Ltd* [1920] AC 508 (HL).
[42] See **3.37** *et seq*.

committed a criminal offence under s 11 of the Care Standards Act 2000. That Act says: 'Any person who carries on or manages an establishment or agency of any description without being registered under this Part in respect of it … shall be guilty of an offence.'

10.17 While this caused the Justices some concern, they held that the court could still permit such a placement under the inherent jurisdiction. Lady Black argued simply that there was 'no alternative'[43] – a curious approach to Parliament's decision to criminalise an activity. Lady Black also relied on Practice Guidance issued by the President of the Family Division.[44] The Guidance, no longer in effect,[45] set out how the inherent jurisdiction should be used in DOL cases, and addressed failure to register the chosen accommodation. Reliance on this Guidance is hard to understand. Lady Black seems to argue that the court is justified in using the inherent jurisdiction because the Guidance (the legal status of which is murky at best[46]) did not 'outlaw' the placement of children in unregistered accommodation.[47] What 'outlaw' means here is unclear. Plainly the Guidance could not itself create a criminal offence, so presumably it means that the *practice* was not prohibited by the Guidance – but that must be beside the point where criminal liability already arises. In any case, the reasoning is circular: Practice Guidance cannot change the law, and in so far as it is legally wrong it is ultra vires.[48] The Supreme Court cannot rely on the Guidance in determining what the law is, because the very question was whether the President's approach (in the Court of Appeal, and reflected in his subsequent Guidance) was correct.

10.18 Lord Stephens addressed the criminal offence issue in this way:

> It is no part of the court's function to 'authorise' the commission of any criminal offence. Any order under the inherent jurisdiction does not do so. Rather, if the inherent

[43] ibid [145].

[44] Practice Guidance: *Placements in Unregistered Children's Homes in England or Unregistered Care Home Services in Wales* (November 2019).

[45] It was replaced by the far less extensive *Revised Practice Guidance on the Court's Approach to Unregistered Placements* (September 2023), which extols the court to 'restrict its considerations and orders to its own functions' (para 7). It limits the court's enquiry to asking the LA whether a proposed placement is registered or not and, if not, why an unregistered placement is in the child's best interests (para 8).

[46] Whereas Practice *Directions* are issued pursuant to s 81 of the Courts Act 2003 to supplement the Family Procedure Rules 2010, Practice *Guidance* is a newer creation with no obvious legal standing. David Burrows describes the entire category of President's Guidance as 'undemocratic': 'Practice Directions and President's Guidance' (4 November 2019), online at dbfamilylaw.wordpress.com/2019/11/04/practice-directions-and-presidents-guidance/ (accessed 1 June 2024), and D Burrows, '"Guidance" as Law' (25 March 2019), online at www.iclr.co.uk/blog/commentary/guidance-as-law/ (accessed 1 June 2024). See more general discussion in J Masson, 'Disruptive Judgments' [2017] *CFLQ* 401 and G Douglas and S Gilmore, 'The (Il)legitimacy of Guideline Judgments in Family Law: The Case for Foundational Principles' (2020) 31 *King's Law Journal* 88, focusing on concerns around using judgments to give practice guidance.

[47] *Re T* (n 11) [147].

[48] Even Practice *Directions* do not have force of law, and in so far as they are wrong in law, they carry no force at all: *Re NY (Abduction: Inherent Jurisdiction)* [2019] UKSC 49, [2019] 2 FLR 1247, [38]. This principle applies a fortiori to Practice Guidance.

> jurisdiction is used, then the court 'authorises' but does not 'require' the placement by a local authority of a child in an unregistered children's home despite the potential that a person may be prosecuted for and convicted of an offence under section 11 of the Care Standards Act 2000.[49]

This argument is unconvincing. It is obvious, when an LA applies for DOL authorisation, that the consequence is virtually certain to be that the child is, in fact, deprived of their liberty. No offence is committed unless a child is actually placed in the accommodation – and that cannot happen without court authorisation. The court is complicit in the criminal offence that inevitably flows from its decision, yet Lord Stephens seems to deny responsibility for this outcome.

10.19 Lady Arden's approach is even harder to understand. She said, 'In my judgment …, if section 11 had criminalised the *use* of unregistered homes, the court could not have exercised its inherent jurisdiction.'[50] Given that the Act criminalises a person who 'carries on or manages' an unregistered children's home, it follows that such homes cannot lawfully operate. It is therefore merely playing with words to say that the *use* of an unregistered home is not criminalised. A property only becomes a 'children's home' once it 'provides care and accommodation wholly or mainly for children',[51] so the offence occurs when a child is placed in the unregistered home. Until then, the property is not providing care and accommodation so, contrary to Lady Arden's suggestion, it is the *use* of unregistered children's homes that is forbidden by the Act (though only the operators of the home incur liability).

10.20 The Supreme Court's analysis of the criminality issue was therefore unconvincing. It is a remarkable feature of the inherent jurisdiction that it can apparently be used even when the consequence is to create a situation that Parliament has forbidden by way of criminal sanction.

Civil Restrictions

10.21 If criminal liability does not stop the inherent jurisdiction, can civil restrictions affect its use? Part of Lady Arden's judgment is relevant to this issue. Prior to the judgment in *Re T*, Parliament had passed new Regulations that prohibited LAs from placing children under the age of 16 in unregistered placements.[52] The Regulations were not yet in force when *Re T* was decided, but Lady Arden noted that she was proceeding 'on the basis that the Secretary of State is not asking the court to exercise its jurisdiction in this appeal to authorise the placement of a child

[49] *Re T* (n 11) [162].
[50] ibid [192] (original emphasis).
[51] Care Standards Act 2000, s 1(2).
[52] Care Planning, Placement and Case Review (England) (Amendment) Regulations 2021 (SI 2021/161).

under that age in an unregistered home'.[53] That assumption was quickly challenged in later litigation.[54]

10.22 The 2021 Regulations reference s 22C of the CA 1989, which addresses ways in which children looked after by LAs should be accommodated. If a looked-after child is not placed with their parents or another holder of parental responsibility, the LA 'must' (per sub-section (5)) choose the 'most appropriate' placement from four options listed in sub-section (6):

> (a) placement with an individual who is a relative, friend or other person connected with C and who is also a local authority foster parent;
> (b) placement with a local authority foster parent who does not fall within paragraph (a);
> (c) placement in a children's home in respect of which a person is registered under Part 2 of the Care Standards Act 2000 or Part 1 of the Regulation and Inspection of Social Care (Wales) Act 2016; or
> (d) … placement in accordance with other arrangements which comply with any regulations made for the purposes of this section.

Options (a) and (b) cannot amount to secure accommodation; (c) could be, but the 'bespoke' placements that cause particular concern would all fall under (d).

10.23 Against this background, r 27A of the 2021 Regulations provides:

> **27A Prohibition on placing a child under 16 in other arrangements**
>
> A responsible authority [i.e. the LA] may only place a child under 16 in accommodation in accordance with other arrangements under section 22C(6)(d), where the accommodation is—
>
> (a) in relation to placements in England, in—
>
> (i) a care home;
> (ii) a hospital …;
> (iii) a residential family centre …;
> (iv) a school … providing accommodation …;
> (v) an establishment that provides care and accommodation for children as a holiday scheme for disabled children …

There are equivalent provisions for placements in accommodation in Wales or Scotland. While the provisions themselves are complex, the purpose is clear: unregulated accommodation for children under 16 is prohibited. The LA may only place a child under 16 with their parents or other holder of PR; with an LA foster carer; in a children's home; or, if under s 22C(6)(d), in one of the five types of accommodation listed in r 27A.

10.24 This was Parliament's intention. During Committee scrutiny of the Regulations, the Minister, Michelle Donelan MP, stated that the Regulations

[53] *Re T* (n 11) [182].
[54] The following analysis draws from R George, 'Vulnerable Children in Unregulated Care: The Unstoppable Inherent Jurisdiction' (2021) 44 *JSWFL* 254.

'*ban the practice* of placing children under the age of 16 in unregulated independent and semi-independent settings'.[55] Likewise in the Lords Debates on the Regulation, Baroness Berridge spoke for the government in saying that 'Children should be placed in children's homes or foster care, which is why we have laid these regulations that will *ban the practice* of placing children under the age of 16 in unregulated independent and semi-independent settings'.[56] The Explanatory Memorandum to the Regulations states that the purpose of the Regulations is 'to ensure that looked after children under the age of 16 are *only* placed in children's homes or foster care'.[57] It continues:

> The effect of the amendments will be that looked after children under 16 *can no longer be placed in unregulated settings* .... Unregulated independent and semi-independent settings cannot meet the needs of looked after children under the age of 16 who are very vulnerable and often have complex needs which require the care and support provided by regulated settings.[58]

10.25 Once the Regulations entered force in September 2021, after the decision in *Re T*, the Court of Appeal came to consider them in *Derby CC v BA*.[59] The question, as formulated by MacDonald J at first instance, was 'whether it remains open to the High Court to authorise, under its inherent jurisdiction, the deprivation of liberty of a child under the age of 16 where the placement in which the restrictions that are the subject of that authorisation will be applied is prohibited by the terms of the amended statutory scheme'.[60]

10.26 Given the background as set out, the answer would appear to be straightforwardly 'no': Parliament specifically prohibited the placement of children under 16 in unregulated accommodation, so self-evidently the court cannot circumvent that prohibition by using its inherent jurisdiction to authorise the exact thing that Parliament has forbidden. However, that was not the answer reached by MacDonald J or by the Court of Appeal (McFarlane P, Baker and Simler LJJ).

10.27 The Regulation, as seen, is directed to the 'responsible authority', ie, the LA. The court took the view, therefore, that this prohibition did not affect its own powers – the court can make an order that leads to a breach of r 27A because, building on Lord Stephens' comments in *Re T*,[61] the court itself is not placing the child or *requiring* the child's placement in contravention of the Regulation; it is only *authorising* it. The court therefore could authorise such placements under the inherent jurisdiction. In so holding, the court effectively nullified the new Regulation, since the LA required the court's authorisation for secure

[55] Hansard, Delegated Legislation Committee, 20 July 2021 (emphasis added).
[56] Hansard, HL Deb, 22 March 2021, Vol 811, Col 701 (emphasis added).
[57] Explanatory Memorandum to the Care Planning, Placement and Case Review (England) (Amendment) Regulations 2021 (2021 No. 161), para 2.2 (emphasis added).
[58] bid para 6.7 (emphasis added).
[59] *Derby CC v BA* [2021] EWCA Civ 1867, [2022] Fam 351.
[60] [2021] EWHC 2472 (Fam), [1].
[61] *Re T* (n 11) [168].

accommodation in any event. But how can the LA act on that authorisation without itself breaching the Regulations?

10.28 McFarlane P's answer was that 'placement in an unregistered children's home is, and has always been, wholly outside the statutory scheme, and not therefore within s 22C(6)(d) [of the CA 1989]'.[62] Given that s 22C applies 'where a local authority are looking after a child' (which they undoubtedly are in all these cases) and the LA 'must' place the child in one of the listed types of placement, this is a dubious claim. While an unregulated placement may indeed be outside paragraph (d), the LA breach subsection (5) by placing a child in such accommodation. How can the court authorise a placement when the LA placing the child there would be contrary to the Act?

10.29 That leads to McFarlane P's second reason for concluding that the placement is nonetheless permissible, namely that the Supreme Court in *Re T* said so: 'All of the Justices agreed with Lady Black that, where it is necessary to do so to meet the overarching needs of the child (or to protect the safety of others), the inherent jurisdiction of the High Court must be available, notwithstanding that the underlying placement is prohibited by statute.'[63] This reasoning is problematic. First, Lady Arden expressly said that she was working on the basis that the new Regulation would change things.[64] More generally, the Supreme Court considered that a potential criminal offence committed *by a third party*, namely the private operator of an unregistered children's home, did not prevent the use of the inherent jurisdiction to authorise accommodation, in circumstances where it was clear that there was no direct limitation on the actions of the LA. Here, the Regulation explicitly limits *the LA's* ability to place a child in this way, and is described in the title to r 27A as a 'prohibition'. The court's authorisation cannot simply circumvent the statutory scheme. The wording of the Regulation, and Parliament's intention behind it, is clear: it is not permissible to place children under 16 in these unregulated placements, and the court's continued complicity in allowing the use of such placements is unacceptable.

ECHR Article 5

10.30 The final aspect of DOL to address is the requirement that it comply with Article 5 of the ECHR. Article 5(1)(d) states:[65]

> 1. Everyone has the right to liberty and security of person. No one shall be deprived of his liberty save in the following cases and in accordance with a procedure prescribed by law: …

[62] *Derby CC v BA* [2021] EWCA Civ 1867, [2022] Fam 351, [73].
[63] ibid [74].
[64] See **10.21**.
[65] Sub-paras (a), (b) and (c) relate to criminal law matters, and (f) concerns deportation or extradition, none of which is relevant here. Sub-para (e) is about mental health and infectious diseases, which

(d) the detention of a minor by lawful order for the purpose of educational supervision or his lawful detention for the purpose of bringing him before the competent legal authority; …

10.31 Article 5 is in 'the first rank of fundamental rights … and as such its importance is paramount'.[66] No DOL will be lawful unless it falls within one of the permissible grounds specified in subparagraphs (a)–(f); it is a closed list. Any DOL must be 'in accordance with a procedure prescribed by law', which must be sufficiently legally certain that it protects the individual from arbitrary state decision-making; it must be 'sufficiently accessible, precise and foreseeable'.[67] Provisions concerning the liberty of the individual should be clear, precise, governed by detailed rules, and subject to significant safeguards.[68]

10.32 These are precisely the qualities that s 25 of the CA 1989 and the accompanying Regulations have. There is a strict legal test for placing children in secure accommodation; rules govern the types of placements that can be used; the Secretary of State must approve accommodation; children under 13 cannot be placed in such accommodation save with the specific approval of the Secretary of State / Welsh Ministers; there is a duty on placements to give information to the relevant authority; there are maximum periods of authorisation on both first and subsequent orders; there is a duty to inform parents and other relevant individuals; specified people (at least one being independent of the LA) must be appointed to review the keeping of the child in the accommodation; a formal system of frequent reviews to monitor the deprivation of liberty exists; and records must be kept. By contrast, the inherent jurisdiction has none of these qualities. However, with the exception of Lady Arden (see below), the Supreme Court in *Re T* appeared unconcerned by Article 5.

10.33 When the state puts in place a system to deal with DOL, as it has with s 25, the ECHR requires that it put sufficient resources into that system to make it operate effectively in practice.[69] Using the inherent jurisdiction to authorise an *alternative* because the statutory system is inadequately resourced does not fulfil the requirement of the DOL being 'in accordance with the law'. There is a strong analogy with *DG v Ireland*,[70] which concerned whether DOL authorised by the Irish court's inherent jurisdiction met the requirements of Article 5 in

can be relevant, but is generally considered under the Mental Health Acts rather than the inherent jurisdiction in the child law context; for adults, see **13.17–13.19** and **14.52–14.62**.

[66] *Winterwerp v The Netherlands* (App No 6301/73) [1979] ECHR 4, [39].

[67] *Grabowski v Poland* (App No 57722/12) (2015) 68 EHRR 1129, [45]; see the summary in *R (Khan) v Secretary of State for Justice* [2020] EWHC 2084 (Admin), [2020] 1 WLR 3932 (Fulford LJ and Garnham J).

[68] See generally *J v Welsh Ministers (Mind intervening)* [2018] UKSC 66, [2020] AC 757, [27]–[28] (Lady Hale P).

[69] See *Bouamar v Belgium* (App No 9106/80) (1989) 11 EHRR 1.

[70] *DG v Ireland* (App No 39474/98) (2002) 35 EHRR 1153.

circumstances where the Irish state had set up a statutory system for penal detention of children. The European Court held that:

> If the Irish State chose a constitutional [statutory] system of educational supervision implemented through court orders to deal with juvenile delinquency, it was obliged to put in place appropriate institutional facilities which met the security and educational demands of that system in order to satisfy the requirements of art 5(1)(d).[71]

The fact that the alternative placements were authorised under the Irish court's inherent jurisdiction did not absolve the Irish state of its obligations under Article 5.

10.34 Lady Arden (who has sat as a Judge of the European Court of Human Rights) specifically reserved her position on this issue,[72] and was the only Justice to mention the appellant's reliance on *DG v Ireland*, commenting that '[i]t is not satisfactory that the courts should be used to address not just a specific gap but a systemic gap in the provision of care for children'.[73] Conversely, Lady Black's failure to engage with the issue gives context to her sweeping comment that '[o]nce a court order authorising the deprivation of liberty in this way [ie under the inherent jurisdiction] is made, I do not see how the deprivation can be said to be not in accordance with the domestic law for article 5 purposes'.[74] *DG v Ireland* says, precisely, that court authorisation per se is not enough to make a DOL be 'in accordance with the law', so her failure to consider it is extraordinary. The court also fails to join up the issues before it: how can the court's decision to rely on accommodation provided in such a way that a criminal offence is inevitably committed be said to be 'in accordance with the law'?

10.35 Lady Black went on to say that, since numerous High Court judgments authorised DOL under the inherent jurisdiction, '[t]he law as to the exercise of the inherent jurisdiction in this area is, in my view, sufficiently accessible and foreseeable with advice'.[75] This is a self-fulfilling argument (how did these cases begin?), but even Lady Black makes no claim that the law is 'precise', the other term used by the European Court. Under the inherent jurisdiction, there are no criteria at all before DOL can be authorised, other than the welfare of the child – an approach that lacks the precision required by the statutory criteria. Consequently, even if (which I rather doubt) the law is sufficiently accessible and foreseeable, there is no realistic argument that it is precise.

10.36 The Supreme Court's approach in *Re T* is concerningly complacent. A court process per se is not 'sufficiently accessible, precise and foreseeable'[76] for Article 5 and, as *DG v Ireland* shows, the requirements on the state can be

[71] ibid [79].
[72] *Re T* (n 11) [196].
[73] ibid [185].
[74] ibid [150].
[75] ibid [152].
[76] *Grabowski v Poland* (App No 57722/12) (2015) 68 EHRR 1129, [45].

heightened where there is a detailed statutory scheme in place to achieve the same outcome. That detailed statutory scheme is found in s 25 and the accompanying Regulations.[77] The fact that the scheme is inadequately resourced is a failure by the UK state, and for Article 5 purposes that failure is not 'made good' by the court purporting to authorise DOL in an alternative placement outside the statutory scheme.[78] These are not mere technical concerns. As a 'first rank' right, Article 5 reflects a fundamental protection that is guaranteed to every individual, and the court has overridden this protection in the context of some of society's most vulnerable children.

Conclusion

10.37 The underlying concerns that lead the court to rely on the inherent jurisdiction to deprive children of their liberty are of the utmost seriousness, and there are no easy answers. The court accepts that it 'cannot replicate the official safety net that the regulatory framework provides',[79] and that it 'is not a regulator and cannot inspect potential placements or oversee care regimes'.[80] Yet despite these serious shortcomings, the court has presumed to provide a long-term policy answer in an area that it is ill-equipped to regulate.

10.38 The court's view that the use of the inherent jurisdiction in this context is 'a temporary solution, developed by the courts in extremis'[81] is at best wishful thinking and at worst disingenuous. Given the lack of resources for statutory placements, DOL orders will be made under the inherent jurisdiction in the majority of cases[82] for the foreseeable future, and the orders in individual cases will neither be, nor feel, 'temporary'. The court knows little about the placements it is authorising, and following the 2023 *Revised Practice Guidance on the Court's Approach to Unregistered Placements*, the High Court will not even attempt to investigate – the court need not even take steps to ensure that placements are registered as children's homes, but should merely ask, if they are unregistered, why that placement is sought. The court's *decreasing* involvement in over-seeing these placements only increases the concern about their use.

[77] The fact that the court has now disregarded aspects of the Regulations when authorising placements under the inherent jurisdiction adds to the concern about failure to comply with Art 5: see **10.21** *et seq*.

[78] *Bouamar v Belgium* (App No 9106/80) (1989) 11 EHRR 1; *DG v Ireland* (App No 39474/98) (2002) 35 EHRR 1153.

[79] *Re T* (n 11) [142].

[80] *Re J (Deprivation of Liberty: Hospital)* [2022] EWHC 2687 (Fam), [36] (Poole J).

[81] *Re T* (n 11) [142].

[82] See **10.3**. The court thinks that its decision applies to 'a relatively narrow group of cases': *Re T* (n 11) [17].

10.39 Moreover, the underlying problems will not be addressed, in part because the court – driven by its *protective imperative*[83] – has removed the policy imperative for Parliament, government and LAs to address the systemic failings that lead to these cases. The protective imperative operates to allow the court to authorise what are actually impermissible and harmful placements, on the basis that there is 'no alternative'. But there is an alternative. As Lady Arden pointedly noted, 'it is not entirely clear to me from the Secretary of State's submissions why the Secretary of State cannot or cannot yet enable all children who need to do so to enjoy the security of a registered home'.[84] It is a policy choice not to make proper provision for these vulnerable children, and the court's complicity by invoking its inherent jurisdiction is inappropriate.

10.40 A better solution would have been for the court to set a time limit on how long it would permit this use of the inherent jurisdiction to continue. Giving the government a notice period – a year, say – would allow the immediate welfare of the individual children concerned to be safeguarded,[85] while making it clear that this problem requires a properly funded and coherent policy solution that the court cannot and should not seek to try to provide.[86]

[83] This rationale is explicit: 'It is such imperative considerations of necessity that have led me to conclude that the inherent jurisdiction must be available in these cases. There is presently no alternative that will safeguard the children who require its protection': *Re T* (n 11) [145].

[84] *Re T* (n 11) [185].

[85] *Cf* by analogy *Walden v Lichtenstein* (App No 33916/96), discussed in *R (Steinfeld) v Secretary of State for International Development* [2018] UKSC 32, [2020] AC 1, [43]–[44]: refusing to quash a discriminatory law pending amendment meets a legitimate aim of maintaining legal certainty while legislative reform is enacted.

[86] *Cf* **1.24**: this proposed approach 'recognise[s] the boundaries of [the court's] role and the need to accord proper respect to the respective roles of the other two branches of state': N Phillips, *The Lord Chief Justice's Review of the Administration of Justice in the Courts*, HC 448 (London: TSO, 2008), para 1.4.

11

Adoption and Surrogacy

11.1 Amongst the most significant legal consequences of invoking the inherent jurisdiction are those affecting parent-child relationships, seen in both adoption and surrogacy cases. Some instances appear to be legitimate examples of the inherent jurisdiction filling unintended legislative gaps. Others involve the court subverting core legislative principles and, beyond merely 'cutting across' a statutory scheme, show the inherent jurisdiction being used to override statutes.

Adoption

11.2 Adoption is a legal process that severs a child's legal relationship with their birth family[1] and creates a new legal relationship between the child and their adoptive parent(s) (and, by extension, the adoptive parents' wider family). An adopted child is deemed, in law, *always* to have been the child of the adoptive parent(s).[2] There is no statutory power to 'un-do' an adoption, save in one very limited situation;[3] the life-long status of parent and child created by adoption can only be removed if the child is adopted a second time.

11.3 Most children enter the adoption system following care proceedings, the birth family typically opposing the local authority ('LA') plan for adoption. The adoption process has two stages.[4] The first, previously known as 'freeing' the child for adoption, involves a 'placement order', allowing the LA to place the child in a suitable home pending adoption. After a placement order has been made, the Adoption and Children Act 2002 ('ACA 2002') allows a birth parent to oppose the adoption only in limited circumstances,[5] and the court will make a final adoption order where doing so is in the best interests of the child throughout their life.[6]

[1] Step-parent adoption is slightly different: the legal relationship with one birth parent is severed but the relationship with the other parent is unaffected and that parent's partner is added as the child's second legal parent.

[2] ACA 2002, s 67(1).

[3] ibid s 55: adoption in favour of one natural parent can be revoked if the child is 'legitimated' by the subsequent marriage or civil partnership of the child's natural parents.

[4] For detail, see R George, S Thompson and J Miles, *Family Law: Text, Cases, and Materials*, 5th edn (Oxford: OUP, 2023), ch 13.

[5] ACA 2002, s 24.

[6] ibid s 1(2).

11.4 Adoption is entirely regulated by statute;[7] there is no 'common law adoption', and the legislation is 'a self-contained statutory code' (as Wall J once put it).[8] It might therefore be thought that the statute is the beginning and the end of the court's powers in relation to adoption, but that is not so. There are several areas where the court has invoked its inherent jurisdiction.[9]

Recognition of Foreign Adoptions

11.5 Cases where a child is adopted in a foreign country fall into several categories.[10] Some are recognised *automatically* in English law, including what are termed 'Convention adoptions' (governed by the 1993 Hague Convention on Protection of Children and Co-operation in Respect of Intercountry Adoption) and 'overseas adoptions' (regulated by the Adoption (Recognition of Overseas Adoptions) Order 2013, which applies if the adoption took place in a listed country). Other foreign adoptions are not automatically recognised in English law; nevertheless, the ACA 2002 provides scope for a category of 'adoption recognised by the law of England and Wales and effected under the law of any other country'.[11]

11.6 There is no statutory mechanism for recognising foreign adoptions that are not 'Convention' or 'overseas adoptions'. Consequently, although most authorities make no express reference to the legal basis for the recognition, Cobb J must be right to say that the court relies in its inherent jurisdiction to determine these applications.[12]

11.7 The court's approach was summarised by Hedley J as a series of questions:

> first, was the adoption order obtained wholly lawfully in the foreign jurisdiction; secondly, if it was, did the concept of adoption in that jurisdiction substantially conform to the English concept; and thirdly, if so, is there any public policy consideration that should mitigate against recognition?[13]

[7] Adoption Act 1976; ACA 2002; CAA 2006.

[8] *Re C (Adoption: Freeing Order)* [1999] Fam 240, 253; *Re X and Y (Revocation of Adoption Orders)* [2024] EWHC 1059 (Fam), [74] (Lieven J).

[9] Under the pre-2002 legislation, the court used the inherent jurisdiction to make and vary contact orders in relation to children who had been placed for adoption, when the legislation did not provide any power to do so: see *Re C (Minors) (Contact: Jurisdiction)* [1996] Fam 79 (CoA). The court now has power to address this issue under ACA 2002, s 26.

[10] For an adoption taking place prior to the ACA 2002, the issue is governed by the Adoption Act 1976: see ACA 2002, s 66(2) and (3); *Re T and M (Adoption)* [2010] EWHC 964 (Fam), [2011] 1 FLR 1487, [11] (Hedley J).

[11] ACA 2002, s 66(1)(e).

[12] *Re G (Recognition of Brazilian Adoption)* [2014] EWHC 2605 (Fam), [2015] 1 FLR 1402, [3].

[13] *Re T and M (Adoption)* [2010] EWHC 964 (Fam), [2011] 1 FLR 1487, [12], summarising *Re Valentine's Settlement* [1965] 1 Ch 831 (CoA); see also *Re G (Recognition of Brazilian Adoption)* [2014] EWHC 2605 (Fam), [2015] 1 FLR 1402, [21].

Despite suggestions to the contrary,[14] the preponderance of authority suggests that there is no role for a separate welfare analysis conducted by the English court[15] – presumably on the basis that recognising an existing decision of foreign authorities is not in itself a 'decision relating to the adoption of a child'.[16] This is therefore an unusual example where the child's welfare is not the court's paramount consideration when making an inherent jurisdiction decision,[17] which raises questions about what principles actually apply to the decision-making process.

11.8 This limited role that the English court is performing in these cases is significant – the adoption has already happened; the decision whether to change the child's legal status and parentage has already been taken, and the English court is merely recognising that existing decision. Moreover, given that ACA 2002, s 66(1)(e) makes specific reference to foreign adoptions being *recognised* by English law, there is clear evidence that Parliament intended such recognition to occur. Absent any statutory power, there is clear implied justification for the court to use its inherent jurisdiction. This is a legislative gap where the inherent jurisdiction is appropriately deployed. However, a clear statutory power setting out the relevant requirements before recognition could be granted would be more satisfactory than the ad hoc process available under the inherent jurisdiction, particularly as the issue relates to the fundamental status of the parent-child relationship.

Revoking Placement Orders

11.9 The inherent jurisdiction has been deployed to *revoke a placement order*, previously termed a freeing order. Under the pre-2002 legislation, if a mother signed a declaration stating that she did not wish to be consulted further about her child's future, she could not then apply to revoke the freeing order. In *Re C (Adoption: Freeing Order)*,[18] it became clear that no final adoption order would be made and that it would be in the child's interests for the freeing order to be revoked. However, because of the mother's signed declaration, the statutory provisions prevented her (or anyone else) from applying to revoke the freeing order. Wall J held that it could not have been Parliament's intention to leave a child in 'adoption limbo', and '[a]ccordingly it is … open to me to exercise the inherent jurisdiction to fill the gap and to protect [the child] by acting in what is plainly in

[14] See, eg, *A County Council v M and Others (No 4) (Foreign Adoption: Refusal of Recognition)* 2013] EWHC 1501 (Fam), [2014] 1 FLR 881, [85] (Jackson J); *S v S (No 3) (Foreign Adoption Order: Recognition)* [2016] EWHC 2470 (Fam), [2017] Fam 167 (MacDonald J).

[15] See, eg, *Re G (Recognition of Brazilian Adoption)* [2014] EWHC 2605 (Fam), [2015] 1 FLR 1402, [22] (Cobb J); *Re N (A Child) (Secretary of State for the Home Department intervening)* [2016] EWHC 3085 (Fam), [2018] Fam 117, [129] (Munby P).

[16] ACA 2002, s 1(7) gives guidance on the meaning of 'coming to a decision', but the recognition of an existing foreign order is not specified; the issue could be argued either way.

[17] See **3.7**.

[18] *Re C (Adoption: Freeing Order)* [1999] Fam 240.

his best interests by discharging the freeing order'.[19] This approach was followed in other cases.[20] Though viewed by some as a pragmatic solution to an unsatisfactory statutory position,[21] Robin Spon-Smith suggested that this use of the inherent jurisdiction amounted to judicial legislation and was therefore wrong.[22]

11.10 The approach taken in *Re C* remains available,[23] though the circumstances in which it would be required were significantly reduced by the ACA 2002, since anyone can now seek leave to apply to revoke a placement order.[24] In cases where the original order was made in the Family Court, there is also a statutory power under s 31F(6) of the Matrimonial and Family Proceedings Act 1984 to 'rescind' any order made by it.[25] Given the statutory changes with the 2002 Act, and the general power available under the 1984 Act, it is hard to see circumstances where using the inherent jurisdiction in this context would now be justified.

Revoking Final Adoption Orders

11.11 By far the most controversial use of the inherent jurisdiction in the adoption context is the claim that the court can use it to *un-do an adoption order* that has been fully made and implemented. The starting point is that, other than in one extremely limited situation,[26] there is no statutory power to revoke an adoption order;[27] the only way to dissolve the parent-child relationship created by adoption is to make a further adoption order.

11.12 This fundamental aspect of adoption is illustrated by *Re B (Adoption: Jurisdiction to Set Aside)*.[28] A child born to a Roman Catholic mother and a Muslim father was mistakenly adopted by a Jewish couple. Relying on this fundamental mistake about his racial and ethnic origins, the child sought the adoption to be set aside under the court's inherent jurisdiction. The Court of Appeal refused the application, describing it as facing 'insurmountable hurdles'.[29] While the court

[19] ibid 257.

[20] See *Re J (Freeing for Adoption)* [2000] 2 FLR 58 (Black J); *Oldham MBC v D* [2000] 2 FLR 382 (Bracewell J).

[21] C Bridge, 'Adoption – Re C (Adoption: Freeing Order)' [1999] *Family Law* 11.

[22] R Spon-Smith, 'The Inherent Jurisdiction and Revocation of Freeing Orders' [2000] *Family Law* 43.

[23] See, eg, *A City Council v C* [2013] 2 EWHC 8 (Fam), [2013] 1 WLR 3009 (King J).

[24] ACA 2002, s 24(1).

[25] On the approach to s 31F(6), see *Re A and B (Rescission of Order: Change of Circumstances)* [2021] EWFC 76, [2022] 1 FLR 1143, esp [39] (Cobb J), approved in *Cazalet v Abu-Zalaf* [2023] EWCA Civ 1065, [24]; *cf* fn 27 on the position regarding final adoption orders, which raises some doubt about this point as well.

[26] ACA 2002, s 55: child adopted by a sole natural parent who subsequently marries the other natural parent. The existence of this exception 'shows that Parliament did consider the issue of revocation when making this ACA, but only created this one, very narrow, ground for revocation': *Re X and Y (Revocation of Adoption Orders)* [2024] EWHC 1059 (Fam), [29] (Lieven J).

[27] Lieven J rejected the suggestion that Matrimonial and Family Proceedings Act 1984, s 31F(6), noted at **11.10**, could be used to revoke a final adoption order: *Re X and Y*, ibid [89]–[92].

[28] *Re B (Adoption: Jurisdiction to Set Aside)* [1995] Fam 239 (CoA).

[29] ibid 245.

noted that there were examples of adoptions being set aside on the basis of procedural irregularities, it was not possible to set aside an adoption based on mistake of fact, no matter how fundamental:

> There is no case which has been brought to our attention in which it has been held that the court has an inherent power to set aside an adoption order by reason of a misapprehension or mistake. To allow considerations such as those put forward in this case to invalidate an otherwise properly made adoption order would … undermine the whole basis on which adoption orders are made, namely that they are final and for life as regards the adopters, the natural parents, and the child. … [I]t would gravely damage the lifelong commitment of adopters to their adoptive children if there is a possibility of the child, or indeed the parents, subsequently challenging the validity of the order. I am satisfied that there is no inherent power in the courts in circumstances such as arise in this case to set aside an adoption order.[30]

This statement of principle appears uncompromising: despite the context of 'misapprehension or mistake', the court's conclusion is framed more broadly, namely that it does not have an inherent jurisdiction to allow adoptions to be undone.[31]

11.13 However, although the court purports to apply the principles from *Re B*, there has been a marked change of approach. First, the court is increasingly willing to allow appeals long out of time,[32] in cases where there are 'highly exceptional circumstances' such as 'a fundamental breach of natural justice';[33] these cases focus on procedural errors, and are not my concern.[34] More problematic is a second group of cases where, in direct contradiction to *Re B*, the court has held that it can use its inherent jurisdiction to undo an adoption.

11.14 The subsequent authorities start with *Re W (Inherent Jurisdiction: Permission Application: Revocation and Adoption Order)*, where Bodey J cited *Re B* as authority for the proposition that 'the inherent jurisdiction can be used for revocation, but only in exceptional circumstances'.[35] This proposition entirely re-wrote *Re B*, which went from being clear, binding authority that the court did *not* have an inherent jurisdiction to revoke an adoption order, to being used as authority for the opposite proposition. The second and third sentences of the passage from *Re B* quoted above were cited in *Re W*, but not the first or the fourth. In other words, the cautionary reasons were included, but the actual legal principle was omitted. Bodey J refused the application on its facts, but his decision was picked up in *PK v Mr and Mrs K*.[36]

[30] ibid 249 (Swinton Thomas LJ).

[31] See also *Webster v Norfolk CC* [2009] EWCA Civ 59, [2009] 1 FLR 1378; *Re PW (Adoption)* [2013] 1 FLR 96 (Parker J).

[32] This is the preferred approach when there is a challenge to the original process that led to the adoption order: *Re J (Adoption: Appeal)* [2018] EWFC 8, [2018] 4 WLR 38 (Cobb J).

[33] *AX v SX (Adoption: Revocation)* [2021] EWHC 1121, [2021] 4 WLR 80, [80].

[34] See generally P Morgan, 'Three Groups of Revocation Cases' (2020) 42 *JSWFL* 246.

[35] *Re W (Inherent Jurisdiction: Permission Application: Revocation and Adoption Order)* [2013] EWHC 1957 (Fam), [2013] 2 FLR 1609, [6].

[36] *PK v Mr and Mrs K* [2015] EWHC 2316 (Fam), [2016] 2 FLR 576 (Pauffley J).

11.15 The application to revoke the adoption in *PK* was made by the child herself, a 14-year-old girl who had been adopted ten years earlier. Two years after the adoption, she was sent to live abroad with extended family where she was seriously abused. Later, she was reunited with her birth mother and grandmother. She applied to make herself a ward of court, and her birth mother was given interim care and control.[37] Pauffley J subsequently revoked the adoption order using the inherent jurisdiction. The judge did not refer to *Re B* directly, only to the misleading extract quoted in *Re W* which omitted the core legal principles. The respondents did not engage with the case, and the court did not appoint an advocate to the court or invite the Attorney General to intervene, so the issue was also not the subject of argument. Polly Morgan describes *PK* as an 'outlier' because, unlike other cases where adoptions have been set aside, there were no factors that undermined the basis for the original order.[38] While I agree with that, for my purposes the bigger issue is the legal vehicle used to achieve the outcome. The court disregarded clear Court of Appeal authority, creating for itself a power not provided for by statute to overturn a statutory adoption. The statutory provisions on adoption plainly constitute a complete statutory code; it is extraordinary for the court to consider that it can step in and change the statutory rules under the inherent jurisdiction.

11.16 Despite these concerns, the general approach in *PK* became enmeshed in subsequent cases. Munby P relied on *PK* and *Re W* to assert that '[u]nder the inherent jurisdiction, the High Court can, in an appropriate case, revoke an adoption order'.[39] The Court of Appeal has also approved a summary of the applicable principles given by MacDonald J, which included the statement that 'the court's discretion under the inherent jurisdiction to revoke a lawfully made adoption order is severely curtailed and can only be exercised in highly exceptional and very particular circumstances'.[40] Baker LJ held that 'the better course' was 'to file a notice of appeal seeking permission to appeal within the time period prescribed in the rules rather than bring an application at a later date under the inherent jurisdiction to revoke the order',[41] but accepted that the inherent jurisdiction was a viable legal mechanism to set aside an adoption.[42]

[37] A child arrangements order would have sufficed, giving the birth mother parental responsibility for PK as well: CA 1989, s 12(2). There is no discussion of why wardship was required, nor why it was continued by the court.

[38] Morgan (n 34) 247.

[39] *Re O (A Child) (Human Fertilisation and Embryology Act: Adoption Revocation)* [2016] EWHC 2273 (Fam), [2016] 4 WLR 148, [27(i)]. Munby P specifically rejected Parker J's view in *Re PW (Adoption)* [2013] 1 FLR 96 that the only way to challenge an adoption was by way of an appeal out of time.

[40] *HX v A Local Authority* [2020] EWHC 1287 (Fam), [2021] 1 FLR 82, [38(iii)], approved by *Re I-A (Children) (Revocation of Adoption Order)* [2021] EWCA Civ 1222, [2021] 4 WLR 139, [15] (Baker LJ).

[41] *Re I-A*, ibid [27].

[42] See also *AX v SX (Adoption: Revocation)* [2021] EWHC 1121 (Fam), [2021] 4 WLR 80 (Theis J).

11.17 These cases are highly concerning. Adoption is a permanent, fundamental change of a person's legal identity, and yet, as Morgan argues, the authorities on revocation under the inherent jurisdiction reveal 'no single unifying thread other than exceptionality – and exceptionality as an argument can only go so far when the cases start to stack up'.[43] Exceptionality should describe a pattern of outcomes rather than purportedly being used as a test in its own right,[44] because without more 'exceptionality' contains no principled guidance and therefore lacks predictive quality. Possible though it may be to sympathise with the applicants in these cases, the court is ill-equipped to identify principles that might govern the question of when adoptions should be set aside. That is a policy decision requiring broader input from more stakeholders than a court can get in individual cases. This failure to be able to identify the principles applicable in these cases is a common feature of the court's (mis-)use of its inherent jurisdiction when it strays into novel areas.[45]

11.18 Aside from the question of the basis on which the power should be exercised, a more fundamental issue is whether the inherent jurisdiction power to revoke adoption orders exists at all. The current approach is underpinned by a fundamental error that has been built upon and restated so as to introduce a major change in the law. The court has claimed for itself a hugely significant power that Parliament chose not to grant it, in doing so both cutting across a statutory scheme and disregarding precedent. Notably, Lieven J reached the same conclusion in *Re X and Y (Revocation of Adoption Orders)*, holding that there is no power under the inherent jurisdiction to order the revocation of adoptions on the basis of the children's best interests.[46] *Re X and Y* is an unusual example of judicial restraint, and even retrenchment, in the use of the inherent jurisdiction. Lieven J relied explicitly on the *De Keyser* principle,[47] holding that the ACA 2002 is 'a comprehensive scheme, which covers the entire process of legal adoption' and, crucially, one which expressly considered the role for revocation within the statutory scheme.[48] At time of going to press, this decision was under appeal, so it remains to be seen whether Lieven J's reasoning will be upheld by the Court of Appeal.

11.19 Given the permanent and irrevocable nature of adoption, it is also not clear why the inherent jurisdiction should be able to change legal parentage in this context (and, as seen below, in surrogacy cases[49]), but not others. Can a child use the inherent jurisdiction to cause themselves to be legally 'orphaned' on similar

[43] Morgan (n 34) 248.

[44] See *Re W (Abuse: Oral Evidence)* [2010] UKSC 12, [2010] 1 WLR 701, [30] (Lady Hale); *Manchester CC v Pinnock* [2010] UKSC 45, [2011] 2 AC 104, [51] (Lord Neuberger); *Re A, B and C (Adoption: Notification of Fathers and Relatives)* [2020] EWCA Civ 41, [2020] Fam 325, [89(7)] (Jackson LJ).

[45] See also **15.20–15.23**.

[46] *Re X and Y (Revocation of Adoption Orders)* [2024] EWHC 1059 (Fam), [73].

[47] ibid [80]; see **3.37** *et seq*.

[48] ibid [81].

[49] See **11.25–11.27**.

facts to *PK*, but where the birth parents had since died? Or where no adoption took place and the breakdown of the parent-child relationship is within the birth family? Can parents seek such an order? The instinctive answer to all these examples is 'no', but it is not clear what the difference of principle is. True, the adopted child regains the legal parentage of the birth parents, but it is worth noting that those parents were deemed so unsuitable that adoption was ordered in the first place (and regarding surrogacy the situation is different again, as below). This analogy serves to cast further doubt on the existence and scope of the inherent jurisdiction to revoke adoption orders.

Surrogacy

11.20 A surrogacy arrangement involves a child being carried during pregnancy by a woman (the surrogate), with the intention that the child will be raised not by her but by the 'intended parent(s)'. Under the current law,[50] the surrogate is automatically the child's legal mother at birth (and if she is married, her spouse will usually be the other legal parent); the intended parent(s) must apply for a *parental order* ('PO') after the child's birth to extinguish the surrogate's legal parenthood and recognise their own. Drawing on adoption orders, a PO terminates all the child's existing legal parental relationships and vests legal parenthood and PR in the intended parent(s).[51] The law is set out in s 54 / 54A of the Human Fertilisation and Embryology Act 2008 ('HFEA 2008').[52] Under a PO, the child is 'treated in law as the child of the applicants',[53] as if originally born to the intended parents.[54] Various requirements must be met,[55] though the court has 'stretched and manipulated' the statutory wording (in Claire Fenton-Glynn's words[56]) to allow POs to be made in cases where many of the requirements, strictly interpreted, are not satisfied.

11.21 Despite this broad approach, there are requirements within the HFEA 2008 that the court cannot override – including the need for the surrogate to consent to the making of the order,[57] the need for the applicants to be in a continuing relationship with one another at the time of the application,[58] and the need for

[50] See George, Thompson and Miles (n 4) 657–671.
[51] HFEA 2008, s 55; Human Fertilisation and Embryology (Parental Order) Regulations (SI 2018/1412), Sch 1.
[52] S 54 applies to applications by couples, while s 54A is for applications by single people.
[53] HFEA 2008, s 54(1) / 54A(1).
[54] ACA 2002, s 67 (applied to surrogacy by Human Fertilisation and Embryology (Parental Order) Regulations (SI 2010/985), Sch 1, para 12).
[55] HFEA 2008, s 54(1)–(8A) / s 54A(1)–(8).
[56] C Fenton-Glynn, 'The Regulation and Recognition of Surrogacy Under English Law: An Overview of the Case Law' [2015] *CFLQ* 83, 83.
[57] *Re C (Surrogacy: Consent)* [2023] EWCA Civ 16, [2023] 2 FLR 109.
[58] *AB v CD (Surrogacy)* [2018] EWHC 1590 (Fam), (2018) 167 NLJ 7800.

at least one of the applicants to be domiciled in the UK.[59] Against this background, two situations have arisen where the court has used its inherent jurisdiction. The first is in cases where the statutory criteria for a PO are not met, and the second is to revoke POs that have already been made.

Surrogacy Outside the Statutory Scheme

11.22 If the court cannot make a PO, the intended parents have limited options. The only other mechanism to change legal parentage is adoption, the criteria for which may or may not be met on the facts of the case;[60] but even when adoption is available, the court suggests that adoption is 'not an attractive solution' because in every surrogacy at least one of the intended parents must be the biological parent of the child already.[61] Alternatively, the court can make private law orders under the Children Act 1989 ('CA 1989'). Private law orders cannot change legal parentage, but can: (i) order that the child lives with the intended parents,[62] which automatically grants them PR for the child,[63] and (ii) restrict the ability of the surrogate (and her partner, if applicable) to exercise any aspect of their PR.[64] However, the court's default reaction in these cases is not to rely on the CA 1989 alone, but to make orders under its inherent jurisdiction (sometimes in combination with s 8 orders).

11.23 The court makes use of wardship and inherent jurisdiction powers both as interim measures[65] and for final orders. In *JP v LP (Surrogacy Arrangement: Wardship)*,[66] King J endorsed an approach of making s 8 orders and also making the child a ward of court for the remainder of their minority: 'given the wholly exceptional circumstances of this case, wardship is the most appropriate way in

[59] *Y v Z* [2017] EWFC 60.

[60] Particular challenges arise from ACA 2002, ss 83 (restriction on bringing a child into the UK for the purposes of adoption) and 95 (restrictions on making payments in relation to adoption). See also *Re Z (Surrogacy: Step-Parent Adoption)* [2024] EWFC 20, refusing step-parent adoption for an intended parent where a PO was not available.

[61] *Re X (A Child) (Parental Order: Time Limit)* [2014] EWHC 3135 (Fam), [2015] Fam 186, [7] (Munby P). Query why the legal fiction of adoption is more undesirable than the alternative, which is that the child remains legally unrelated to the intended parent(s) at all.

[62] CA 1989, s 8 (child arrangements orders).

[63] CA 1989, s 10(2).

[64] The court can use specific issue orders and prohibited steps orders to provide that surrogate cannot exercise any aspect of PR, and that the intended parents can make all decisions about the child using their PR: see, by analogy, cases like *Re B and C (Change of Names: Parental Responsibility: Evidence)* [2017] EWHC 3250 (Fam), [2018] 4 WLR 19 (Cobb J). The court cannot revoke PR from the surrogate, nor from her partner if they were married or in a civil partnership: *Re A (Parental Responsibility)* [2023] EWCA Civ 689, [2024] 1 FLR 1.

[65] See, eg, *Re A (A Child: Surrogacy: Section 54 Criteria)* [2020] EWHC 1426 (Fam), [2021] 1 FLR 357: final orders were made under s 54, with no explanation why wardship was used on an interim basis.

[66] On the facts, the court would now make a parental order: *Re X (A Child) (Parental Order: Time Limit)* [2014] EWHC 3135 (Fam), [2015] Fam 186 (Munby P).

which to manage the overall use of parental responsibility as between the father, the legal mother and the psychological mother of this child'.[67] Quite what wardship added to this case is unclear. King J noted that the CA 1989 incorporated the key features of wardship and that she could use prohibited steps orders 'to regulate the use made by the surrogate mother of her parental responsibility',[68] but did not explain why this approach was inadequate.[69] Warding the child also technically introduced a (presumably unwanted) requirement to get the High Court's endorsement of any significant decision about the child's upbringing.[70]

11.24 Invoking wardship or the inherent jurisdiction in these cases has no discernible benefit. The failure to explain the value of wardship in the cases is particularly notable when other judges, finding themselves unable to make a PO, have simply used the CA 1989's private law provisions.[71] The statutory powers under the CA 1989 are entirely adequate to these cases, and avoid the unfortunate consequence of technically being required to obtain court authorisation in relation to significant decisions about the child's upbringing.

Revoking Parental Orders

11.25 The HFEA 2008 provides no mechanism to revoke a PO. However, in *G v G (Parental Order: Revocation)*,[72] Hedley J held that the inherent jurisdiction could be used to do just that.

11.26 Having obtained a PO, the intended parents' relationship soon ended. Contact between the father and the child was restricted by the mother, with whom the child was living; the father, who was the child's biological parent, applied for the PO to be revoked. If a revocation order was granted, the father would remain the child's legal father by virtue of his genetic connection, but the intended mother would become a legal stranger to the child. The father argued that the intended mother had deceived him, the surrogate and the court when the PO was made because she had already decided to end her relationship with him, but concealed her intentions in order to secure the PO. He therefore contended that the PO had been made on a false premise, and that he would have opposed the PO had he known the truth. Hedley J refused the application but, applying the case law on revocation of adoption orders by analogy,[73] held that there was a power under the

[67] ibid [37].
[68] ibid.
[69] See similarly *Re D (A Child)* [2014] EWHC 2121 (Fam), [27] (Moylan J); *AB v CD (Surrogacy)* [2018] EWHC 1590 (Fam), (2018) 167 NLJ 7800, [73] (Keehan J).
[70] See **3.15–3.17**.
[71] See, eg, *A and B v X and Z* [2016] EWFC 34 (Russell J); *F v S (Foreign Surrogacy: Parental Responsibility)* [2016] EWFC 70 (Theis J).
[72] *G v G (Parental Order: Revocation)* [2012] EWHC 1979 (Fam), [2013] 1 FLR 286 (Hedley J).
[73] See **11.11** *et seq.*

inherent jurisdiction to revoke a PO. *G v G* does not appear to have been applied in any other cases, although Munby P twice cited it with apparent approval, once in relation to the court's powers in surrogacy cases generally,[74] and once regarding adoption revocation.[75]

11.27 As with adoption, the court's claim to have power to revoke an order made by statutory power, when the statute itself makes no such provision, is remarkable. The analysis builds on the adoption cases, but in some ways the idea of revoking a PO is more extreme. Whereas birth parents in adoption cases may be happy to regain parental status and PR over 'their' child, the position of the surrogate (and possibly her partner) is very different. Typically, surrogates never intend to be the child's (legal) parent, and so the idea that she might have legal parenthood 'restored' to her is extraordinary. The court might therefore conclude that the circumstances leading to a PO simply do not lend themselves to post-order revocation. Again, the court is ill-equipped to embark on policy-making in this area, and the inability to identify what principles might apply shows that the court should not be using its inherent jurisdiction in this way.

Conclusion

11.28 The use of the inherent jurisdiction in adoption and surrogacy cases is particularly striking because, in both instances, the court is creating powers that alter perhaps the most fundamental part of a child's social and legal identity: legal parents and lineage.

11.29 The recognition of foreign adoptions is justified because the court is merely declaring what has already taken place abroad to be legally effective here, and the ACA 2002 envisages that there should be such a power. In principle, it may be justified for the court to be able to undo a freeing / placement order if no adoption is going to take place, but the court's existing statutory power under the Matrimonial and Family Proceedings Act 1984, s 31F(6) is adequate to do this for any order made by the Family Court, so the inherent jurisdiction is not needed.

11.30 But more troubling is the court's view – with the exception of *Re X and Y*[76] – that it can undo substantive orders for adoption or surrogacy after they have been made. It is concerning enough that the authorities so markedly fail to follow precedent. More fundamentally, Parliament set out detailed statutory schemes giving the court powers to make changes to life-long parent-child relationships by way of

[74] *Re X (A Child) (Parental Order: Time Limit)* [2014] EWHC 3135 (Fam), [2015] Fam 186, [54].
[75] See *Re O (A Child) (Human Fertilisation and Embryology Act: Adoption Revocation)* [2016] EWHC 2273 (Fam), [2016] 4 WLR 148, [26].
[76] *Re X and Y (Revocation of Adoption Orders)* [2024] EWHC 1059 (Fam); see **11.18**.

adoption and parental orders, and chose not to provide any power to undo them once made. The creation of such a power under the inherent jurisdiction goes beyond the appropriate constitutional role of judges,[77] cutting across a statutory scheme and thereby, at least implicitly, contradicting parliamentary will. Further, the court's inability to identify any meaningful principles that apply in revocation of adoption and PO cases, other than 'exceptionality', highlights the unsuitability of judges to the process of policy-making via the inherent jurisdiction.

[77] See **1.22–1.27**.

12

Miscellaneous Uses of the Inherent Jurisdiction in Relation to Children

12.1 This chapter addresses miscellaneous uses of the inherent jurisdiction. The overall themes are similar. There are occasions where there seems genuinely to be no alternative to the inherent jurisdiction, and where its use fits with both the court's protective imperative and 'goes with the grain' of general legislation.[1] However, many of the uses of the inherent jurisdiction are more questionable, cutting across statutory schemes and extending the court's power beyond the limitations imposed by Parliament.

Undesirable Associations

12.2 Attempts to protect children from undesirable associations using wardship or the broader inherent jurisdiction have a long history.[2] Hale LJ set out the historic and modern uses, observing that 'the inherent jurisdiction has long been used to protect children from undesirable associations, traditionally with fortune hunters and more recently with paedophiles, drug pushers and pimps'.[3] While comparatively rare, these orders are the second listed use of the inherent jurisdiction in Practice Direction 12D – Inherent Jurisdiction (Including Wardship) Proceedings.[4]

12.3 The protections in question have two forms. The first is to ward the child. Historically, one consequence of wardship was that the ward could not be married without court consent.[5] That prohibition is now irrelevant since no minor can lawfully be married,[6] so any value of wardship in such cases is doubtful. The second protection, more commonly seen, involves injunctive orders against the person considered to be an undesirable associate, prohibiting them from seeing

[1] *Ghaidan v Godin-Mendoza* [2004] UKHL 30, [2004] 2 AC 557, [33]; see **1.22–1.27**.
[2] See, eg, *Iredell v Iredell* (1885) 1 TLR 260 (HC).
[3] *Re S (A Child) (Identification: Restriction on Publication)* [2003] EWCA Civ 963, [2004] Fam 43, [24].
[4] Para 1.2(b).
[5] N Lowe and R White, *Wards of Court*, 2nd edn (London: Barry Rose, 1986), paras 2.1–2.2.
[6] Marriage and Civil Partnership (Minimum Age) Act 2022.

or contacting the child, or restricting their movements to keep them away from the child.

12.4 How effective these protections are is questionable.[7] One example illustrating the potential futility is *Re R (A Minor) (Contempt)*.[8] A man in his 30s was committed to prison for contempt on two occasions for breaching inherent jurisdiction injunctions prohibiting him from having contact with a 14-year-old girl, who was also a ward of court. His breaches included, after the first period of imprisonment, spending multiple nights with the girl and impregnating her – a sign that the court's injunctions did little to protect her.

12.5 In some cases, the conduct of the associate is unlawful, as in *Re R*, such that remedies might be available other than the inherent jurisdiction – involving the police, or seeking an injunction under the Protection from Harassment Act 1997, for example. In other cases, no criminal activity is taking place, yet the child is thought to be at risk.[9] As Hale LJ noted, the court has under its inherent jurisdiction 'a power to protect children from the otherwise lawful activities of third parties which goes beyond anything which parents could achieve'.[10]

12.6 Recently, the court has used the inherent jurisdiction to protect vulnerable young people (mostly girls) who have been the victims of sexual exploitation by gangs of men. In *Birmingham CC v Riaz*,[11] the local authority ('LA') obtained injunctive orders against various named individuals whom the High Court found to have sexually exploited a 17-year-old girl, AB. AB did not consider herself to be a victim, but she consented to the making of a secure accommodation order under s 25 of the CA 1989.[12] The police considered that there was no realistic prospect of successful prosecutions against the men, and the LA took what Keehan J described as 'a bold and novel step' in seeking inherent jurisdiction injunctions to protect AB.[13] Having concluded that the remedies sought by the LA could not be obtained by using statutory powers, the judge granted injunctions to prevent child sexual exploitation, holding this remedy to be at 'the heart of the *parens*

[7] In 1967, Cross J wrote extra-judicially that 'the court can achieve little or nothing' in cases where the young person favoured the association: G Cross, 'Wards of Court' (1967) 83 *LQR* 200, 202; see also J Mitchell, 'Whatever Happened to Wardship? Part II' [2001] *Family Law* 212, 213.

[8] *Re R (A Minor) (Contempt)* [1994] 2 FLR 185 (CoA). See also *Re H (A Minor) (Guardian Ad Litem: Requirement)* [1994] Fam 11 (Booth J): a 15-year-old boy developed what the judge called a 'morally unhealthy' relationship with his dance teacher; injunctions were eventually discharged as they were ineffective.

[9] See, eg, *Kelly v British Broadcasting Corporation* [2001] 1 FLR 197 (Munby J): wardship used to protect a teenage boy who had run away from home to join a religious cult.

[10] *Re S (A Child) (Identification: Restriction on Publication)* [2003] EWCA Civ 963, [2004] Fam 43, [24].

[11] *Birmingham CC v Riaz* [2014] EWHC 4247 (Fam), [2015] 2 FLR 763.

[12] See generally **ch 10**.

[13] [2014] EWHC 4247 (Fam), [2015] 2 FLR 763, [7]. *Cf Rotherham MBC v M* [2016] EWHC 2660 (Fam), [2017] 2 FLR 366 (Cobb J).

patriae jurisdiction of the High Court'.[14] Notably, the police could have obtained a *sexual risk order* under s 122A of the Sexual Offences Act 2003 (which prohibits the named person from doing, or requires them to do, anything specified in the order, and can be issued without the person having been convicted of any offence), but had not done so.[15] At the time, therefore, the inherent jurisdiction was the only available option. It is possible that the court could now make an injunction under the Domestic Abuse Act 2021: AB was aged 16 or over[16] and had been in an 'intimate personal relationship' with the named men;[17] the LA would likely be granted permission to bring an application,[18] and AB's opposition to the making of the order would be a factor to consider but would not prevent the order being made.[19] Had AB been under 16, though, that remedy would not be available; the lack of any civil injunction in such cases is a significant omission, at least potentially justifying the use of the inherent jurisdiction. However, Parliament's decision to make orders under the 2021 Act's remedies available only to those over the age of 16 is a reason to think that there was a policy decision to exclude younger children (perhaps on the basis that such children can be protected by parental intervention or, failing that, through care proceedings).

12.7 However, the orders in *Riaz* went beyond merely protecting AB. More controversially, they also prevented the named men from approaching *any female* under the age of 18 not already associated with them in a public place. This final provision was considered by Hayden J in *Redbridge LBC v A*, who declined to follow *Riaz*.[20] *Redbridge* concerned a man who had been found to have systematically groomed and later raped his step-daughter. The step-daughter was protected by existing orders but the man posed a risk to other girls – the LA sought to restrain him from contacting, approaching, being in the company of, or residing in the same home as, any female under 18 years of age. Hayden J refused the application, holding that the inherent jurisdiction could be used to protect only to an identified or known child who was the subject of proceedings.

12.8 Two points arise. First, inherent jurisdiction proceedings are essentially private law cases, so it is problematic to suggest that the inherent jurisdiction can perform a public protection role. As Hayden J concluded, its function is to protect the subject child; wider risks posed by respondents to those proceedings need to be addressed by the police or other public processes. Second, there may be other legal remedies available, whether in the criminal, family or civil court;[21] the court

[14] ibid [46].
[15] Of course, that remedy would be no use in a case where the issue was not sexual exploitation but was, for example, involvement with a drugs gang.
[16] DAA 2021, s 33(1).
[17] ibid s 1(1)(e).
[18] ibid s 28(2)(d).
[19] ibid s 33(1)(b) and s 33(3).
[20] *Redbridge LBC v A* [2015] EWHC 2140 (Fam), [2015] Fam 335.
[21] ibid [47]–[48], referring to a *sexual risk order* under Sexual Offences Act 2003, s 122A; see also now remedies under the DAA 2021.

should bear in mind the general principle that the inherent jurisdiction should be used only when no suitable statutory remedy exists.

12.9 The importance of this second point was underlined in *Re T (A Child) (Non-Molestation Order)*.[22] The child was placed in long-term foster care under a care order. The child's mother made several attempts to abduct the child from his carers, and the LA sought inherent jurisdiction injunctions to prevent her going to specified locations. The judge granted the applications, but the Court of Appeal reversed that decision and made non-molestation orders in their place.[23] While the application itself had been appropriate, the court could resolve the issue by making a statutory order of its own motion.[24] The conduct of the mother was within the definition of 'molestation', and the statutory injunction had the further advantage that breach automatically amounts to a criminal offence.

12.10 These cases represent an old usage of wardship and the inherent jurisdiction being repurposed by the court to address modern problems. While in some instances the jurisdiction has been invoked where alternative, more effective statutory remedies are available, a notable feature of the undesirable association case law is that in at least some instances the court has, correctly, resisted using the inherent jurisdiction for that same reason.

Private Law Parenting Disputes

12.11 The court rarely invokes the inherent jurisdiction in private law parenting disputes.[25] The CA 1989 deliberately set out to incorporate the beneficial features of wardship into the statutory scheme, and the historic reasons why wardship was preferred – for example, non-parents not having standing in relation to children,[26] and the incoherence of the statutory powers available in different sets of proceedings[27] – were addressed in the CA 1989. In the vast majority of private law parenting disputes, therefore, it is hard to see what benefit would arise from using wardship or the inherent jurisdiction.

12.12 One example of uses that can be made of the inherent jurisdiction is in preventing child abduction in certain circumstances. For instance, if the child holds a non-British passport, Tipstaff orders (only available under the inherent

[22] *Re T (A Child) (Non-Molestation Order)* [2017] EWCA Civ 1889, [2018] Fam 290.
[23] FLA 1996, s 42.
[24] ibid s 42(2)(b).
[25] *Cf* the approach in New Zealand: see **5.27**.
[26] Law Commission, *Review of Child Law: Wards of Court*, WP No 101 (London: HMSO, 1987) (hereafter, 'Law Com WP 101'), paras 3.24 and 4.41.
[27] ibid para 3.9; Law Commission, *Review of Child Law: Guardianship and Custody*. Law Com 172 (London: HMSO, 1988) ('Law Com 172'), para 4.25. See **2.25**.

jurisdiction) are required to seize those documents;[28] alternatively, if the person concerned about abduction risk does not have PR, invoking wardship can ensure that their rights in relation to the child are recognised.[29] Outside these niche contexts, though, wardship or inherent jurisdiction orders offer no tangible benefit to private law cases that cannot be addressed under CA 1989, s 8.[30] The court can use the CA 1989 to determine arrangements for the child, regulate the exercise of PR, and impose conditions or make directions as to how any s 8 order is to be implemented.[31]

12.13 Despite legal remedies under the CA 1989 that 'incorporate the most valuable features of wardship',[32] the court seems unable to accept that wardship has no benefits in private children cases. For example, wardship is presented by Munby P as a possible legal response to a parent 'alienating the child from the other parent and denying contact between them',[33] though with no explanation of what wardship would add. This approach was applied in *Re T (Parental Alienation)*.[34] The parents separated when T was a year old. Contact with the father stopped. Psychological assessments were ordered, with interim contact to be supervised by an independent social worker, though she was unable to persuade T (now aged four) to see her father. HHJ Raeside then records: '[t]he father recognised that since T did not have a relationship with him, any application for a change of residence would have to be supported by a bridging placement and an application for Wardship', which was granted at an early hearing.[35] A plan to resume contact was then agreed, and the wardship discharged. There is no explanation of what wardship added, or why orders under the CA 1989 were inadequate.[36]

12.14 The inherent jurisdiction was also used in a private law parenting dispute in *Re K (Adoption and Wardship)*.[37] A young Muslim girl was taken from Bosnia during the Balkans War by an English couple. The child's mother and grandmother were killed; her father's whereabouts remained unknown. The English couple initially sought to adopt; following substantial evidence of bad faith, they withdrew their adoption application but sought to retain care of the child. Sir Stephen Brown P made long-term wardship orders placing her in the English couple's care and allowing contact with her Bosnian family. Aside from the rather shocking

[28] See **7.40–7.46**.
[29] See **7.37–7.39**.
[30] See, eg, *C v Salford CC* [1994] 2 FLR 926: foster carers sought wardship orders, but Hale J held that there was 'no reason' for wardship to be used in preference to CA 1989 proceedings.
[31] CA 1989, ss 8 and 11(7).
[32] Law Com 172 (n 27) para 1.4. See **2.30** *et seq*.
[33] *Re A (Children) (Contact: Ultra-Orthodox Judaism: Transgender Parent)*, sub nom *Re M (Children) (Ultra-Orthodox Judaism: Transgender Parent)* [2017] EWCA Civ 2164, [2018] 4 WLR 60, [64].
[34] *Re T (Parental Alienation)* [2019] EWHC 3854 (Fam) (HHJ Raeside).
[35] ibid [20].
[36] *Cf* Lieven J's decision to refuse wardship in a private law children dispute, reported by the Transparency Project: transparencyproject.org.uk/observing-a-private-law-children-case-in-the-high-court/.
[37] *Re K (Adoption and Wardship)* [1997] 2 FLR 221 (Brown P).

decision on its facts, wardship was plainly inappropriate when the same outcome could have been achieved under CA 1989, s 8. The President did not explain what wardship added; no mention was made of the statutory remedies or any deficiency in them that justified the inherent jurisdiction being used. By using wardship, although the child was placed under the care and control of the English couple, no one gained PR. The child, who was presumptively an orphan, was therefore left with no person having PR for her, and all significant decisions about her upbringing, at least in theory, required the court's approval.

12.15 *T v S* is another example.[38] Hedley J made entirely unremarkable private law orders in a high conflict parenting case, but did so in wardship, saying that 'care and control' arrangements in wardship were 'in the gift of the court' (as if care arrangements under s 8 were not).[39] The judge refused to make a residence order under s 8 because he considered that it had taken on 'totemic' importance for the parents (hardly unusual in high conflict cases),[40] and used the inherent jurisdiction to place restrictions on further applications when s 91(14) of the CA 1989 would have sufficed.

12.16 These cases show the court reaching for the inherent jurisdiction in complex private children cases, but no lacunae in the statutory powers are identified, and the claimed benefits arising from wardship were at best rhetorical.[41] Private law children cases do not need the inherent jurisdiction, and the court should simply make use of its statutory powers.

Financial Provision

12.17 Schedule 1 of the CA 1989 allows the court to make orders for the financial provision of a child. Following a recommendation of the Law Commission,[42] para 1(7) of Schedule 1 of the CA 1989 provides: 'Where a child is a ward of court, the court may exercise any of its powers under this Schedule even though no application has been made to it.' This provision widened the court's powers in relation to the financial maintenance of a ward, which under the previous legislation were limited to requiring one or both parents to pay periodical payments to whoever was caring for the ward (though illegitimate children were excluded from this provision).[43] There do not appear to be any reported cases where this power has been used.[44]

[38] *T v S* [2011] EWHC 1608 (Fam), [2012] 1 FLR 230.

[39] ibid [22].

[40] ibid.

[41] *Cf* N Lowe, 'Inherently Disposed to Protect Children: The Continuing Role of Wardship' in R Probert and C Barton (eds), *Fifty Years in Family Law* (Cambridge: Intersentia, 2012), 173.

[42] Law Com 172 (n 27) para 4.69.

[43] Family Law Reform Act 1969, s 6 (as enacted).

[44] It has significant potential use in non-Hague child abduction cases to allow interim financial support for a child during proceedings or to make 'soft landing' provisions if a return order is made; see generally **ch 7**.

12.18 While it is not strictly a decision in relation to children, this is a convenient place to address Sir James Munby's decision in *FS v RS and JS*.[45] The applicant was a 41-year-old man with various alleged vulnerabilities, seeking financial support from his parents under numerous provisions, including the inherent jurisdiction.[46] The court rejected the claim for three reasons. First, the proposed order was 'far outside the accepted parameters of the [relevant] branch of the inherent jurisdiction',[47] namely that in relation to capacitous but vulnerable adults (as discussed in chapter fourteen). That jurisdiction, Sir James said, existed to support autonomous adults and to facilitate their exercise of autonomy,[48] which did not describe the applicant's claim. Second, there was a 'fundamental principle' that the inherent jurisdiction 'cannot be used to compel an unwilling third party to provide money or services',[49] though whether the respondent parents are really 'third parties' is questionable. Finally, the proposed use of the inherent jurisdiction was ousted by the combined statutory schemes of the Matrimonial Causes Act 1973 and the CA 1989, between them 'dealing … with the circumstances in which a child, including, as here, an adult child, can make a financial claim against a living parent'.[50] This reasoning is an exemplary application of the fundamental principles of the inherent jurisdiction, and is notable given Sir James Munby's role in creating and expanding the inherent jurisdiction in relation to vulnerable adults.[51]

Restrictions on Publicity

12.19 Issues about restrictions on publicity regarding a child arise in two situations. The more common is where a child is the subject of existing litigation, and the question concerns reporting of the case. Here, there are extensive statutory limitations on what can be reported, which depend on the nature of the case; the issue for the court is whether to vary those restrictions. The second, less common situation is where an application is made to restrict the publication of information about a child which does not arise out of existing family court litigation. The classic example is *Re X (A Minor) (Wardship: Jurisdiction)*,[52] where orders were sought (but refused) to stop the publication of a book that contained information about the deceased father of a ward, where it was said that the information would be distressing to the child if it came to her attention.

[45] *FS v RS and JS* [2020] EWFC 63, [2020] 4 WLR 139.
[46] ibid [110].
[47] ibid [112].
[48] ibid [114].
[49] ibid [123]; see **3.66**.
[50] ibid [137].
[51] See **2.55** *et seq* and **ch 14**.
[52] *Re X (A Minor) (Wardship: Jurisdiction)* [1975] Fam 47 (CoA).

12.20 Historically, the inherent jurisdiction was the mechanism for such restrictions,[53] but the House of Lords in *Re S (A Child) (Identification: Restriction on Publication)*[54] held that such cases should be determined as applications under the Human Rights Act 1998 and not under the inherent jurisdiction. In *Re S*, a mother was due to stand trial for murder of the subject child's brother. The guardian for S in care proceedings sought inherent jurisdiction orders preventing the identification of S, including that any report of the criminal proceedings not include the names or photographs of the mother or the deceased child. While the restrictions were initially made, they were relaxed after challenge by the media. The House of Lords dismissed the guardian's appeal against the relaxation of the restrictions. Whereas the Court of Appeal held that the inherent jurisdiction provided 'the vehicle' by which the court could balance the ECHR rights in such a case,[55] the House of Lords disagreed. Lord Steyn explained:

> since the 1998 [Human Rights] Act came into force …, the earlier case law about the existence and scope of inherent jurisdiction need not be considered in this case or in similar cases. The foundation of the jurisdiction to restrain publicity in a case such as the present is now derived from Convention rights under the ECHR. This is the simple and direct way to approach such cases.[56]

Consequently, while the historic precedents were inherent jurisdiction cases, there is no reason for the modern authorities to invoke the inherent jurisdiction at all; the application can and should be made under the HRA 1998.

12.21 Nevertheless, despite this House of Lords authority on the point, Practice Direction 12D – Inherent Jurisdiction (Including Wardship) Proceedings lists 'orders to restrain publicity' as the first item in the list of most common uses of the inherent jurisdiction.[57] And the President of the Family Division has stated in his *Guidance as to Reporting in the Family Courts* that, in addition to the various statutory restrictions on the reporting of family court proceedings, 'the court has the power to extend reporting restrictions in appropriate cases using its inherent jurisdiction'.[58] Not only is this likely to lead applicants (and judges) astray, but it reveals something about the court's unwillingness to give up on its inherent jurisdiction as an available remedy, even when the highest court has ruled that recourse to the inherent jurisdiction in these circumstances is inappropriate and unnecessary.

[53] See, eg, *Re W (A Minor) (Wardship: Restrictions on Publicity)* [1992] 1 WLR 100 (CoA), *R v Central Independent Television Plc* [1994] Fam 192 (CoA), *Re Z (A Minor) (Identification: Restrictions on Publication)* [1997] Fam 1 (CoA), *Nottingham CC v October Films* [1999] 2 FLR 347 (Brown P).

[54] *Re S (A Child) (Identification: Restriction on Publication)* [2004] UKHL 47, [2005] 1 AC 593.

[55] *Re S (A Child) (Identification: Restriction on Publication)* [2003] EWCA Civ 963, [2004] Fam 43, [40].

[56] [2004] UKHL 47, [2005] 1 AC 593, [23].

[57] Para 1.2(a).

[58] A McFarlane, *President's Guidance: Guidance as to Reporting in the Family Courts* (3 October 2019), [5], online at www.judiciary.uk/wp-content/uploads/2019/10/Presidents-Guidance-reporting-restrictions-Final-Oct-2019-1.pdf (accessed 1 June 2024).

Disposal of a Deceased Child's Body

12.22 Orders under the CA 1989 cannot take effect or continue after the death of the subject child.[59] Similarly, it is doubtful whether the court's *parens patriae* inherent jurisdiction could be exercised after a child's death,[60] for the same reasons that it cannot be invoked before the child's birth.[61] Nonetheless, the court has invoked the wider inherent jurisdiction in these cases, separate from its welfare-based jurisdiction in relation to children's upbringing.[62]

12.23 Relatedly, the court has invoked the inherent jurisdiction when a child's parents disagreed about how their child's body should be disposed of after death.[63] In *Re JS (Disposal of Body)*,[64] the subject child (a 14-year-old girl) had been diagnosed with terminal cancer and sought a court direction to have her body cryo-preserved after death. Under the Non-contentious Probate Rules 1987, a child's legal parents have a shared right to determine what happens to their child's remains after death; JS's mother supported her daughter's wish, but JS's estranged father did not. While the court has power under s 116 of the Senior Courts Act 1981 to regulate the exercise of that right when 'special circumstances' exist, its scope is unclear. Because of JS's wish for cryo-preservation, it was essential for a decision to be made prior to death, because the steps required for preservation must be undertaken immediately on death. Peter Jackson J held that s 116 could be used to substitute one parent for both within the 1987 Rules, or alternatively 'that the same result could be achieved by the court's use of its inherent jurisdiction'.[65] The court further held that it could exercise this power prospectively on the facts of the case.[66] The court therefore granted: (i) specific issue orders to allow the mother to take the necessary steps *prior to* JS's death, and (ii) a prospective order under s 116 *or alternatively under the inherent jurisdiction* appointing the mother as sole administrator of JS's estate, so that she could make arrangements for the disposal of JS's body after death.[67] *Re JS* highlights an ambiguity in the scope of s 116 that the court did not resolve, including whether the statutory jurisdiction

[59] *R v Gwynedd CC, ex p B* [1991] 2 FLR 365 (CoA), decided under the Child Care Act 1980 but applicable by analogy: see also *Re JS (Disposal of Body)* [2016] EWHC 2859 (Fam), [2017] 4 WLR 1, [45] (Peter Jackson J).

[60] *Cf Re K (A Child: Deceased)* [2017] EWHC 1083 (Fam), [2018] 1 FLR 96; Hayden J's reasoning shows that he was purporting to apply the *parens patriae* inherent jurisdiction in relation to a deceased child.

[61] See **4.23** *et seq*.

[62] See *Hartshorne v Gardner* [2008] EWHC 3675 (Ch), [2008] 2 FLR 1681 (DHCJ Proudman QC); *Anstey v Mundle* [2016] EWHC 1073 (Ch) (Klein J).

[63] See, eg, *Re E (A Child: Burial Arrangements)* [2019] EWHC 3639 (Fam) (HHJ Gareth Jones).

[64] *Re JS (Disposal of Body)* [2016] EWHC 2859 (Fam), [2017] 4 WLR 1. I was counsel for the applicant child, led by Frances Judd QC (as she then was). See comment in R George, 'Making Determinations During Life about the Disposal of a Body after Death' (2017) 39 *JSWFL* 109.

[65] ibid [53].

[66] ibid [59].

[67] ibid [41].

can be engaged prior to death. The combination of that ambiguity, the urgency and novelty of the issue, the prospective nature of the application, and the need for certainty about the legality of the proposed actions (particularly for the hospital trust) perhaps justifies the use of the inherent jurisdiction in this case.

12.24 The relationship between s 116 and the inherent jurisdiction is somewhat fluid. While directions under s 116 will often be sufficient, in other cases the appointment of an administrator will not resolve the problem. For example, in *Re K (A Child: Deceased)*, the parents did not make any arrangements for the child's burial,[68] and so Hayden J used the inherent jurisdiction to direct the local authority to do so.[69] In this limited context, the inherent jurisdiction plays an important role in filling a legislative gap, and ensuring that arrangements are made for a child after death; but a better solution would be for a statutory power to exist to resolve cases like these.

Conclusion

12.25 The five issues discussed in this chapter raise a common theme: with some limited exceptions, use of the inherent jurisdiction in these instances is difficult to justify, but financial provision is the only area where the court has firmly stated that conclusion.

12.26 In relation to private children cases there are no identified benefits from the inherent jurisdiction, and statutory remedies are available. The High Court should refuse to hear these applications, re-allocating them to the appropriate level of the Family Court to make orders under the CA 1989.[70] Applications in relation to publicity should not be heard under the inherent jurisdiction, given the House of Lords authority on this issue, and the Practice Direction should be amended to remove this issue from the list of 'common uses' of the inherent jurisdiction.

12.27 Injunctions against 'undesirable associations' are the most complex of the issues, directly engaging the court's 'protective imperative'. The wider scope proposed in *Riaz*, allowing public protection orders under the inherent jurisdiction, must be beyond the acceptable scope of the court's power in family litigation. As to injunctions against individuals, the balance of factors is complex. In cases where a statutory power exists that is available in the civil court, it should be used in preference to the inherent jurisdiction, but where the only available remedy is on police application to the criminal court, the High Court is unlikely to resist its protective imperative if the police choose not to act.

[68] See generally C Sharp, 'The Family Court's Jurisdiction to Direct the Burial of a Child' [2017] *Family Law* 844.

[69] [2017] EWHC 1083 (Fam), [2018] 1 FLR 96, [13].

[70] Inherent jurisdiction cases are 'family proceedings' and therefore the court can resolve the case by making orders under the CA 1989.

13

Adults without Mental Capacity

13.1 This chapter considers the court's powers in relation to adults who lack mental capacity to make a relevant decision at the particular time. The court's separate jurisdiction in relation to adults who have capacity but who are 'vulnerable' is addressed in the next chapter. Many of the reported cases refer somewhat indiscriminately to 'incapacitous or vulnerable' adults, or use the terms interchangeably – care is consequently needed to ensure that the cases are actually authority in relation to the particular issue, since the legal principles applicable to the two areas are very different.

13.2 As James Munby has written extra-judicially, in cases concerning an adult without capacity, that person ('P') is undoubtedly vulnerable in significant ways, but it is P's lack of decision-making capacity that founds the court's inherent jurisdiction.[1] The practical use of the inherent jurisdiction in these cases is limited – and arguably should be seen as entirely dormant – because Parliament has intervened with the Mental Capacity Act 2005 ('MCA 2005'). The MCA 2005 applies where P does not have capacity to make a relevant decision 'because of an impairment of, or a disturbance in the functioning of, the mind or brain'.[2] The Act expressly assumes that P *does* have capacity unless shown otherwise, and the assessment must be of P's capacity to make the specific decision.[3] In cases where P does not have capacity to make a particular decision, the Act provides:

(i) a defence against liability in respect of acts connected to the care and treatment of people who are reasonably believed to lack capacity;[4]
(ii) a range of possible orders that can be made,[5] and
(iii) general principles applicable to decision-making for P, including that the decision must be in P's best interests and that there should be consideration of whether the purpose could be achieved in a way that is less restrictive of P's rights and freedom of action.[6]

[1] J Munby, 'Whither the Inherent Jurisdiction? Part I' [2021] *Fam Law* 215, 217.
[2] MCA 2005, s 2(1).
[3] ibid ss 1(2) and 4.
[4] ibid s 5.
[5] See, eg, ibid ss 4A, 15 and 16.
[6] ibid s 1(5) and (6).

13.3 The inherent jurisdiction does *not* apply to cases that are within the scope of the MCA 2005 – though as I explore below, at times the court has taken a surprisingly narrow view of the Act's scope.

The Existence of the Inherent Jurisdiction Over Incapacitous Adults

13.4 The detailed history of the inherent jurisdiction of the High Court in relation to incapacitous adults is set out earlier in this book.[7] In summary, the court's powers arose by delegation from the Crown, repeated by each new monarch by Royal Warrant at the start of their reign. As such, it was delegated prerogative power; 'The jurisdiction cannot therefore be regarded as one which is 'inherent' in the High Court.'[8] However, the last such Warrant was withdrawn when the Mental Health Act 1959 ('MHA 1959') entered force. That Act and its successor in 1983 were considered a 'complete code' – they made no provision (unlike earlier legislation) for the continued exercise of the Royal prerogative, and repealed all existing legislation dealing with the prerogative over idiots and lunatics regarding both property and welfare issues.[9] Parliamentary and Crown intention was to abolish *parens patriae* powers in relation to incapacitous adults, and in *Re F (Mental Patient: Sterilisation)* the House of Lords was clear that 'the *parens patriae* jurisdiction with respect to adults of unsound mind no longer exists'.[10]

13.5 The Law Commission's work on mental incapacity in the 1990s specifically rejected attempting to revive the inherent jurisdiction.[11] The Law Commission thought that there were 'complex technical arguments which lead us to doubt whether [reviving the inherent jurisdiction] could in fact be done', but also considered such an approach to be 'quite out of step with our policy aims'.[12] The Law Commission's proposed statutory scheme in relation to incapacitous adults was intended to be 'a single *comprehensive piece of legislation* to make new provision for people who lack mental capacity' which could be used 'when *any decision* (whether personal, medical or financial) needs to be made' for a person lacking capacity.[13] And the Joint Committee on the Mental Incapacity Bill 'endorse[d] the

[7] See **2.39–2.55**.

[8] B Hoggett, 'The Royal Prerogative in Relation to the Mentally Disordered: Resurrection, Resuscitation, or Rejection?' in M Freeman (ed), *Medicine, Ethics and the Law* (London: UCL Press, 1988) ('Hoggett'), 92.

[9] MHA 1959, ss 1 and 149(2) and Sch 8; Hoggett (n 8) 94.

[10] *Re F (Mental Patient: Sterilisation)* [1990] 2 AC 1 (HoL), 63 (Lord Brandon); see also at 70 (Lord Griffiths) and 71 (Lord Goff).

[11] Law Commission, *Mental Incapacity*, Law Com 231 (London: TSO, 1995), para 2.48; see also the House of Lords Select Committee on Medical Ethics (1993–94), HL 21-I (London: HMSO, 1994), paras 169–171.

[12] Law Commission (n 11) para 2.48.

[13] ibid para 1.2 (emphasis added).

draft Bill's widely-supported aim of replacing common law uncertainties by *a comprehensive statutory framework*'[14] – in effect, with no place for the inherent jurisdiction. The Commission's proposals were adopted and brought into effect by the MCA 2005.

13.6 The Law Commission's report gave no consideration to how its proposed scheme would interact with the inherent jurisdiction. Why would it? The jurisdiction did not exist when the report was written, and the court's 'rediscovery' of its inherent jurisdiction over incapacitous adults prior to 2005 went unnoticed by Parliament.[15] Consequently, the MCA 2005 makes no reference to the prerogative, to *parens patriae*, or to any inherent jurisdiction[16] – because it did not exist; it had not existed since the last Royal Warrant was withdrawn when the MHA 1959 entered into force.

13.7 However, as set out earlier,[17] between the Commission's report in 1995 and the passage of the MCA 2005, the court had in effect replaced the old jurisdiction over incapacitous adults with a newly-created 'inherent jurisdiction' – what James Munby later extra-judicially termed 'a full-blown welfare-based *parens patriae* jurisdiction … which, except in one respect (there is no power to make an adult a ward of court) is indistinguishable from the long established *parens patriae* jurisdiction in relation to children'.[18] This was nothing short of a vast power-grab by the court, what Munby accepts was an 'invention' by the High Court that 'bears no relation to the declaratory jurisdiction as reinvigorated by the House of Lords in 1989'.[19]

13.8 When the issue first came to the court in *Westminster CC v C*,[20] the Court of Appeal refused permission to appeal a High Court decision that the inherent jurisdiction remained available 'alongside' the Act. Wall LJ approved Wood J's judgment: the court 'can exercise its inherent jurisdiction in relation to mentally handicapped adults alongside, as appropriate, the [MCA] 2005'.[21] Thorpe LJ

[14] Joint Committee on the Draft Mental Incapacity Bill, HL189-I / HC 1083-I (London: TSO, 2003), 5 (emphasis added); see also paras 30, 86 and 214 and the conclusions at 95, para 3.

[15] See, eg, House of Commons Library Research Paper, *The Mental Capacity Bill* (Research Paper 04/73, 5 October 2004). Likewise, the Joint Committee (n 14) makes only one reference to the inherent jurisdiction, at para 202. It recommends allowing advanced decision to refuse medical treatment, thus avoiding the need to use the inherent jurisdiction which 'would be contrary to the Bill's intentions … to create a comprehensive and accessible framework of statutory legislation'. The proposal became MCA 2005, ss 24–26.

[16] *Cf Re L (Vulnerable Adults with Capacity: Court's Jurisdiction)* [2012] EWCA Civ 253, [2013] Fam 1, [61]: McFarlane LJ suggested that Parliament could have included express consideration of the inherent jurisdiction under the MCA 2005, as it had done under the CA 1989. Given the state of the law when the MCA was being developed, the omission is both unsurprising and unrevealing.

[17] See **2.48** *et seq.*

[18] Munby (n 1) 225.

[19] ibid; see further **2.53**.

[20] *Westminster CC v C* [2008] EWCA Civ 198, [2009] Fam 11. See also the summary by Baker LJ in *A Local Authority v BF* [2018] EWCA Civ 2963, [2019] COPLR 150, [22(1)].

[21] *Westminster CC v C*, ibid [55], citing *City of Westminster v IC* [2007] EWHC 3096 (Fam), [119].

dismissed the challenge to the continuing existence of the inherent jurisdiction based on a lack of contrary authority.[22] That was surely the wrong question: a new statutory scheme – clearly intended to be comprehensive and passed in the context of there being no inherent jurisdiction then in existence – placed the onus on those seeking to establish that this novel, non-statutory jurisdiction had in fact survived (or rather, been re-created).

13.9 The foundations of what is now called 'the inherent jurisdiction' in relation to incapacitous adults are thus remarkably shallow. The court *never* had an untrammelled 'inherent' jurisdiction over incapacitous adults – when it existed, it was delegated by Royal Warrant (not 'inherent' in the court), and it was highly regulated by numerous Acts of Parliament. Most significantly, it was categorically revoked in 1960, and the Law Commission and Parliament proceeded on that basis when designing and implementing the MCA 2005. The court's newly-created jurisdiction is a blatant example of the court legislating from scratch[23] – of judges granting themselves extensive and unregulated powers which Parliament had specifically not given them. And for this reason, the entire line of authority is arguably wrongly decided.

Uses of the Inherent Jurisdiction Alongside the MCA 2005

13.10 Against this background of concern over the very existence of the inherent jurisdiction in relation to incapacitous adults, I turn to examples where the inherent jurisdiction has been used.

Relocation and Travel Abroad

13.11 The *Westminster CC v C* decision discussed above concerned the foreign marriage of a British man who was found to lack capacity to marry, the ceremony having already purportedly taken place by telephone.[24] The court held it had no power to declare a marriage to be void unless a petition for nullity were made,[25] and turned its focus to preventing P's removal from this country to live abroad. The court addressed this issue under its inherent jurisdiction because it considered that '[n]o part of the 2005 [Act] deals with the issue of preventing the mentally incapacitated person from leaving the country'.[26]

[22] ibid [12]. Thorpe LJ also relied on *Re MM; Local Authority X v MM* [2007] EWHC 2003 (Fam), [2009] 1 FLR 443 (Munby J), but the case is not authority on this issue.

[23] See **1.22–1.27**.

[24] *Westminster CC v C* [2008] EWCA Civ 198, [2009] Fam 11.

[25] Matrimonial Causes Act 1973, s 12(c); Family Law Act 1986, ss 55(1) and 58(5). See further **13.13**.

[26] *Westminster CC v C* [2008] EWCA Civ 198, [2009] Fam 11, [55], quoting with approval *City of Westminster v IC* [2007] EWHC 3096 (Fam), [121].

13.12 That view must be wrong, and is expressly contrary to the orders later made by Roberts J and upheld on appeal in *J v Luton BC*.[27] A 'personal welfare decision' under the MCA includes 'deciding where P is to live',[28] and an ordinary reading of those words would include whether P should go to live abroad.[29] The scope of s 16 is also not limited,[30] and so, for example, a decision for P to travel abroad on holiday is also readily available within s 16. The only use for the inherent jurisdiction in these cases is to manage an urgent abduction risk using Tipstaff orders to prevent P's removal from the country pending judicial determination of the matter.[31]

Non-Recognition of Marriage and Nullity

13.13 The court has held that foreign marriages concerning incapacitous adults do not fall within the MCA 2005, but can be addressed under the inherent jurisdiction.

13.14 *X County Council v AA* concerned the court's powers in relation to a purported marriage ceremony for P undertaken seven years earlier.[32] Parker J held that both an order declaring the marriage to be void, and a declaration that it was in P's best interests for a nullity application to be issued, were outside the scope of the MCA 2005 – 'it is not a personal welfare decision'[33] – therefore the court could invoke the inherent jurisdiction. Parker J specifically rejected the submission that the MCA was 'a complete statutory code … [and that] there is no gap to be filled', holding that it was possible to rely on the inherent jurisdiction to grant a declaration of non-recognition of the marriage.[34]

13.15 Parker J is clearly right that a declaration of non-recognition of marriage cannot be made under the MCA 2005.[35] However, it is more problematic to say that this issue is not within the scope of a 'personal welfare decision' under the MCA. Section 16 is headed simply 'Powers to make decisions and appoint deputies: general'. Sub-section (1) provides that the section applies if P lacks capacity in relation to a matter or matters relating to 'personal welfare' or 'property and affairs'. Sub-section (2) broadly states that the court may, 'by making an order,

[27] *J v Luton BC* [2024] EWCA Civ 3.
[28] MCA 2005, s 17(1)(a).
[29] See also *UR v Derby CC* [2021] EWCOP 10, [2021] COPLR 314 (Hayden VP), granting permission for permanent relocation to Poland under the MCA 2005.
[30] See further **13.15**.
[31] See **7.40–7.46**.
[32] *X CC v AA* [2012] EWHC 2183 (COP), [2013] 2 All ER 988. *Cf* A Ruck Keene, 'The Inherent Jurisdiction: Where Are We Now?' [2013] *Elder LJ* 88, 90.
[33] *X CC v AA*, ibid [48].
[34] ibid [52].
[35] See *Westminster CC v C* [2008] EWCA Civ 198, [2009] Fam 11 and *Re SA (Declaration of Non-Recognition of Marriage)* [2023] EWCA Civ 1003.

make the decision or decisions on P's behalf in relation to the matter or matters' (or appoint a Deputy to do so for P). The power under s 16 is subject to the Act's general principles in s 1, and the best interests approach mandated in s 4, neither of which limits the scope of s 16. Some guidance is found in s 17 which sets out a list of issues to which the s 16 powers 'extend *in particular*' – in other words, it is non-exhaustive. The s 17 list includes living arrangements, contact, and health care – but there is no reason to take a narrow approach.[36] The Court of Protection can, for example, make a determination that it is in P's best interests for divorce proceedings to be commenced on P's behalf.[37] Likewise, s 16 could be used to authorise an application for nullity to be made on P's behalf.

13.16 A better solution to the problem in *X County Council v AA* would therefore to have been a fuller consideration of the scope of the MCA 2005, which readily lends itself to allowing the remedy that Parker J sought, without unnecessary recourse to the inherent jurisdiction.

Deprivation of Liberty

13.17 The provisions for deprivation of liberty ('DOL') under the MCA 2005, principally in s 16A and Sch 1A, are 'almost incomprehensible' and 'characterised by extreme opacity'.[38] Unsurprisingly therefore, they have created some difficulty.

13.18 *An NHS Trust v A* concerned a DOL application,[39] in circumstances not covered by the amended provisions of the MCA 2005.[40] The case concerned a hospital patient, 'Dr A', who was refusing to eat or drink in protest at a failed asylum claim. While at times his stay was voluntary, he was being detained at the relevant time. He did not meet the statutory criteria for DOL, and Baker J held that it was impermissible to 'read down' the relevant provisions of the Act using s 3 of the Human Rights Act 1998 – doing so would fundamentally alter the meaning of the words.[41] It might have been expected that that was the end of the case. However, despite acknowledging that 'the 2005 Act was intended to provide a comprehensive code for the care of mentally incapacitated adults',[42] Baker J went on to hold that the inherent jurisdiction remained available and could be used to

[36] Note the Parliamentary intentions: see **13.5–13.7**.
[37] *D v S* [2023] EWCOP 8 (Hayden J).
[38] *An NHS Trust v A* [2015] EWCOP 71 (Mostyn J), [12] and [8] respectively.
[39] *An NHS Trust v A* [2013] EWHC 2442 (Fam), [2014] Fam 161. For a similar case where the patient had capacity, see *JK v A Local Health Board* [2019] EWHC 67 (Fam), [2020] COPLR 246: Lieven J accepted a concession that the inherent jurisdiction was not available in that case.
[40] MCA 2005, ss 4A and 16A and Schs A1, AA1 and 1A.
[41] The authors of the 39 Essex blog suggest an alternative solution, based on 'residual liberty': see Anon, 'An NHS Trust v Dr A', 27 March 2013, online at www.39essex.com/information-hub/case/nhs-trust-v-dr (accessed 1 June 2024), relying on discussion in *Munjaz v United Kingdom* (App No 2913/06) [2012] ECHR 1704.
[42] *An NHS Trust v A* [2013] EWHC 2442 (Fam), [2014] Fam 161, [90].

authorise a DOL in circumstances where the same was prohibited by the MCA 2005.[43] Why interpreting the MCA 2005 in this way using the HRA 1998 was 'impermissible', but achieving the exact same outcome under the inherent jurisdiction was acceptable, is unexplained.

13.19 Baker J placed reliance on *Westminster CC v C* and *Re L (Vulnerable Adults with Capacity: Court's Jurisdiction)*.[44] *Re L* was of limited application to Dr A's case in two important respects. First, *Re L* concerned a *vulnerable* adult who had capacity, and so comments about the scope of the MCA were made in that context, not in the context of an *incapacitous* adult. Second, obiter comments from Davis LJ in a short concurring judgment in *Re L* did suggest that 'in the case of an adult who lacks capacity within the meaning of the 2005 Act, it appears that the inherent jurisdiction remains available to cover situations not precisely within the reach of the statute'.[45] However, Dr A's case *was* 'precisely within the reach of the statute' – and the statute forbade the outcome that Baker J wished to achieve.[46] This is a clear example of the court violating the *De Keyser* principle:[47] Parliament regulated this situation and held, as part of a comprehensive scheme, that DOL was impermissible,[48] yet the court used its inherent jurisdiction to disregard that restriction.[49] Parliament's decision not to permit DOL in these circumstances was not a minor oversight that it was open to the court to 'fix', even if the outcome was one with which many people would agree. As Lieven J put it in obiter comments in a case where the application under the inherent jurisdiction had been withdrawn, '[t]he inherent jurisdiction cannot be used to simply reverse the outcome under a statutory scheme, which deals with the very situation in issue, on the basis that the court disagrees'.[50]

13.20 As with the cases on DOL affecting children,[51] this issue raises various concerns. It is necessary not only that the order is in P's best interests, but also that the DOL complies with ECHR Article 5. Whether the inherent jurisdiction amounts to 'a procedure prescribed by law'[52] is doubtful – particularly

[43] The conclusion is 'rather surprising': J Herring, *Vulnerable Adults and the Law* (Oxford: OUP, 2016), 79.

[44] *Westminster CC v C* [2008] EWCA Civ 198, [2009] Fam 11and *Re L (Vulnerable Adults with Capacity: Court's Jurisdiction)* [2012] EWCA Civ 253, [2013] Fam 1.

[45] ibid [70].

[46] *Cf An NHS Trust v A* [2015] EWCOP 71 (Mostyn J) and *A Hospital Trust v CD* [2015] EWCOP 74 (Mostyn J): the MCA 2005 could be used for DOL on the facts, so the inherent jurisdiction was not needed.

[47] See **3.33** *et seq*.

[48] Arguably this outcome reflects poor drafting, rather than a specific policy decision – but when the liberty of the subject is at stake, a strict reading of the language used is required.

[49] R Hughes, 'Inherent Jurisdiction: Artificial Nutrition and Hydration' [2013] *Elder LJ* 346 supports this outcome, despite being 'somewhat surprised' at 'an order which appears to be expressly prohibited by the MCA 2005'.

[50] *JK v A Local Health Board* [2019] EWHC 67 (Fam), [2020] COPLR 246, [57].

[51] See **ch 10**.

[52] ECHR, Art 5(1).

when it is being used to circumvent clear restrictions and limitations imposed by Parliament in an extensive statutory scheme.[53] The court's approach to DOL, and the continued use of an extra-statutory mechanism, looks to be another example of the court deploying its 'protective imperative' at the expense of legal principle.[54] Parliament has decided which incapacitous adults may and which may not be subject to DOL, and it is not for the court to override that policy.

Nationality-Based Jurisdiction

13.21 Territorial jurisdiction to make orders under the MCA 2005 is addressed by the Hague Convention on the International Protection of Adults 2000, though the rules are given effect in domestic law[55] by the Act itself. The relevant provisions grant the court jurisdiction in relation to: (a) any adult habitually resident in England and Wales, (b) any adult's property in England and Wales, (c) any adult physically present in England and Wales or who has property there, if the matter is urgent, and (d) any adult physically present in England and Wales, where a protective measure is both temporary and limited in its effects to England and Wales.[56] The court cannot therefore exercise its MCA 2005 powers in relation to an adult who does not meet these criteria, such as a British national adult presently abroad, who is not habitually resident in England and Wales and who does not have property here. The question then arises: can the court nonetheless use its inherent jurisdiction in such cases on the basis of P's British nationality?

13.22 The court held in *Al-Jeffrey* that it can exercise jurisdiction in respect of a *vulnerable* adult (with capacity) abroad based only on their nationality,[57] akin to the position in relation to children.[58] Alex Ruck Keene has argued that the same approach would apply to an *incapacitous* adult who is not habitually resident in England and Wales.

> In such cases, the Court of Protection – a court deriving its powers from statute – will have no jurisdiction over the welfare of the person. However, and in line with the approach taken elsewhere by the judges where there is a statutory lacuna in relation to those lacking capacity …, I would suggest that it is equally appropriate for a judge of the High Court to have recourse to the inherent jurisdiction if the circumstances warrant it.[59]

[53] *Cf DG v Ireland* (App No 39474/98) (2002) 35 EHRR 1153, discussed at **10.33–10.34**.
[54] See **1.19–1.21**.
[55] In Scotland, the Convention is fully ratified.
[56] MCA 2005, Sch 3, para 7(1).
[57] *Al-Jeffrey v Al-Jeffrey (Vulnerable Adult: British Citizen)* [2016] EWHC 2151 (Fam), [2018] 4 WLR 136; see also **14.66–14.68**.
[58] See **ch 6**.
[59] A Ruck Keene, 'Extending the Great Safety Net' [2016] *Elder LJ* 401, 404.

13.23 Subsequent authority, however, appears to go against this approach. While not stating that there is no nationality-based jurisdiction, the court has on at least two occasions declined to exercise it on the basis that doing so would 'subvert the predictable and clear framework of the [MCA] in an unprincipled way', as Cobb J put it in *Re QD (Jurisdiction: Habitual Residence)*.[60] A similar approach was taken by Lieven J in *AB v XS*,[61] where P was habitually resident in Lebanon and a relative sought orders requiring P to be brought to the UK. Citing *Re QD*, Lieven J held that it was 'plainly inappropriate to exercise the inherent jurisdiction to make an order to return [P] to England because it would … cut across the carefully crafted statutory scheme applicable to precisely people in [P's] situation, and as such would be a misuse of the inherent jurisdiction'.[62]

13.24 Lieven J did not entirely close the door to nationality-based jurisdiction being invoked in other cases: 'in a case concerning the inherent jurisdiction it is necessary to consider each case on its own particular facts, and the court must always retain an element of flexibility'.[63] Authors at 39 Essex Chambers suggest that Lieven J might have invoked the jurisdiction had she taken the view, on the merits, that P should have been brought to England – 'at that point, it would be logical to see the use of the inherent jurisdiction as plugging a protection gap'[64] – but that would be contrary to the judge's arguments of principle.

Conclusion

13.25 This chapter has explored four applications of the inherent jurisdiction in relation to incapacitous adults – supposing it exists at all. Relocation and travel abroad are plainly within the scope of the MCA 2005 and do not require the inherent jurisdiction. The issue of non-recognition of (foreign) marriages and applications for nullity are not expressly within the Act, but it is no stretch of language for 'personal welfare' matters to include this issue, just as applications for divorce have been covered.

13.26 The court's use of the inherent jurisdiction to make DOL orders and leave open the possibility of a nationality-based jurisdiction over incapacitous adults abroad undermines the MCA's position as a 'complete code'. The 'gaps' identified

[60] *Re QD (Jurisdiction: Habitual Residence)* [2019] EWCOP 56, [2020] COPLR 633, [31]. Cobb J distinguished *Re Mrs Ann Clarke* [2016] EWCOP 46 (Peter Jackson J), which assumed there was potential nationality-based jurisdiction regarding a woman presumed habitually resident in Spain.
[61] *AB v XS* [2021] EWCOP 57, [2022] 4 WLR 13.
[62] ibid [35].
[63] ibid [36].
[64] Anon, 'AB and XS (P, by her Litigation Friend the Official Solicitor)', 15 November 2021, online at www.39essex.com/information-hub/case/ab-and-xs-p-her-litigation-friend-official-solicitor (accessed 1 June 2024).

are part of the fabric of the overall framework – they reflect deliberate policy choices by Parliament, such that resort to the inherent jurisdiction is impermissible. In relation to DOL, the court's prioritisation of the 'protective imperative' over the principled limitations imposed by Parliament through the MCA is particularly concerning, affecting the liberty of the subject. These issues raise serious questions about the appropriate role for the inherent jurisdiction, again representing examples of the *De Keyser* principle being jettisoned by the court.[65]

[65] See **3.37** *et seq.*

14

Vulnerable Adults with Mental Capacity

14.1 Chapter thirteen addressed the inherent jurisdiction in relation to adults who do not have capacity to make a relevant decision. This chapter is about a newly-created jurisdiction with respect to adults who *have* mental capacity, but over whom the court nonetheless says it can exercise a protective jurisdiction on the basis of their *vulnerability*. As I noted in Chapter thirteen, many cases in this area use the language of (in)capacity and vulnerability interchangeably, which creates the risk that the principles that apply to one are inappropriately, or accidentally, applied to the other.[1]

14.2 Vulnerable adult cases have received significant attention and criticism in the academic literature.[2] The court has responded to situations involving at-risk adults who are (or are suspected of) being exploited and abused, reflecting the court's underlying *protective imperative*.[3] However, unlike for children or incapacitous adults, the justification for intervening in the lives of *capacitous* adults is not straightforward, and the court has done a poor job of explaining the basis for intervention. While some cases expressly claim 'protection' as the core rationale,[4] others take a narrower approach, focused on enabling the vulnerable adult to exercise their own autonomy.[5] The lack of coherent reasoning, coupled with the court's general unsuitability to policy-making and the proper constitutional limitations on the court's role,[6] lead to the concerns explored in this chapter.

14.3 Laura Pritchard-Jones identifies 'three areas of concern or confusion' in the law on vulnerable adults: 'when it should apply, what it should do, and on what

[1] The risk is highlighted by J Munby, 'Whither the Inherent Jurisdiction? Parts II and III' [2021] *Fam Law* 365 and 508 ('Munby (2021)'), esp 369–373.

[2] Some commentators are more positive: see, eg, M Hall, 'The Vulnerability Jurisdiction: Equity, Parens Patriae, and the Inherent Jurisdiction of the Court' (2016) 2 *Canadian Journal of Comparative and Contemporary Law* 185; E Cave and H Cave, 'Skeleton Keys to Hospital Doors: Adolescent Adults who Refuse Life-Sustaining Medical Treatment' (2023) 86 *MLR* 984, 1006–1007.

[3] See **1.19–1.21**.

[4] *Re SA (Vulnerable Adult with Capacity: Marriage)* [2005] EWHC 2942 (Fam), [2006] 1 FLR 867, [37] (Munby J); *Re L (Vulnerable Adults with Capacity: Court's Jurisdiction)* [2012] EWCA Civ 253, [2013] Fam 1, [65] (McFarlane LJ) and [79] (Kay LJ).

[5] *FS v RS and JS* [2020] EWFC 63, [2020] 4 WLR 139, [114] (Sir James Munby).

[6] See **1.22–1.27**.

basis judges decide what it should do'.[7] She argues that the law is 'characterised by incoherence, inconsistency, and historical accident', and considers that the problems are 'now woven into the fabric of the common law'.[8] I return to these themes throughout this chapter. The first question is: does the court actually have these powers at all?

The Law Commission's 1995 Report

14.4 In considering the inherent jurisdiction over capacitous but vulnerable adults, I start by looking at the statute that never was: the Law Commission's proposals in relation to vulnerable adults within its 1995 *Mental Incapacity* report. The Commission proposed the following definition of vulnerable adults:

> a 'vulnerable person' should mean any person of 16 or over who (1) is or may be in need of community care services by reason of mental or other disability, age or illness and who (2) is or may be unable to take care of himself or herself, or unable to protect himself or herself against significant harm or serious exploitation.[9]

14.5 The Commission proposed a definition of 'harm' for these purposes,[10] and 'stressed that "merely vulnerable" clients, as opposed to mentally disordered clients or those who lack capacity, should be able to reject intervention by the authorities'.[11] A series of powers was recommended.

(i) Local authorities ('LAs') would have power to enter premises and interview a vulnerable person ('P') who was thought to be at risk of harm. The power could not be exercised if the LA knew or believed that P would object, unless there was reasonable cause to believe that P was suffering from mental disability.[12]
(ii) If entry was prevented by a third party, a court warrant could authorise police to enter the premises accompanied by an LA officer.[13]
(iii) The court could make an 'assessment order' allowing the LA to assess whether P was in fact at risk and, if so, what services or protective steps were appropriate. The assessment period would be no longer than eight days, and P could object to any part of the assessment. P could not be removed from their home unless authorised by the court order, and only if necessary for the assessment.[14]

[7] L Pritchard-Jones, '"Palm Tree Justice": The Inherent Jurisdiction in Adult Welfare Cases' (2023) 86 *MLR* 1358, 1359.
[8] ibid 1360.
[9] Law Commission, *Mental Incapacity*, Law Com 231 (London: TSO, 1995), para 9.6.
[10] ibid para 9.8.
[11] ibid para 9.10.
[12] ibid para 9.19.
[13] ibid para 9.21.
[14] ibid paras 9.24–7.

(iv) The court could make a 'temporary protection order' if: (1) P was likely to be 'at risk' unless placed or kept in protective accommodation for a short period, and (2) the applicant did not know or believe that P would object to the order (except in cases where there was reasonable cause to believe that P was suffering from a mental disability). The order would last a maximum of eight days, and the LA would have had a duty to return P to their home as soon as practicable and consistent with P's interests.[15]

14.6 There are two points to emphasise. First, the scheme was tightly defined in terms of who would be covered and what potential interventions were permitted. It included a threshold for intervention when a third party was the cause for concern, being 'significant harm or serious exploitation'; the parallel with care proceedings for children is obvious.[16] Second, there were significant safeguards, reflecting P's autonomy as a person with mental capacity. Most significantly, if P objected *or it was believed that they would object*, the interventions immediately ended – competent adults could reject 'help' that they did not want, even when they were considered vulnerable.

14.7 The government's response to the Commission's proposals was tepid. The 1997 consultation Green Paper stated that the government was 'not convinced that there is a pressing need for reform'.[17] By the time of the White Paper, all mention of this part of the Commission's report had disappeared.[18] The matter was given further thought – and again rejected – by the Joint Parliamentary Committee on the draft Bill:

> Professor John Williams suggested to us another approach to extend the scope of the Bill to cover the lack of capacity to make a free choice as a result of undue influence (or unacceptable pressure). … As Professor Williams acknowledged, drafting such a clause would be "immensely complex" and would have to contain significant safeguards to avoid unnecessary intervention. We do not feel confident in recommending such an approach.[19]

In other words, having consulted on the issue, lawmakers made a clear policy decision not to legislate in relation to vulnerable, capacitous adults – as David Lock puts it, it was 'deliberately left out' of the Mental Capacity Act 2005 ('MCA 2005') scheme.[20]

14.8 Although providing quite different legal remedies, it is also worth brief consideration of the Care Act 2014. The Act addresses LA duties in respect of

[15] ibid paras 9.28–32.
[16] Children Act 1989 ('CA 1989'), s 31.
[17] Lord Chancellor's Department, *Who Decides? Making Decisions on Behalf of Mentally Incapacitated Adults*, Cm 3803 (London: TSO, 1997), para 8.6.
[18] Lord Chancellor's Department, *Making Decisions: The Government's Proposals for Making Decisions on Behalf of Mentally Incapacitated Adults*, Cm 4465 (London: TSO, 1999).
[19] Joint Committee on the Draft Mental Incapacity Bill, HL189-I / HC 1083-I (London: TSO, 2003), para 270.
[20] D Lock, 'Decision Making, Mental Capacity and Undue Influence: Do Hard Cases Make Bad – Or Least Fuzzy-Edged Law?' [2020] *Family Law* 1624, 1629.

meeting the needs of adults, where they meet specified eligibility criteria. 'Needs' fall within the Act if: (i) they 'arise from or are related to a physical or mental impairment or illness'; (ii) they result in two or more of a list of outcomes being unachievable for the individual; and, in consequence (iii) there is or is likely to be a significant impact on the adult's well-being.[21] Various principles guide LA actions, the most important for present purposes being:

(i) 'the assumption that the individual is best-placed to judge their own well-being';
(ii) the importance of 'the individual's views, wishes, feelings and beliefs';
(iii) 'the need to protect people from abuse and neglect'; and
(iv) 'the need to ensure that any restriction on the individual's rights or freedom of action that is involved in the exercise of the function is kept to the minimum necessary for achieving the purpose for which the function is being exercised'.[22]

The Care Act sets out various means by which needs may be met,[23] giving LAs both duties and powers[24] – most relevant for present purposes is the LA's duty of enquiry. Under s 42, the LA must make enquiries 'to enable it to decide whether any action should be taken in the adult's case' in any case where it has reasonable cause to believe that an adult: (i) has needs for care and support; (ii) is experiencing or is at risk of abuse or neglect; and (iii) is unable to protect themselves from that abuse or neglect as a result of their needs. However, this legislation is aimed at regulating existing service-providers in relation to specified needs for care or support.[25] Its scope and its definition of those adults affected are both narrower than apply in relation to the inherent jurisdiction and so, while the Act is significant, it addresses only a narrow range of the issues that concern the court.

14.9 The court's action in creating and expanding an entire jurisdiction over vulnerable adults must be seen against the background of the Law Commission's proposals that were never enacted, and the limited scope of the Care Act.

The Rise of the Inherent Jurisdiction in Relation to Vulnerable Adults

14.10 The history of the inherent jurisdiction regarding capacitous but vulnerable adults is set out in chapter two.[26] To summarise, as late as November 2003,

[21] Care and Support (Eligibility Criteria) Regulations 2015, r 2.
[22] Care Act 2014, s 1(3)(a), (b), (g) and (h).
[23] ibid s 8.
[24] ibid ss 18–20.
[25] For example, every LA must have a Safeguarding Adults Board, which safeguards adults 'by co-ordinating and ensuring the effectiveness of what each of its members does': Care Act 2014, s 43(3).
[26] See **2.56–2.63**.

Butler-Sloss P expressly disavowed the existence of an inherent jurisdiction over capacitous adults.[27] However, a new 'inherent' jurisdiction over *vulnerable* adults was created by the court as an off-shoot of the reactivated inherent jurisdiction over *incapacitous* adults. The inherent jurisdiction over *incapacitous* adults was itself built on the shakiest of foundations.[28] Using it as a springboard to create an entirely new jurisdiction over *vulnerable* adults – an area where the prerogative jurisdiction never historically existed[29] – really was nothing less than a sprinkle of 'magic sparkle powers' by the court.[30] Notably, this new creation occurred alongside the passage of the MCA 2005 – but only once it was apparent that the Act excluded provision for capacitous, vulnerable adults. Far from deferring to Parliament, the court embarked on a process of judicial law-making covering the same ground that was rejected during the policy-making process – and, as discussed below, the court's scheme is far wider than the Law Commission's proposals, yet contains none of its proposed safeguards.

14.11 The general principles that apply in vulnerable adult cases are discussed in chapter three.[31] Because the vulnerable person (P) has capacity in relation to the relevant decision, the MCA 2005 is not applicable.[32] The court's approach is thus vividly described by McFarlane LJ as operating in 'a jurisdictional hinterland [that] exists outside [the MCA's] borders to deal with cases of "vulnerable adults" who fall outside that Act'.[33] While Baker LJ has warned in this context of the need to avoid the *protective imperative*,[34] I suggest that the court is, to the contrary, entirely focused on this aspect – to the detriment of any principled consideration of the proper role of the court when imposing decisions on people who, by definition, have capacity to decide for themselves.

Existing Statutory Remedies

14.12 Before I address the inherent jurisdiction, it is helpful to consider the statutory remedies that may be available when a capacitous adult is perceived to be at risk of undue influence or coercion from a third party. The court asserts that it is operating in a legal lacuna,[35] and that this justifies using the inherent jurisdiction.

[27] *Re A Local Authority (Inquiry: Restraint on Publication)* [2003] EWHC 2746 (Fam), [2004] Fam 96 (Butler-Sloss P); see **2.58–2.60**.

[28] See **2.39–2.55**.

[29] As noted at **2.44**, the historic cases actively resisted any suggestion of jurisdiction existing without a commission of lunacy having first taken place.

[30] Andrew Pack's phrase to describe the inherent jurisdiction generally on his Seusspicious Minds blog, suesspiciousminds.com (accessed 1 June 2024).

[31] See in particular **3.20–3.26**.

[32] See **13.2**.

[33] *Re L (Vulnerable Adults with Capacity: Court's Jurisdiction)* [2012] EWCA Civ 253, [2013] Fam 1, [1].

[34] *A Local Authority v BF* [2018] EWCA Civ 2962, [2019] COPLR 150, [22(10)].

[35] See, eg, *Re L (Vulnerable Adults: Non-Molestation Injunction)* [2010] EWHC 2675 (Fam), [2011] Fam 189, [14] (Wall P).

But the wish to have a remedy does not in itself justify the court claiming jurisdiction over the issue.[36] And, as Joanna Miles explains:

> [L]ocal authority and court frustration at being unable to intervene does not necessarily mean that there is a gap in the law. The lack of statutory third party power to act on behalf of competent adults [who are] opposed to the proposed action and where no minors require protection may reflect a proper determination that the balance of rights and interests here weighs in favour of victims' rights to respect for family and private life.[37]

14.13 The most obvious potential remedy in the case of a capacitous adult who is at risk of undue influence or coercion is a non-molestation order ('NMO'). This injunctive protection, breach of which is a criminal offence,[38] prohibits an identified person ('D') – who must be a relative or (former) partner of P[39] – from molesting P. In practice, NMOs prohibit specified conduct – this can ban particular behaviour directed to P, or impose a geographic restriction on D to keep them from named locations such as P's home. NMOs offer significant protection, but are available only when P makes the application or is a party to existing 'family proceedings'.[40] This requirement is a substantial limitation on the utility of NMOs in vulnerable adult cases, whose subjects may not want, or recognise that they need, protecting – but this is not an oversight. The government consulted on making NMOs available on third party applications[41] – but research on the merits of this idea led to the conclusion not to add such a power.[42]

14.14 Civil injunctions under the Protection from Harassment Act 1997 also have limited utility in vulnerable adult cases. While the remedy might be useful for some situations currently addressed by the inherent jurisdiction, the Act's requirements are hard to meet, and ordinarily the application must, again, be made by P.[43] The criminal remedies under the 1997 Act are available without the consent or cooperation of the victim, but such proceedings are retrospective and cannot protect from future risk.

14.15 More relevant may be the court's new power to make Domestic Abuse Protection Orders ('DAPOs') under the Domestic Abuse Act 2021 ('DAA 2021'),[44]

[36] See also B Hewson, '"Neither Midwives nor Rainmakers": Why DL Is Wrong' [2013] *Public Law* 451, 458.

[37] J Miles, 'Family Abuse, Privacy and State Intervention' [2011] *CLJ* 31, 33.

[38] Family Law Act 1996 ('FLA 1996'), s 42A.

[39] ibid s 62.

[40] ibid s 42(2).

[41] There is power to do so by secondary legislation: FLA 1996, s 60.

[42] M Burton, 'Third Party Applications for Protection Orders in England and Wales: Service Providers' Views on Implementing Section 60 of the Family Law Act 1996' (2003) 25 *JSWFL* 137. The only exception relates to forced marriage, where protective orders are available on application by third parties: FLA 1996, s 63C(2).

[43] The general provisions are in s 3. *Cf* the wider provisions of s 3A, but the conditions require harassment of two or more persons which is intended to persuade any person (whether one of those or not) not to do something that they are entitled to do, or to do something that they have no obligation to do – but only the people being harassed can apply.

[44] DAPOs can be of any duration set by the court (any requirement of electronic monitoring can last for only 12 months): DAA 2021, s 38.

which had not entered into force at time of writing. DAPOs allow the court to either prohibit or require certain actions by D.[45] DAPOs can be made on application by P, by the appropriate Chief Constable, by third parties specified in Regulations, or by 'any other person with the leave of the court'.[46] Three conditions must be met.[47] First, the court must be satisfied on the balance of probabilities that D (who is aged 18 or over) has been abusive towards P (who is aged 16 or over). Second, D and P must be 'personally connected', which generally means being, or having been, partners or relatives.[48] And third, the DAPO must be 'necessary and proportionate to protect [P] from domestic abuse, or the risk of domestic abuse' from D.[49] Domestic abuse includes controlling or coercive behaviour, economic abuse, and physical, emotional 'or other abuse'.[50]

14.16 DAPOs will clearly not cover every situation where the inherent jurisdiction is presently used. While the broad definition of abuse will often cover the third party's behaviour towards P, the relationship between D and P will not satisfy the 'personally connected' test in all cases.[51] Further, it is unclear if the court will consider the range of powers under the Act sufficient to protect P. The Act allows the court to 'impose any requirements' on D that are necessary to protect P – this expressly includes eviction or exclusion from property, prohibiting D from contacting P, and zonal restrictions preventing D coming within a specified distance of particular premises.[52] Although these powers are wide, the court currently takes a far broader view of the orders it can make under the inherent jurisdiction, as addressed later.

14.17 Drawing these statutory threads together, other than in relation to DAPOs (once in force),[53] the scope of the powers that have been enacted to protect vulnerable adults are limited to private law actions – they do not give the state or third parties power to intervene, except through criminal law actions. The limited role that LAs and the court are given under statute makes the court's assertion that it has an 'inherent' jurisdiction to make orders in relation to vulnerable adults on the application of any third party look highly questionable.

Procedure

14.18 It is instructive at the outset to consider a few procedural issues. Much of chapter four applies also to vulnerable adults.

[45] DAA 2021, s 27(1). The Act refers to the person against whom DAPOs are being made as P, but I am using terminology consistent with the rest of this chapter.
[46] DAA 2021, s 28(2). The court can also make the order of its own motion within certain existing proceedings.
[47] DAA 2021, s 32.
[48] ibid, s 2(1).
[49] ibid s 32(3).
[50] ibid s 1.
[51] Abusive relationships between friends or neighbours, for example, will not qualify.
[52] DAA 2021, s 35.
[53] And forced marriage.

14.19 First, there is no separate application form to bring an inherent jurisdiction application with respect to a vulnerable adult – Form C66 is used, despite being headed 'Application for inherent jurisdiction order *in relation to children*' (emphasis added). The fact that there is not even a court form, 20 years after the cases started, underlines the fragile basis of the newly-invented jurisdiction.

14.20 Second, there is no list identifying who has standing to bring an application. Clearly a vulnerable adult could, in theory, bring an action of their own accord, but the nature of the cases tends to involve third parties bringing claims. David Lock suggests that the test is 'akin to a judicial review test, namely that the person who brings the proceedings must have a legitimate interest in the matter',[54] though the analogy seems unduly complex – the inherent jurisdiction regarding children has a straightforward 'genuine interest' test.[55]

14.21 The Court of Appeal has set out general guidance on applications,[56] particularly regarding *without notice* applications. The following requirement is notable:

> A party who seeks to invoke the inherent jurisdiction with regard to vulnerable adults must provide the court with their reasons for taking that course and identify the circumstances which it is contended empower the court to make the order.[57]

This point – entirely sensible in its own terms – reveals the court's uncertainty about the scope of its powers over vulnerable adults. There are no guidelines on the circumstances in which the court can intervene, and this requirement reads as a judicial plea for help – perhaps if litigants identify some principles, the court could adopt them.

Who is a Vulnerable Adult?

The Court's Definition

14.22 The court is concerned with the vague and under-theorised idea of the so-called 'vulnerable adult'. This person has mental capacity to make the relevant decision – but they are 'vulnerable' because they are (or are suspected of being) the victim of coercion or duress, or for some other reason they are unable to make an autonomous decision.[58] Because P has capacity, the MCA 2005 does not apply; the

[54] D Lock, 'Decision-making, Mental Capacity and Undue Influence: Action by Public Bodies to Explore the Grey Areas between Capacity and Incapacity' [2015] *Judicial Review* 42, 46.

[55] FPR 2010, r 12.3. See **4.5**.

[56] *Mazhar v Birmingham Community Healthcare Foundation NHS Trust* [2020] EWCA Civ 1377, [2021] 1 WLR 1207.

[57] ibid [74(4)].

[58] On meanings of 'autonomy', see J Lewis, 'Safeguarding Vulnerable Autonomy? Situational Vulnerability, the Inherent Jurisdiction, and Insights from Feminist Philosophy' (2021) 29 *Medical Law Review* 306 and J Herring, *Vulnerable Adults and the Law* (Oxford: OUP, 2016), 88–93.

inherent jurisdiction is 'targeted solely at those adults whose ability to make decisions for themselves has been compromised by matters other than those covered by the 2005 Act'.[59]

14.23 The leading authority is *Re SA (Vulnerable Adult with Capacity: Marriage)* ('*Re SA*').[60] Munby J described the 'vulnerable adults' who are within the court's jurisdiction:

> the inherent jurisdiction can be exercised in relation to a vulnerable adult who, even if not incapacitated by mental disorder or mental illness, is, or is reasonably believed to be, either: (i) under constraint; or (ii) subject to coercion or undue influence; or (iii) for some other reason deprived of the capacity to make the relevant decision, or disabled from making a free choice, or incapacitated or disabled from giving or expressing real and genuine consent.[61]

14.24 The term 'vulnerable' is being used in a specific sense here. A person may be *vulnerable* in an everyday sense but not meet the criteria for legal intervention: as Cobb J held, it is 'a question of fact [whether] his decision-making in relation to [the relevant issue] has been 'vitiated' or so overborn by his circumstances … that he should be regarded as requiring the intervention of the High Court exercising its inherent jurisdiction'.[62] However, without clear criteria for court involvement, the definition is circular: the court can intervene if the circumstances justify court intervention.

14.25 Munby J attempted to address this issue in *Re SA*, though he oscillates concerningly between adults who do and do not have capacity:

> In the context of the inherent jurisdiction I would treat as a vulnerable adult someone who, whether or not mentally incapacitated, and whether or not suffering from any mental illness or mental disorder, is or may be unable to take care of him or herself, or unable to protect him or herself against significant harm or exploitation, or who is deaf, blind or dumb, or who is substantially handicapped by illness, injury or congenital deformity. This, I emphasise, is not and is not intended to be a definition. It is descriptive, not definitive; indicative rather than prescriptive.[63]

This list is both vague and over-inclusive. For example, the idea that the court has jurisdiction to make orders in relation to a capacitous adult merely on the basis, without more, of them being deaf or blind is extraordinary. Indeed, various judges have explicitly rejected the idea,[64] Lieven J commenting: '[t]he fact that [P]

[59] *Re L (Vulnerable Adults with Capacity: Court's Jurisdiction)* [2012] EWCA Civ 253, [2013] Fam 1 ('*Re L*'), [53].

[60] *Re SA (Vulnerable Adult with Capacity: Marriage)* [2005] EWHC 2942 (Fam), [2006] 1 FLR 867 ('*Re SA*').

[61] ibid [77]. *Cf Ealing LBC v KS* [2008] EWHC 636 (Fam), [2008] 2 FLR 720, [148] (Sumner J).

[62] *Wakefield MBC v DN and MN* [2019] EWHC 2306 (Fam), [2019] COPLR 525, [45].

[63] *Re SA* (n 60) [82]. Despite stating that this was not a definition, it was described as exactly that in *Re L* (n 59) [23].

[64] See, eg, *Southend-on-Sea BC v Meyers* [2019] EWHC 399 (Fam), [2019] COPLR 202, [33] (Hayden VP).

is physically vulnerable cannot possibly be sufficient to incur the use of the inherent jurisdiction'.[65]

14.26 Munby J went on in *Re SA* to say:

> The significance … of the concept of a vulnerable adult is pragmatic and evidential: it is simply that an adult who is vulnerable is more likely to fall into the category of the incapacitated in relation to whom the inherent jurisdiction is exercisable, than an adult who is not vulnerable. So it is likely to be easier to persuade the court that there is a case calling for investigation where the adult is apparently vulnerable than where the adult is not on the face of it vulnerable.[66]

Herring rightly notes that this passage suggests that 'being vulnerable is neither a necessary nor a sufficient condition to fall within the jurisdiction',[67] and the implication within it that the court might be persuaded to intervene when a person was *not* vulnerable is truly extraordinary. Munby J also appears to be drawing a wider, non-medical definition of (in)capacity – presumably to justify this expansion of the court's jurisdiction, cloaking it in the apparent legitimacy of the inherent jurisdiction over incapacitous adults.[68]

14.27 Munby J's judgment, albeit effective in expanding the reach of the inherent jurisdiction, therefore created serious and still unanswered questions about the scope of the law. Nevertheless, his approach was expressly approved by the Court of Appeal in *Re L* in 2012 – and because the Court of Appeal added little to Munby J's judgment, *Re SA* remains the leading authority on the meaning of 'vulnerability'.

Analysis

14.28 There are four significant problems with the court's definition of 'vulnerable' adults.

14.29 First, the cases offer no clear explanation of what characteristics a person must have to qualify as 'vulnerable'.[69] In trying to identify what the court is doing in practice, Pritchard-Jones suggests 'that "vulnerability" for the purposes of invoking the inherent jurisdiction … relies on evidencing that a person['s] … decision-making about something has been "vitiated", or that their will has become

[65] *London Borough of Croydon v KR* [2019] EWHC 2498 (Fam), [2020] COPLR 285, [60].
[66] *Re SA* (n 60) [83].
[67] Herring (n 58) 81.
[68] On why I say 'apparent', see **13.4–13.9**.
[69] See L Pritchard-Jones, 'The Good, the Bad, and the "Vulnerable Older Adult"' (2013) 38 *JSWFL* 51, criticising the narrow focus on an inherent characteristic combined with a risk of harm, without assessing the particular individual's *experience* of their vulnerability: 'internal characteristics *themselves* do not generate vulnerability; it is inadequate support mechanisms that generate the experience of vulnerability.'

so overborne that the decision is no longer freely made'.[70] This definition reflects Jonathan Herring's interpretation of the authorities, that the inherent jurisdiction 'is available for those who have the capacity to make the decision, but are unable to make an autonomous choice'.[71] However, as I will explore, the position is more complicated and the authorities do not consistently apply this definition.

14.30 The inability to identify even the most basic qualifying criteria is exemplified by the Court of Appeal decision of *Re L* itself. Maurice Kay LJ, concurring with McFarlane LJ's leading judgment, thought that it would be 'most unfortunate' if the court had no power to protect a person 'against unscrupulous manipulation' of an 'oppressor' because of arguments about the person's personal autonomy.[72] Yet no explanation of these powers or their limitations was set out – it is simply that the court wants there to be a remedy to what it perceives as an unacceptable situation. Davis LJ, also agreeing, noted that it was 'the essence of humanity that adults are entitled to be eccentric, entitled to be unorthodox, entitled to be obstinate, entitled to be irrational', and that 'there can be no power of public intervention simply because an adult proposes to make a decision, or to tolerate a state of affairs, which most would consider neither wise nor sensible'[73] – yet he offered no explanation as to when or why the court could interfere. Davis LJ concluded that:

> Cases which are close to the line can safely be left to be dealt with under the inherent jurisdiction by the judges of the Family Division on the particular facts and circumstances arising in each instance.[74]

In other words: trust the judges.

14.31 The second problem with the court's definition comes from eliding 'vulnerability' with 'incapacity'.[75] In his suggested third category of people who fall within the definition, quoted earlier, Munby J used the words 'deprived of the capacity' and 'incapacitated'. The same issue arises in Macur J's judgment in *LBL v RYJ and VJ*:

> I do not doubt the availability of the inherent jurisdiction to supplement the protection afforded by the Mental Capacity Act 2005 for those who, whilst 'capacitous' for the purposes of the Act, are 'incapacitated' by external forces – whatever they may be – outside their control from reaching a decision.[76]

[70] Pritchard-Jones (n 7) 1372. I have removed the words 'is incapacitated in the sense that their' because the term 'incapacitated' is apt to confuse.

[71] J Herring, 'Protecting Vulnerable Adults: A Critical Review of Recent Case Law' [2009] *CFLQ* 498, 502.

[72] *Re L* (n 59) [79]. Hewson (n 36) highlights the emotive language of this judgment.

[73] ibid [76].

[74] ibid. *Cf* Peter Harris's tongue-in-cheek remark that the inherent jurisdiction is seen as unproblematic because High Court judges are 'nice chaps in London': see **1.7**.

[75] Concerningly, the court also often equates *unwise decisions* with *incapacity*, 'identifying a perceived unwise decision first – [such as] the decision to remain in an abusive situation – and declaring a person therefore lacks capacity to make the decision': Pritchard-Jones (n 7) 1368.

[76] *LBL v RYJ and VJ* [2010] EWHC 2665 (COP), [2011] 1 FLR 1279, [62]; this passage is expressly approved in *Re L* (n 59).

Describing a person as 'incapacitated' despite being 'capacitous' (for the purposes of the MCA 2005) introduces confusion into the law between the categories of 'vulnerable' but capacitous adults, and adults without capacity.[77] It is also not clear that Macur J is right to say that the person is *unable* to reach a decision – more accurate may be Herring's language, that P is 'unable to make an autonomous choice'.[78]

14.32 Third, as Pritchard-Jones explains, Munby J's definition of 'vulnerability' 'was exceptionally broad and potentially covered an exponential number of situations'.[79] While Herring may be right that the court should not attempt 'anything that is like a precise statutory definition' given its constitutional role,[80] the lack of definition leaves the jurisdiction's boundaries unclear. Is it compatible with the rule of law – or with the requirement in Article 8 of the ECHR that interferences with the right to respect for private and family life be 'in accordance with the law' – that it is impossible to say in advance whether a particular person in a particular situation is or is not liable to have orders made about them?

14.33 Finally, Munby J's definition of a 'vulnerable adult' is incoherent. Internally, it incorporates three separate categories of people with no universally applicable explanation or rationale that justifies the court's power to intervene in their private and family lives. It is also inconsistent with the private law concepts of duress and undue influence.

14.34 Taking the latter point first, Munby J's first two 'categories' of vulnerable adult – that P is '(i) under constraint; or (ii) subject to coercion or undue influence'[81] – bear close resemblance to the private (contract) law concepts of duress and undue influence. As explored in chapter two, in private law, duress, unconscionability and undue influence are equitable remedies that act as a shield (and not a sword) within existing proceedings; they are not jurisdictional triggers that justify state intervention in people's lives.[82] Contract law sets a high bar for what must be shown to establish duress, unconscionability or undue influence;[83] and the defences arise after the event, when the wrongful conduct has actually taken place and affected P's behaviour.

14.35 Despite defining vulnerable adults (in part) by reference to these private law concepts, the inherent jurisdiction over vulnerable adults has entirely different legal consequences. Being judged to be at risk of duress or undue influence in the vulnerable adult case law gives rise to a general jurisdiction in the court – available

[77] See further in relation to deprivation of liberty at **14.52** *et seq*, and in the conclusions at **14.69**.
[78] Herring (n 71) 502.
[79] Pritchard-Jones (n 7) 1365.
[80] Herring (n 58) 85; see **1.22–1.27**.
[81] *Re SA* (n 60) [77].
[82] See **2.62**. See also Hewson (n 36) 458.
[83] Lock (n 20) 1633; see generally E McKendrick, *Contract Law: Text, Cases, and Materials*, 10th edn (Oxford: OUP, 2022), chs 18–20.

at the behest of interested third parties (LAs, healthcare providers, relatives, neighbours, landlords?) – to take action that P may or may not want, and where the orders made often directly affect P as well as D. The duress or undue influence may not yet have prevented P from doing what they wish to do;[84] and the court's view of what amounts to duress or undue influence is 'entirely more flexible' than in the private law context.[85] As Lock explains, the logical implication of using these terms to justify pre-emptive intervention by the court is that 'if this were to be a private law action where P was later seeking to avoid legal responsibility for his or her decisions, the court would grant P a remedy' because of D's undue influence or duress.[86] Consequently, Lock persuasively concludes that vulnerability per se is not the basis for the court's jurisdiction in these cases – rather, it is 'vulnerability coupled with decisions which could later be set aside on established legal grounds or where there is [actual or] threatened future wrongdoing which can be restrained by an injunction'.[87]

14.36 Munby J's third category of persons is different from the first two: adults who are 'for some other reason deprived of the capacity to make the relevant decision, or disabled from making a free choice, or incapacitated or disabled from giving or expressing real and genuine consent'.[88] Herring suggests a possible explanation for the jurisdiction extending into this third category – the state may have positive obligation to act to protect people from breach of their rights under Articles 2 and 3 of the ECHR.[89] This approach, protecting people from death, or from torture or inhuman or degrading treatment, also fits Lock's general thesis – that it is defensible for the court to claim jurisdiction over capacitous adults where a legal wrong is being done to them.[90] If Articles 2 or 3 are engaged, an actionable wrong is (at least potentially) taking place, requiring the state to protect P. However, if this if the rationale, the court must say so explicitly and, as Herring argues, limit itself to cases that meet those criteria. Certainly that is not presently the situation, hence the concern that the law stretches to cover 'not only those who are not able to make autonomous decisions, but also those who do not, for some reason, exercise their autonomy to protect themselves from exploitation or neglect'.[91]

[84] Some cases clearly involve P being prevented from taking the decision that they wish to by D, such as *Al-Jeffrey v Al-Jeffrey (Vulnerable Adult: British Citizen) (No 3)* [2017] EWHC 774 (Fam) (Holman J) where P was allegedly being held against her will in Saudi Arabia and wished to return to the UK. But most cases do not fall into this category – mostly, the claim is that D's influence means that P's decision does not reflect their *true* wish – even when P says otherwise. See Pritchard-Jones (n 7) 1375–6.

[85] Lock (n 20) 1633. See also Pritchard-Jones (n 7) 1374: 'the courts have given a limited indication as to what exactly they are looking for in such coercion or undue influence'.

[86] ibid.

[87] ibid.

[88] *Re SA*, (n 60) [77].

[89] Herring (n 71) 503.

[90] Lock (n 20) 1632. He argues this in relation to duress and undue influence specifically.

[91] Herring (n 71) 502.

14.37 The problem is that the court is singly ill-equipped to create a coherent definition.[92] Ad hoc decision-making on a case-by-case basis of the kind that the court does is not the way for a principled general policy to be established from scratch, particularly not in an area of social policy where views will legitimately differ as to the appropriate role for the state.[93] As Miles puts it, this area 'raise[s] questions of principle which should ideally be resolved after full consultation with key stakeholders, not by a court … in one difficult case'.[94]

14.38 In light of these significant problems with the court's definition of vulnerability, it is hard not to sympathise with Pritchard-Jones's suggestion that the cases show:

> an attempt to circumnavigate the technicalities of the MCA 2005 in having to prove that it is the disturbance of the mind or brain that is causing the incapacity so that pre-decided protective measures can be put in place around the person either way.[95]

This links to her further concern that the cases suggest that the court is simply imposing 'better' outcomes on people who 'should' want different things from what they claim to be wanting[96] – the opposite of promoting autonomy.

The Scope of the Court's Powers and its Guiding Principles

14.39 The next issue is what the court can actually do concerning a vulnerable adult. Munby J in *Re SA* said that, as with the inherent jurisdiction in relation to children, there are *theoretically* no limitations:

> Just as there are, in theory, no limits to the court's powers when exercising the wardship jurisdiction I suspect that there are, in theory, few if any limits to the court's powers when exercising the inherent jurisdiction in relation to adults.[97]

Since the jurisdiction has no history or principles of its own, just those borrowed from children and incapacitous adult cases, this may be right. It also follows that this theoretical power is subject to significant restrictions in practice as to how the court will exercise it.[98]

14.40 However, there are two problems. First, in the context of children and of incapacitous adults, the subject of the application *requires* the court to make

[92] See **1.22–1.27**.
[93] Hence the differences of opinion during the policy-making process leading to the MCA 2005: see **14.4–14.7**.
[94] Miles (n 37) 34.
[95] Pritchard-Jones (n 7) 1374.
[96] ibid 1376.
[97] *Re SA* (n 60) [84].
[98] See **3.35** *et seq*.

a decision because they cannot make it themselves, and it may relate to all kinds of things – education / training, medical and healthcare, personal care, interpersonal relationships / contact, living arrangements, and so on. It is doubtful that this range of orders is available, or appropriate, in relation to a *capacitous* adult: the law should be more restricted, reflecting P's capacity and autonomy. Second, a major limitation on the exercise of the court's power over children / incapacitous adults is that the best interests of the child / adult must be the court's paramount consideration.[99] There are detailed guidelines in the MCA 2005 as to what must be done to determine P's best interests, including considering P's past and present wishes, values and beliefs.[100] However, the statutory best interests principle has no application to *capacitous* but vulnerable adults, and the substituted decision-making it involves is inappropriate[101] – so what are the guiding principles?

14.41 McFarlane LJ, in *Re L*, emphasised the 'facilitative, rather than dictatorial, approach of the court' in accordance with 'the re-establishment of the individual's autonomy of decision-making in a manner which enhances, rather than breaches, their Article 8 rights'.[102] This passage is crucial, yet ambiguous. It seems to involve P's views being given significant weight, but that is never actually stated – nor is there any mention (as there was in the Law Commission's proposals, for example) of P having a right of veto over any intervention. McFarlane LJ quoted from Theis J's judgment at first instance in *Re L*, where she said that the 'primary purpose [of the inherent jurisdiction over vulnerable adults] is to create a situation where the person concerned can receive outside help free of coercion, to enable him or her to weigh things up and decide freely what he or she wishes to do'[103] – but if this is the approach (it was not endorsed, just quoted), the consequences are not followed through. There is no time limit set on interventions; there is no requirement that interventions are limited to creating 'breathing room' for P to express a free view; and there is no mechanism to assess whether P's expressed views are 'genuine' or not. These are all failings arising from the court taking on the role of policy-maker for which it is ill-suited.[104]

14.42 High Court judges have attempted to give substance to this general principle, with significant variations in approach. At one end, Cobb J and Lieven J have given the inherent jurisdiction a limited role in relation to capacitous adults. For instance, in relation to orders about a person's place of residence, Cobb J has suggested that the inherent jurisdiction can be used only 'as an interim measure

[99] This is required by statute in children cases, applying CA 1989, s 1(1); for *incapacitous* adults, the MCA 2005 is applied by analogy.
[100] MCA 2005, s 4. There is authority that at least some of these principles should be applied to vulnerable adult cases: see, eg, *London Borough of Croydon v KR* [2019] EWHC 2498 (Fam), [2020] COPLR 285, [52] (Lieven J); *London Borough of Islington v EF* [2022] EWHC 803 (Fam) (DHCJ Verdan QC).
[101] Pritchard-Jones (n 7) 1381.
[102] [2012] EWCA Civ 253, [2013] Fam 1, [67].
[103] Quoted in *Re L* (n 59) [26]; see also *FS v RS and JS* [2020] EWFC 63, [2020] 4 WLR 139, [114] (Sir James Munby).
[104] *Cf* **14.7**: legislators thought that drawing the lines in this area was too difficult.

while proper inquiries are made', allowing the court to determine whether there is a situation that justifies the court's intervention.[105] Conversely, Hayden VP has used the inherent jurisdiction to make long-term orders about P's place of residence and the people with whom P could live, against P's express wishes.[106] Consequently, the case law is mixed – and it is unclear that McFarlane LJ's benign-sounding approach is an accurate description of what the court is in fact doing. While there are general limitations on the power of the court, as set out in chapter three,[107] and some cases suggest specific limitations,[108] Pritchard-Jones is right that 'clarity has, unfortunately, not been forthcoming about what [the inherent jurisdiction] *can* be used to do'.[109]

14.43 There are four further, specific concerns with the court's approach stemming from the fact that no clear principles underpin the new jurisdiction over capacitous adults. First, the claim that orders are 'facilitative' rather than 'dictatorial' is, at best, a matter of perspective:[110] the court's facilitative order is P's dictatorial restriction on their autonomy. Lock[111] illustrates this concern with *Re D (Vulnerable Adult) (Injunction: Power of Arrest)*.[112] P was an 18-year-old woman and the local authority sought injunctions preventing her father (AD) and a male friend (GH) going to her home. Both AD and GH misused drugs, and GH alleged made P take heroin, was physically violent towards her, and took money from her. A psychiatric report concluded that P had capacity, but that she was susceptible to influence by both AD and GH. P did not accept that she was vulnerable, and she had insight into the fact that spending time with AD and GH was not good for her – but she wished to do so anyway, even after a period in which the court's injunctions had been in place to give her space away from them. As Lock says, therefore:

> The court did not limit the injunctions to cover a period of reflection but continued them for as long as [P] maintained an oppositionist stance. So it was simply taking decisions away from [P] despite the fact that she had capacity to make her own (unwise) decisions.[113]

[105] *Wakefield MBC v DN and MN* [2019] EWHC 2306 (Fam), [2019] COPLR 525, [47], endorsed by *London Borough of Croydon v KR* [2019] EWHC 2498 (Fam), [2020] COPLR 285, [44] (Lieven J).

[106] *Southend-on-Sea BC v Meyers* [2019] EWHC 399 (Fam), [2019] COPLR 202. Munby (2021) (n 1) is highly critical of this case. See further **14.49** and **14.58** *et seq.*

[107] See **3.35** *et seq.*

[108] For example, contra *Re SA* (n 60), the court cannot impose a power of arrest under the inherent jurisdiction: *Re D (Vulnerable Adult) (Injunction: Power of Arrest)* [2016] EWHC 2358 (Fam), [2017] Fam 105 (HHJ Bellamy).

[109] Pritchard-Jones (n 7) 1379 (original emphasis).

[110] See ibid 1379–81.

[111] Lock (n 20) 1634.

[112] *Re D (Vulnerable Adult) (Injunction: Power of Arrest)* [2016] EWHC 2358 (Fam), [2017] Fam 105 (HHJ Bellamy).

[113] Lock (n 20) 1634.

14.44 Second, while some cases reflect the 'facilitative' principle,[114] there are cases that impose orders *against* P (rather than against D).[115] If the aim is to allow P to make choices free from undue influence, why are orders being made against P?[116] In the related fields of NMOs or forced marriage protection orders, the law clearly differentiates between D, against whom the injunctive orders are made, and 'the person for whose benefit such an order … is made' / 'the person to be protected' respectively.[117] It would be non-sensical (as well as contrary to the statutory provisions) for these orders to be made *against* P – yet that is exactly what happens under the inherent jurisdiction in some cases.

14.45 Third, there is inadequate focus on safeguards. Even the safeguards that exist under the MCA 2005 in relation to incapacitous adults – for instance, the requirement to focus on whether P has capacity to make a *particular* decision – are not reflected in the court's approach to vulnerable adults.[118] Certainly there is no consideration of the wider safeguards (a right to veto intervention) that the Law Commission proposed.[119]

14.46 Finally, the compatibility of the court's approach with Article 8 of the ECHR is questionable. The Court of Appeal in *Re L* sated that the court's orders must be necessary and proportionate[120] – but what that means in this context was not articulated.[121] Nor did the court ask whether this newly-created inherent jurisdiction, under which the court has entirely unclear and unpredictable powers in circumstances where Parliament declined to legislate, is 'in accordance with the law', as required by Article 8. I rather doubt that it is.

Application to Specific Issues

14.47 I turn to address various specific circumstances in which the court has used its inherent jurisdiction regarding vulnerable adults. I do not intend this as a comprehensive analysis, but focus on areas of particular interest.

[114] See, eg, *LBL v RYJ and VJ* [2010] EWHC 2665 (COP), [2011] 1 FLR 1279 (Macur J); *London Borough of Islington v EF* [2022] EWHC 803 (Fam) (DHCJ Verdan QC); *cf* D Bedford and P Bremner, 'Falling Through the Great Safety Net of the Inherent Jurisdiction' (2023) 31 *Medical Law Review* 441.
[115] Munby (2021) (n 1) 513, argues that the inherent jurisdiction cannot be used to prevent a vulnerable adult from doing anything that would otherwise be lawful.
[116] See, eg, *Southend-on-Sea BC v Meyers* [2019] EWHC 399 (Fam), [2019] COPLR 202 (Hayden VP), discussed at **14.51**; *Mazhar v Birmingham Community Healthcare Foundation NHS Trust* [2020] EWCA Civ 1377, [2021] 1 WLR 1207, accepting the idea that the court could order P to be removed from his home and taken to hospital for treatment against his will.
[117] FLA 1996, ss 42(4B) and 63A(2).
[118] Pritchard-Jones (n 7) 1366.
[119] See **14.5**.
[120] ibid [66] (McFarlane LJ) and [76] (Davis LJ).
[121] See Pritchard-Jones (n 7) 1381–3 and Bedford and Bremner (n 114) 447–8.

Accommodation

14.48 The court says it can, at least on a short-term basis, make injunctive restrictions on P's place of residence – in other words, require P to leave their home and reside at a specified location such as a care home. An example is *Wakefield MBC v DN and MN*.[122] Cobb J held that it was 'entirely proper for the inherent jurisdiction to be invoked as an interim measure while proper inquiries are made',[123] including ordering that P be removed from their home for the purposes of assessing whether they needed court assistance. For Cobb J, this was a short-term measure while assessments were made, enabling P to express their views free from potential influence. Referencing Cobb J's similar decision in *Redcar and Cleveland BC v PR*,[124] the authors of the 39 Essex blog suggest that the decision will provide 'some reassurance to statutory bodies faced with difficult and urgent situations concerning safeguarding people with capacity that the court will exercise its powers, at least on a temporary basis'.[125] However, the court's approach raises serious questions.

14.49 It is true that LAs have various duties, including to 'make enquiries' if they have reasonable cause to think that an adult with care and support needs is experiencing (or is at risk of experiencing) abuse or neglect[126] – but it is questionable whether the inherent jurisdiction should be used to regulate P's accommodation to facilitate those enquiries. In the context of children thought to be at risk of harm, Parliament provided LAs with investigatory powers and gave the court powers to support those investigations, including to remove a child from their home if necessary for the purposes of assessment.[127] These powers are strictly defined and regulated, both as to the circumstances in which they can be invoked and their duration. By contrast, the Care Act 2014 provides no equivalent powers in relation to vulnerable adults, and – more strikingly still – it *repealed* a previous statutory power to remove 'aged, infirm or physically incapacitated' persons from their homes when they were not receiving adequate care there.[128] The court appears to have not only disregarded the removal of this power, but indeed to have expanded the scope of it – the inherent jurisdiction is used without any apparent restrictions, other than general (usually unparticularised and rarely analysed) references to necessity and proportionality.

[122] *Wakefield MBC v DN and MN* [2019] EWHC 2306 (Fam), [2019] COPLR 525.

[123] ibid [47]. Inherent jurisdiction applications are used as a mechanism for a capacity assessment to be ordered, the case then transferred to the Court of Protection if P lacks capacity: see, eg, *London Borough of Redbridge v G* [2014] EWCOP 485 (Russell J).

[124] *Redcar and Cleveland BC v PR* [2019] EWHC 2305 (Fam) [2020] 1 FLR 827.

[125] Anon, 'Redcar and Cleveland BC v PR and others', 5 September 2019, online at www.39essex.com/information-hub/case/redcar-and-cleveland-bc-v-pr-and-others (accessed 1 June 2024).

[126] Care Act 2014, s 42.

[127] CA 1989, ss 43(9) and 48(3).

[128] National Assistance Act 1948, s 47, repealed by Care Act 2014, s 46.

14.50 Even for short-term investigations of P's potential vulnerability, therefore, the court's intervention is questionable. For the court to remove P from their own property – as opposed to removing D from P's property, or preventing D from contacting P, for example – is plainly a violation of Article 8. I doubt this interference is 'in accordance with the law', given that this judicial power is entirely unenumerated, created on an ad hoc basis, and flies in the face of a similar statutory power having been repealed. I also question whether such orders are necessary and proportionate, given that less intrusive remedies (against D) are probably available.

14.51 More controversial still is the court's use of the inherent jurisdiction to make longer-term orders regulating a capacitous adult's living arrangements. Once a short-term order has been used to give P space to make their own autonomous decision, can the court interfere further? The authorities are contradictory. Lieven J has (surely rightly) held that the court will normally struggle to justify this type of order.[129] On the other hand, in *Southend-on-Sea v Meyers*,[130] Hayden VP did exactly that – an approach that has been subjected to significant criticism.[131] It is difficult to see how the court is justified in imposing decisions about *anything* against a capacitous adult's wishes, let alone something as fundamental as where they live and with whom they spend their time. Hayden VP was clearly deeply concerned that one consequence for Mr Meyers of returning home to live with his son might have been Mr Meyers' death. Nevertheless, it is not clear that this risk justifies state intervention when the adult is cognisant of the risk, capable of weighing the consequences, has alternative choices available to them, and wishes to make the decision for themselves.

Deprivation of Liberty

14.52 The concerns about the court's approach to P's accommodation become even more acute if the court's order amounts to the deprivation of liberty ('DOL') of a vulnerable adult, which some authorities suggest that the inherent jurisdiction can do.[132] I consider these cases to be wrong and the orders made to be unlawful.

14.53 The starting point is Article 5 of the ECHR, and in particular para 1(e):

> (1) Everyone has the right to liberty and security of person. No one shall be deprived of his liberty save in the following cases and in accordance with a procedure prescribed by law: …

[129] *London Borough of Croydon v KR* [2019] EWHC 2498 (Fam), [2020] COPLR 285, [63].
[130] *Southend-on-Sea v Meyers* [2019] EWHC 399 (Fam), [2019] COPLR 202.
[131] See especially Munby (2021) (n 1).
[132] See *Hertfordshire CC v AB* [2018] EWHC 3103 (Fam), [2019] Fam 291 (Knowles J); *A Local Authority v BF* [2018] EWCA Civ 2962, [2019] COPLR 150 (Baker LJ, a reported permission to appeal decision), and the same case at a further hearing in *Southend-on-Sea BC v Meyers* [2019] EWHC 399 (Fam), [2019] COPLR 202 (Hayden VP). See also obiter comments in *NCC v PB and TB* [2014] EWCOP 14, [2015] COPLR 118, [113] and [122] (Parker J).

> (e) the lawful detention of persons for the prevention of the spreading of infectious diseases, *of persons of unsound mind*, alcoholics or drug addicts or vagrants; … (emphasis added).

14.54 The European Court of Human Rights has set out three criteria that must be met for this provision to be satisfied:

> The very nature of what has to be established before the competent national authority – that is, a true mental disorder – calls for objective medical evidence. Further, the mental disorder must be of a kind or degree warranting compulsory confinement. What is more, the validity of continued confinement depends on the persistence of such a disorder.[133]

Reference to 'persons of unsound mind' must be given a narrow interpretation.[134] Derogations from these requirements are permitted in cases of a genuine emergency,[135] in particular when the state has reason to doubt capacity but has not yet had opportunity to make a determination. In such circumstances, emergency detention is lawful only for a short period of time – medical assessment must be undertaken as soon as possible if detention is to continue.[136] Beyond a short-term emergency response, DOL is permissible only when supported by clear medical evidence[137] – and for a *capacitous* but vulnerable adult, by definition there will not be medical evidence demonstrating 'a true mental disorder'.

14.55 The language of the Convention in discussing 'unsound mind' and the more modern language of the English court in thinking about capacity has created a degree of inconsistency – just one of the 'troubling pockets of confusion' relating to the inherent jurisdiction over vulnerable adults.[138] This difficulty arises, in my view, from the court's frequent elision of the words *capacity* and *vulnerability*.[139] By choosing to describe a person whose will is overborne as 'incapacitated', the court creates an unhelpful grey area, opening a space for this non-medical version of 'incapacity' to meet (or rather, circumvent) the requirements of Article 5. As Amber Pugh says, this approach to Article 5 is 'extremely artificial': 'An approach to unsound mind that is devoid of any internal mental impairment and is instead premised solely on external constraints to capacity is far beyond the scope of Article 5(1)(e).'[140]

[133] *Winterwerp v The Netherlands* (App No 6301/73) [1979] ECHR 4, [39]. On the applicability of these criteria in domestic law, see *M v Secretary of State for Justice* [2018] UKSC 60, [2019] AC 712, [8].
[134] *Ilnseher v Germany* (App No 10211/12) [2019] MHLR 278, [129].
[135] *X v United Kingdom* (App No 7215/75) [1981] ECHR 6, [40]–[41].
[136] ibid [44]–[45]; *Varbanov v Bulgaria* (App No 31365/96) [2000] ECHR 457, [47].
[137] See A Pugh, 'Emergencies and Equivocality under the Inherent Jurisdiction' (2019) 27 *Medical Law Review* 675, 679–80, for an excellent analysis of these requirements.
[138] ibid 686.
[139] See **14.31**.
[140] Pugh (n 137) 682.

14.56 Not only would such an approach be outside a plain reading of the words 'of unsound mind', it is the opposite of the required narrow approach.[141] This view accords with Cobb J in *Wakefield MBC v DN and MN*.[142] In determining the approach to take in relation to the *vulnerable* P, Cobb J distinguished the cases on *incapacitous* adults – 'the inherent jurisdiction *cannot* properly be deployed to authorise a deprivation of [P]'s liberty (as opposed to a restriction of his liberty)'.[143]

14.57 The Court of Appeal declined to rule on this issue in *Mazhar v Birmingham Community Healthcare Foundation NHS Trust* because the appeal was resolved on other grounds.[144] Baker LJ's obiter analysis of the issue is nonetheless problematic, failing to differentiate between cases on *vulnerable* versus *incapacitous* adults.[145] *Mazhar* should therefore not be relied on as authority for the proposition that an adult with capacity can be deprived of their liberty using the inherent jurisdiction.

14.58 By contrast, Hayden VP's decision in *Southend-on-Sea BC v Meyers* is undoubtedly authority that a vulnerable but capacitous adult can be subject to DOL using the inherent jurisdiction.[146] Mr Meyers was an elderly man, blind and with diabetes and osteoarthritis. It was accepted that he was capacitous within the meaning of the MCA 2005, and that his physical disabilities did not make him 'vulnerable' so as to justify court intervention. However, he lived with his son who had drug and alcohol addiction and was so abusive towards care staff that they refused to attend the home. Mr Meyers was found partially clothed, not having eaten or drunk liquid for days, and his home squalid. He was removed to residential care and an urgent order prevented him from returning home. Pausing there, this order was justified: the evidence showed that Mr Meyers at that stage probably lacked capacity, and the situation constituted an emergency such as to justify a temporary deprivation of liberty while further assessments were made.[147] With treatment having been provided, however, Mr Meyers quickly regained capacity and he expressed a wish to return home to live with his son.

14.59 Despite the LA not seeking further restrictions, Hayden VP continued the orders preventing Mr Meyers from returning home. Permission to appeal against those orders was refused by Baker LJ.[148] Baker LJ appears to have treated the 'emergency' stage as ongoing, though this is doubtful: as Pugh comments, 'there was adequate evidence available to Baker LJ to militate against a finding of

[141] *Ilnseher v Germany* (Application No 10211/12) [2019] MHLR 278, [129].
[142] [2019] EWHC 2306 (Fam), [2019] COPLR 525. See also *CD v London Borough of Croydon* [2019] EWHC 2943 (Fam) (Cobb J).
[143] [2019] EWHC 2306 (Fam), [2019] COPLR 525, [27] (original emphasis).
[144] *Mazhar v Birmingham Community Healthcare Foundation NHS Trust* [2020] EWCA Civ 1377, [2021] 1 WLR 1207.
[145] See Munby (2021) (n 1) 369–73.
[146] *Southend-on-Sea BC v Meyers* [2019] EWHC 399 (Fam), [2019] COPLR 202.
[147] Pugh (n 137) 678.
[148] *A Local Authority v BF* [2018] EWCA Civ 2962, [2019] COPLR 150.

unsound mind and … the situation before Baker LJ could no longer be properly regarded as an emergency'.[149] An alternative is that Baker LJ failed to resist what Peter Jackson J once termed '[t]he temptation to base a judgment of a person's capacity upon whether they seem to have made a good or bad decision':[150] Mr Meyers' decision was objectively questionable, and it may have been tempting, while proceedings were on-going, to approach it on the basis of a lack of capacity. Ironically, Baker LJ remarked that 'where someone is not found to be of unsound mind, they cannot, of course, be detained in circumstances which amount to a deprivation of liberty'[151] – yet he refused Mr Meyers' application for permission to appeal an order that did exactly that.

14.60 At the final hearing, the evidence showed that Mr Meyers had capacity and was not under duress or coercion from his son. The court nevertheless held that Mr Meyers was within the court's jurisdiction over vulnerable adults on the basis of his son's malign influence. Orders were made (framed as a 'restriction on movement', rather than a DOL) allowing Mr Meyers to live where he wanted – but not with his son.

14.61 It is doubtful that this order truly did not amount to a DOL.[152] As Pugh has noted, the European Court has been sceptical of attempts to differentiate 'deprivation of liberty' from 'restriction of movement' – the difference is 'merely one of degree and intensity, and not one of nature and substance'.[153] Pugh observes that Hayden VP's decision (that Mr Meyers' son could not live with him) was only enforceable by regular monitoring, and cites the Ministry of Justice's former *Code of Practice* which indicated that similar factual scenarios would amount to a DOL.[154] If the restrictions did amount to a DOL, the order breached Article 5.

14.62 Despite this authority to the contrary, Cobb J must be right in his conclusion in *Wakefield MBC v DN and MN* that the inherent jurisdiction cannot be used to authorise DOL of a capacitous adult.[155] While the court *may* be able to make restrictions on liberty, there are two significant limitations. First, since there

[149] Pugh (n 137) 680.
[150] *Heart of England NHS Foundation Trust v JB* [2014] EWHC 342 (COP), 137 BMLR 232, [7].
[151] *A Local Authority v BF* [2018] EWCA Civ 2962, [2019] COPLR 150, [35].
[152] Anon, 'Southend-on-Sea Borough Council v Meyers', 20 February 2019, online at www.39essex.com/information-hub/case/southend-sea-borough-council-v-meyers (accessed 1June 2024). Sir James Munby expressed 'some doubt' about *Meyers*; '*if correct*, it must … mark the extremity of what can be done in exercise of the jurisdiction': *FS v RS and JS* [2020] EWFC 63, [2020] 4 WLR 139, [122] (original emphasis).
[153] *Guzzardi v Italy* (App No 7367/76) [1980] ECHR 5, [93]; Pugh (n 137) 683.
[154] Pugh (n 137) 684, citing Ministry of Justice, *Mental Capacity Act 2005: Deprivation of Liberty Safeguards* (London: TSO, 2008), para 2.5. This guidance is no longer current, but gave indicative examples, including 'A decision has been taken by the institution that the person will not be released into the care of others, or permitted to live elsewhere, unless the staff in the institution consider it appropriate', 'The person is unable to maintain social contacts because of restrictions placed on their access to other people' and 'The person loses autonomy because they are under continuous supervision and control.'
[155] [2019] EWHC 2306 (Fam), [2019] COPLR 525.

is no bright-line demarcation between DOL and restriction on liberty, the court must analyse the issue specifically in each case. It is not enough simply to assert that any orders amount 'only' to a restriction – the question is what actual effect they have on P. Second, even 'mere' restrictions must be the least interventionist measure possible to achieve a legitimate aim. Since the legitimacy of the aim of imposing orders on capacitous adults is itself dubious, there is an additional onus to ensure that restrictions are objectively necessary and proportionate – and to provide proper analysis to support that conclusion.

Contact and Family Relationships

14.63 Many vulnerable adult cases concern the regulation of inter-personal relationships. This is unsurprising, given that a central part of the justification for the court's involvement in the lives of capacitous adults is that they are being subjected to coercion, duress or undue influence. I take some illustrative examples here.

14.64 The Court of Appeal's decision in *Re L* itself is an obvious example. The LA was concerned about the treatment of an elderly couple by their son, with whom they lived, including physical assault, verbal abuse, controlling behaviour towards the mother (and towards care professionals attempting to support her), and financial abuse. The court granted orders restraining the son's behaviour towards his parents.[156] If the court has power to intervene in these cases at all, orders like these – responding directly to the cause of the problem – seem appropriate; the only question is about duration. If the purpose of the inherent jurisdiction is to give P space to make autonomous decisions, the nature of the decisions that are being restricted or influenced by D should determine the duration of the restrictions, alongside consideration of whether P is able to obtain other effective protection. Once the DAA 2021 is in force, for example, the parents in *Re L* would be eligible for a DAPO;[157] if the parents choose not to make such an application (or if the court refused to make the DAPO), it is inappropriate for inherent jurisdiction orders to continue.

14.65 At the other end of the age spectrum, the court may also be concerned with young adults, for example those who are at risk of grooming and where the aim is to extend protections that were in place while P was a minor. An example is *London Borough of Islington v EF*.[158] The LA's principal application was for a

[156] The orders also included injunctions against D in respect of care staff and other professionals. It is easy to see why D's action against a care-giver could affect P; it is harder to see the jurisdictional basis for any orders to protect that professional directly, rather than (say) an order preventing D from going within 100 meters of P's property, thus ensuring that professionals can attend if P wished them to. If needed, injunctive protection was probably available to the care workers under the Protection from Harassment Act 1997.

[157] See **14.15**.

[158] *London Borough of Islington v EF* [2022] EWHC 803 (Fam) (DHCJ Verdan QC).

restriction on P's ability to travel abroad, where she sought to meet D. The court rightly refused to restrict P's movement. D was already abroad (and could not enter the UK for legal reasons), so his influence over P was not so immediate that she could not seek assistance had she wanted it – certainly this was a long way from the threshold for duress or undue influence in the private (contract) law field. Going to meet D abroad may have been an unwise decision, but seeking restrictions on P herself (rather than protecting P by imposing restrictions on D) was inappropriate in the case of a capacitous adult who had various choices open to her and the ability to make her own decision.[159] On different facts, though, if D was in this country, the court might consider orders restricting D from contacting or approaching P for a limited period of time, to allow P to make applications for other protective orders if she wished.[160] Again, under the DAA 2021, P could apply for a DAPO if there was a previous intimate relationship; alternatively, P could likely obtain an injunction under the Protection from Harassment Act 1997 if she chose to apply for one.[161]

Nationality-Based Jurisdiction

14.66 The court takes the view that it can exercise jurisdiction over a vulnerable but capacitous adult if they are a British national, even when they are not physically present or habitually resident in this country. Nationality-based jurisdiction in relation to children is addressed in detail in chapter six – in so far as the court has an equivalent jurisdiction over vulnerable adults, the same principles must apply.

14.67 In *Al-Jeffrey v Al-Jeffrey (Vulnerable Adult: British Citizen)*,[162] the applicant was a dual British and Saudi Arabian national, born and raised in Wales. Shortly before turning 18, P was forced to travel to Saudi Arabia by her father. Proceedings commenced shortly after her removal but were withdrawn on her application. Four years later P re-applied, contending that her father had coerced or deceived her into withdrawing the previous application, and that she was being abused and constrained by him and prevented from leaving Saudi Arabia. Holman J invoked a nationality-based jurisdiction by analogy with the approach to children,[163] and made orders requiring the father to facilitate P's return to England and Wales.

14.68 *Al-Jeffrey* is undoubtedly authority for the proposition that the court can exercise jurisdiction based on P's nationality, though it has not been applied in any

[159] *Cf* Bedford and Bremner (n 121).

[160] See, eg, *Re D (Vulnerable Adult) (Injunction: Power of Arrest)* [2016] EWHC 2358 (Fam), [2017] Fam 105 (HHJ Bellamy). However, the orders were made on a long-term basis, an inappropriate use of the jurisdiction. See also Lock (n 20) 1634, and discussion at **14.43**.

[161] See **14.14**.

[162] *Al-Jeffrey v Al-Jeffrey (Vulnerable Adult: British Citizen)* [2016] EWHC 2151 (Fam), [2018] 4 WLR 136.

[163] See **ch 6**.

other vulnerable adult cases.[164] While it is possible to sympathise with the decision, it is somewhat remarkable. By comparison, judges have refused to exercise nationality-based jurisdiction in relation to *incapacitous* adults in several cases because it would cut across the statutory scheme of the MCA 2005.[165] The MCA 2005 by definition does not apply to a capacitous adult, but it nevertheless seems odd for the court to be able to exercise power over a *capacitous* adult who is physically present in another country and not habitually resident here, when the same power is denied in the case of an *incapacitous* adult.

Conclusion

14.69 The entire existence of the inherent jurisdiction in relation to vulnerable adults is difficult to justify. It has no historical basis – as recently as 2003, the authorities were categorically against there being such a jurisdiction.[166] As Hewson noted, '[a] perceived need for a remedy does not thereby endow judges with power, however worthy their motives',[167] and some of the authorities deployed in support are used in a positively misleading way, cited to support points in direct opposition to their ratio.

14.70 The jurisdiction in relation to vulnerable adults is the archetypal example of the *protective imperative* in action – and of the dangers of this 'intuitively appealing' approach.[168] The subjects of the applications are invariably in sympathetic situations, where human instinct is to want to help – but from this desire to protect, the court has created an entire jurisdiction with no clear definition as to who may be subject to it, no established principles, no predictability of application, and no safeguards. While potentially well-meaning, it is dangerous and constitutionally inappropriate: it should be 'no function of the courts to legislate in a new field' in this way.[169] If there is to be such a jurisdiction, it should come from Parliament. There should be a clear structure; those who fall within its scope should be known and predictable; coherent principles must exist addressing how the powers can be exercised; and limitations on the court's powers should be expressly stated (including P's right of veto). These requirements are ill-suited to development by the judiciary from scratch, as the existing state of the law demonstrates.

[164] *Al-Jeffrey* is cited in *Re M (Exercise of Inherent Jurisdiction)* [2020] EWCA Civ 922, [2021] Fam 163 in relation to the threshold for invoking nationality-based jurisdiction; *Re M* concerned children, and the fact that *Al-Jeffrey* was about an adult was not analysed. Holman J himself declined to invoke nationality-based jurisdiction in *Re KBH (Forced Marriage Protection Order: Non-resident British Citizen)* [2018] EWHC 2611 (Fam), [2018] 4 WLR 137, and Lieven J expressed doubt about it in *AB v XS* [2021] EWCOP 57, [2022] 4 WLR 13, [36].

[165] See **13.21–13.24**.

[166] See **2.58–2.60**.

[167] Hewson (n 36) 458.

[168] Pritchard-Jones (n 69) 58.

[169] *Malone v Metropolitan Police Comr* [1979] Ch 344, 372–3 (Megarry V-C); see **1.26**.

15

Conclusions

15.1 I set out in this book to map the ways in which the English High Court uses its so-called inherent jurisdiction in relation to children and certain categories of adult, and to ask whether those uses are justified. My overall argument is that the court makes excessive use of the inherent jurisdiction. In some cases, adequate statutory remedies exist, such that recourse to the inherent jurisdiction is unnecessary and inappropriate: when Parliament has provided statutory powers with specific criteria, the court should not encroach on the legislative function and use its own powers to create similar remedies by another procedural route, usually with less exacting criteria. More concerning still are the areas where the court has *created* powers – and, over adults, entire areas of law – that fly in the face of parliamentary decisions. Here, the court is policy-making from scratch, which is undemocratic and a task to which the court is practically ill-suited.

15.2 The sheer number of cases, and the enormous range of issues, in which the court invokes its inherent jurisdiction is remarkable. Almost every aspect of child law is engaged, with particularly frequent examples in relation to child abduction,[1] medical treatment,[2] child protection,[3] and orders depriving children of their liberty for their own safety.[4] Equally, the two jurisdictions over adults show the court engaging in a huge range of issues. In all cases, the court insists that its powers are theoretically limitless – a claim that is particularly concerning when made in relation to *capacitous* adults since, no matter how 'vulnerable' they may be, such people have capacity and the right to make autonomous choices about their own lives.

15.3 This final chapter draws together some of the threads of the book and asks what conclusions flow from them. Despite some suggestions that the inherent jurisdiction might have out-lived its usefulness following the passage of the CA 1989,[5] it not only survived but has experienced a significant renaissance over the last 25 years; Waite LJ's warning in 1992 – that '[i]t would be rash to start writing

[1] **ch 7**.
[2] **ch 8**.
[3] **ch 9**.
[4] **ch 10**.
[5] See, eg, A Bainham, 'The Children Act 1989: The Future of Wardship' [1990] *Family Law* 270.

obituaries today for a jurisdiction which has survived with protean tenacity down the centuries'[6] – has stronger resonance today than when he wrote it. I do not think that the inherent jurisdiction is likely to disappear entirely – nor is that necessarily the outcome I seek.[7] But it should play a far less significant role than it presently does.

Fundamental Principles of the Inherent Jurisdiction

15.4 It is perhaps an inevitable feature of a 'theoretically limitless' jurisdiction that its limits are hard to draw. But in a liberal democracy, in which legislative functions are primarily carried out by the politically accountable legislature and executive, such a judicial power requires boundaries and principles. To that end, clear principles are identified as set out in chapter three, and it is worth reviewing some of them in light of the rest of the book.

15.5 The most explicit restrictive principle is in s 100 of the Children Act 1989 ('CA 1989'),[8] which limits the court's and local authorities' ('LAs') use of the inherent jurisdiction. Generally speaking, s 100 has effectively limited the use of the inherent jurisdiction in child protection, which was its focus[9] – but, somewhat ironically, its wording has also been used as an argument for an unnecessarily expansive use of the inherent jurisdiction elsewhere. The court's approach seems to be that s 100 acts as a form of 'ouster clause', limiting use of the inherent jurisdiction *only* in relation to child protection.

15.6 The Law Commission, though, had a broader policy aim – in both public *and private law*, that the CA 1989 would 'incorporate the most valuable features of wardship into … a new statutory scheme' and thus 'reduce the need to resort to wardship proceedings save in the most unusual and complex cases'.[10] The child protection focus of s 100 allowed Lord Wilson in *Re NY (Abduction: Inherent Jurisdiction)* to assert that 'Parliament … nowhere sought to preclude exercise of the inherent jurisdiction so as to make orders equivalent to those for which sections 8 and 10 of [the CA 1989] provide'.[11] Although perhaps technically true, this approach is entirely contrary to the spirit of the Act – as Waite LJ aptly said in *Re T (Child: Representation)*,[12] the court should permit use of the inherent

[6] *Re X (Wardship: Disclosure of Documents)* [1992] Fam 124 (CoA), 137.

[7] *Cf* Law Commission, *Wards of Court*, WP No 101 (London: HMSO, 1987) ('Law Com WP 101'), para 1.6, querying whether it is 'justifiable to have a universal jurisdiction capable of overriding or transcending the ordinary limits set by Parliament'.

[8] See **3.27**.

[9] See **2.30** *et seq*.

[10] Law Commission, *Review of Child Law: Guardianship and Custody*. Law Com 172 (London: HMSO, 1988) ('Law Com 172'), para 1.4.

[11] *Re NY (Abduction: Inherent Jurisdiction)* [2019] UKSC 49, [2019] 2 FLR 1247, [40].

[12] *Re T (Child: Representation)* [1994] Fam 49 (CoA), 282.

jurisdiction only when the issue cannot be resolved by making orders under the CA 1989. That principle has been almost entirely abandoned in the more recent cases.[13]

15.7 If, as Lord Wilson says, orders under s 8 and under the inherent jurisdiction are truly 'equivalent' – and I think they are – why is the inherent jurisdiction needed? It adds nothing, yet its use violates the *De Keyser* principle.[14] When Parliament has provided a set of powers in statute, along with provisions about when and how those powers should be exercised,[15] the court must use those powers and not invoke the inherent jurisdiction.[16] Yet the courts seem, at best, ambivalent about applying this principle,[17] relying on the fact that s 100 *specifically* excludes the inherent jurisdiction in some contexts to argue that therefore it remains *generally* available – even though the statutory provisions do the same job. The Law Commission focused on the main problem at the time – over-use of the inherent jurisdiction by LAs[18] – but the court has since shifted its focus to private law. Perhaps a better approach would therefore have been for the CA 1989 to impose a *general* restriction on *the court.* To adapt the language of s 100:

> No court shall exercise the High Court's inherent jurisdiction with respect to children unless the result which the court seeks to achieve cannot be achieved by the making of an order otherwise than in the exercise of the court's inherent jurisdiction.

15.8 The general principles that the court has set out are, in my view, sound. But they are not applied consistently, with the *protective imperative* overriding judicial restraint in many cases.

Nationality-Based Jurisdiction

15.9 The court's approach to its nationality-based jurisdiction is unhelpfully opaque, with numerous judgments that offer similar, but subtly conflicting, approaches.[19] The connection between this specific basis for the court to claim

[13] Various of Lieven J's judgments form a notable exception: see, eg, *JK v A Local Health Board* [2019] EWHC 67 (Fam), [2020] COPLR 246, [57] ('[t]he inherent jurisdiction cannot be used to simply reverse the outcome under a statutory scheme, which deals with the very situation in issue, on the basis that the court disagrees'); *Article 39 v Secretary of State for the Home Department* [2023] EWHC 1398 (Fam), [2023] 4 WLR 58, [33] (the inherent jurisdiction 'cannot and should not be used where there are statutory powers in place that can essentially do the same job'); *Re X and Y (Revocation of Adoption Orders)* [2024] EWHC 1059 (Fam), [80] ('the inherent jurisdiction cannot be used where there is a statutory scheme which covers the same ground').

[14] See **3.37** *et seq.*

[15] Examples here include the core principles in CA 1989, s 1, along with the standing rules in s 10.

[16] *Attorney-General v De Keyser's Royal Hotel Ltd* [1920] AC 508 (HL); *Richards v Richards* [1984] AC 174 (HL), 199.

[17] See **3.41** *et seq.*

[18] Law Com WP 101 (n 7) paras 3.3 and 3.30–3.47.

[19] See **ch 6**.

authority-jurisdiction (the authority to make decisions about the issues in question) and the general statutory criteria for authority-jurisdiction is both unclear and unsatisfactory, creating arbitrary results that the court has to avoid with artificial interpretations of the legislative rules. This area requires a detailed and coherent scheme, probably best conducted by the Law Commission.

Wardship

15.10 The continued existence of wardship in English law is an anachronism. There is no way to know how often children are made wards of court, since the High Court appears to keep no record of who becomes (and who ceases to be) a ward – despite the specific requirement to do so.[20] But it remains a frequently-used legal tool, even though no one has yet provided a convincing answer to the challenge set by Mostyn J to identify what actual benefits flow from making a child a ward of court in the vast majority of cases.[21] In a small minority of child abduction cases, practical benefits arise if the child was a ward before the abduction, or if they are made one afterwards.[22] But this is a real minority. Mostly, there is no identifiable benefit, and in many cases where wardship is invoked, its primary legal consequences – in particular, the parents' parental responsibility being suspended, and the rule that 'no important steps' can be taken in the child's life without the court's approval[23] – are positively unwanted. Why, then, is it still used? Is it, as Mostyn J suggests, merely 'a reflex',[24] or is there more to it?

15.11 On a purely pragmatic level, legal aid policy probably provides part of the answer. While it is truly the tail wagging the dog, the relative ease of obtaining legal aid when the child has been made a ward likely explains at least some applicants' interest in seeking or continuing wardship.[25] This reality makes resort to the inherent jurisdiction understandable in each individual case, but it makes no sense to allow legal aid policy to drive the substantive law. The answer is obvious and straightforward: the Legal Aid Agency rules should be changed to govern CA 1989 applications on the same basis as applications under the inherent jurisdiction.

15.12 More substantively, it might be suggested that the immediate imposition of wardship, arising as soon as the application is issued and without the need

[20] FPR 2010, r 12.41; see **1.3**.
[21] *AS v CPW* [2020] EWHC 1238 (Fam), [31]–[32] (Mostyn J); *A v B (Port Alert)* [2021] EWHC 1716 (Fam), [2021] 4 WLR 108, [8] (Mostyn J).
[22] See **7.37–7.39**.
[23] See **3.15** *et seq*.
[24] *AS v CPW* [2020] EWHC 1238 (Fam), [2020] 4 WLR 127, [31].
[25] My experience is that some judges are sympathetic to this reality and will continue wardship as a way of ensuring that legal aid remains in place, while others are hostile to the suggestion of using wardship for this purpose.

for a court hearing,[26] is a significant benefit that is not achievable in other ways. In one sense, that is true. But in reality, how useful is it for the child to be technically a ward if there is no court order to that effect with which someone could be served? A purported *legal* change in relation to a ward – a deed poll change of name, for example – might be considered a nullity if the court had not permitted it.[27] But in practical terms it would still require an order to undo it, and the court would then need to consider whether undoing the change was in the child's best interests. And most changes that might be made in relation to a child are not so easily undone – a change of school or geographic location cannot simply be declared a nullity, regardless of whether the person who effected it had court authorisation or not.

15.13 It is said that breaching the rule against removing a ward from the country or the 'no important steps' rule amounts to a contempt. Munby J once suggested that contempt proceedings can be brought if there is 'proof of knowledge that the child in question is a ward of court',[28] but the strictness of the requirements for a contempt application have increased since then. It is notable, for example, that this claim is not reflected in the Family Procedure Rules – and generally, unless the respondent had been served with a court order that included a penal notice,[29] a contempt application will founder. So it seems unlikely that the mere fact that an application has been issued such that the child technically became a ward could, without a court order, underpin contempt proceedings.

15.14 Moreover, when a child is actually at immediate risk, wardship is always supplemented with other, more practically effective orders – in the child abduction context, for example, a Tipstaff passport order and the accompanying port alert.[30] Here, wardship is not the operative element providing protection – and the more practical orders that are doing the work require a court hearing to take place before they can be imposed. Urgent hearings can take place at any time, including out of hours if required,[31] so these more potent remedies are easily available, with or without wardship. The benefit of having wardship's 'cloak of protection' imposed immediately is almost certainly therefore only theoretical.

15.15 It is hard therefore to see that wardship should be retained save for that tiny minority of child abduction cases where there is an identifiable tangible benefit to the child of having that status (and where it is used, wardship should be recorded and data made public about its use).[32] For the vast majority of cases it is an anachronism, adding nothing to the substantive orders that are available, yet carrying significant and often unwanted legal consequences.

[26] Senior Courts Act 1981, s 41(2); see **4.16**.
[27] I am not aware of any authority on this point.
[28] *Kelly v British Broadcasting Corporation* [2001] Fam 59, 75.
[29] FPR 2010, r 37.4(2)(e).
[30] See **7.42–7.43**.
[31] PD12E – Urgent Business.
[32] *Cf* Law Com 172 (n 10) para 4.40, identifying 'the objective of limiting wardship to cases where the continuing parental responsibility of the court is genuinely needed'.

The Wider Inherent Jurisdiction Over Children

15.16 Aside from wardship specifically, there are serious questions about the wider inherent jurisdiction in relation to children. I have identified through this book some areas where the court is using the inherent jurisdiction to fill genuine unintended statutory lacunae.[33] An example is the recognition of foreign adoptions: the legislation clearly envisages that the court will do this, but provides no mechanism.[34] Using the inherent jurisdiction goes 'with the grain' of the legislation,[35] supporting it and providing a means by which Parliament's intended outcome is achieved. Similarly, when a child is in LA care but a dispute arises about a substantial issue regarding the child's welfare, the developing understanding of Article 8 rights has created a statutory lacuna in the CA 1989.[36] Because the standard remedy of a s 8 order is unavailable when a care order is in force,[37] but – applying Article 8 – the LA should not simply decide the issue using its own parental responsibility, the court has no choice but to engage the inherent jurisdiction. While a statutory amendment to the CA 1989 would be preferable – allowing LAs (but no one else) to apply for s 8 orders concerning children in their care – in the absence of that change, the use of the inherent jurisdiction in this context is unobjectionable. Somewhat akin to the consequences of the court declaring legislation to be incompatible with human rights obligations,[38] I would favour a power (or perhaps rather a duty) for the court to notify the government when it considers that it has identified an accidental lacuna in legislation, to give Parliament opportunity to put it right. Unlike the human rights context, though, I think it is acceptable for the court to 'patch' the law on at least an interim basis using the inherent jurisdiction.[39]

15.17 There are also uses of the inherent jurisdiction that support other legislative policies, even though the particular examples appear to go beyond the powers generally given to the court. The Tipstaff powers to locate children, seize passports, and deliver children physically to a named individual are examples.[40] There are significant statutory powers that apply in related areas, but they fail to offer the extent of the protection available under the inherent jurisdiction.[41] Despite potentially going against the limitations set by the legislative powers, the

[33] This was an intended residual use for the inherent jurisdiction alongside the CA 1989: see Law Com 172 (n 10).

[34] See **11.5–11.8**.

[35] *Ghaidan v Godin-Mendoza* [2004] UKHL 30, [2004] 2 AC 557, [33]; see **1.5**.

[36] See **9.20–9.25**.

[37] CA 1989, s 9(1).

[38] Human Rights Act 1998 (HRA 1998), s 4.

[39] *Cf* the approach in Canada: see **5.14**.

[40] See **7.40–7.45**.

[41] See **7.46**.

generally strong international policy response against child abduction, including in domestic legislation, may justify the use of these wider powers in that context.

15.18 Far harder to justify is the court's extensive use of the inherent jurisdiction to make orders that can be just as well made under statutory powers – examples include child abduction,[42] medical treatment,[43] and private law children disputes.[44] As noted above, these cases violate the *De Keyser* principle, yet offer no benefit: as the court accepts, the orders are 'equivalent',[45] which as a matter of fundamental principle should make the inherent jurisdiction unavailable. The court's approach here reveals its attitude: the addiction to the inherent jurisdiction is so strong that the court insists that those powers must be available even when the exact same remedy is available under the CA 1989. This attitude, which is far from new,[46] has limited practical consequences in areas where the court is simply duplicating existing statutory remedies under its inherent jurisdiction. One might be forgiven for thinking that this issue is not particularly concerning, appearing more theoretical than real. But the same attitude informs the court's thinking in other areas, where the consequences are far more problematic.

15.19 The real concern in the children context is where the court uses its inherent jurisdiction to legislate from scratch, creating new policy and even undermining express statutory provisions. The least concerning of these examples is the 'undesirable association' cases,[47] where the court imposes injunctions against individuals that would not be available under any statutory power. Parliament has created remedies for some of these situations, but which are not in the hands of the family judiciary. The court's use of injunctions in this context has a long lineage, but in the modern era it must be questionable whether the court should really have this power. Likewise with deprivation of liberty cases,[48] the court's use of its inherent jurisdiction not only violates the *De Keyser* principle, but also Article 5 of the ECHR. The court, driven by its *protective imperative*, is using the inherent jurisdiction to 'patch up' a major policy failing by government – the failure to provide and fund adequate statutory facilities for vulnerable children. But in doing so, the court has provided its own policy answer when it is woefully ill-equipped to do so,[49] failing to 'recognise the boundaries of [the court's] role'.[50] The consequence is that the court

[42] See **ch 7**.
[43] See **ch 8**.
[44] See **12.11–12.15**.
[45] *Re NY (Abduction: Inherent Jurisdiction)* [2019] UKSC 49, [2019] 2 FLR 1247, [40].
[46] *Cf* the responses of the High Court Judges to the Law Commission's proposal to abolish wardship in 1987: see **2.26–2.28**.
[47] See **12.2–12.10**.
[48] See **ch 10**.
[49] See **10.37–10.38**.
[50] N Phillips, *The Lord Chief Justice's Review of the Administration of Justice in the Courts*, HC 448 (London: TSO, 2008), para 1.4; see **1.25**.

now allows the liberty of the child to be taken based solely on its view of that person's 'best interests' and in circumstances where Parliament has not permitted that to happen. Moreover, it is far from clear that the accommodation used for this purpose is actually improving the situation of the individual children involved;[51] the court accepts it is not in a position to assess or regulate that accommodation;[52] and, perhaps most significantly, the court's use of its inherent jurisdiction has removed the imperative for government, Parliament and LAs to act. Recognising that it would be unacceptable to leave the individual child unprotected at a time of extreme vulnerability, the court could have set a time limit on the use of the inherent jurisdiction, in effect demanding action from the other branches of government which are the ones properly equipped to address this issue.

15.20 Most straightforwardly inappropriate are the cases where the court expressly undermines statutory powers. For example, the court's claim that it can use the inherent jurisdiction to 'authorise actions which fall outside statutory obligation or may … be *directly contrary to it*' regarding LA duties to provide information to parents regarding children in care,[53] is obviously improper. Likewise, it is extraordinary to use the inherent jurisdiction to un-do adoption orders[54] and – even more strikingly – parental orders in surrogacy cases,[55] when legislation that is a 'complete code'[56] does not allow that to happen. These cases take the court far beyond its appropriate constitutional role. But they also reveal a major problem seen throughout this book – the court's ill-suitedness to acting as a policy-maker[57] is reflected in its inability to identify coherent (or sometimes any) qualifying criteria or guiding principles that apply when it starts legislating in novel areas. The answer to the question of when an adoption can be set aside is no more informative than 'in exceptional circumstances'. But 'exceptionality' is not a principle: it is a description of a pattern of outcomes,[58] revealing nothing about when this legal remedy is available in principle nor about the criteria that will be applied to deciding whether to apply it to particular facts.[59]

[51] Children's Commissioner, *Unregulated: Children in Care Living in Semi-Independent Accommodation* (London: CCE, 2020).

[52] See **10.37**.

[53] *Re O (A Child) (Care Proceedings: Issues Resolution Hearing)* [2015] EWCA Civ 1169, [2016] 1 WLR 512, [24]; see **9.26–9.30**.

[54] See **11.11–11.19**.

[55] See **11.25–11.27**.

[56] *Re C (Adoption: Freeing Order)* [1999] Fam 240, 253 (Wall J).

[57] See **1.26**.

[58] *Re W (Abuse: Oral Evidence)* [2010] UKSC 12, [2010] 1 WLR 701, [30] (Lady Hale); *Manchester CC v Pinnock* [2010] UKSC 45, [2011] 2 AC 104, [51] (Lord Neuberger); *Re A, B and C (Adoption: Notification of Fathers and Relatives)* [2020] EWCA Civ 41, [2020] Fam 325, [89(7)] (Jackson LJ).

[59] *Cf* Law Com WP 101 (n 7) para 4.17: 'exceptional circumstances are likely to be construed to mean either "not covered by the statutory code" or, perhaps worse, "covered by the statutory code but exceptional even so".'

The Inherent Jurisdictions Over Adults

15.21 The development of the inherent jurisdictions in relation to *incapacitous* and *vulnerable* adults over the last two decades is nothing less than shocking, and a complete disregard for the proper role of judges in our constitution.[60]

15.22 Regarding *incapacitous* adults, the High Court has completely disregarded express, binding House of Lords authority.[61] James Munby's extra-judicial writings are right to accept that the High Court (though principally he himself) 'invent[ed] … a novel jurisdiction',[62] entirely unrelated to the limited declaratory power that the House of Lords held to be all that was available.[63] While the Mental Capacity Act 2005 ('MCA 2005') has reduced the use that the court now makes of this self-created power, the examples of where the inherent jurisdiction is still used are concerning, undermining the deliberate policy choices that are at the heart of the legislative framework.[64]

15.23 The approach to *vulnerable* adults is far worse. The inherent jurisdiction *never* stretched into this field, and was conjured from the air by the High Court, relying on an actively misleading use of previous authorities. This happened just as it was clear that Parliament had chosen, against the recommendation of the Law Commission,[65] *not* to legislate in this area. In other words, the court disregarded Parliament's decision not to provide it with powers over capacitous but vulnerable adults, instead creating that power for itself. But in doing so, it has singularly failed to identify any coherent principles about: who is subject to the court's power; what the court can do; or the basis on which it does it.[66] Still less are there any safeguards in place. Whereas the Law Commission scheme included detailed definitions and specific safeguards, the court's scheme is vague and incoherent. Again, the court is simply ill-equipped to make policy from scratch, and it is far beyond the scope of the judges' constitutional role for them to attempt to do so.[67]

15.24 The first step in putting this right is for confirmation – from the Supreme Court, or from Parliament – that this so-called inherent jurisdiction does not exist. Doing so is no more than to repeat what the House of Lords already held in relation to *incapacitous* adults – but it apparently needs re-stating, and also extending to the new context of *vulnerable* adults, because this 'progeny' of which James Munby claims to be the 'proud father'[68] is, in every sense, illegitimate. If there is to

[60] See **1.22–1.27**.
[61] *Re F (Mental Patient: Sterilisation)* [1990] 2 AC 1 (HL); see **2.48–2.54**.
[62] J Munby, 'Protecting the Rights of Vulnerable and Incapacitous Adults – The Role of the Courts: An Example of Judicial Law Making' [2014] *CFLQ* 64, 64.
[63] J Munby, 'Whither the Inherent Jurisdiction? Part I' [2021] *Family Law* 215, 225.
[64] See **13.10** *et seq*.
[65] Law Commission, *Mental Incapacity*, Law Com 231 (London: TSO, 1995); see **14.7**.
[66] See **14.42–14.46**.
[67] See **1.22–1.27**.
[68] J Munby, 'Whither the Inherent Jurisdiction? Part II' [2021] *Family Law* 365, 367.

be a court power to intervene in the private and family lives of *capacitous* adults, that must be a democratically created power that comes from Parliament, with clear eligibility criteria, principles for how the power is applied, and safeguards to allow the adult to say no to 'help' they do not want.

Final Thoughts

15.25 The inherent jurisdiction is woven so deep within the fabric of English law that it is difficult to imagine doing without it.[69] The Law Commission hoped that 'the true scope for a residual power for the courts' would become apparent following the enactment of the CA 1989,[70] but the reality has been that the courts have stretched and expanded that 'residual' power far beyond what could have been imagined in 1988. The current state of wardship and the inherent jurisdiction is a mess – it is used *unnecessarily* when statutory remedies exist, and it is used *inappropriately*, undermining legislation in some cases and being used as a tool for the court to legislate from scratch in others. Looking at the approaches of other jurisdictions,[71] the striking difference is that they invoke their inherent jurisdictions far less frequently, and in far more restrained ways, than the English court. There needs to be a wholesale review, and a substantial 'pruning' of the court's use of its inherent jurisdiction.

15.26 Much of this could be done by the courts themselves, but only if they focus on a principled approach that is not led purely by the *protective imperative*. Recent attempts to get the Supreme Court to limit unnecessary[72] and inappropriate[73] uses of its inherent jurisdiction do not inspire confidence. So while the court could do this, more likely it requires legislation, potentially informed by the Law Commission report on the inherent jurisdiction that was proposed but never taken forward when the CA 1989 was introduced.[74]

15.27 I hope that this book has drawn attention to the court's actions in an area that has been given little attention for the best part of 40 years. There are serious questions about the way that the court has developed the law, and this book should provoke significant reflection on the appropriateness or otherwise of the modern use of the inherent jurisdiction. Most notably, I hope that the effect of the book is to scale back the court's use of its inherent jurisdiction. As I have shown, much of its use is *unnecessary* and *inappropriate*, and in a modern liberal democracy it is not acceptable that major judicial powers are created by the whims of the judges.

[69] Though well worth the effort, as Humphrey Lyttelton might have joked.
[70] Law Com 172 (n 10) para 1.4.
[71] See **ch 5**.
[72] *Re NY (Abduction: Inherent Jurisdiction)* [2019] UKSC 49, [2019] 2 FLR 1247.
[73] *Re T (Secure Accommodation)* [2021] UKSC 35, [2022] AC 723.
[74] Law Com 172 (n 10) para 1.4.

BIBLIOGRAPHY

Anon, 'AB and XS (P, by her Litigation Friend the Official Solicitor)', 15 November 2021, online at www.39essex.com/information-hub/case/ab-and-xs-p-her-litigation-friend-official-solicitor

Anon, 'An NHS Trust v Dr A', 27 March 2013, online at www.39essex.com/information-hub/case/nhs-trust-v-dr

Anon, 'Redcar and Cleveland BC v PR and others', 5 September 2019, online at www.39essex.com/information-hub/case/redcar-and-cleveland-bc-v-pr-and-others

Anon, 'Southend-on-Sea Borough Council v Meyers', 20 February 2019, online at www.39essex.com/information-hub/case/southend-sea-borough-council-v-meyers

Bagehot, W, *The English Constitution* (Oxford: OUP, 2001 [1867])

Bainham, A, 'The Children Act 1989: The Future of Wardship' [1990] *Family Law* 270

Baker, J, *Introduction to English Legal History*, 5th edn (Oxford: OUP, 2019)

Bedford, D, and Bremner, P, 'Falling Through the Great Safety Net of the Inherent Jurisdiction' (2023) 31 *Medical Law Review* 441

Bell, H, *An Introduction to the History and Records of the Court of Wards and Liveries* (Cambridge: CUP, 2011 [1953])

Betts, A, 'The Tipstaff' (1918) 30 *Juridical Review* 342

Bicknell, B, *The Law and Practice in Relation to Infants* (London: Solicitors' Law Stationery Society, 1928)

Bingham, T, *The Rule of Law* (London: Allen Lane, 2010)

Blackstone, W, *Commentaries on the Law of England*, 11th edn (Oxford: Clarendon Press, 1811), 303–5

Bridge, C, 'Adoption – Re C (Adoption: Freeing Order)' [1999] *Family Law* 11

Bridgeman, J, 'Beyond Best Interests: A Question of Professional Conscience?' in I Goold, J Herring and C Auckland (eds), *Parental Rights, Best Interests and Significant Harms* (Oxford: Hart Publishing, 2019)

Bridgeman, J, 'The provision of Healthcare to Young and Dependent Children: The Principles, Concepts, and Utility of the Children Act 1989' (2017) 25 *Medical Law Review* 363

Buckley-Thomson, L, 'What Place Does Wardship Have in Modern Family Proceedings?' (2013), online at www.familylawweek.co.uk/articles/what-place-does-wardship-have-in-modern-family-proceedings

Burrows, D, '"Guidance" as Law' (25 March 2019), online at www.iclr.co.uk/blog/commentary/guidance-as-law

Burrows, D, 'Practice Directions and President's Guidance' (4 November 2019), online at dbfamilylaw.wordpress.com/2019/11/04/practice-directions-and-presidents-guidance

Burton, M, 'Third Party Applications for Protection Orders in England and Wales: Service Providers' Views on Implementing Section 60 of the Family Law Act 1996' (2003) 25 *JSWFL* 137

Cave, E, and Cave, H, 'Skeleton Keys to Hospital Doors: Adolescent Adults who Refuse Life-Sustaining Medical Treatment' (2023) 86 *MLR* 984

Chambers, J, *A Practical Treatise on the Jurisdiction of the High Court of Chancery over the Persons and Property of Infants* (London: Saunders and Benning, 1842)

Child Law Project, 'Ten Young People Before Wards List in High Court' (2022), online at www.childlawproject.ie/latest-volume/ten-young-people-before-wards-list-in-high-court

Children's Commissioner, *Unregulated: Children in Care Living in Semi-Independent Accommodation* (London: CCE, 2020)

Cleary, A, *The Family Court Practice 2017* (Bristol: Jordan Publishing, 2017)

Courts Service, *Annual Report 2022* (Dublin: Office of the Courts Service, 2023)
Cretney, S, *Family Law in the Twentieth Century: A History* (Oxford: OUP, 2003)
Cretney, S, *Principles of Family Law*, 4th edn (London: Sweet and Maxwell, 1984)
Cross, G, 'Wards of Court' (1967) 83 *LQR* 200
Devlin, P, 'Judges and Lawmakers' (1976) 39 *MLR* 1
Dickey, A, *Family Law*, 6th edn (Sydney: Lawbook Co, 2014)
Donnelly, J, 'Inherent Jurisdiction and Inherent Powers of Irish Courts' (2009) 9 *Judicial Studies Institute Journal* 122
Douglas, G, and Gilmore, S, 'The (Il)legitimacy of Guideline Judgments in Family Law: The Case for Foundational Principles' (2020) 31 *King's Law Journal* 88
Eekelaar, J, 'Do Parents have a Duty to Consult?' (1998) 114 *LQR* 337
Eekelaar, J and Dingwall, R, *The Reform of Child Care Law* (London: Routledge, 1990)
Elliott, M, and Thomas, R. *Public Law*, 5th edn (Oxford: OUP, 2024)
Fenton-Glynn, C, 'The Regulation and Recognition of Surrogacy Under English Law: An Overview of the Case Law' [2015] CFLQ 83
Finlay, H, *Family Law in Australia*, 2nd edn (Sydney: Butterworths, 1979)
Freeman, M, 'Controlling Local Authorities in Child Care Cases' (1982) 146 *Justice of the Peace* 188
Freeman, M, *Parental Child Abduction: The Long-Term Effects* (London: International Centre for Family Law, Policy and Practice, 2016)
George, R, 'Changing Names, Changing Places: Rethinking s 13 of the Children Act 1989' [2008] *Family Law* 1121
George, R, 'Making Determinations During Life about the Disposal of a Body after Death" (2017) 39 *JSWFL* 109
George, R, 'Parental Responsibility, Vaccination, and the Role of the Court' (2021) 136 *LQR* 559
George, R, 'The Legal Basis of the Court's Jurisdiction to Authorise Medical Treatment of Children' in I Goold, J Herring and C Auckland (eds), *Parental Rights, Best Interests and Significant Harms* (Oxford: Hart Publishing, 2019)
George, R, 'Vulnerable Children in Unregulated Care: The Unstoppable Inherent Jurisdiction' (2021) 44 *JSWFL* 254
George, R, and Laing, A, 'Return Orders and the Inherent Jurisdiction after Re NY' [2020] *Family Law* 271
George, R, and Netto, J, 'Concurrent Convention and Non-Convention Cases: Child Abduction in England and Wales' (2023) 12 *Laws* 70
George, R, Thompson, S, and Miles, J, *Family Law: Text, Cases, and Materials*, 5th edn (Oxford: OUP, 2023)
Gilmore, S, 'The Limits of Parental Responsibility' in R Probert, S Gilmore and J Herring (eds), *Responsible Parents and Parental Responsibility* (Oxford: Hart Publishing, 2014)
Gilmore, S, 'The Nature, Scope, and Use of the Specific Issue Order' [2004] *CFLQ* 367
Goold, I, Auckland, C, and Herring, J, 'Medical Decision-Making on Behalf of Children in England and Welsh Law: A Child-Centred Best Interests Approach' in I Goold, C Auckland and J Herring (eds), *Medical Decision-Making on Behalf of Young Children: A Comparative Perspective* (Oxford: Hart Publishing, 2020)
Gulati, G, et al, 'The Inherent Jurisdiction of the Irish High Court: Interface with Psychiatry' (2020) 69 *International Journal of Law and Psychiatry* 101533
Hall, M, 'The Vulnerability Jurisdiction: Equity, Parens Patriae, and the Inherent Jurisdiction of the Court' (2016) 2 *Canadian Journal of Comparative and Contemporary Law* 185
Hayes, M, 'Relatives, Care Proceedings and Wardship' [1984] *Family Law* 234
Hayes, M, 'The Proper Role of Courts in Child Care Cases' [1996] *CFLQ* 210
Henaghan, M, Atkin, B, Burnhill, S, and Chapman, A, *Family Law in New Zealand*, 21st edn (Wellington: LexisNexis, 2023)
Herring, J, 'Protecting Vulnerable Adults: A Critical Review of Recent Case Law' [2009] *CFLQ* 498
Herring, J, *Vulnerable Adults and the Law* (Oxford: OUP, 2016)

Hewson, B, '"Neither Midwives nor Rainmakers": Why DL Is Wrong' [2013] *Public Law* 451
Heywood, K, 'Safeguarding Reproductive Health? The Inherent Jurisdiction, Contraception and Metal Incapacity' (2011) 19 *Medical Law Review* 326
Hoggett, B, 'The Royal Prerogative in Relation to the Mentally Disordered: Resurrection, Resuscitation, or Rejection?' in M Freeman (ed), *Medicine, Ethics and the Law* (London: UCL Press, 1988)
Holdsworth, W, *History of English Law*, Vol 1 (London: Methuen and Co, 1922)
Holdsworth, W, *History of English Law*, Vol V (London: Methuen and Co, 1924)
Holdsworth, W, *History of English Law*, Vol VI (London: Methuen and Co, 1924)
Home Office, *The Cautioning of Offenders*, Circular No 14/1985
Hood Phillips, O, 'A Constitutional Myth: Separation of Powers' (1977) 93 *LQR* 11
House of Commons Library Research Paper, *The Mental Capacity Bill* (Research Paper 04/73, 5 October 2004)
House of Lords Select Committee on Medical Ethics (1993–94), HL 21-I (London: HMSO, 1994)
House of Lords Select Committee, *Children and Families Act 2014: A Failure of Implementation*, HL 100 (London: TSO, 2022)
Hughes, R, 'Inherent Jurisdiction: Artificial Nutrition and Hydration' [2013] *Elder LJ* 346
Jacob, I, 'The Inherent Jurisdiction of the Courts' [1970] *Current Legal Problems* 23
Jaffe, L, *English and American Judges as Lawmakers* (Oxford: OUP, 1970)
Joint Committee on the Draft Mental Incapacity Bill, HL189-I / HC 1083-I (London: TSO, 2003)
Jones, M, 'Deprivation of a Child's Liberty: Section 25 and the Need for Legislative Reform' [2017] *Family Law* 645
Joseph, P, *Constitutional and Administrative Law in New Zealand*, 3rd edn (Wellington: Brookers, 2007)
Kahn-Freud, O, 'Law Reform (Miscellaneous Provisions) Act 1949' (1950) 12 *MLR* 222
Law Commission, *Mental Incapacity*, Law Com 231, (London: HMSO, 1995)
Law Commission, *Review of Child Law: Guardianship and Custody*, Law Com 172 (London: HMSO, 1988)
Law Commission, *Wards of Court*, WP No 101 (London: HMSO, 1987)
Law Commission, *Custody of Children: Jurisdiction and Enforcement within the United Kingdom*, Law Com 138, (London: HMSO, 1984)
Legal Aid Agency, *Scope of Family Proceedings Under LASPO* (January 2021), assets.publishing.service.gov.uk/government/uploads/system/uploads/attachment_data/file/948249/Scope_of_Family_Proceedings_Under_LASPO__January_2021_.pdf
Lewis, J, 'Safeguarding Vulnerable Autonomy? Situational Vulnerability, the Inherent Jurisdiction, and Insights from Feminist Philosophy' (2021) 29 *Medical Law Review* 306
Lindsay, 'Children: The Parens Patriae, and Supervisory, Jurisdiction of the Supreme Court of NSW', *Child Representation Conference* (Terrigal NSW, 18 November 2017)
Lock, D, 'Decision Making, Mental Capacity and Undue Influence: Do Hard Cases Make Bad – Or Least Fuzzy-Edged Law?' [2020] *Family Law* 1624
Lock, D, 'Decision-making, Mental Capacity and Undue Influence: Action by Public Bodies to Explore the Grey Areas between Capacity and Incapacity' [2015] *Judicial Review* 42
Lord Chancellor's Department, *Making Decisions: The Government's Proposals for Making Decisions on Behalf of Mentally Incapacitated Adults*, Cm 4465 (London: TSO, 1999)
Lord Chancellor's Department, *Who Decides? Making Decisions on Behalf of Mentally Incapacitated Adults*, Cm 3803 (London: TSO, 1997)
Lowe, N, 'Inherently Disposed to Protect Children: The Continuing Role of Wardship' in R Probert and C Barton (eds), *Fifty Years in Family Law* (Cambridge: Intersentia, 2012)
Lowe, N, 'The Family Law Act 1986: A Critique' [2002] *Family Law* 39
Lowe, N, 'The Limits of the Wardship Jurisdiction Part 1: Who Can Be Made a Ward of Court?' (1988) *J of Child Law* 6
Lowe, N, 'The Limits of the Wardship Jurisdiction Part 2 – The Extent of the Court's Power Over a Ward' (1989) 1 *J of Child Law* 44
Lowe, N, 'To Review or Not to Review?' (1982) 45 *MLR* 96

Lowe, N, and Nicholls, M, *International Movement of Children: Law, Practice and Procedure*, 2nd edn (Bristol: Family Law, 2016)
Lowe, N, and Nicholls, M, *The 1996 Hague Convention on the Protection of Children* (Bristol: Family Law, 2012)
Lowe, N, and White, R, *Wards of Court*, 1st edn (London: Barry Rose, 1979)
Lowe, N, and White, R, *Wards of Court*, 2nd edn (London: Barry Rose, 1986)
Mackay, J, 'Perceptions of the Children Bill and Beyond' (1989) 139 *NLJ* 505
MacPherson, W, *A Treatise on the Law Relating to Infants* (London: Maxwell and Son, 1842)
Masson, J, 'Disruptive Judgments' [2017] *CFLQ* 401
Masson, J, and Prabhat, D, 'Allowing Appeals to Increase High Court Power' (2021) 43 *JSWFL* 327
McKendrick, E, *Contract Law: Text, Cases, and Materials*, 10th edn (Oxford: OUP, 2022)
Miles, J, 'Family Abuse, Privacy and State Intervention' [2011] *CLJ* 31
MoJ, *Family Court Statistics Quarterly* (March 2024), www.gov.uk/government/statistics/family-court-statistics-quarterly-october-to-december-2023
MoJ, *Legal Aid Statistics Quarterly* (March 2024), www.gov.uk/government/statistics/legal-aid-statistics-quarterly-october-to-december-2023
MoJ, *Mental Capacity Act 2005: Deprivation of Liberty Safeguards* (London: TSO, 2008)
Mitchell, J, 'Whatever Happened to Wardship? Part I' [2001] *Family Law* 130
Mitchell, J, 'Whatever Happened to Wardship? Part II' [2001] *Family Law* 212
Monahan, G, and Young, L, *Family Law in Australia*, 6th edn (Sydney: LexisNexis Butterworths, 2006)
Montesquieu, C, *The Spirit of the Laws* (Cambridge: CUP, 1989 [1748])
Morgan, P, 'Three Groups of Revocation Cases' (2020) 42 *JSWFL* 246
Munby, J, 'Protecting the Rights of Vulnerable and Incapacitous Adults – The Role of the Courts: An Example of Judicial Law Making' [2014] *CFLQ* 64
Munby, J, 'Whither the Inherent Jurisdiction? Part I' [2021] *Family Law* 215
Munby, J, 'Whither the Inherent Jurisdiction? Part II' [2021] *Family Law* 365
Munby, J, 'Whither the Inherent Jurisdiction? Part III' [2021] *Family Law* 508
Phillips, N, *The Lord Chief Justice's Review of the Administration of Justice in the Courts*, HC 448 (London: TSO, 2008)
Pidd, H, 'Councils in England and Wales Pay £1m a Year to House Child in Private Care Home', *The Guardian*, 28 August 2022
Pope, H, *The Law and Practice of Lunacy*, 2nd edn (London: Sweet and Maxwell, 1890)
Prest, C, *The Family Court Practice* (London: LexisNexis, 2023)
Pritchard-Jones, J, 'The Good, the Bad, and the "Vulnerable Older Adult"' (2013) 38 *JSWFL* 51
Pritchard-Jones, L, '"Palm Tree Justice": The Inherent Jurisdiction in Adult Welfare Cases' (2023) 86 *MLR* 1358
Pugh, A, 'Emergencies and Equivocality under the Inherent Jurisdiction' (2019) 27 *Medical Law Review* 675
Raz, J, *The Authority of Law* (Oxford: OUP, 1979)
Reid, J, 'The Judge as Law Maker' (1972–3) 12 *Soc of Public Teachers of Law* 22
Roe, A, *Children Subject to Deprivation of Liberty Orders* (London: Nuffield Family Justice Observatory, 2023)
Ruck Keene, A, 'Extending the Great Safety Net' [2016] *Elder LJ* 401
Ruck Keene, A, 'The Inherent Jurisdiction: Where Are We Now?' [2013] *Elder LJ* 88
Seymour, J, 'Parens Patriae and Wardship Powers: Their Nature and Origin' (1994) 14 *OJLS* 159
Sharp, C, 'The Family Court's Jurisdiction to Direct the Burial of a Child' [2017] *Family Law* 844
Simpson, A, *A Treatise on the Law and Practice Relating to Infants* (London: Stevens and Haynes, 1875)
Smith, C, 'Judicial Power and Local Authority Discretion – The Contested Frontier' [1997] *CFLQ* 243
Spon-Smith, R, 'The Inherent Jurisdiction and Revocation of Freeing Orders' [2000] *Family Law* 43
Stebbings, C, 'Protecting the Property of the Mentally Ill: The Judicial Solution in Nineteenth Century Lunacy Law' [2012] *CLJ* 384

Taylor, R, 'Parental Decisions and Court Jurisdiction: Best Interests or Significant Harm?' [2020] *CFLQ* 141

Theobald, H, *The Law Relating to Lunacy* (London: Stevens and Sons, 1924)

Thomson, S, *The Nobile Officium: The Extraordinary Equitable Jurisdiction of the Supreme Courts of Scotland* (Edinburgh: Edinburgh University Press, 2015)

Tickle, L, and Summers, H, 'Siblings of Sara Sharif, Found Dead at her Father's Home, Are Made Wards of Court', *The Guardian*, 24 December 2023

Wall, T, 'Hundreds of Vulnerable Children Sent to Illegal and Unregulated Care Homes in England', *The Observer*, 13 April 2024

Watson Committee Report, *Wardship, Guardianship, Custody, Access, Change of Name* (Canberra: Australian Government, 1982)

White, R, Carr, P, and Lowe, N, *The Children Act in Practice* 3rd edn (Oxford: Butterworths, 2002)

Williams, D, Gration, M, and Wright, M, 'Habitual Residence and the 'Parens Patriae' Jurisdiction after Re B [2016] UKSC 4' [2016] *International Family Law* 239

INDEX

Note: Unless otherwise indicated all entries relate to the inherent jurisdiction / wardship, and to the practice in England and Wales.

www.ingramcontent.com/pod-product-compliance
Ingram Content Group UK Ltd.
Pitfield, Milton Keynes, MK11 3LW, UK
UKHW020246290926
15470UKWH00002B/775

9 781509 972142